Talk, Text and Technology

Literacy and Social Practice in a Remote Indigenous Community

Inge Kral

MULTILINGUAL MATTERS
Bristol • Buffalo • Toronto

Library of Congress Cataloging in Publication Data
A catalog record for this book is available from the Library of Congress.
Kral, Inge.
Talk, Text and Technology: Literacy and Social Practice in a Remote Indigenous
Community/IngeKral.
Critical Language and Literacy Studies: 14
Includes bibliographical references and index.
1. Literacy--Australia--History--20th century. 2. Literacy--Technological innovations--
Australia. 3. Literacy--Social aspects--Australia. 4. Language and languages--Australia. I.
Title.
LC159.K73 2012
302.2'2440994–dc232012009344

British Library Cataloguing in Publication Data
A catalogue entry for this book is available from the British Library.

ISBN-13: 978-1-84769-759-2 (hbk)
ISBN-13: 978-1-84769-758-5 (pbk)

Multilingual Matters
UK: St Nicholas House, 31–34 High Street, Bristol BS1 2AW, UK.
USA: UTP, 2250 Military Road, Tonawanda, NY 14150, USA.
Canada: UTP, 5201 Dufferin Street, North York, Ontario M3H 5T8, Canada.

Typeset by the Charlesworth Group.
Printed and bound in Great Britain by the MPG Books Group.

Contents

Acknowledgements

I wish to acknowledge, first and foremost, the Ngaanyatjarra, Ngaatjatjarra and Pitjantjatjara people of the Ngaanyatjarra Lands, who since my first interactions in 1997 have supported my growing research inquiry. Your stories have inspired me and I feel privileged to have been able to document your history.

In the Ngaanyatjarra world my heartfelt gratitude goes to Lizzie Ellis, Daisy Ward, Harvey Murray, Bernard Newberry, Robyn Smythe, Lynley Green, Jasmine Lawson, Delvina Lawson and Kresna Cameron. There are too many people to mention everyone by name, however I would like to thank the Murray family, Gerald Porter, Cyril Simms, Livingston West, June Richards, Beryl Jennings, Terry Robinson, Margaret Davies, Stewart Davies, Dulcie Watson, Andrew Watson, Rhoda Watson, Jayden Smith, Elizabeth Holland, Lynette Smith, Michelle Green, Dorothy Ward, Maimie Butler, Roxanne Laidlaw, Danny Harris, Andrew Jones, Neil Carnegie, Paul Carnegie, Phillip West, Betty West, Christine West, Debra West, Alisha West, Jodie West, Phillipa Butler and Lowanna Smythe. A special thank you to the youth arts project, especially Dorothy Smith, Noelene Landers, Lana Porter, Rosequeen Ward, Elfreda Ward, Clarabelle Ward, Shirley Frazer, Cherelle Robertson, Maria Duncan, Gino Ward, Cliff Davies, Casey Jones, Michael Carnegie, Carl Smith and Nathan Smith, and at Ngaanyatjarra Media Belle Davidson, Noelie Roberts, Natalie O'Toole, Chris Reid and Nathan Brown. I wish also to thank colleagues associated with the Ngaanyatjarra Lands, past and present, for their support, in particular Damian McLean, Pam Collier, Fay Paget, Albie Viegas, Elves Brites, Peter Allsop, Sophie Staughton, Nina Tsernjavski, Gary Proctor and Gillian Shaw. A special thank you goes to Amee Glass, Dorothy Hackett, Jan Mountney, Herbert Howell, Murray Wells and Sam Mollenhauer for their early advice and comments on language and history. Lastly, I am indebted to David Brooks for his ongoing support and insights (published, unpublished and in conversation) that have informed my thinking.

I wish to express deep gratitude to the people who have taught me much about the Aboriginal world over many decades. I would particularly like to thank the Strelley, Camp 61 and Yipirinya communities, as well as Jenny Green, Linda Rive, Jeannie Devitt, Maureen Tehan, John and Gwen Bucknall, Cliff Goddard, David Wilkins and Tim Rowse. And lately, for giving me a crash course in media technology, I am grateful to Daniel Featherstone, Anna Cadden and Jason Gibson. Thank you also to my colleagues at the Centre for Aboriginal Economic Policy Research at The Australian National University, especially Jerry Schwab and Bill Fogarty. Important in this list are my colleagues and friends Margaret Carew, Samantha Disbray, Josie Douglas, Angela Harrison, Carmel O'Shannessy, Myf Turpin and Gail Woods. Finally, I thank my mother Shirley Kral, and other wonderful friends (too numerous to mention but they know who they are).

This book builds on my long-term perspective as an educator and researcher in the field of Indigenous education, language and literacy in remote Australia. Ideas were further developed during my PhD dissertation, completed at The Australian National University in 2007 and fieldwork undertaken while a Post Doctoral Research Fellow (2007–2010) on an Australian Research Council Linkage Project. Additional funding from The Fred Hollows Foundation and the Centre for Aboriginal Economic Policy Research supported the writing of the book. An International Research Fellowship from The Australian Academy of the Humanities allowed me to travel to the United States in 2010 to work with Shirley Brice Heath whose continuing inspiration, support and valued friendship has been my good fortune. For their useful comments on early drafts I thank Harvey Murray, Lizzie Ellis, Linda Rive, Shirley Brice Heath, David Brooks, Jenny Green, Sarah Holcombe and Shivaun Inglis. Thanks also to John Hughes, Gillian Cosgrove and Brenda Thornley for assistance with the graphics.

I dedicate this volume to Ian Ward whose insights were always profound, Gerald Porter who took hold of literacy in a unique way, June Richards who inspired everyone. And to Margaret and Stewart Davies, and Andrew Watson. Their passing is our loss.

Abbreviations

AAEM	Australian Aborigines Evangelical Mission
AAPA	Aboriginal Affairs Planning Authority (Western Australia)
ATSIC	Aboriginal and Torres Strait Islander Commission
AEW	Aboriginal Education Worker
CAPS	Christian Aboriginal Parent-directed Schools
CDEP	Community Development Employment Projects Scheme
CNA	Commissioner of Native Affairs (Western Australia)
CNW	Commissioner of Native Welfare (Western Australia)
DAA	Department of Aboriginal Affairs (Commonwealth)
DCW	Department of Community Welfare (Western Australia)
DNA	Department of Native Affairs (Western Australia)
DNW	Department of Native Welfare (Western Australia)
DSS	Department of Social Services (Commonwealth)
EGHS	Eastern Goldfields High School (Kalgoorlie-Boulder, Western Australia)
GBTI	Gnowangerup Bible Translation Institute
MNA	Minister of Native Affairs (Western Australia)
MNW	Minister of Native Welfare (Western Australia)
NPYWC	Ngaanyatjarra Pitjantjatjara Yankunytjatjara Women's Council
NRS	National Reporting System
NT	Northern Territory
SA	South Australia
SIL	Summer Institute of Linguistics
UAM	United Aborigines Mission
UB	Unemployment Benefits
WA	Western Australia
WASRO	Western Australia State Records Office
WYAP	Warburton Youth Arts Project

Historical Chronology

Protectionist Policy

1905–1936 *Aborigines Act 1905* (WA).
1915–1936 A.O. Neville, Chief Protector Department of Aborigines, WA.
1921–1953 Mt Margaret Mission, established by United Aborigines Mission (UAM).
1934 *Western Australian Royal Commission into the Status and Conditions of Aborigines*, led by M.D. Moseley.
1934 Warburton Ranges Mission established by UAM.
1936 Introduction of the *Native Administration Act* (WA).
1936–1940 A.O. Neville, Commissioner of Native Affairs.
1944–1971 *Native (Citizenship Rights) Act* (amended 1950 and 1951).
1948–1954 Stanley G. Middleton, Commissioner of Native Affairs.
1953 Cosmo Newbery Settlement handed over to the UAM.

Assimilationist Policy

1954 *Native Welfare Act* (WA) introduced. Department of Native Affairs renamed Department of Native Welfare.
1954–1962 S.G. Middleton, Commissioner of Native Welfare.
1959 Amendments made to the *Commonwealth Social Services Act* – child endowment available to mothers and pension available for aged, widowed and invalid people under the care of missions, settlements and cattle stations.
1963 Amendments made to the *Native Welfare Act* (WA).
1967 Commonwealth constitutional referendum on Aboriginal citizenship question.
1968 *Federal Pastoral Industry Award* amended, leading to equal wages for Aboriginal pastoral workers.

Self-Determination

1971 Labor government elected in WA. Functions of Department of Native Welfare absorbed by Department of Community Welfare.
The *Native (Citizenship Rights) Act* is repealed in WA.

1972   *Aboriginal Affairs Planning Authority Act* (WA) introduced.
            Remaining functions of Department of Community Welfare
            are absorbed by Aboriginal Affairs Planning Authority.
1972   Federal Labor Party elected under Prime Minister Gough
            Whitlam. Policy of self-determination introduced under new
            Commonwealth Department of Aboriginal Affairs (DAA).
1973   UAM relinquishes Warburton Ranges Mission.
1974   Commonwealth DAA takes responsibility for most aspects of
            Aboriginal affairs in WA and is the main service provider to
            remote communities. Commissioner of Native Welfare is now
            Director of DAA.
1975–1983   Federal Liberal government under Prime Minister Malcolm
            Fraser.
1977   Four Ngaanyatjarra communities recommended under early
            phase of CDEP.
1981   Ngaanyatjarra Council established.
1989   Functions of DAA taken over by the Commonwealth Aborigi-
            nal and Torres Strait Islander Commission (ATSIC).

Mainstreaming

2004   ATSIC abolished by federal Liberal Prime Minister, John
            Howard. Welfare Reform Agenda commences.
2008   National Indigenous Reform Agreement under federal Labor
            Prime Minister, Kevin Rudd.
2009   Phasing out of CDEP commences.

Series Editors' Preface

This is the second book in the *Critical Language and Literacy* Studies series with a focus on language and literacy in Indigenous communities. *The Struggle for Legitimacy: Indigenized Englishes in Settler Schools* by Andrea Sterzuk (2011) looks at the discrimination faced by indigenous pupils in a school in rural Saskatchewan, Canada. Among some of the white teachers in the school, Sterzuk identifies a "color-blind discourse" that allows them to maintain a stance in favour of a standard English that allows no space for localized varieties. For Sterzuk, the goal in this context, and in the broader Canadian context, is to "decolonize society," to battle against the discourses and ideologies that continue to construct Indigenous students and teachers and the language they use in negative ways. "Learning to deconstruct colonial discourses about identities, nations, languages and literacy is a necessary step in moving towards equitable practices in schools." (2011: 48)

To connect these two books of course begs a number of questions. On the one hand, it is certainly and shamefully true that many of the accounts of Indigenous lives in Canada echo those of Australia. When we wrote in the preface to Sterzuk's book of "the paternalistic accounts of welfare dependency, drug and alcohol abuse, and child neglect that surface in the mainstream media, or in the anger and impatience of white residents caught up in land claim disputes that remain unresolved due to government inaction and obfuscation" (Morgan, Pennycook and Kubota, 2011: .ix), we might have easily been talking about Australia. Inadequate housing, sanitation and education, unemployment, poverty, poor health, high levels of incarceration, deaths in custody, removal of children from the parents, and subsequent schooling (and abuse) in boarding schools, and much more connect Indigenous communities in Canada and Australia (and the USA, and New Zealand and many other such settler colonies across the world).

On the other hand, it is important to emphasize first that the label 'Indigenous' runs the danger of concealing vast differences among very different people, lives and conditions. We need to be careful not to define similarity along lines of what has been done to people within colonial societies. White colonizers may be guilty of similar and sustained racial discrimination against different people, often with similar outcomes, but those people remain fundamentally different. In this regard, the term 'Indigenous' conflates and elides by linking not only Aboriginal Australians (forced themselves into a commonality which was never considered until the European invasion) and a diversity of Canadian First Nations, but also many others defined as Indigenous (people identified as still living in a region in which they are known as having the first historical connection) – Basques and Sami in Europe, Palestinians in the Middle East (controversial, of course, but see Nasser, Berlin and Wong, 2011), Orang Asli in Malaysia, the Palawan in the Philippines, Zapotec in Mexico, Guarani across regions of South America, Zulu in Southern Africa and many hundreds of others. Indeed, it is clear that it is more the claim to historical primacy rather than social or cultural similarity that unites Indigenous people. Second, however, despite such diversity, it is important to observe that that there are also many positive commonalities among Indigenous people – intimate knowledge of land, flora and fauna, story traditions that link people to these landscapes, linguistic and cultural practices that have evolved over thousands of years, forms of knowledge and wisdom that could greatly inform contemporary modern life. Indigenous activists have also found commonalities in their struggles around the world and may, like the Aboriginal Australian activist Bobbi Sykes, be skeptical of easy talk of postcolonialism: "What? Postcolonialism? Have they left?" (cited in Smith, 1999: 24).

It is into this mixed space – Indigenous lives in the remote present – that Kral takes us in this detailed study of literacy practices in Ngaanyatjarra communities in the Western Desert region of Australia. While Sterzuk's central context of study is the school, Kral's focus is more generally on questions of out-of-school literacy, or the literacy practices of the community. This focus matters in part because a continuing question for education in remote communities is what is literacy for? Who uses it in what languages for what purposes? Is there a place for literacy in Indigenous literacies aside from a stepping-stone towards the schooled literacies of English? And what roles do new technologies and literacies play? What are the consequences for oral and written communication and learning of the introduced language and literacy practices of the Western world? Kral looks at the different social and physical spaces for literacy amid a community undergoing rapid change. This is not to suggest, of course, that such communities were locked in some traditional, unchanging past prior to colonization, but rather that the incursions of modern Australia, from welfare to schooling, from popular culture to digital communication, are bringing about more rapid change than was often the case in the past.

These changes are not limited to the physical conditions of their lives but also include many social and cultural changes. With the arrival of missionaries at Warburton Ranges in the early 1930s came both new language and religion. Perhaps more important, however, have been the interrelated social, linguistic and educational shifts. Whereas in earlier times, linguistic practices were linked to the particular social and cultural practices of a nomadic lifestyle, missionary and 'native welfare' changes eroded the influence of Ngaanyatjarra Elders and parents by reducing sustained interactions between the young and the old. Thus intergenerational cultural and learning patterns changed, leading to profound shifts in socialisation and learning processes, from former practices of observation and imitation of Elders to sedentary and institutionalized learning and socialization practices. Kral is careful here to locate these shifts within the context of a much longer historical trajectory of changing Ngaanyatjarra social practices and forms of communication, a long historical process of change, adoption, adjustment and adaptation.

Just as Sterzuk found positive accounts of pedagogical practice particularly among the Indigenous teachers in her school, so Kral is able here to show how cultural resilience can occur within a process of change. This is not a rose-tinted account of language maintenance, nor of cultural preservation, but rather of the ways in which communities can nonetheless adapt within contexts of change. As Mufwene has noted, "the ideal world in which (rich) linguistic diversity can be sustained is far from being ours. There are really no language rights. Many people who are struggling to improve their living conditions in the current ever-changing socioeconomic ecologies are not concerned with maintaining languages and heritages, which are more properly archived in libraries and museums" (2010: 927). Thus, as Mufwene goes on, it is incumbent on linguists to "address issues arising from the real world of socioeconomic inequality more globally and not just from the point of view of languages as maps of world views and illustrations of mental/cognitive variation" (2010: 927). As Kral notes, the problem remains that it is English literacy that predominates. Although Ngaanyatjarra literacy was introduced quite early, the focus in school is on English literacy, and there is little vernacular literacy. Nonetheless, as Ober and Bell (2012) point out, although many Aboriginal languages have been wiped out, Aboriginal people have been able to adapt their cultural identities by "shaping, moulding and manipulating the English language into something of their own. Whether we like it or not, Aboriginal English is the first language for the majority of Aboriginal Australians and it is here to stay". For them it is the juggernaut that is Standard Australian English that needs to be "confronted, tamed and disempowered" (Ober and Bell, 2012)

Kral's work is informed by a view of literacy as a social practice, a view shared by a number of other books in this series, such as Stroud and Wee

(2011) and Hernandez-Zamora (2010). It is this view of language or literacy practices as things people do in particular places at particular times with a variety of linguistic and non-linguistic resources that helps us see language and literacy not as cognitive processes to be measured but as social practices embedded in human life and history. As Hernandez-Zamora reminds us, "we cannot forget that education and language policies have historically been at the heart of colonialism and neocolonialism" (2010: 188). Discussing the Mexican context, he points out that the "very creation of a school system was thought as a strategy to instill the symbols and rituals of the new postcolonial nation, and to homogenize a population who spoke dozens of native indigenous languages through the compulsory teaching of Spanish-based literacy" (Hernandez-Zamora, 2010: 188). Aligned with formal schooling, we should not ignore the role of linguistics in homogenizing indigenous diversity. As Nakata (2007) argues, "the inability of linguists to give primacy to language speakers and to the history of a language" is "a fundamental limitation of linguistic practice to this day. This shortcoming has come about because scholars have taken for granted an approach that single-mindedly submerges and subjugates the presence of people and their community. Such an approach affords little priority to language formation in its socio-historical context" (39).

"If the history of a language and its users is not factored into the theory as a primary standpoint" argues (Nakata, 2007: 37), "then any knowledge generated about that language is flawed." This is not, as Nakata points out, to reject the whole body or work carried out by linguists – this would be foolish in the extreme – but it is to point to the problem that a linguistic focus on formal aspects of a language "fundamentally separates the language from the people; it falsely separates the act of speaking from what is being spoken." Understanding the locality of language, therefore, is not merely about accurate descriptions of language systems – "as if languages were floating in a vacuum, 'ready-made' within a system of phonetic, grammatical and lexical forms and divorced from the social context in which the speech is being uttered" (Nakata, 2007: 37) but about people and place. The ways in which languages are described, legislated for and against, policed, and taught have major effects on many people. In trying to develop a perspective on languages as local practices (Pennycook, 2010), therefore, we need to appreciate that language cannot be dealt with separately from speakers, histories, cultures, places, ideologies. This is why both Kral's historical work as well as her close ethnographic study are crucial here, showing how any understanding of language and literacy practices has to be set in the context of people's lives, their communities and of their historical trajectories.

Neither of these books – Sterzuk or Kral – has been written by an Indigenous researcher. Although the definition of Indigenous is, as noted above, a difficult one, it is also clear that neither of these writers makes any claim to an Indigenous background. One of the aims of this book series was to encourage writing by researchers less well represented in the mainstream: We hoped to encourage younger, newer researchers, with backgrounds other than English, from different regions of the world, with new and different and critical topics. Researchers with Indigenous backgrounds would be an important addition to this agenda. The issue, of course, is not only the background but also the agenda of the research. As Smith (1999) and Nakata (2007) observe, the problem has been one of the historical and disciplinary fixing of Indigenous people in the colonial knowledge archive. For Smith – writing from "the vantage point of the colonized" – "the term 'research' is inextricably linked to European imperialism and colonialism. The word itself, 'research', is probably one of the dirtiest words in the indigenous world's vocabulary" (1). Smith nonetheless sees a role for non-Indigenous researchers if their work can also help privilege "indigenous values, attitudes and practices rather than disguising them within Westernized labels such as 'collaborative research'" (125). These two books, we hope, contribute in important ways to Indigenous interests. Sterzuk's project is one of decolonizing White knowledge, of revealing the assumptions and colour-blindness of settler education. This remains part of the decolonizing project. Kral's project is a different one; it is a closer investigation of Indigenous practices. It works because of the long association Kral has developed with Ngaanyatjarra people, because of the long historical trajectory and close knowledge she brings to the account, and because the project is not one of contributing yet another block of knowledge in the colonial archive but rather of fostering knowledge that can help these desert communities move forward in their quest for a life of decency in a country that constantly denies it to its first inhabitants.

Alastair Pennycook
Brian Morgan
Ryuko Kubota

References

Hernandez-Zamora, G. (2010) *Decolonizing Literacy: Mexican lives in the era of global capitalism.* Bristol: Multilingual Matters.

Mufwene, S. (2010) The role of mother-tongue schooling in eradicating poverty: A response to Language and poverty. *Language* 86 (4), 910–932.

Nakata, M. (2007) *Disciplining the Savages: Savaging the Disciplines.* Canberra: Aboriginal Studies Press.

Nasser, I., Berlin, L. and Wong, S. (Eds) (2011) *Examining education, media and dialogue under occupation: The case of Palestine and Israel.* Bristol: Multilingual Matters.

Ober, R. and Bell, J. (2012) English Language as Juggernaut and Aboriginal English in Australia. In V. Rapatahana and P. Bunce (Eds). *English as hydra: Its impacts on non-English language cultures.* Bristol: Multilingual Matters.

Pennycook, A. (2010) *Language as a local practice.* London: Routledge.

Smith, L.T. (1999) *Decolonizing methodologies: Research and indigenous peoples.* London: Zed Books.

Sterzuk, A. (2011) *The Struggle for Legitimacy: Indigenized Englishes in Settler Schools.* Bristol: Multilingual Matters.

Stroud, C. and Wee, L. (2011) *Style, identity and literacy: English in Singapore.* Bristol: Multilingual Matters.

Introduction

This book has emerged out of my 30-year learning journey in remote Indigenous Australia. In 1981, I first visited a remote community in the Anangu Pitjantjatjara Yankunytjatjara Lands in the north-west of South Australia. Significantly, I went with a linguist, and this has coloured my perspective on language, learning and literacy in this domain ever since. Over the intervening years, I have lived and worked as an educator and researcher in Indigenous communities in the Pilbara, Alice Springs, the Top End and, most importantly, the Ngaanyatjarra Lands. I have taught Aboriginal children from remote contexts to read and write in English and assisted Aboriginal language speakers to teach literacy in the mother tongue. I have imbued students with the expectation that through schooling they would 'succeed' in creating the kind of life their parents and grandparents (and the wider society) envisaged for them. Subsequently, I have seen them evolve into adults. Although some have become community leaders and others are good parents giving their children the best opportunities they can, many have floundered. In spite of schooling and their personal strengths and qualities, they have been ground down by the vicissitudes of everyday life and had their expectations thwarted by circumstances beyond their control.

Over the years, I have grown uneasy with the relentless pessimism of public and policy commentary in relation to literacy, education and the future of youth in remote Indigenous communities. In this discourse, youth are typically portrayed as illiterate. Their failure to achieve in the education and training system, we are informed, is leaving them unemployable and descending into a vortex of anomie, substance abuse and violence. Accordingly, solutions to this intractable 'problem' have included the re-introduction of a 'back to basics' approach to literacy teaching and comprehensive reporting through school-based national literacy and numeracy benchmark testing, accompanied by (sometimes punitive) reforms to the welfare system.[1]

I suggest that certain commentary (Beadman, 2004; Cleary, 2005; Hughes, 2005; Hughes, 2009; Storry, 2006) reveals only an aspect of what is a nuanced and complex story, impacted on by historical contingencies and context-specific differences. Missing in this discourse, most notably, is a scholarly perspective informed by understandings drawn from linguistics, anthropology and social learning theory. Absent, also, is a historical or lifespan perspective on language and literacy acquisition and socialisation that takes account of individual and collective histories, and cultural differences. Absent, as well, is a perspective that gives voice to Aboriginal people's own perspectives and experiences and at the same time addresses the ideological or political and economic contingencies that have enabled or disabled them once they move beyond institutional learning.

In fact, most accounts of literacy in remote Indigenous Australia focus solely on pedagogy and, accordingly, conceptualise literacy acquisition as 'a universal constant whose acquisition, once individual problems can be overcome by proper diagnosis and pedagogy, will lead to higher cognitive skills' (Street, 1993b: 11), where, by implication, employment and 'successful' futures will automatically follow. Such conceptualisations disregard the social, cultural and ideological character of the process of acquisition and the social meaning associated with literacy in different cultural contexts, allowing us to consider why some literacies have 'taken hold' and not others. By contrast, I consider that literacy in the newly literate remote Indigenous Australian context cannot be understood simply in terms of schooling or individual technical skills competence – it is also a cultural process. Moreover, literacy cannot be analysed in isolation from the ideological and socio-economic circumstances and conditions that precipitate its development, nor can it be removed from the cultural conceptions and social meanings associated with reading and writing in both historical and contemporary contexts.

What follows is an ethnographic study, informed by the theoretical fields of anthropology, sociolinguistics, language socialisation, ethnography of communication and social learning theory. Based on fieldwork undertaken in the Ngaanyatjarra Lands in remote south-eastern Western Australia (see Figure 1), this study addresses anthropological concerns associated with culture contact and language and culture shift; identity formation; socialisation and learning; and cultural transmission and reproduction across the generations.[2] As the title *Talk, Text and Technology* indicates, I view literacy as one facet of a rich and nuanced language environment that embraces a vast spectrum of multimodal – oral, written, visual, gestural and symbolic – forms of communication. I am concerned not with language or literacy 'competence', but with 'performance' (Hymes, 1972) – what people do with a range of multimodal communicative possibilities in everyday practice and how material resources and new technologies have impacted upon communication and social practice.

As noted earlier, I have observed first-hand the ebb and flow of change over the generations. It is from this long-term vantage point that I reflect on intergenerational change and examine the consequences for language, literacy and learning in one setting in remote Aboriginal Australia. In this study, I focus on individual identities, families and the community. I trace the introduction of literacy in the 'mission time' up to the digital literacy practices of the current youth generation. I do not look at classrooms or address literacy as pedagogy. There are *many* other studies that deal with schools, methodology and curriculum in the Indigenous Australian field. However, few examine language, literacy and learning from a social practice, historical or life-course perspective.[3] I consider, also, the adaptations that one small Indigenous Australian desert society has made in the 'ontological shift' (Austin-Broos, 2009; Myers, 2011; Poirier, 2005) from a hunter-gatherer existence to modernity. Importantly, this is not a comparative study of other similar contexts in remote Australia; rather, it is a close ethnographic consideration of one setting that illuminates practice, rather than pedagogy. I trace the acquisition of new social and cultural practices over four generations and consider how the Ngaanyatjarra have integrated some European norms and attitudes into their own cultural processes, but not others. The approach taken in this volume examines how knowledge, beliefs, habits, values and practices, associated with language, literacy and learning, have been transmitted and reproduced across the generations. By viewing the Ngaanyatjarra context as newly literate, this study takes account of the fact that it has taken millennia for literacy in Western society to reach the point where it is at now. Yet, this important fact is often left unexamined in the remote Indigenous Australian context. In part, this is because introduced Anglo-European cultural practices and institutional processes (education, employment and governance) are taken for granted, perceived as the norm and, thus, left unexamined, 'due to their dominance and pervasiveness' (Rogoff *et al.*, 2003: 85).

In this volume, I analyse the introduced practices of the Western world and reflect on their consequences for oral and written communication, and for learning. Contexts, spaces and places for language and literacy socialisation and sociocultural learning in a community of practice undergoing language and culture shift are examined. Ngaanyatjarra social practices, forms of communication and modes of production are looked at contextually and viewed as part of a historical process of intergenerational change, adoption, adjustment and adaptation. Addressed, also, is the manner in which material and spatio temporal aspects and the acquisition of new habits, values and dispositions have factored in Ngaanyatjarra people's growing 'sense of being literate' (Heath, 1991) in new 'figured worlds' (Clammer *et al.*, 2004) *and* how the recent introduction of digital technolo-gies has generated new communication modes and channels, especially among the youth generation.

Practice-Based Ethnography

This analysis has been informed by theoretical strands drawn from anthropology and linguistics. By looking at language and literacy not only as a set of symbolic resources that can be used to represent the world, but also as a set of social and cultural practices, this study falls into the tradition of what is known as 'practice-based' ethnographic research. Practice theory, according to Sherry Ortner (1989: 200), is 'a theory of the conversion or translation between internal dynamics and external forces' that is concerned with 'the ways in which a given social and cultural order mediates the impact of external events by shaping the ways in which actors experience and respond to those events'. By drawing on Ortner and other anthropologists, I seek to understand *practice* and the 'configuration of cultural forms, social relations, and historical processes that move people to act in ways' that produce or determine certain effects (Ortner, 1989: 12). Practice theorists commonly use Pierre Bourdieu's notion of 'habitus' to reflect on the nature of social reproduction and transformation (Bourdieu, 1977; Bourdieu, [1980] 1990). Habitus, according to Bourdieu, is 'a system of lasting, transposable dispositions which, integrating past experiences, functions at every moment as a *matrix of perceptions, appreciations, and actions*' (Bourdieu, 1977: 82–83 [emphasis in original]). I use Ortner's notion that underlying 'cultural schemas' determine the reproduction of practice in the new habitus (Ortner, 1989: 60). Her concept of 'cultural schemas' embraces the 'organized schemas for enacting (culturally typical) relations and situations' that often take on 'an ordering function, achieving a degree of generality and transferability across a range of somewhat disparate social situations' (Ortner, 1989: 60). I integrate a practice-oriented approach to consider how the habitus of a colonising culture is taken on and transformed into practices that are redolent of the underlying cultural values and processes of the receiving group (Ortner, 1984). A recursive theme throughout this book is the enduring influence of deeply embedded Ngaanyatjarra cultural processes in contemporary everyday practice, signalling what Marshall Sahlins terms the 'structures of the long run' (Sahlins, 1981: 9). Similarly, Ortner asserts that 'a theory of practice is a theory of history', because 'the playing out of effects of culturally organized practices is essentially processual and often very slow' (Ortner, 2006: 9). Ethno-historical approaches to anthropology (Appadurai, 1986; Comaroff, 1985; Harries, 1994; Sahlins, 1981) reveal 'the way in which the impact of external forces is internally mediated, not only by social structural arrangements... but also by cultural patterns and structures' (Ortner, 1989: 14). Therefore, a practice approach offers a model that 'implicitly unifies both historical and anthropological studies' (Ortner, 1984: 159).

By viewing language, literacy and learning from an ethno-historical perspective that embraces 'practice', ontological issues are confronted. This is because the ontologies – that is, the 'figured worlds' – in which practice is shaped 'constitute the largest or most fundamental frame out of which culture is shaped' (Clammer *et al.*, 2004: 4). A 'figured world', according to Clammer *et al.* (2004), is a system of meaning comprising historically produced norms and practices, as well as individual sense-making, as one 'figures' one's self into a new world of interpretation. From this perspective, the concept 'figured worlds' also embraces the 'socially produced, culturally constituted activities', whereby people come to conceptually and materially produce and perform new understandings of self or identities (Holland *et al.*, 1998: 40–41). In this light, I look also to sociologists Berger and Luckmann, who focus on the socially constructed nature of social action and posit that frequently repeated action – 'practice' – can become 'habitualised' and reproduced as routines. They assert, however, that such routines are transmitted to the next generation *only* when experienced as 'a reality that confronts the individual as an external and coercive fact' and suggest that when transmitted practices become taken for granted cultural processes a form of 'legitimation' has taken place (Berger & Luckmann, [1966] 1975: 70–85). I use Berger and Luckmann's model to understand how new practices have been formed, in response to the impact of external ideological influences such as the church and the state on language, cultural forms and practice.

Social theorists Dorothy Holland and Jean Lave consider that social practice theory embraces 'the historical production of persons in practice' (Holland & Lave, 2009: 1), as well as the processes of social formation and cultural production (Holland & Lave, 2001). Therefore, how people participate in social processes – including the production of their lives, work and relationships – depends, in part, on 'the changing historical circumstances that have shaped and do shape the ongoing social world they inhabit' (Holland & Lave, 2009: 1). Accordingly, attention must be paid to 'how material economic practices, power relations, and the production of meaning and difference constantly play upon one another' (Holland & Lave, 2009: 3). 'Local practice', Holland and Lave assert (2009: 3), comes about in response to 'the encounters between people as they address and respond to each other while enacting cultural activities under conditions of political-economic and cultural-historical conjuncture'. Following Holland and Lave, I examine how the Ngaanyatjarra are, in part, fashioned and have fashioned themselves in 'historically and culturally specific ways' (Holland & Lave, 2001: 5). In this case, social practice theory is used to reflect on the consequences of change for contemporary Ngaanyatjarra practice. As anthropologist Fred Myers suggests, approaches that look at the 'new Aboriginal cultural formations' and Aboriginal practices 'contextually in historical process' also illuminate the way in which meanings are 'reshaped and contested' (Myers, 2002: 117). In this study, the interrelationship between the historical production of persons, contested local practice and the ideological struggles associated with language, literacy and learning in one complex intercultural space are examined.

The Evolution of a Social Practice Approach to Literacy

In the early development of anthropological thought, 'literacy' was emblematic of the 'great divide' between orality and literacy, the binary division between 'civilised and primitive', 'literate and illiterate' and the determinant of difference between 'us' and 'them' (Goody, 1968; Ong, 1982). From this purview, literacy reached its 'apogee' only in the West, and in the non-Western world, illiteracy was a signifier of inferior or primitive cultures (Besnier, 1995: 1). Where early anthropological studies explored the 'consequences' of the introduction of literacy and the 'impact' of literacy on the receiving culture (Levy-Bruhl, 1923; Wogan, 1994), later research examined the acceptance or rejection of literacy in the local vernacular, or the introduced language, by assessing whether literacy 'took hold' in preliterate cultures and under what conditions (Ferguson, 1987; Huebner, 1987; Kulick & Stroud, 1993; Spolsky *et al.*, 1983). According to anthropologist Brian Street, early exponents of what he terms the 'autonomous' model of literacy (Goody, 1968; Goody, 1977; Olson, 1977; Ong, 1982) tended to conceptualise literacy 'in technical terms, treating it as independent of social context, an autonomous variable whose consequences for society and cognition can be derived from its intrinsic character' (Street, 1993b: 5). In this 'autonomous' model, certain inherent properties of alphabetic literacy are believed to explain the differences between preliterate and literate societies and individuals and to cause changes at a societal and individual level (Besnier, 1995: 2–3).

Over recent decades, studies in education anthropology (Levinson *et al.*, 2000; Philips, 1983; Spindler, 1974; Varenne & McDermott, 1999; Wolcott, 1967) and sociolinguistics have shifted the emphasis away from a traditional, cognitivist view of literacy as a set of technical skills possessed, or conversely lacked, towards studies of the social and cultural behaviour associated with literacy. While some researchers (Cole & Scribner, 1981; Luria, 1976; Street, 1984) separated 'schooling' and 'literacy' and examined the cognitive 'consequences' of schooled and non-schooled literacies, others have used developments in sociolinguistics and anthropology to look at the relationship between language and literacy use in social contexts (Cook-Gumperz, 1986b; Levine, 1986; Maybin, 1994; Prinsloo & Breier, 1996). Accordingly, scholars began to look outside of schools to family and community to better understand and provide programmes to support learners from non-mainstream cultural, linguistic or socio-economic backgrounds. These new perspectives were significant in that they started to shift the discourse beyond deficit theories that attributed school failure to individuals, family environment or non-standard language use. Importantly, research began to take account of the discontinuities between school and home, especially in minority contexts where non-standard language forms were used, with linguists arguing that no language was deficient (Labov, 1972). In tandem, ethnographic methods have been used to study how children are acculturated into the ways that adults in the home environment use spoken and written language. Important studies in this field (Heath, 1982b; Heath, 1983; Taylor & Dorsey-Gaines, 1988) have highlighted the strengths of diverse language and literacy socialisation contexts.

Linguists and anthropologists have further opened up new under-standings with the application of ethnographic methods to the study of communication. Theories of the 'ethnography of communication' (Gumperz & Hymes, 1964; Hymes, 1964; Gumperz & Hymes, 1972) and 'communicative practices' (Grillo, 1989) blended anthropology and linguistics and explored the links between culture, language and society. As sociolinguists and linguistic anthropologists were unable to separate language from sociocultural practice, a less stark divide between orality and literacy emerged (Heath, 1982a; Heath, 1984), allowing scholars to also draw on studies of performance (Bauman, 1986). Performance-based studies have challenged dominant Western conceptions by prompting researchers to stress the cultural organisation of communicative processes, by calling attention to 'the dialectic between performance and its wider sociocultural and political-economic context' (Bauman & Briggs, 1990: 61).

Practice theory has, in turn, influenced a social practice approach to literacy. Scholars from the so-called 'New Literacy Studies' have drawn on the various developments in anthropology and sociolinguistics to view literacy as social practice (Gee, 2000; Street, 1993b). Significantly, ethnographic methodology was used to document literacy activities in communities and link the meanings of local events to broader cultural institutions and practices (Barton & Padmore, 1994; Barton & Hamilton, 1998; Barton et al., 2000; Ivanic & Hamilton, 1990). In this field, researchers conceptualise literacy not in terms of skills and competencies, but as integral components of social 'events' and 'practices'. The term 'literacy event' has been used by Shirley Brice Heath to encompass speech events that have social interactional rules around text (Heath, 1983: 386), whereas Street points out that 'literacy practices' incorporate 'literacy events' and refer to both behaviour and conceptualisations related to the use of reading and/or writing (Street, 1993b: 12–13). Axiomatic is Heath's notion that being literate involves more than having the individual technical literacy skills that 'enable one to disconnect from the interpretation or production of a text as a whole, discrete elements, such as letters, graphemes, words, grammar rules, main ideas, and topic sentences' (Heath, 1991: 3). Being literate, Heath states, also depends upon 'an essential harmony of core language behaviors and certain critical supporting social relations and cultural practices' and an individual's 'sense of being literate derives from the ability to also exhibit *literate behaviors*' (Heath, 1991: 3–6 [emphasis in original]).

The ideas of Heath and Street are in accord with other scholars, who suggest that literacy practices are what people do with literacy every day and, thus, 'cultural ways of utilising literacy' may be more abstract and 'cannot be wholly contained in observable tasks and activities' (Barton *et al.*, 2000: 8). David Barton and Mary Hamilton suggest the following useful set of propositions to encompass the 'literacy as social practice' approach (Barton & Hamilton, 1998: 7):

- There are different literacies associated with different domains of life.
- Literacy practices are patterned by social institutions and power relationships, and some literacies become more dominant, visible and influential than others.
- Literacy practices are purposeful and embedded in broader social goals and cultural practices.
- Literacy is historically situated.
- Literacy practices change and new ones are frequently acquired through processes of informal learning and sense-making.

Researchers have also examined literacy from a social practice perspective in cross-cultural, minority language and newly literate contexts (Besnier, 1995; Kulick, 1992; Schieffelin & Gilmore, 1986; Scollon & Scollon, 1981; Street, 1993a). They have investigated why literacy has acquired certain cultural meanings and how value has been attributed in a range of different situations by turning their attention to the 'creative and original ways in which people transform literacy to their own cultural concerns and interests' (Street, 1993b: 1). Significantly, in these studies, the culturally shaped nature of literacy acquisition and use in newly literate groups is foregrounded, and literacy acquisition is situated as a social and cultural process within the dynamic of social change. Importantly, these studies address the lacuna in our knowledge about literacy in minority languages, third or fourth world societies and how people in newly literate contexts have shaped the creative and cultural uses of literacy and why.

Finally, fundamental to an anthropological perspective on literacy is the notion that 'illiteracy' is not primarily a technical skills issue, but is 'relational' or 'ideological' (Cook-Gumperz, 1986a; Smith, 1986). As Street contends (1995: 24), literacy practices are specific to political and ideological contexts and their consequences 'vary situationally'. Writers assert that many people who would be labelled 'illiterate', within Street's 'autonomous model', do, in fact, derive meaning from, and make use of, different *literacies* in various contexts (Barton *et al.*, 2000; Gee, 1996; Street, 1995). An alternative literacy discourse emphasises the multiplicity of 'literacies' that the term literacy encompasses to signify that there can be no single definition of literacy. Scholars from the 'New London Group' have furthered thinking around the concept of 'multiliteracies' (Cope & Kalantzis, 2000; New London Group, 1996). As literacies are 'situated' and context-dependent, a singular criterion for what literacy competence entails is unattainable, as competence differs according to domain and function. Street argues that as linguists, such as Ralph Grillo, propose the acceptance of 'language varieties' outside the dominant norm (Grillo, 1989), there is also a need to accept 'literacy varieties' (Street, 1994). Thus, the definition of what constitutes literacy has been broadened to see what is accomplished with literacy, rather than what is deficient (Street, 2001; Prinsloo & Breier, 1996). Lastly, as I discuss in detail in Chapter 7, fresh thinking about literacy has been ushered in by the arrival of digital technologies and the emergence of new social practices surrounding electronic media, digital film/photography and mobile phone technology.

A Social Theory of Learning

As theorists have been unable to separate language from sociocultural practice, this has led to new thinking around learning and language socialisation. Barbara Rogoff posits that learning is a 'process of changing participation' in community activities (Rogoff, 2003: 284). Moreover, she states, human development is 'a process of *people's changing participation in sociocultural activities of their communities*', where '[p]eople of each generation, as they engage in sociocultural endeavours with other people, make use of and extend cultural tools and practices inherited from previous generations' (Rogoff, 2003: 52 [emphasis in original]). Accordingly, children and other novices learn by taking part in everyday activities with family members or are apprenticed through observation and imitation (Greenfield, 1999; Rogoff, 1990; Rogoff *et al.*, 1993). Jean Lave and Etienne Wenger emphasise 'shifting the analytic focus from the individual as learner to learning as participation in the social world, and from the concept of cognitive process to the more-encompassing view of social practice' (Lave & Wenger, 1991: 43) where the learner is a member of a sociocultural community or a 'community of practice' (Wenger, 1998). From this perspective, social practices are in a process of 'reproduction, transformation, and change', and human lives are seen as trajectories through multiple social practices across the lifespan (Lave & Wenger, 1991: 123). Literacy, they contend, is also a cultural process, and 'everyday practice' is 'a more powerful source of socialization than intentional pedagogy' (Lave, 1988: 14). This situated and social perspective broadens learning beyond formal instruction, advancing the notion of learning and literacy as purposeful, context-specific and socially organised practice (Barton *et al.*, 2000; Engestrom, 1990; Gee, 2004; Lave, 1996; Paradise & Rogoff, 2009; Rogoff & Lave, 1984; Rogoff *et al.*, 2003).

Language Socialisation

Language socialisation researchers have drawn on theory from anthropology and sociolinguistics (and human development) to examine how learners acquire the knowledge, practices and dispositions required to function as competent members of their social groups and cultural communities. Language socialisation, according to Bambi Schieffelin and Elinor Ochs (1986), is the process by which cultural practices and understandings shape the way that people acquire language within the local culture. As each local culture has its own norms, preferences and expectations associated with language and literacy practices, resources and ideologies, these factors influence the ways of communicating and participating specific to the local speech community or 'community of practice'. Importantly, language socialisation research in cross-cultural contexts (Ochs, 1988; Ochs, 1993; Schieffelin & Ochs, 1986; Schieffelin, 1990) highlights diverse language socialisation contexts and provides insights into the manner in which everyday language activities – as socialising activities – form the basis for the transmission and reproduction of culture that are linked to the social practices and symbolic forms of that community.

Furthermore, language socialisation is a lifelong process. Participating in society and using language are intertwined activities (Ochs, 1996), as the acquisition of sociocultural competence is gained through the acquisition of language, as well as other relevant meaning systems and symbolic structuring, including literacy. Language socialisation, according to Heath, 'perhaps more than any other aspect of growing up, frames our way of being in the social worlds in which we will live' (Heath, 2008a: xiii). This factor notwithstanding, while many studies have focused on child language acquisition and socialisation, the language socialisation of adolescents and young adults has received relatively little attention. International studies indicate that language socialisation and learning continues well into the adolescent years (Eckert, 1988; Heath, 2008b; Hoyle & Adger, 1998; Mendoza-Denton, 2007; Rampton, 1995; Shuman, 1986), as verbal and written registers and styles are acquired according to emerging roles, identities and practices. For many young people today, their way of being in the world – that is, their language socialisation framework – 'involves not only the co-existence of more than one language or dialect, it may also be mediated by new information and communication technologies (ICTs), and may involve the development of related oral, written and multimodal, as well as cultural, practices intertwined with new intercultural or "hybrid" identities' (Duff, 2008: xvi). When considering young people's ways of learning, using and adapting communication forms, ethnographers around the world emphasise the embeddedness of youth in global culture, including youth in Third World and Indigenous contexts (Ito et al., 2010; Katz, 2004; Wyman, 2012).

What is apparent, in the literature surveyed above, is the absence of Indigenous Australian case studies. Significantly, linguists in Australia have studied the impact of sociocultural change and the implications for language shift, socialisation and transmission (Langlois, 2004; McConvell, 1991; Schmidt, 1985; Schmidt, 1990), and researchers have addressed child language acquisition and socialisation (Bavin, 1993; Jacobs, 1988; O'Shannessy, 2011; Simpson & Wigglesworth, 2008). However, few scholars have addressed intergenerational change and the adolescent language socialisation context. Furthermore, few studies in the anthropological literature have considered the impact of change on the life trajectory for Aboriginal youth in remote Australia. Youth have typically been referred to in relation to the life-cycle paradigm (Burbank, 1988; Hamilton, 1981; Myers, 1986; Tonkinson, 1978). More recently, anthropologists have examined the tension between cultural continuity and change (Brady, 1992; Eickelkamp, 2011a; Fietz, 2008; Merlan, 2005), and education anthropologists have addressed Indigenous concerns (Fogarty, 2010; Schwab, 2001). This volume seeks to contribute to this literature by considering the relational aspect of historical, social, cultural and ideological factors and how these have impacted on and influenced language and literacy socialisation in one community of practice over a number of generations in a time of culture change and language shift. It will examine the consequences of these factors for Ngaanyatjarra youth, as they make the transition from adolescence to adulthood with the communicative and sociocultural competence to operate effectively in their own, and other, communities.

An Ethnography of Changing Social Practice in the Ngaanyatjarra World

What follows is an ethnographic consideration of changing social practice and how literate habits, assumptions, dispositions and behaviours have been developed, transmitted and transformed across the generations (Barton *et al.*, 2000; Clanchy, 1979; Heath, 1991). Importantly, this ethnography is not a study of individual literacy skills and competencies. As Barton and Hamilton state, 'shifting away from literacy as an individual attribute is one of the most important implications of a practice account of literacy' (Barton & Hamilton, 1998: 12). Rather, it is about finding out what people do with text and how an array of 'literacies' are used in everyday contexts to communicate what matters to individuals, families and the community.

At another level, this book is about how the Ngaanyatjarra have adapted to the interventions and the intrusions of settler society and the state and how they have adopted, or otherwise, new forms of Western practice. The generational approach displays the temporal unfolding of an expanded range of sociocultural practices and processes, embedded within 'an historically shaped material world' (Goodwin, 2000: 1492). The historical forces that shaped the Ngaanyatjarra world provide insights into the ideological frames that have created the habitus – the normative practices associated with language, learning and literacy today. In this way, this book is also a study of the social process of learning and how people adapt as cultures change and technologies alter. Furthermore, it is a reflection on how globalization has 'excavated' traditional contexts of action (Giddens, 1994: 95) and altered the meaning of 'things' in time and space. In this respect, it is also an exploration of changing subjectivities. I trace the generations as they articulate from a preliterate society to modernity and observe how people deal with the consequences of altered life-course trajectories, noting the subtle shifts in core cultural concepts and Ngaanyatjarra conceptions of personhood.

Finally, this volume is an exploration of cultural production, transmission and reproduction across the generations and the implications of change for language socialisation and the cultural production of the literate person in the 'globalised media world' (United Nations, 2005). By examining Nganyatjarra people's sociocultural and communicative practices and how they have acquired new skills and competencies from a generational perspective, two aspects become clear. Firstly, the extent to which all forms of communication and expression – oral, written, gestural, visual and, now, computer-mediated – are interdependent and can never be extracted from the social, cultural, historical, political and economic context from which they emerge, in which they change and for which they exist. Of emphasis, also, is the manner in which these forms are learned or acquired and how the conditions of their use is multifaceted, lifelong and 'lifewide' (Duff, 2008: xv). In other words, to draw on Patricia Greenfield, as cultures change over historical time, 'the very process of cultural learning and cultural transmission also change' (Greenfield, 1999: 57).

Structure of the Book

The book is divided into three parts. In Part 1, the focus is on the present. Through detailed 'thick description' (Geertz, 1973: 14), a richly textured picture of everyday Ngaanyatjarra social practices and cultural processes is painted, revealing the way in which new modes of communication have permeated the 'practice of everyday life' (de Certeau, 1984). Culture change and language shift are signalled in the exploration of altered cultural processes and practices. A practice-oriented approach is used to foreshadow how current practices are historically produced and redolent of underlying Ngaanyatjarra cultural schemas. I signal here Barton and Hamilton's proposition that 'literacy practices are culturally constructed, and like all cultural phenomena, they have their roots in the past' (Barton & Hamilton, 2000: 13–14). The values, attitudes and feelings associated with individual, family and community literacy practices, and the meaning attributed to text, are discussed in this light.

In Part 2, I develop further the notion that any contemporary understanding of the ideology, culture and traditions in which current practices are based must be underpinned by a historical approach as a background to describing the present by exploring how the Ngaanyatjarra negotiated the profound period of change from the 1930s up to the present. Using personal narratives and historical data, I introduce the first generation to experience European practices during the 'mission time', as well as the subsequent generation, who experienced the encounter with the state during 'Native Welfare time' from the 1950s to the early 1970s, and the impact of 'self-determination' after 1972. I trace the introduction, transmission and development of literacy and learning across the generations to consider the interconnection between a complexity of factors, of which pedagogy is but a part. I consider how two prevailing ideologies – the Christian commitment to providing the written Word of God to adults in Ngaanyatjarra and the new state narrative of advancement through education in English – impacted on literacy development from the late 1950s to the early 1970s. I explore the development of literate habits, assumptions, dispositions and behaviours in the shift towards a literate mentality (Clanchy, 1979; Heath, 1991). Lastly, I show how the Ngaanyatjarra began using written language to address pressing social and cultural needs, such as the establishment of outstation communities and the emergence of a Ngaanyatjarra community of interest.

In Part 3, a practice-centred approach is used to consider anthropological aspects, such as the social construction of lived space: the habits and attitudes of time and space usage, literate systems and the materiality required to enact literate processes (Hanks, 1990; Lefebvre, [1974] 1991; Ochs, 1988). By focusing on literacy and the spatio-temporal determinants of social practice, I consider the ways in which these are in accord with, and mutually reinforce, other cultural patterns and the implications for language and literacy socialisation. Lastly, I turn to the adolescent and young-adult generation. I consider how the developmental trajectory of Ngaanyatjarra youth is diverging from both cultural and mainstream norms. Where young people were constrained by the tools of alphabetic literacy production, new digital technologies have catalysed a wave of intense, focused creativity and communication in a form that suits the context.

Introducing the Ngaanyatjarra

This book is about one remote Aboriginal group in the Western Desert of Australia. I focus on the Ngaanyatjarra and some Pitjantjatjara people who came into the United Aborigines Mission (UAM) at Warburton Ranges from the early 1930s. I also introduce the Ngaatjatjarra – the last of the nomads to come out of the desert in the 1960s. These groups still occupy the same region, known today as the 'Ngaanyatjarra Lands', in the south-east of Western Australia. This large area comprises some 250,000 square kilometres (approximately 3% of mainland Australia) of the Gibson, Great Sandy and Great Victoria deserts and the Central Ranges, fanning out from the tri-state border with South Australia and the Northern Territory (see Figure 1).

Today, the Ngaanyatjarra Lands operate as a cohesive and cooperative set of 11 communities under the umbrella of the Ngaanyatjarra Council.

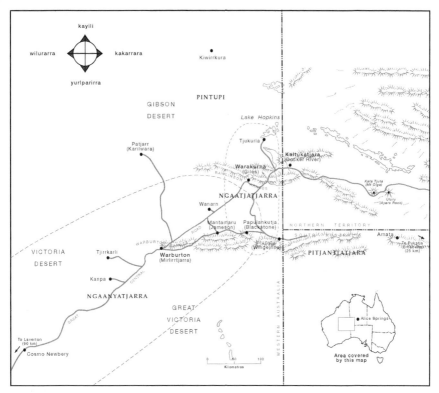

Figure 1 The Western Desert region.
Map by Brenda Thornley. © The Institute for Aboriginal Development

Warburton (*Mirlirrtjarra*) – the original site of the United Aborigines Mission – came under community control in 1973. The communities of Wingellina (*Irrunytju*), Blackstone (*Papulankutja*), Jameson (*Mantamaru*) and Giles (*Warakurna*) were established in the mid-1970s by Ngaanyatjarra, Ngaatjatjarra and Pitjantjatjara people returning to their traditional homelands. Permanent settlements were established at Tjukurla, Tjirrkarli, Wanarn and Kiwirrkura in the 1980s. Cosmo Newbery, previously under the United Aborigines Mission, was re-established under the Ngaanyatjarra Council after 1989, by families whose historical links are to Mt Margaret and Laverton in the Eastern 'Goldfields' region of Western Australia. Patjarr community was settled by the so-called 'Gibson Desert families' returning from the town of Wiluna in the 1990s. As will become clear throughout this volume, the temporary movement of Ngaanyatjarra people west to the towns, schools and pastoral stations of 'the Goldfields' is an integral aspect of the Ngaanyatjarra story (see Figure 2).

Enumerating accurate population data in this region is difficult, nevertheless, it is estimated that the Ngaanyatjarra Lands has a population of some 1600 permanent residents, plus a large and mobile visitor population (Brooks & Kral, 2007). Community facilities typically include a store, clinic, school and, often, a small church, an arts project and a media centre (operated by Ngaanyatjarra Media, the locally controlled remote Indigenous media organisation). Warburton, as the largest of the Ngaanyatjarra communities, also has a youth arts project, a swimming pool and a roadhouse nearby. Local government services are provided by the Shire of Ngaanyatjarraku and include a regional art gallery located nearby on the Great Central Road – the main arterial between the towns of Alice Spring to the east and Kalgoorlie to the west.

Ngaanyatjarra Language and Culture

Prior to contact with European society, Aboriginal people in the broader Western Desert region of Central Australia lived a relatively unchanged existence for thousands of years. Archaeological research dates human occupation in this region at some 10,000 years (Gould, 1980: 35) and in the broader Western Desert, at more than 24,000 years (Veth, 1996, cited in Rose, 2001: 35). Anthropologists talk of a 'Western Desert cultural bloc', including what is now the tri-state border region of the Northern Territory, South Australia and Western Australia. This cultural bloc comprises a single social system and relative cultural homogeneity extending in an arc from Woomera in the south-east of South Australia to Kalgoorlie in the south-west of Western Australia and north through to Wiluna, Jigalong and Balgo (Berndt & Berndt, 1980; Tonkinson, 1978).

Linguists collectively term the mutually intelligible dialects spoken across this large region as the Western Desert group of languages, within the Wati subgroup of the south-west group of the Pama-Nyungan family of languages (Glass & Hackett, 2003). The contemporary speech community of the Ngaanyatjarra Lands is not homogeneous. Although residents are predominantly Ngaanyatjarra speakers, the region comprises speakers of other mutually intelligible Western Desert dialects, predominantly Ngaatjatjarra, Pitjantjatjara and Pintupi. Other related dialects include Yankunytjatjara spoken further east of the Pitjantjarra region in South Australia and Manyjilyjarra, Gugadja and Wangkatja to the north and west. Many adults in the Ngaanyatjarra Lands have multi-lectal competence in

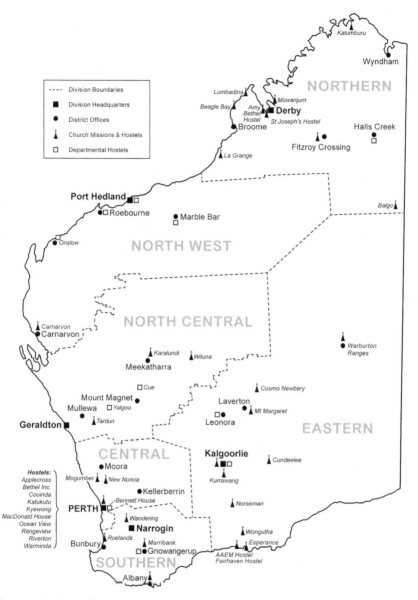

Figure 2 Native Welfare Department Western Australia – Divisions, Offices, Hostels and Church Missions.

Map by John Hughes and Gillian Cosgrove. Source: Department of Native Welfare Newsletter Vol. 2 No. 2 1971

other Western Desert dialects and English. Ngaanyatjarra is spoken around Warburton and east towards the Jameson Range; Ngaatjatjarra is spoken around the Jameson Range, Blackstone Range and Rawlinson Ranges; and Pitjantjatjara is spoken around the tri-state border region from around Wingellina in Western Australia east to the Mann Ranges in South Australia and into the Northern Territory. Pintupi, Ngaatjatjarra and Pitjantjatjara dialects are spoken at Tjukurla. At Kiwirrkura, the most northerly of the communities under the Ngaanyatjarra Council, the main language is Pintupi. Varieties of spoken English range between, at one end of the language continuum, English as a Second Language (a form resembling Standard Australian English) and, at the other end, a form of 'Aboriginal English' spoken as a first language (by a small group who have grown up in the Eastern Goldfields, some of whom retain a passive knowledge of Ngaanyatjarra).[4] The 2005 National Indigenous Language Survey rates Ngaanyatjarra as 'critically endangered' (AIATSIS/FATSIL, 2005: 193). Whether or not this assessment is accurate is, as yet, unclear. It is evident, nonetheless, that changed linguistic and cultural factors have impacted on spoken Ngaanyatjarra. Throughout this volume, I refer collectively to all language speakers as 'the Ngaanyatjarra' (or *yarnangu* – 'people'), unless referring to specific dialect groups.

Social organisation

Undergirding all social practice in this region is the continuity of the kinship system that operates at a symbolic level and as an actual framework of protocols that governs relatedness between affinal and consanguinal kin. Distinctive features of relatedness are found among consanguinal or 'close' kin, and similar kin terms are applied to affinal or 'distant' kin. Overall 'relatedness' between Ngaanyatjarra people (and across the broader Western Desert) is held together by the underpinning structure of a classificatory section system.

The section system represents a form of social organisation particular to a number of desert groups in Central Australia. The six section system (often referred to as 'skin names' as a shorthand for the system of relatedness) is of the Aluridja type and acts as a guide to the protocols employed in funerals, in the structure of some ceremonies and as a framework for marriage options (Brooks, 2002b; Glass, 1997). In this system (see Figure 3):

A *Tjarurru* man can marry either a *Panaka* or a *Yiparrka* woman (and has *Purungu* children).
A *Purungu* man can marry either a *Karimarra* or *Milangka* woman (and has *Tjarurru* children).

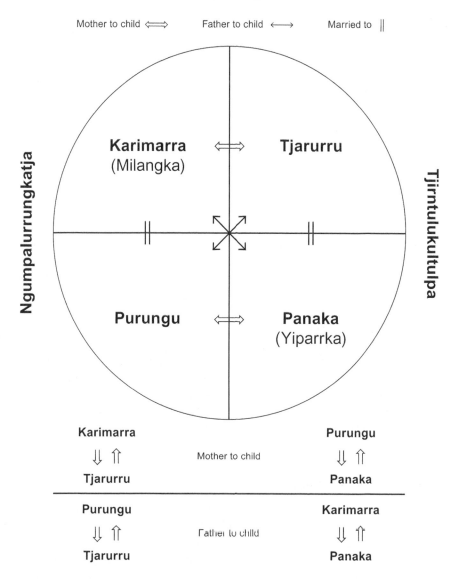

Figure 3 Ngaanyatjarra/Ngaatjatjarra section or skin name system.

Whereas:

A *Panaka* man can only marry a *Tjarurru* woman (and has *Karimarra* children).
A *Karimarra* man can only marry a *Purungu* woman (and has *Panaka* children).
A *Yiparrka* man marries a *Tjarurru* woman (and has *Milangka* children).
A *Milangka* man marries a *Purungu* woman (and has *Yiparrka* children).

The Ngaanyatjarra also have a horizontal moiety system. The group as a whole is divided into two parts, based on sets of alternating generations:

Tjirntulukultul(pa) – the 'sun side' social grouping consisting of *Tjarurru, Panaka, Yiparrka.*
Ngumpalurrungkatja – the 'shade side' social grouping consisting of the *Karimarra, Milangka, Purungu.*

Generational moiety division is central to the social and symbolic order of Ngaanyatjarra life and is deeply embedded in cultural processes. This division unites all the people of one set of alternating generations and places them in opposition to the people of the other set. Not only does 'each person inalienably belong, from birth, to one "side" or the other, but ceremony grounds, ceremonial activity and sacred sites are spatially divided into two parts on this basis' (Brooks, 2002b: 39–41). The cyclic nature of the system means that one's grandparents (*tjamu/kaparli*) and one's grandchildren (*tjamu/kaparli*) are in the same generational moiety as one's own generation, whereas one's children and one's parents are in the other generational moiety. The 'worst violation' of rules, relating to marriage partners, involves partnering '*yinyurrpa* way', that is, to a person of the other generational moiety (Brooks, 2002b).[5]

Tjukurrpa: The 'Dreaming'

To understand contemporary Ngaanyatjarra identity, in relation to the overarching cultural schema and framework of symbols that the Ngaanyatjarra draw on in their oral and written practices, requires paying attention to the underlying connection to the worlds within which current actions, practices and assumptions make sense. For the Ngaanyatjarra, their most fundamental ontological premises or conceptions of being-in-the-world (Clammer *et al.*, 2004) derive from the *tjukurrpa* (that is, the 'Dreaming' or the 'Law') – the spiritual framework that provides the overarching cultural schema within which contemporary life is played out.

Fundamental to Ngaanyatjarra, social unity and cultural life was, and still is, the *tjukurrpa*. In the Western Desert, the *tjukurrpa* provides an underpinning metaphysics that anthropologists Fred Myers and Annette Hamilton consider to embrace a sense of 'changeless, timeless, permanence' (Myers, 1986) or 'timeless transformation' (Hamilton, 1979). David Brooks, an anthropologist who has worked with the Ngaanyatjarra since 1988, suggests that all Ngaanyatjarra people share a world of meaning that basically derives from the *tjukurrpa*. This is manifest in the way in which people interpret aspects of the world and conceive the links between people, country, events and phenomena. Much of their habitual thinking about the world takes place through the lens of the *tjukurrpa*, in a manner that distinguishes them from 'whitefellas' or non-Aboriginal people. Moreover, even Ngaanyatjarra youth, despite their contemporary demeanour and ways of being in the world, have imbibed this worldview from their elders and maintain an underlying cultural propensity for what Brooks (2011b) terms '*tjukurrpa*-thinking' in everyday life.

It is believed that in the *tjukurrpa*, the Ancestral Beings created the landscape:

> The Dreaming Beings created the animals and plants which provided food for people; and they gave names to these animals and plants and to all things. They taught people how to hunt, gather, cook and share out the various types of food; as well as how to make implements such as spears, water carrying vessels and the like. They laid down the roles to be played by people, men and women in the course of their life cycles, and the methods by which the successive transformations through the life cycle were to be achieved. They established different groupings within the body corporate of Ngaanyatjarra people as well as various roles to facilitate the conduct of an orderly life in the sphere of material production and to govern social relationships generally. All these creative acts which the Dreaming Beings performed were sacred (*miirl-miirlpa* or *mayaka*); and as well as performing them for the first time they taught the people to regularly reproduce their original acts, and thereby to keep the energising sacredness alive. (Brooks, 2002c: 12)

Tjukurrpa-related performance, interlinked with connection to country, undergirds the contemporary cultural identity of Ngaanyatjarra people. 'Country' is 'first and foremost' a matter of *tjukurrpa* relationships:

It is in and through the cycle of sacred creation, which was initiated by the Dreaming Beings and continued through the generations by living people, that Ngaanyatjarra people's common relationship to the land is constituted and maintained. This relationship, which has spiritual and emotional dimensions, and entails responsibilities and obligations as well as rights and interest, is in a sense the birthright or inheritance of all Ngaanyatjarra people. (Brooks, 2002c: 18)

The Dreaming tracks laid down by the Ancestral Beings permeate the contemporary consciousness as a symbolic map not only to the physical locations in 'country' traversed for thousands of years by their forebears, but also to the telling and re-telling of the *tjukurrpa* stories. Regenerative re-enactments of the *tjukurrpa*, through ritual and ceremony, remain critical to the well-being of the Ngaanyatjarra. A complex web of cultural meaning is embedded in the rich semiotic resources of the *tjukurrpa*. In the Western Desert, sacred texts and performances 'encode the system of land ownership and resource exchange', thus, 'encrypting' information, that has been indispensable to social and material well-being over great distances and deep time (Rose, 2001: 29). These, and other sociocultural systems, have been reproduced through time as social situations that are 'realised as texts of various types, including verbal exchanges, instructions, narratives, songs, rituals, paintings' (Rose, 2001: 49). Narratives from the *tjukurrpa* have varying discursive strengths and restrictions, depending on the secular or sacred nature of context and audience, and provide enduring models for human behaviour. Language thus forms the nexus between *tjukurrpa,* identity and well-being in the construction of reality that makes sense in the Ngaanyatjarra world.

In the classical past, there were perhaps 2000 people widely dispersed over a large region of the Great Victoria Desert (Brooks & Shaw, 2003: 2–3), roughly equivalent to the population of the Ngaanyatjarra Lands today.[6] Within the construct of social-relatedness, the rhythm of desert life was an 'irregularly alternating aggregation and dispersal of social groups' (Tonkinson, 1978: 29). Individuals were either within the smaller band grouping all bounded by attachments to particular country or within the broader collective for ceremonial gatherings. The 'Ngaanyatjarra' probably spent most of their time in bands of around 12 to 20 people, and the 'tendency' was for senior men and their families to roam on their own country, with sets of brothers usually sharing a common broad country, thus creating an anchor point to specific areas. Each brother would have one or two wives, and the group would consist of the children and probably a grandparent, perhaps a widow or two and a couple of young men (Brooks, 2011a). The regulatory capacity of senior Law men was respected and feared, and the flaunting of rules resulted in retribution, often by spearing. It was, and still is, the role of men to protect or 'hold' (*kanyira*) the people. They do this mainly through having primary responsibility for the performance of ceremony, 'which keeps the physical and metaphysical world in harmony and balance, for the benefit of all people' (Brooks & Shaw, 2003: 23). The internal trust of this small kin-based society was counterbalanced by the external distrust of *malikitja* or 'strangers or persons from another place', often in the form of *warrmarla* or 'revenge parties'. Revenge parties were either the secret travel-by-night *tjina karrpilpa* (featherfeet) or the more open, confrontational *warrmarla* (warrior groups) who came in groups to raid or take wives (Brooks & Shaw, 2003; Glass & Hackett, 2003). Revenge killings were a 'sanction against individuals transgressing the common good' and, by such means, the Law has enabled the 'smooth running of the society on a large scale, and its reproduction through deep time' (Rose, 2001: 28).

Survival in the physically harsh environment of the Western Desert provided a subsistence challenge (Gould, 1969; Hamilton, 1979; Myers, 1986). In times of rain, people moved through the broader stretches of country to forage for food and other resources. In times of drought, people were less mobile and exploited a tighter locus of water sources. Myers suggests that the unreliability of rainfall necessitated a 'continual interdependence' among a network of people across the Western Desert and 'social isolation' was 'ecologically impossible' (Myers, 1986: 27). Large gatherings of people would come together for ceremonies in locations where food and water were sufficiently abundant to last a few weeks (Brooks & Shaw, 2003). One of the most important was the young men's manhood-making ceremonies, now referred to in English as the '[Law] Business' (Peterson, 2000; Sackett, 1978b; Tonkinson, 1974). Ritual and ceremony involved a complex network of social relatedness extant through marriage, economic exchange and the reciprocal transmission of knowledge. Still today, during the annual Law Business ceremonial activity, kin across the Western Desert are tied into a system of reciprocal rights and obligations where the Law provides a set of socially sanctioned norms of conduct or rules that govern behaviour. The *tjukurrpa* remains the enduring moral authority that lies outside individuals and underpins everyday life in this 'symbolic space' (Myers, 1986) where control is maintained by persistent, collective cultural belief systems. Sorcery and the supernatural (manifest in a fear of unknown or malevolent forces) are part of the perceived reality, and spirits – *mamu, mitjunu, wurna-wurna* – lurk on the periphery of everyday events and activities. Such beliefs are interpreted as the causational factors behind illness, hence, traditional healers (*ngangkari* or *maparntjarra*) still play an important role. The worldview of the Ngaanyatjarra remains premised on the social system organised through the *tjukurrpa*. Social relations remain relatively lightly transformed from pre-settlement times (Peterson, 2000) and immense social value continues to be placed on 'relatedness with others' (Myers, 1986: 107–9).

The Ngaanyatjarra have come through the trauma of colonisation relatively unscathed. This is not to say that in their struggle to embrace modernity, they have also not been affected by socio-economic disadvantage, poverty, alcohol, substance abuse, imprisonment, death of close relatives through accident or illness and the monotonous regularity of funerals that leads to a foreboding sense of a foreshortened life expectancy. Nevertheless, the Ngaanyatjarra, as a group, have never left their country, nor has their country been annexed or occupied by outsiders. These factors have contributed to the strong collective identity evident today.

Yarnangu – The People

This ethnographic study of intergenerational change and transmission focuses on the people of the Ngaanyatjarra Lands, predominantly, the families connected to the Warburton area – the locus of continuous contact with European practices since the 1930s – but also those with historical links west to Mt Margaret Mission, Cosmo Newbery and the Eastern Goldfields and east to Ernabella (see Figure 1). I use close ethnographic observations and archival sources to capture the unfolding of this rich multi-layered complexity. I interweave intergenerational narratives to illustrate language and literacy socialisation as a 'generational cultural process' (Rogoff, 2003) and to display individual and collective 'trajectories of identity formation' (Holland & Lave, 2009). Life-course narratives, using people's own words, sit alongside the main body of the text. Pseudonyms are used to protect the anonymity of individual Ngaanyatjarra people. Interviews were conducted in English, transcribed and occasionally translated from Ngaanyatjarra. Real names are used for places and events, as Ngaanyatjarra people are proud of their history and want it told accurately. The real names of non-Aboriginal people ('whitefellas') are used to anchor the history in real time. Ngaanyatjarra words and phrases are used throughout, and translations are found either in the body of the text or in the Glossary. For ease of reference, the people whose narratives I use are grouped together in Table 1, in generational categories, in family groupings.

Table 1 Intergenerational chart

Generation 1 (Mission)	Generation 2 (Native Welfare)	Generation 3 (Self-Determination)	Generation 4 (Now)
Valcie b.1930 m.	**Helen** b.1955		
husband (Mt Margaret Mission)	**Wesley** b.1961	Children	Grandchildren
Katherine b.1937		Children	Grandchildren
Arthur b.1949		Daughter	Granddaughter
Mary b.1935 m. Jack (born around 1926)	**Jacinta** b.1965 m. Patricia's brother	**Troy** b.1982	
Horace b.1932	**Silas** b. 1951	Children	Grandchildren
Harold b.1934 m. W1 - **Rosie** b.1941	Daughter	**Rosemary** b.1985	
	Carmel b.1963 m. **George b.1956**	Son m. **Adina** b. 1982	**Rosina** b.1999
		Nancy b.1987	
	Eileen b.1967 m. **Darren** b.1956	Son Kenny b. 1972 (Darren's nephew)	Grandchildren
(Phyllis b.1954 is Nina's FM)	**Pamela** b.1976 m. **Mick** b.1966	**Nina** b.1998	
Harold m. W2 - **Daphne** b.1944		Grandson m. **Leanne** b.1985	
April's mother b.1940 m. father b.1925	**April** b.1955 m. **Marlon** b.1942	Children	Grandchildren
Patricia's father b.1940 m. W1 b.1940	**Patricia** b.1963 **Jennifer** b.1966	**Lucy** b.1980	**Shantoya** b.1998
Molly b.1940	Children	Grandchildren	
	Clem b.1953	Children	Grandchildren

Table 1 continued

Generation 1 (Mission)	Generation 2 (Native Welfare)	Generation 3 (Self-Determination)	Generation 4 (Now)
Nomadic	Joshua b.1936 m. (W1 – Rosie's sister) W2 – Dawn b.1958	Naomi b.1978 Leah b.1981 m. Mick's brother b.1981	Grandchildren
Una's father b.1923 m. mother b.1937	Una b.1951	Children	Grandchildren
	Maisie b.1947 (Mt Margaret Mission)		
Warburton Ranges Mission	Jim b.1953 m. W1 b.1954	Clarrie b.1979	Grandchildren
Warburton Ranges Mission	Jane b.1956 m. David b.1946 Kayleen b.1972 m. Clifford b.1968	Children	Grandchildren
Nomadic	Louisa b.1959	Jake b.1983 Darleen b.1987	Children
Nomadic	Wingellina	John b. 1985 m. Tinpulya b. 1985	Children
Ernabella Mission	Ernabella		

Key: W1 = Wife 1; W2 = Wife 2 (i.e. co-wives)

Notes

(1) Indigenous students from remote schools are now benchmarked using the National Assessment Program – Literacy and Numeracy (NAPLAN). In the NAPLAN tests, Years 3, 5, 7 and 9 are assessed using national tests in reading, writing, language conventions (spelling, grammar and punctuation) and numeracy and are compared with student achievement in other Australian states and territories.

(2) My methodology (2003–2010) included life history interviews with more than 60 Ngaanyatjarra adults across three generational cohorts (older, middle-aged and young adults); non-Indigenous key informant interviews; participant observation; the collection of literacy artefacts; and data from the Ngaanyatjarra Council 2004

CDEP skills audit and interviews from a review of education and training (Kral & Ward, 2000).

(3)   As exemplified in Shirley Brice Heath's (1983) ethnographic study, *Ways with Words*, and her follow-up study across the generations of spoken and written language in social change (Heath, 1990; Heath, 2012), and Patricia Greenfield's intergenerational study of cultural learning and cultural transmission in an indigenous Mexican community (Greenfield, 1999; Greenfield, 2004).

(4)   *Wangkayi*, or *Wongai*, tends to be used to refer to people from the Eastern Goldfields, whereas Ngaanyatjarra people are referred to as *yarnangu*. Wangkayi derives from *wangka*, meaning 'speech' or 'language'. People are also termed *wangkatja*, sometimes rendered as *Wangkatha*, *Wongatha* or *Wongutha* (Douglas, 1964).

(5)   See, also, Goddard (1983), Hamilton, (1979), White (1981) and Myers (1986) for discussions on social organisation in the Western Desert.

(6)   Classical, here, refers to the pre-contact past, when desert people maintained their original hunter-gatherer existence.

Part 1
Living in the Now

This book begins in the present: *Living in the Now*. The first chapter, 'From Forgetting to Remembering', is a consideration of how the Ngaanyatjarra have adapted, adopted and modified to living in the new kind of present that prevails today in the desert communities of the Ngaanyatjarra Lands. Culture change and language shift are signalled in three practices: funerals, birthdays and naming. Over time, new practices and altered protocols have become taken-for-granted ways of being in this transformed sociocultural space. In this chapter, we see young people embracing the new technologies that enable permanency. For the youth generation, the classical life belongs to an unknowable past, and they accept 'the now' as normative. In effect, Chapter 1 introduces the cultural ways in which literacy is utilised, and the abstract cultural conceptions and social meanings associated with reading and writing are emphasised. Whereas, in Chapter 2, 'Transmitting Orality and Literacy as Cultural Practice', I turn to the settings of everyday life in one community, and the observable tasks and activities associated with literacy are described. Literacy is discussed in terms of the alphabetic literacies enacted in both domestic and public domains. I discuss the oral and literate practices that form the backdrop to everyday social interactions that children observe in this community of practice. I illuminate how literacy has permeated the practice of everyday life and bring to the fore the practices of the more visible literates in the community of Warburton. Typically, these individuals are from the 'mission families', who have been integrating literacy into social practice for up to four generations. I identify, also, how many Ngaanyatjarra live without needing to read or write much at all. Lastly, I explore the mismatch in expectations surrounding literacy practice in institutional settings, by indicating the consequences of illiteracy.

Importantly, Part 1 reveals the extent to which a literate orientation and literate behaviours (Heath, 1991) have become part of the habitus of contemporary Ngaanyatjarra life (Bourdieu, 1977; Ortner, 1989).

1 From Forgetting to Remembering

In Loving Memory of...[1]

A *Panaka* relative has passed away and various kin have gathered together to help prepare the funeral text or *'pipa' (pipa kurrakurra)* for the church service in five days' time. An atmosphere of sadness pervades the small room, intermingled with an air of respectful, industrious, focused productivity emanating from the different generations of the one extended family. Five women are huddled around a computer. All eyes are focused on the screen as one young woman responds to the instructions issued by her elders. It is a scene that exemplifies the collaborative, historically constituted and essentially social nature of cultural production elemental to everyday practice in the Ngaanyatjarra Lands' communities today.

Among the Ngaanyatjarra, everyone is regarded as being related to everyone else. Social organisation is the core force in the structuring of funerals and distinct protocols are respected. All *yarnangu* belong to one of six sections in the kinship system: *Purungu, Karimarra, Milangka, Tjarurru, Yiparrka* and *Panaka* (see Figure 3 in the Introduction). The section system defines everyone's relationship to each other and acts as a guide to protocols at funerals and other ceremonies. This funeral is organised by those of the *Tjarurru* section, who are the designated *tilitjartu* or traditional undertakers. The *tilitjartu* (the husband, or wife, and brothers-in-law and sisters-in-law of the deceased) are those who take on the role of the 'workers' at funerals. It is the role of the *tilitjartu* to communicate the 'sad news' to distant kin and inform them when the funeral will be held and where. Funeral notices are faxed to locations hundreds of kilometres away, and kin travel long distances to attend to the social obligations and responsibilities associated with the funeral. Families who are unable to attend fax their condolences, and these are read out at the funeral service. It is also the role of the *tilitjartu* (or others who assume the role if *tilitjartu* are unavailable) to negotiate, write and produce the funeral text.

On the day of the funeral, the *tilitjartu* escort the family to the church. After the service, the *tilitjartu* go ahead with the coffin and take responsibility for the burial at the cemetery on the outskirts of the community. In times past, upon completion of the burial, the *tilitjartu* would return to the wailing mourners and throw gum leaves over them, followed by a ritual exchange of gifts such as spears, coolamons, resin, ochre or hair-belts. Nowadays, once the burial is complete, mourners shake hands with the *tilitjartu* to thank them for their work, and contemporary objects, such as blankets, are exchanged.

Funerals in Warburton and the other Ngaanyatjarra communities occur with an unsettling regularity – an unnerving reminder of the high mortality rate among Indigenous people in Australia. Since the mid-1980s, with the establishment of community cemeteries, funeral rites in the Ngaanyatjarra Lands have taken on many features typical of Christian funerals. This is manifest in the textual dimension and the manner in which Christian symbols and values permeate the discourse. Funerals signal the ever-evolving nature of social practice in this remote Aboriginal Australian context. Moreover, this contemporary ritual exemplifies how introduced practices have been adopted, adapted and merged with remnant practices of the past. This, in turn, has generated new cultural practices and altered social protocols that have become the new norm for successive generations.

Textual practice as cultural practice

Over the last decade or so, funerals have become textually mediated events. Nowhere is this more evident than in the emergence of *'pipa'*: written eulogies in the form of small booklets that are handed out to mourners at the church service. These texts represent one of the more vivid examples of the textual dimension of changing social practice in the desert communities of the Ngaanyatjarra Lands.

The eulogy production process has undergone a rapid and profound transformation in less than a decade. Prior to this, written eulogies, if they existed at all, were simple, handwritten texts, inclusive of errors in grammar and spelling. By the early 2000s, computer technology had become commonplace. It was, however, typically located within the sphere of non-Aboriginal control. Access to computers was generally negotiated through personal relationships with non-Aboriginal staff who worked in office locations or non-Aboriginal friends who assisted on their home computers. The writing process was thus typically mediated through a literate person (generally non-Aboriginal). Simple templates were often constructed in Microsoft Word, enabling quick layout and production in busy offices. As I discuss in Chapter 7, increased access to computers in public spaces over the last five years has led to greater Ngaanyatjarra autonomy in the writing and production of increasingly complex documents. Now, many young people have computer competence and are independently able to produce ever more sophisticated documents, inclusive of graphics and photographs. Although a typical practice in Warburton, computer-mediated texts are, however, less common in the smaller, more traditional communities, where a simple handwritten 'Order of Service' may suffice.

The process of writing the *pipa* is communal. It brings the sociality of related kin together in textual form. The relationship with the deceased continues on, living in the text 'so the children continue thinking of him, being with him'. In this collaborative literacy event, everyone can contribute ideas on how the text should be constructed, what images and symbols should be used and, importantly, how the list of grieving relatives should be ordered. As a literacy event, the production of the funeral text involves, firstly, research – finding accurate dates of birth, names of extended family, and details of personal histories and selecting appropriate verses from the Bible in English or Ngaanyatjarra. Next, the text is drafted on paper, keyed into the computer, edited and borders and symbols are inserted. Previous funeral texts are also referred to, thus, features of this new written genre, including layout and formulaic phrases, are modelled, imitated and transmitted. Older relatives dictate recounts of significant events that younger writers attempt to structure into a cohesive written narrative, usually in English and occasionally Ngaanyatjarra. Young people with computer skills may take on the role of writers, but they defer to their elders who have the authority to approve the content:

> That's a big gap in there from when he was a boy to when he was working on stations. I'll print it and have a look. They should explain it to us properly so we can write it down, they shouldn't talk in riddles. Can't jump from little kid to working straight away. Go and see XX, she'll know.

The order of the funeral service, including Bible readings, hymns and prayers in English and Ngaanyatjarra, is listed in the text. The affective significance of the text foregrounds not only the continuing and binding obligation that kin have to the deceased, but also the protocols of social interaction. The list of mourning relations is a key feature of the genre and is marked by a specific protocol. Oral memory is used to compile the extensive kinship web – living and deceased – with older people, recollecting the intricacies of the genealogical connections in the written listing of some 200 named relatives or more. Close relatives are individually named and more distant kin are listed in surname groupings, often followed by a cautious addition: 'and many more too numerous to name' – in case some names have been forgotten. These texts enable younger people, or kin from urban centres in the Eastern Goldfields, to see genealogical links they may have forgotten or have never known. The process of negotiating the text can take days: deciding which kin should be listed, in what order: 'put *kurta* and *tjurtu* (older siblings) and their kids first', suggests one woman. Those who prepare the written list must ensure that no-one is left out and that the list is written in the 'right way'. A writer comments on the structure of one such list: 'He might get wild and spear me if his name's not there!' she jokes in a half-serious manner.

The prominent inclusion of *turlku* (hymns) and excerpts from the translated Bible highlights the symbolic significance of Ngaanyatjarra as a written language. It also allows the older 'mission generation' to show off their deep knowledge of passages from the Bible. A touching aspect of many of these texts is the foregrounding of significant relationships with non-Aboriginal people who have played an important role in the historical memory. As such, the texts are emblematic of the respectful and positive relationships between Ngaanyatjarra and 'whitefellas' that have developed in this region.

Symbolic structuring

The multilayered symbol system of the Ngaanyatjarra social and cultural world is powerfully indexed in the funeral texts and expressed in a complex interplay between the rich imagery of Christianity intertwined with the cultural emblems of contemporary Ngaanyatjarra identity and sentiment. The cultural organisation of Ngaanyatjarra communicative processes and oral genres is apparent in the texts, as is the overarching framework of symbols that draw on Ngaanyatjarra cultural schemas. A rich interplay of symbolic references is revealed in the layering of text, images, icons and colour in specific ways, in accordance with the affective recalled image of the individual. Gentle images of flowers and birds frame the photos of softer personalities, whereas strong leaders are framed by defining lines and the Aboriginal colours of red, yellow and black ochre. Christian symbols, such as the Bible, an angel or cross are commonly used. Such attention to detail flows into the funeral service: 'Gotta make the funeral in a good way so people can see what he was doing in this community'.

In this new narrative, the sentiment of nurturance, 'looking after' or 'caring for' kin, as a core value in the framework of social relatedness – expressed in Ngaanyatjarra as *kanyilku* or *miranykanyilku* – is symbolised in the poetic tenderness of the messages:

To our loving uncle, We will miss you. Our hearts are breaking knowing that you are not here with us.

We never wanted memories, we only wanted you. A million times we needed you, A million times we cried.

Gone are the happy days we shared but not the memories; they last forever. When thoughts go back as they often do, I will treasure the memories I have of you.

To you my son-in-law, You went away from us so quick. We will always remember you in our hearts. So many sad tears I've shed.

We all miss you and love you very much. And the memories are deep in our hearts forever.

Concern for the well-being of kin is typically expressed by the close family in a message on the last page of the booklet, thanking mourners for sharing their sorrow and wishing them a safe journey home. In one text, the family gives:

... thanks to everyone for their help and support during this very sad time, if we have left any one's names out, we are sorry please forgive us.

Pipa, as a written record, marks not only cultural change, but also language shift. It used to be that even the use of the written form of the name of the deceased challenged oral protocols. The sad news was, and often still is, announced by referring to the status of the bereaved: '*Karirrkanya pirnkurringu* – Karirrka has become a bereaved sister' or '*Nuninya wangulyararringu* – Nuni has become an orphan' (Glass, 1997: 39). In oral discourse, *yarnangu* still announce the news from the perspective of the bereaved: 'Have you heard the sad news? Barbara*nya kutjurringu* – Barbara has become one'. Whereas, in the new written genre, relatives are referred to from the perspective of the deceased: the 'loving uncle of', 'nephew and cousin to'. Moreover, loose Aboriginal English kin terms are seeping in from the urban towns of the Eastern Goldfields. The English term 'uncle', for example, is now commonly used to refer both to '*mama*' (father's brother), as well as '*kamuru*' (mother's brother).

Historical memory

Funerals, like so many aspects of Ngaanyatjarra social practice, have undergone profound change in only a few decades. In this modified rite of passage, we see not only a documentation of accelerated change, exemplified most poignantly in the changing practice associated with names and images of the deceased, but also amplification of memory.

In the classical past, protocols associated with death and burial were strictly observed. Sorrow was such a powerful emotion that it caused the bereaved to wail, keen and hit themselves with grief. The 'sad news' was communicated by word of mouth, gesture and ritual wailing. Close relatives would cut their hair short as a sign of sorrow, a practice still evident today. In the past, people were so grief-stricken after a death that possessions belonging to the deceased were burned or given away, and people moved away from the location where the death had occurred. According to Brooks, this allowed people to 'survive in the kind of present that prevails in the desert', as prolonged grieving for the deceased was seen to hamper ongoing life (Brooks, 2011a). In the past, the grieving process involved an erasure of any memory of the deceased, including avoiding the name of someone who had recently passed away. When referring to the deceased (or someone with the same name), individuals used the term *kunmarnarra* (as a substitute name), until a suitable period of mourning had elapsed. A new term was also temporarily substituted for any other words that sounded similar to the name of the deceased. Today, the term *kunmarnarra* is still used. Families also leave the house of the recently deceased and move into a temporary camp, known as a 'sorry camp', until the funeral takes place, often not returning to the house where they previously resided, because they are 'too sorry'.

New cultural orthodoxies

With the arrival of photography and film, new cultural orthodoxies have emerged. The insertion of photographs of the deceased in the funeral text is a recent innovation, although a reluctance to incorporate images of the deceased remains an issue for some older *yarnangu*. Prior to the arrival of cameras, images of the deceased were non-existent. Until recently, hard-copy images were put away and not viewed until a suitable period of time had elapsed and the family gave permission for the image to be seen once more. In addition, images in newsletters, magazines and other printed matter were covered over. The advent of Aboriginal 'media organisations' has led to the production of locally made videos. As a consequence, new protocols have been developed, and films containing images of the recently deceased are locked away in specially designated cupboards. The community digital database of historical photos – *Ara Irititja* – maintains this practice by having a category of 'sorrow' photos closed off from public view, until the family agrees to have them restored to the 'open' category.[2]

The turning point for considering the inclusion of images in funeral texts may have come in 2001, with the funeral of a significant Ngaanyatjarra leader. This large funeral included many important visitors from outside the local community. The family of the deceased worked on the memorial document for many days, preparing hundreds of copies, each bound with a thin, coloured ribbon. A debate ensued around whether to include a photo; however, his sisters prevailed in their refusal to allow his image to be included.[3] With the introduction of digital cameras over the last decade, a surfeit of images of people has entered the public domain. This is challenging the contemporary cultural orthodoxy associated with the photographic permanency of images of deceased relatives. *Yarnangu* are once more accommodating new transformations by inserting digital images of the recently deceased into funeral texts.

Texts are now commonly mastered by young people with computer skills, who independently produce them in community offices, media centres or the small Youth Arts Project studio in Warburton (see Chapter 7). Young people search for images of the deceased in folders of digital photos and weave the symbols of Ngaanyatjarra sociality into an integrated whole, as noted above. This practice is, nonetheless, still in a state of transformation. In a 2010 funeral text for a woman born in the 1930s, not only was her image on the front cover, but also digital images of 24 of her extended family were embedded in the document. Rather than wanting to forget, digital technologies are allowing *yarnangu* to hold on to images of their loved ones: 'to keep that one for memory'. Families note that holding a copy of the text in their hands is meaningful: 'instead of just having a funeral where they walk out, they have something' as a record, a tangible memory to take away with them. Today, even the name of the deceased (and sometimes his or her relatives) may be inscribed on the headstone of a grave as a permanent marker.

A written record

Funeral texts are becoming not only the repository of oral memory, but also a written record for future generations. The funeral brings written texts to life, for here, oral performances retell the life story, thus representing 'the symbolic construction of discursive continuity with a meaningful past' (Bauman & Briggs, 1990: 78). Unlike in the recent past, when funerals tended to be conducted by non-Aboriginal pastors and the oral eulogy was marked with moral inflections that tended to emphasise the elevation of Christ over the shortcomings of the individual. Now the written genre is bringing a life-cycle cultural perspective to the fore.

The oral 'travelling narrative' story schema, deriving from the traditional oral canon, forms the structuring principle of the narrative in many funeral texts where the life journey and achievements of the deceased are emphasised. The written genre of the funeral text typically uses a chronological structure to situate the individual's unique journey within the shared historical trajectory of momentous sociocultural change experienced by the Ngaanyatjarra over recent decades. Memories are recalled of life before contact with Europeans; of surviving adverse desert conditions and making epic treks by foot; of growing up in the mission at Warburton Ranges, Ernabella or Mt Margaret; of schooling in the Eastern Goldfields towns of Esperance, Kalgoorlie and Leonora during the assimilation era and working on stations near Laverton and Wiluna; of establishing new communities in the 1970s and participating in the Christian Crusades in the 1980s; of being leaders of the people; of protecting the country; and of raising strong and happy families. These narratives are a unique genre, written by *yarnangu* for a *yarnangu* audience. Through these texts, the memories of the lives of the significant leaders, the important elders, the mothers, the fathers, the uncles, the aunts, the cousins, the siblings and the children taken away too young are all preserved for posterity with equal reverence, care and love. Big and small achievements are honoured and immortalised in the text. The life trajectories of individuals are no longer ephemeral. *Yarnangu* are embracing the permanency of cultural memory and reflecting on their own history as individuals, families and as a cultural group. Inadvertently, the texts also reveal the manner in which the defining markers of an individual's lifespan trajectory (education, training and employment) commonly parallel the typical Western life-course paradigm.

In summary, the funeral texts described here illustrate the innovative manner in which *yarnangu* are adapting to altered sociocultural circumstances and modifying cultural practice to meet contemporary circumstances. Funerals are thus an adapted cultural practice, whereby memory is mediated visually and textually through the markers of cultural and linguistic change.

In Celebration of the Birth of . . .

At the other end of the life cycle, *birth* represents regeneration and new life. In classical times, significant rites of passage were oriented around place, seasons and *tjukurrpa*. People's enduring relationship with their *ngurra* or 'country' or 'place' was anchored through birth. Their *ngurra* was their inalienable, intrinsic home, their place of origin, originating from a time when everyone's birth was inextricably linked to country and the overarching cultural schema embedded in the *tjukurrpa*. Moreover, every individual's *tjukurrpa* was determined by their birthplace. When a baby was born, he or she became imbued with the *kuurti* – the 'identity or essence' of the particular *tjukurrpa* associated with that place – and was forever interconnected with the country of a 'grouping' of relatives (Brooks, 2002c: 19–21). In earlier times, a grandmother would 'smoke' (*puyungkatja* or *tjunarntatja*) a newborn baby to ensure that it 'grow up straight':

> When the baby born in the bush, which rockhole, which spirit come from the baby, when the babies have the birthmark on them, grand-mothers have to take responsibility for the baby, put it in a wooden dish in the smoke. Then that man never grow up nuisance, he listen to the mother, never talk back to the family.[4]

Today, babies are generally born in hospitals in the regional towns of Kalgoorlie or Alice Springs, nearly 1000 kilometres away. Nevertheless, youngsters still tend to identify with their community as their *ngurra* or 'place', thereby ensuring that the connection between an individual and their 'country' retains significance. In addition, the celebration of birth based on 'date of birth' is now commonplace, and birthday parties are facilitating a new form of identity socialisation.

Birthday parties as social practice

Nina and Rosina are children from a Warburton family whose lineage extends back to the first encounter with missionaries in 1933 (see Table 1 in the Introduction). The family continues to live in Warburton today. Rosina and Nina have birthdays a few days apart. They expect that a 'birthday party' will be organised to celebrate this event.

Nina is turning six. Her birthday party is organised by all her mothers – her *ngunytju*, that is, her mother and her mother's sisters Carmel, Pamela and Eileen – and her *kaparli*, her grandmother, Rosie. The day before the party, Nina's matri-kin order a birthday cake and sandwiches at the local roadhouse. A birthday card for a six-year-old is also purchased. Nina's adult older sister – her *tjurtu* – asks me to help write the appropriate text, she signs it, then organises for the rest of the family to sign it. On the morning of the party, the cake is collected and crisps, lollies, fruit, cordial and paper cups and plates are purchased. When the women return with the food, all the children are ordered out of the house. Preparations are made in the kitchen, hidden from view. The women cut up the fruit, fill the bowls with potato crisps and sweets and plastic buckets are filled with red cordial. The kitchen table is covered with a cloth, and the food is laid out, with the chocolate cake – inscribed with *Happy Birthday* – taking centrepiece on the table.

When the preparations are complete, the door is opened, and the party fare is revealed. Everyone in the extended family enters the kitchen; attention is focused briefly on Nina, and 'Happy Birthday' is sung. The children are then told to line up, before filing around the table to select a plate of party food. Once all the food is consumed, the guests soon depart. A few days later, Rosina announces: 'It's my happy birthday today, November 9'. Adina has organised a party for her daughter's fifth birthday. Unusually, Adina has done this on her own, since her older matri-kin are absent from the community. Adina has baked special 'cupcakes', cut up fruit, and prepared sandwiches and cordial. She has also bought an ice-cream birthday cake from the store and placed five candles on top, next to the numeral 5 denoted in coloured jelly-beans. Notably, Rosina's party parallels the social routines evident at Nina's birthday party.

As a social event, the birthday party stands in stark contrast to daily food preparation and consumption practices.[5] Typically, most mealtimes involve minimal elaborate preparation and few organised temporal routines. By contrast, birthday parties are planned affairs with unspoken rules about preparation, presentation and the order of events. The planning phase involves saving sufficient money to pay for the party fare, as well as estimating the quantity of food and drink required, then ordering the food in advance. Once the 'preparation and performance' phase commences, birthday parties resemble ceremonial performance in the manner in which the preparation of the event is concealed, followed by revelation when everything is ready, followed by performance, consumption and exit. Under ordinary circumstances, Ngaanyatjarra children are typically not socialised into time-and-space rule-oriented boundaries, contrasting with the discipline expected of children during ceremony time.[6] The birthday party is an atypical social event in that it reinforces delayed gratification and allows adults to enforce discipline and regulatory control, by keeping the children outside until preparations are complete and enforcing 'lining up' and taking food 'one-by-one'. Having been socialised into Western domestic socio-spatial, corporeal and linguistic routines, young mothers are comfortably merging new practices with old in these ritual celebrations with children.

Birthday parties as literacy events

Importantly, the 'birthday party' reveals the extent to which text has permeated this adopted Western cultural practice. As mentioned earlier, birthday cards are bought, written and signed. Although it is still relatively rare for people to receive birthday cards in the mail, people who are related to family in the Eastern Goldfields are likely to receive birthday cards or cards announcing the birth of a new child. Leah, a young mother, says: 'when there's party, [I] get a card and sit down and write', but 'not much people do like that, but I do'. Textual events tend to be English-based, as is the singing of the *Happy Birthday* song. As in Western birthday parties, the 'birthday cake' has become an important signifier, both as a material object and also 'an immaterial sign or symbol of kinship' (Gee, 2004: 33). Birthday cakes have embedded literacy aspects: birthday messages are encoded on the cake, the age of the birthday child is symbolised and candles are counted out. The baking of 'packet cakes' for the birthday party is another literacy event, involving either reading the simplified English instructions on the packet, decoding the graphic symbols or simply guessing. One time when Adina was preparing a party, she bought two packet cakes from the store. Without reading the instructions, she put the two cake mixes into the one cake tin, giving no attention to the cooking time nominated in the instructions. When the mixture spilled over and burned, she responded by exclaiming: 'He be right' in a characteristically Ngaanyatjarra manner.

When Nina and Rosina had their birthdays, their young mothers were involved in the Warburton Youth Arts Project (see Chapter 7). They were learning how to make slumped 'art glass' platters, fired in a large kiln at the Arts Project. Spontaneously, one evening, the mothers decided to make large plates inscribed with birthday messages. Nina's mother, Pamela, encoded her plate with 'Happy Birthday Nina'. Pamela gave this memento to Phyllis, Nina's *kaparli* – father's mother – to take home with her when she returned to her community, some 500 kilometres away. A few nights later, Adina also made a glass plate and inscribed a textual message with the glass acting as a surface for the emblazoning of names and dates emblematic of the celebrated *individual*:

Happy Birthday Rosina
November 9 2004

Socialisation into a new identity

Previously, Ngaanyatjarra systems of classification, or taxonomies, were oriented around the socio-spatial co-ordinates of *tjukurrpa* – place, seasons and events (Brooks, 2002c; Douglas, 1976). A 'time-since-birth' measure of age and development was not a significant cultural marker in classical times. As mentioned earlier, of greater significance was the connection between an individual and their birth *place*. More important, also, than a time-since-birth measure of age and development, was the core cultural concept of seniority or being led by one's elders, demonstrated lexically by the terms *kurta* – for senior or elder brother – and *tjurtu* – for elder sister – contrasting with the term *marlany (pa)* – for younger brother or sister (literally meaning, the one coming behind). Cultural concepts, such as being led by one's elders and being led 'straight' (*tjukarurru*), that is, metaphorically, along the straight path or the 'right way', were, and still are, used as structuring principles in narratives. Stories of two brothers – *tjuma kurtararra-pula* (i.e. 'story of brother-pair') – are typically found in the Ngaanyatjarra canon (Glass & Newberry, [1979] 1990; Murray, [1969] 1979). Here, the story schema thematically incorporates the seniority and leadership of the *kurta* ('elder brother') over the *marlany (pa)* ('younger brother') and is emphasised both as an organising principle of the narrative and a socio-structural metaphor.

In contrast to this, the celebration of 'date of birth', supported by the birthday party ritual, is used as a social mechanism for individual identity formation in Western society. Yet, the focus on age as a way to divide the life stream is a recent practice, in terms of the history of humanity. In Western society, people often did not know or have records of their birthdate before the middle of the 1800s, and it was not until the 20th century that birthdays began to be celebrated (Rogoff, 2003: 154–6). Now, in the Western cultural frame, a child must 'learn a temporal biography of self that will enter him within the continuous flow of cultural time' (i.e. linear, segmented time) and make him 'responsive to the taxonomic break between age-categories based on the units of the year' (Shamgar-Handelman & Handelman, 1991: 293–4). By participating in birthday parties as a social practice, Ngaanyatjarra children are acquiring the practice of enumerating their age and date of birth. Although identity still remains strongly connected to 'place', as will be discussed further later, in this event, we can see that some Ngaanyatjarra children are imbibing a Western 'literate' orientation by classifying the self through using individuated temporal age-since-birth, rather than cultural, spatial referents.

The 'individuation' of the birthday child is an important feature of the Western birthday party (Weil, 1986). The out-of-the-ordinary focus on the 'birthday child' and the symbols of the party ritual – the birthday cake, the singing of 'Happy Birthday', the candles, the party, the card and the presents – all accentuate the individual and signify the event as a special occasion, unlike other days. As a new cultural practice, this event runs counter to most other Ngaanyatjarra social norms, where people tend to avoid focusing on the individual person. Furthermore, the celebration of birth is now symbolised by a new materiality – the cake, the cards and the presents. Western consumer culture has brought with it a new form of individualised reciprocity where the symbolic value of kinship and social relatedness is expressed through Western material objects. The availability of affordable items, such as toys, bikes, clothes, books and crayons at the store, means that people have access to the resources required for the Western gift-giving practices associated with birthday parties. Thus, kinship and the ties that bind are now symbolised in a tangible form – in the material objects, as well as the photos that record the experience 'for memory'.

Like the funeral, birth as a rite of passage has undergone a transformation as new innovations have been adopted, adapted and incorporated into everyday cultural practice and is now a taken-for-granted cultural process.

Naming as Social Practice

Naming is another instance of changed social practice that has been incorporated into the sociocultural system and passed on to successive generations as the new normative. Prior to missionisation, naming, in effect, inserted the individual into a collective web of social meaning where almost everyone was a known person and strangers were rarely encountered. Moreover, the knowledge and use of names were part of the system of social organisation itself, not only the 'interface', as anthropologist Laurent Dousset (1997) notes. Personal names were given, but rarely used as a vocative. Rather, an indirect mode was the preferred practice, indexed through the use of demonstratives (e.g. *wati ngaanya* – 'this man here'), 'skin' names (e.g. 'that *Milangka'*) or kin terms (e.g. *Cliffordku kurtaku katjaku yurntalpa* – 'Clifford's older brother's son's daughter'). Kin terms – the vocatives of social relatedness – are still commonly used in direct address (for example, the terms *tjurtu*-older sister, *kurntili*-auntie and so forth). They were also known by their mother's name or father's name, plus the suffix *-kurnu*, as in, 'child of' or they were known by the place (birthplace or traditional living area) that they came from, plus the suffix *-nguru* meaning 'from there' (Dousset, 1997: 51). In the past, people were given 'bush names' or nicknames and often still are. Hence, the emphasis on the individually named 'birthday child' described above, stands in stark contrast to earlier times, when individuals were referenced only in relation to others or to places and the social system itself.

As will be discussed in Chapter 4, *adults* associated with the mission at Warburton Ranges started to take on English first names in the 1940s. The acquisition of English names may have arisen around finding a form of address that was phonologically dissimilar from an individual's bush name or perhaps to circumvent the substitution of *kunmarnarra*, when kin bearing the same first name had passed away. Surnames were allocated in the mid- to-late 1950s, in response to bureaucratic requirements imposed by the state (see Chapter 4). At that time, the taking-on of English names signified an appropriation of an introduced Western symbolic system that foreshadowed the subsequent subtle, but inexorable shift in identity formation. In retrospect, it appears that Anglo-Australian surnames were 'plucked out of the air' by the missionaries. *Yarnangu* acquired these strange new appellations (distributed randomly at church meetings or when rations were handed out) as permanent identity markers to be passed down the generations. To this day, they remain the identity markers, devoid of their origin stories, that define family groups and still cause confusion for the collection of census data.[7]

Alphabetic initials – representative of full names – often become the permanent vocative used in situations requiring respect for the deceased or when distance makes speech impractical. Nowadays, alphabetic icons or paralinguistic tags are mouthed or signed in the air, signifying a nuanced substitution used when the voiced full name of the recently deceased cannot be spoken. Other changes in naming practices include the shift from Biblical first names – Josiah, Zedekiah, Elijah, Ezekial – to contemporary youth culture names, such as 'Akon' (named after the Afro-American hip-hop artist),[8] as well as the use of innovative, often idiosyncratic, invented first names (e.g. Telisha, Donnisha, Shemiah, Tanesha and so on). Noticeable, also, is the recent practice of a newborn being given the oftentimes old-fashioned name of a deceased grandparent as a homage to the past – 'for memory'.

Mirlpatjunku

From early on, Ngaanyatjarra children are socialised into the web of relationships that will sustain them for life. Naming and social relationships are inculcated through oral narrative, sand storytelling and echoed in adolescent graffiti. *Mirlpatjunku* – the typically female Western Desert storytelling practice – is acquired by young girls observing the practices of older female relatives.[9] *Mirlpa* is now commonly enacted using the sharp end of a bent 'story wire' that is typically carried slung around the neck – fencing wire having replaced the traditional use of twigs and gum leaves. In *mirlpa*, a story is drawn in the sand with fingers and hands or beaten with the wire or a stick on smoothed ground during oral storytelling. In this cultural practice, young girls verbalise stories in harmony with symbols drawn in the sand and gestures made in the air (Green, 2009). Symbols drawn in the sand also represent the cultural schema of social relationships and genealogies (Dousset, 1997). *Mirlpa*, as a cultural practice, plays a 'societal role' as one of the means of inculcating the habitus of Aboriginal society in young people by modelling proper ways of behaving, imparting life skills and transmitting family connections and histories to youngsters (Watson, 1997). Cultural information is thus transmitted to the next generation as young girls acquire skills, knowledge, social relationships and kinship rules.

Textual and numerical elements and depictions of contemporary objects are also emerging in sand-story iconography. Nowadays, mothers and daughters commonly trace initials and 'names on the ground with story wire' as they narrate. Young girls acquire the habit of story-wire 'writing' and transfer it from the sand to other surfaces with ease. When Rosina was four years' old, I noticed her randomly scribbling alphabet-like letters, in a manner similar to the adolescent graffiti seen around the community:

> R = (initial of first name)
> O = (initial of her father's father's surname)
> M = (initial of her father's mother's surname)
> S = (initial of her mother's father's surname)
> L = (initial of her mother's mother's surname)

Adina tells me that when Rosina was younger, she taught her to write her name using the initials of family names so she would learn the first letters that represent her name. In other words, Rosina learned her tag as a representation of kin on her mother's side and her father's side.[10] Nina's mother also taught her daughter to write her name as the initial letters of her first name, mother's surname and father's surname. Rosina and Nina were both writing their names as 'tags', announcing: 'I'm writing my name'. Patricia also teaches her granddaughter Shantoya to write her name in a similar manner. She considers it important for children to 'know how to read, write and know the family, family lines, family trees, know where my grandparents come from... know where my mother and father country is'.

Here, young girls are learning to write a representation of their name to signal belonging and the intergenerational connection to kin. In this way, the process is more about teaching the sociality of what the name represents, than it is about teaching writing per se. Children are thus imbibing 'the social meaning' traditionally embedded in the oral evocation of names (Dousset, 1997: 53). The manner in which these children are learning a 'tag', which binds them into the complex kinship web, contrasts with Western children, who are inculcated into a first-person subjectivity, where they are more likely to learn to write their name as a representation of the *individual* self. Similarly, three- and four-letter tags representing kinship connectedness can also be found in adolescent graffiti expressions:

NVTW	*APMW*
EQUT	*AKMN*
ONLY 2 FOREVER	*2004*

These coded sequences of four capital letters represent the first letter of an individual's first name, second name, father's surname and their mother's surname.

Graffiti scribbling, as a form of textual play redolent of *mirlpa*, is typically acquired by young girls observing the practices of their older siblings. A few years later, when Nina is seven and Rosina is six, I notice a metal tucker box in their camp, emblazoned with graffiti-like text, evidently written by the two girls:

Nina
Rosina
to
GLy

I realise that these girls are imitating adolescent graffiti writing, and I decode their attempt as:

Nina
Rosina
two
girls only

Reminiscent of the kind of announcements of 'self' emerging in teenage graffiti forms:

ONLY 1 GIRL OKAY
ONLY ONE NO LOVERS

As I describe in Chapter 7, this rendering of orthographic and other symbols in the sand is transferred to other forms of teenage textual play, such as compulsive scribbling, doodling and graffiti tagging. Versatility with this form of textual play and the visual/narrative schemata of *mirlpatjunku* (where symbolic and pictorial representations are integrated with spoken narrative and gesture) may account for young people's rapid take-up of new digital technologies. Young people's quick adaptation to the visual and spatial elements embedded in much new software and their capacity for symbol system production and interpretation (noted earlier, with the funeral texts) and the creation of digital multimedia productions is a point I return to in Chapter 7.

The Speeding Up of Time: An Accelerated Modernity

Culture change and language shift are not new to Ngaanyatjarra culture; it is the pace of change that has accelerated. In classical times, the mythic past was permanently inscribed in the landscape and embedded in the features of the sites left behind by the Ancestral Beings. It was also signified in symbolic representations: the marks and patterns used in ceremonial designs, dances, *tjukurrpa* stories and *mirlpatjunku* – sand drawing. As people traversed the landscape, everyday activities were associated with, and memorialised in, 'place' (Myers, 2002). With little material culture and no alphabetic written record, the signifiers of linguistic and cultural change were subtle and almost imperceptible. The dynamism of change was embedded in oral memory and reproduced and altered over many generations.

Ngaanyatjarra society remained relatively untouched by Western innovations for longer than Aboriginal groups in most parts of settled Australia. The establishment of the United Aborigines Mission at Warburton Ranges in 1934 and the subsequent intervention of the state impacted profoundly on this small desert society, as I explore later. Yet some sociocultural aspects remain only lightly transformed. Nevertheless, with gradual exposure to cars, airplanes and the frequency of travel, time began to speed up and has, as mirrored worldwide, accelerated to a dizzying pace in response to late modernity, globalisation and massive technological changes (Appadurai, 1996; Giddens, 1999; Hulsemeyer, 2003). New communications and digital media technologies are further speeding up an already accelerated modernity (van Dijck, 2007; Tomlinson, 2007). With the proliferation of new recording technologies, *yarnangu* have made a conceptual adjustment to the idea that film and sound recordings transcend death, and social protocols have been adapted accordingly. Technology now immortalises the present, and records change, creating a contemporary version of the collective memory. Memories are mediated through technology, with community digital databases representing a communal photo album. The repatriation of photos of kin long since deceased is compelling older people to remember and reconnect with the forgotten faces of the past. Almost seamlessly, young people are becoming the agents for the recording and transmission of cultural memory in its new forms. As will be discussed later, through the artefacts of new media – laptops and mobile phones – young people are capturing the images of their social world and creating virtual photo albums on Facebook and other forms of online social media. The distance from the past is also allowing young people to reflexively manipulate remnant images as abstractions of a former existence: memorialised in stills and sequences, then distilled through the frame of contemporary technologies in films, photos and digital archival databases.

Conclusion

In this chapter, I have concentrated on representations around two significant rites of passage: death and birth. Here we are seeing the alignment of the generations in a common activity around transformed rituals, many of which are text-based. I have illustrated the cultural ways in which literacy is utilised and the abstract cultural conceptions and social meanings associated with reading and writing. In these examples, the processes of adaptation and modification are amplified. In the new celebrations discussed here, we are seeing the integration of Ngaanyatjarra and Western cultural symbols and schemas. Young people are showing that they are adept at symbol structuring. In the production of funeral texts, they are exploring the generative capacity of new technologies, experimenting with new forms and layering text, images and symbols. In the birthday party, adaptive learning is exemplified in the manner in which a new cultural practice has been acquired to meet contemporary circumstances. In changed naming practices, we are witnessing shifting subjectivities and altered identity formation processes. Through these modified practices and rituals, the Ngaanyatjarra are revealing a great capacity for adaptation, change and innovation. Young people are at the forefront of many of these innovations. They are becoming the agents for the recording and the transmission of cultural memory and as such are agents in the transformation of Ngaanyatjarra society in a time of shifting social paradigms and life circumstances, as I elaborate later.

Notes

(1) Information in this section is sourced from Brooks (2002b) and Glass (1997) and personal communications with Albie Viegas, Linda Rive, Elizabeth Ellis and David Brooks, since 2004.

(2) *Ara Irititja* – a community digital photographic archive, developed for the Pitjantjatjara communities in South Australia – is being introduced into the Ngaanyatjarra communities by Ngaanyatjarra Media – the locally controlled remote Indigenous media organisation, see Hughes and Dallwitz (2007).

(3) Fay Paget (personal communication, April 2004).

(4) Dorothy Ward (personal communication, 2000).

(5) See similar observations in Yasmine Musharbash's anthropological analysis of Warlpiri birthday parties at Yuendumu – an Aboriginal community in the Northern Territory (Musharbash, 2004).

(6) Elizabeth Ellis (personal communication, April 2006). See, also, Burbank (2006), Hamilton (1981) and Shaw (2002) for similar ethnographic observations on Indigenous child-rearing practices.

(7) Linda Rive (personal communication, August 2010).

(8) Daniel Featherstone (personal communication, May 2010).

(9) Other references to Western Desert sand storytelling practice include Eickelkamp (2008, 2011b) and Watson (1997). Also, see examples in Warlpiri (Munn, [1973] 1986), Arrernte (Green, 2009) and Wilkins (1997). A comparable tradition is noted in the Alaskan Eskimo practice of girls telling 'mud knifing stories' (deMarrais *et al.*, 1992).

(10) The letters represent pseudonyms.

2 Transmitting Orality and Literacy as Cultural Practice

Domestic Domains

Households, or 'camps' (*ngurra*), in Warburton are usually occupied by multigenerational members of the one extended family, with often a dozen or more people occupying one house. Camps, encompassing both the house and the surrounds, are noisy social spaces that spill over the boundary of the fenced yard. Day and night people come and go, cars drive in and out, babies cry, children shout, adults call out across the open space between houses, and stereos and TVs resound in the background. Everyday life for *yarnangu* pivots around the negotiation of social relatedness. The social logic of the camp accommodates a cultural sensitivity to avoidance relationships and the approach of strangers. Children wander between households within the parameters of community space, childrearing is shared and babies are rarely left alone. With few structured routines around sleeping and eating: children tend to sleep close to kin in communal spaces and children and teenagers eat 'whatever, whenever and wherever they like' (Shaw, 2002).

Domestic practice is typically oriented outdoors, and activity tends to be communal and public, although an orientation to interior space and a more privatised sociality is emerging. The proliferation of Western consumer items, such as televisions, DVD players and even iPods, is leading to *yarnangu* engaging in more passive, individuated leisure-time activities. Nevertheless, as in the past, when everyday life was conducted in an open camp, the '*waru*', or outside fire or hearth, remains central to family life for cooking, warmth and for providing a sense of well-being. Families can often be found sitting around the fire in winter (or in the shade of verandas and trees in summer) *tjumangkarriku* and *tjumalku* – 'telling stories' and 'gossiping' – and displaying the 'artful use of language in the conduct of social life' (Bauman & Briggs, 1990: 79).

Oral practice

The verbal arts remain central to Ngaanyatjarra social interaction, and language is a salient symbol of Ngaanyatjarra social identity, as emphasised by Maisie:

Ngaanyatjarra is important for everyone because it is their birth, number one language and it's important for them not to lose their language, always keep it, it's their point, their own. Because the English is the second and we only use it when talking to people at the shop, office.

The Ngaanyatjarra use the terms *tjaa yuti, tjaa yartaka* or *wangka yuti*, meaning 'clear' or 'visible' speech, to refer to their richly nuanced language. Storytelling and language play (including speech arts, such as rhyming, metaphor, alliteration and onomatopoeia) are intrinsic to everyday discourse. For older people, status is gained from having a command of high-order oral narrative and oratorical skills: 'whether conversational, controversial, descriptive, hortatory, dramatic or entertaining' (Douglas, 1979: 49). This is mirrored in the attention given to the development of narrative competence, including the primarily female practice of sand storytelling, as well as the oral, written, symbolic, visual and gestural modes of representation and communication displayed in the expressive modalities (music, film, image and narrative) generated by youth in new multimedia productions. The young are immersed in this language-rich environment. They acquire the speech styles and oral narratives of their culture by listening to, and interacting with, those who speak '*tjaa yuti*' and, increasingly, with speakers who 'code-switch' or 'code-mix' between Ngaanyatjarra, Ngaatjatjarra or Pitjantjatjara and English.[1]

Children were, and still are, socialised through social interaction and oral storytelling into cultural understandings. In this way, they acquire the lexical and gestural terms that denote kinship relations and the rules that govern social organisation. In oral narratives, core cultural concepts, such as being led by one's elders and being led 'straight', are used as structuring principles. Through storytelling, speech styles and the rules of appropriate interaction are also acquired. In the 'two brother' genre, mentioned in the last chapter, a *kurta* (older brother) can, for example, talk straight or make direct requests of a *marlanypa* (younger brother), until the younger brother reaches a certain age, after which time, the *kurta* must *tjarlpa watjalku* – communicate indirectly (Lester, 1981: 28).

With the Ngaanyatjarra, social relationships, context and the affective disposition of interlocutors determine the nature of social interaction and these bear a direct indexical relation to linguistic forms. Pragmatic aspects determine the choice of register and style, as well as the prosodic elements of speech. Non-verbal codes, such as gesture, gaze and hand signs – *yurrirra watjara* ('speaking by moving') – are integral to everyday discourse and are also employed in avoidance relationships and sorry-camp interactions (cf Green, 2009; Kendon, 1988). Choice of register is determined by the relationship between interlocutors. A respectful or polite relationship is expected with one's *ngunytju* (mother/mother's sisters), *mama* (father or father's brothers), *kurta* (older brother/male cousins), *tjurtu* (older sister/ female cousins), *marlanypa* (younger brother/sister/cousins), *yurntalpa* (daughter/niece), *katja* (son/nephew) or *watjirra* (cousin / cross-cousin – i.e. son or daughter of father's sister or mother's brother). A joking relationship exists with one's *kamuru* (mother's brother), *kurntili* (father's sister), *tjamu* (grandfather/grandson), *kaparli* (grandmother/granddaughter) and long- way cousins. An avoidance relationship is required with one's *yumari* (son- in-law/mother-in-law) and *waputju* (man's father-in-law or potential father- in-law/son-in-law or potential son-in-law) and in certain ceremonial contexts where a special speech style may be used.

Oral narrative has long been central to instruction and learning in a manner that fosters attention, imagination and metaphoric thinking through the incorporation of core cultural concepts, moral themes and proper ways of behaving for youngsters to emulate. Narrative has thus been critical to the maintenance of a regulatory framework that has bound Ngaanyatjarra society for generations. Children's 'dreamtime stories', or moral tales, were told as simplified versions of the *tjukurrpa*. In the socialisation of children, a fear of *mamu*, or 'bad spirits', was (and still is) inculcated to discipline or keep children obedient (*ngurlutjingalku* or *pinangkatjunku*) and to steer them away from sacred objects or locations (*pikangurlu*). *Mamu tjuma* – stories about 'monsters' or scary spirits – were used to teach children the 'right way' to act. These stories are still told today, but have a diminishing potency (Kral & Ellis, 2008). Through storytelling, Western Desert children are socialised into cultural understandings by taking on 'the role of the receptive and attentive listener and observer who, from informed interpretation, arrives at his or her own conclusions about what is going on' (Klapproth, 2004: 320–321). Klapproth suggests that children learn to discern the ambiguous multilayered complexity of stories through a process of 'retrospective discovery and understanding' of the moral consequences of protagonists' actions.

Despite these continuities, the spatio-temporal settings necessary for the acquisition of cultural processes and language practices have altered markedly, as families have embraced many of the symbols, objects and everyday practices of Western society in the shift to modernity. In the past, complex oral and gestural forms were acquired and used by children, *in situ*. As families traversed familiar country, knowledgeable elders would note signs of seasonal change in the flora and fauna, point out animal and human tracks and employ directional terminology and spatial orientation in the night sky as they navigated land (cf Laughren, 1978; Lewis, 1976; Wilkins,

2004). However, with less time spent hunting and gathering, contextualised occasions for talk, associated with traditional processes and practices, have diminished. Likewise, when families occupied camps 'without walls', *yaarlpirri* – a form of public rhetoric or oratory – was used extensively across the Western Desert as early morning talk to discuss issues, air grievances, disseminate information or organise the day's hunting and gathering (Goddard, 1983: 319–322), as well as praise good deeds or publicly admonish individuals for minor misdemeanours (Liberman, 1985). It used to be 'way back', remembers Molly,

> ...they just sit down like in different camps and they get up and talk *yaarlpirri* and the next person gets up and talks. Sometimes they tell you off for taking off with that boy, how to get a boy or girl right skin way... That's how it happened in our families. Nowadays, most of them, it goes over their head, not our days. Now they don't listen. Now a lot of people close family they living together third cousins, fourth cousins. In old days, you do anything wrong, spear in your leg, woman and man.

Now, in the noisy, built environment of contemporary community life, *yaarlpirri* has faded as a rhetorical device for drawing attention to important matters in the quiet, early morning waking-up time. Prior to the arrival of telephones around 1990, communications technology was primarily the two-way radio 'chatter channel'. Until very recently, the 'two-way' was the preferred mode of communication, particularly for older people, perhaps because it acted as a form of 'publicly available discourse' (Liberman, 1985: 4) redolent of *yaarlpirri*. Now the two-way radio has fallen into disuse, as many households have telephones. In 2009, mobile phone technology – a private form of oral, and textual, communication – became available at Warburton. In 2011, Warburton remains the only Ngaanyatjarra community to have mobile coverage.

Textual practice

In most homes, literacy artefacts are noticeably absent, as are the furnishings that accompany solitary or communal literacy practices, a point I return to in Chapter 6. There are few books and even fewer bookshelves. Filing cabinets for storing documents are rarer still. Bills and important reminders are not kept on pin-boards or stuck to fridges, and children's schoolwork is rarely displayed. Instead, walls are adorned with the symbols of kinship and social relatedness, evident in framed family photos and digital photos printed from the *Ara Irititja* database – the communal family photo album. Internet access has led to a rush of printed, downloaded images of Jesus, for older people, and hip-hop singers, for adolescents, laminated to make home posters.

Although magazines, letters and children's schoolwork are easily discarded, specific texts have been kept over many years. Predominantly, those that hold symbolic value: Bibles, hymn books, the *Ngaanyatjarra Dictionary*, exhibition catalogues and accounts of Ngaanyatjarra history. The Ngaanyatjarra Bible, in particular, represents a 'talisman of continuity' (Csikszentmihalyi & Rochberg-Halton, 1981: 70) with the mission past:

> Some older people who've become Christians, they can't read or write but they'll still carry a Bible around with them because it's the importance, it's God's Word, so they keep it, 'cause it's part of God. It's a Holy Book that they keep with them, along with their Hymn book.[2]

In this highly social world, solitary reading and writing, although a rare sight, does take place. Eileen tries reading alone at home – Christian stories or a *Mills and Boon* from the store – but it is too noisy, whereas Adina reads 'at night when people go sleep'. Adults can be found quietly reading the Bible or magazines amidst the hubbub of public social activity. Clifford and his wife Kayleen are known as readers. When Clifford isn't working, he likes fixing cars and watching television, but 'if I got a book, read a book, all sort of books, newspaper – *Kalgoorlie Miner*'. This young couple keeps books, magazines and newspapers in a basket in their bedroom, as Kayleen explains:

> I've got that big book at home about all the Aboriginal people from the long time ago. You know *Drop in a Bucket*. I read that every night, Mt Margaret stories, about girls been run away. That one, mission one, blue one, little red Bible.

In other words, they keep the little, red English Good News Bible and the blue catalogue from the 'Mission time in Warburton' exhibition (Plant & Viegas, 2002). Clifford's grandmother was a baby in a group that ran away from the Moore River Settlement in 1921 (Dowley, 2000), and he learns his family history by reading about the Mt Margaret Mission and life in the Eastern Goldfields (Morgan, 1986).

April is another avid reader: 'I had that book, that *Drop in a Bucket*, read all that... I got a cupboard there and I got all the books there'. Another old man tells me he reads history books 'like that by Len Beadell', who surveyed and graded the Gunbarrel Highway and other tracks in the Ngaanyatjarra region from the late 1950s (Beadell, 1967). Others read to seek information. Mick reads 'to learn music' and borrows guitar tuition books. While Arthur says:

I had a couple of books about different sorts of Aboriginal way of living. I had that one and I used to read that. That was a really good one. You know, if I might go into another place up this way, north way, well I had to read that book to know, if I'm up there I got to be careful, you know... It's only a book you know, might be whitefella's book that one, but it's really good to read... lent it to someone and it never come back.

Silas reads to expand his knowledge of the world: 'I read history stories... sometimes I read *National Geographic*, learning about other people on the other side of the world'. Others, like Kenny, read 'anything':

I keep reading like book, anything... I get a magazine in the store, *That's Life*, *True Stories* and all that... I read anywhere, college, or if someone's got a book. Get newspapers from office and take them home, look at it over and over, try and get another book and chuck that one away... It's just the way I do it.

'Oh I read anything' echoes Arthur, 'Bible I got there, another book... letters, that police commission sends it here for me, like I lost a number plate, well I'm in trouble':

I pick up a song book in language, another paper there... only been writing song, like translating from the English into language, I can write a couple of *turlku*... if it's a English song, well I write it into Ngaanyatjarra.

At home, older people, like Arthur, commonly write Christian *turlku*, or 'hymns', in English, Ngaanyatjarra or Pitjantjatjara, while younger people compose more contemporary genres. One young couple describe how they write songs together: they buy paper from the store, write the chords and the words in English and keep the songs in a bag at home. Other young musicians pen songs 'in their mind' or on paper, ready to record using the GarageBand recording software on Mac computers available at Warburton Youth Arts Project or Media Centres in other communities.

Functional home reading (food or medication labels or home appliance manuals) is, on the other hand, rare, especially when the function can be figured out by intuitive familiarity, oral instruction or 'reading' graphic symbols. Notes and messages are also superfluous when everyday information can be communicated orally. Some contexts do warrant 'memory aids': telephone numbers are typically scribbled on scraps of paper and cardboard or wall space, inside and outside. Out-of-the-ordinary situations also engender note-writing. Una's brother is deaf, and although she uses sign language to communicate, writing is an alternative modality:

> My brother, he's a deaf man, he comes back and he wants to know what things been happening here. So I have a pad and a pen and I write it down to him and show him... I write words down for him in English, and Ngaanyatjarra... I write lots and lots of little notes for him so he can see. Because we get sorry by using our fingers, I get tired and he keep on asking.

Shopping lists are almost never made. Most people shop using brand loyalty and visual imagery. Despite the dire financial situation of most families, budgeting is uncommon. Items are commonly piled into shopping trolleys with scant estimation of total cost, leaving expensive items discarded at the checkout.

Literacy resources

The enactment of literacy as a social practice is contingent not only on the ability to read or write, but also on the opportunity to obtain and to store literacy artefacts (Bat, 2005; Kral & Falk, 2004). Barton and Hamilton (1998: 191) posit that the opportunities for literacy are provided by the 'range of resources available to people'. In Warburton, although some literacy resources are available for purchase at the store and the roadhouse, many of the less obvious artefacts of literacy, such as stamps, envelopes or reading glasses, are difficult to obtain. Few books, other than the Ngaanyatjarra Bible and hymnal, are stocked in the store: 'not much point', a storekeeper comments, 'locals can't read'. Such comments are typical of the frequent assertions by non-Aboriginal people, regarding what they perceive as the illiteracy of Aboriginal people.

Women's magazines and word puzzle activity books are available locally and sell out fast. Molly likes reading 'anything, any news' and buys *'Take 5, That's Life, Woman's Variety, New Idea* and all that'. Jacinta also buys magazines, but notes how someone always comes and steals them:

> I bought a new one yesterday and it's gone. Someone took it. I don't have any books. I'd love to have a books but people always come in there and take it. I'd like to keep it in my room, locked up.

Naomi and Leah buy 'a lot of magazines every week from the shop, *That's Life* and *Take 5* because they've got the good stories', and sometimes they do the crosswords. When people buy the 'word puzzle' or 'crossword' magazines, they also need to buy a pen, as the storage of writing implements at home is difficult. Magazines with word puzzles and 'find-a-word' activities are popular, because anybody can demonstrate 'literacy-like' behaviour by matching letter shapes, irrespective of alphabetical knowledge. Cheap English children's books are also available at the store, but many are not reader friendly. Leah buys books for her little son, while other mothers borrow children's books from non-Aboriginal friends. Troy buys notebooks, because he likes to write stories:

> I bought it at the roadhouse and I always keeped [sic] it in my bag, but people going through my bag and stealing, that's why. Somebody stole that, I don't know which one. My own diary, but they steal it, one of my brothers steal it.

Eileen notes how she likes writing letters, 'but I got no chance to do that... can't get stamps and envelope'.

Newspapers and other locally produced newsletters are available for free at the community office and read for the photos of local people, the news, the football scores, to find cars to buy or 'just to see who is in prison'. Before it closed (as I discuss later), the community college library in Warburton was also a site where *yarnangu* could access resources. Adults used the computers to prepare funeral texts, type hymns and songs, play computer games and watch videos. Jim regularly visited the library. He would always read the same book, one that described how Ngaanyatjarra people were elected to the Wiluna Shire – a significant event in the Ngaanyatjarra collective memory, to be discussed in Chapter 5. Jim would read this one special book for several hours a day, over several weeks.[3] Young people also liked going to the college library. Troy used to go most days to read books, use the computers and watch videos. Leah liked visiting the library to read 'story one, comedy stories and real life and movie story'. Leah considers that her reading and writing is 'pretty good', nevertheless, she found some of the words difficult 'when you read the long writing'.

Intergenerational transmission of a particular kind of literacy practice

In the mission days at Warburton Ranges, the boundaries of literacy were restricted by the absence of resources, outside of pedagogical or church contexts. As Mary and Jack's daughter, Jacinta, recalls:

There was no books only school books... Some girls used to write
letters, they didn't have biros and all that, pencil and rubber... They
used to go church. Only, what that book, Christian one, song, English
one, Redemption one. For them older peoples.

For many Ngaanyatjarra, their sense of being literate, and their comprehension
of what literacy is, derives from their early exposure to Christian literacy
practices in the mission. Moreover, as I discuss in Chapter 5, the introduction
of the very concept of a 'book' by the missionaries was synonymous with
the Bible and, therefore, 'essentially Christian in nature' (Kulick, 1992: 170).
Wilf Douglas began teaching adults at Warburton to read Ngaanyatjarra
(and English) in the 1950s using portions of Scripture, followed by Amee
Glass and Dorothy Hackett in the 1960s and Jan Mountney in the 1990s.
Glass, Hackett and Mountney have continued this practice by providing
Ngaanyatjarra literacy lessons for adults, as well as after-school informal
literacy activities for children (using Ngaanyatjarra secular and Christian
stories, songs and worksheets). Accordingly, in some families, especially the
'mission families', a very particular type of Christian-imbued family literacy
practice has been transmitted to successive generations.

Mary and Jack learned to read Ngaanyatjarra from Hackett and Glass in
the 1960s. Their daughter, Jacinta, doesn't remember books at home, except
for 'Bibles, that's all, my mum would read' and the songbook in church:

I can read Ngaanyatjarra language from my mother... When she reads I
always see her reading and listening and that's how I got learn.

When Jacinta was a teenager, she continued learning with 'Miss Hackett':
'we would learn every afternoon when she was living here'. In turn, Mary taught
her grandchildren to read: 'I used to teach all the little kids in this house...
teaching the *Mama Godku* book [Ngaanyatjarra Bible]'. Now, she says, her
grandson, Troy, is *ninti purlkanya* (really clever), because he can read the Bible:

I been learning him to do all that... *Yuwa, ngayuku tjamu* (yes, my grandson)... I always sit down and read, sit and read... *ngurrangka* (in camp)...
Yuwa, ngayuku tjamu, he know, *yungarralu* read*tamalpayi* (reading by
himself).

Troy describes his pride in his grandfather's skills:

He know it for English, Ngaanyatjarra, Pitjantjatjara language, three
language, he can read, before he used to read. He read newspaper,
dictionary, that old first one, first language.

Una's interest in reading was stimulated by observing her mother learning Ngaanyatjarra literacy in the 1960s. Later, Una says, she used to 'sit down and read and sometimes write down what I read from the Bible'. In turn, she read to her own children:

> I read them storybooks, like *Three Bears*... We might get it from the secondhand, they come on the truck... some books, not really lot of books... I used to sit down and read: "Oh I've got a lovely little book here for you". Then they sit down and listen. I loved telling stories for my girls when they were little, in English and in Ngaanyatjarra.

Jennifer also remembers learning at home by asking her mother:

> "What is this?" That way I got learn. And I asked her so many question... I used to read, read the Bible, if my mother hasn't got eyeglass I used to help, even my sister, we help her to read. When she reach fullstop and couldn't think what that word is we just say it, we help her out.

Silas also recalls learning as a child:

> In my after school when I go home my mother used to read a story time, like the Christian story, little baby Jesus... so you know I was learning like the education side, school but my mother was learning on the Christian side, Jesus and all the stories. But she also learned me all the Dreamtime stories too.

And now, when his wife reads to the grandchildren, 'bedtime stories like the *Seven Dwarves, Snow White*', Silas explains the characters within the Ngaanyatjarra cultural frame: 'I tell them "No, it's a story, you know dreamtime story what happened in England" and I tell them England is a long way, big place'. Dawn recollects how she used to read and tell stories with her daughters Naomi and Leah in Ngaanyatjarra and English:

> I used to story *watjalpayi, tjukurrpa* read*tamalpayi*, bedtime stories *kuliltjaku,* like books*pa*, you know dreamtime stories. *Watjalpayi yuwa,* read*tamalpayi, tjaa yutilu* and English. From the, books*pa*, Bible*ku* paper with Miss Hackett and Miss Glass and my kids really liked it.

Dawn recalls her children *nyakula nintirringkula* (watching and learning) from her as she read the Bible at home at night. Dawn is repeating the process with the next generation: 'now today my little *tjamu*, he really likes the books, *tirtu nyakupayi* and *nintipukalpayinya*. I teach him how to talk and read and count'. Leah affirms her mother's practices:

> We sit down and listen to her when she reads and she tell a story... Sometimes she sings from that songbook [Ngaanyatjarra hymnbook] and learn her little grandson, *learning him right way.*

Leah also notes the importance of Ngaanyatjarra literacy for young people:

> That lady Miss Glass, she go round every afternoon learning that, learning more language. Yeah [I like to] keep the language going... It's important.

Patricia's daughter, Lucy, says she keeps her reading and writing strong by observing her mother's practices. Lucy is now learning Ngaanyatjarra reading with Hackett, and this, in turn, is providing a catalyst for home reading with her five-year-old daughter, Shantoya.

Thus far, I have shown that Christian texts have remained important across the generations since the 'mission time'. In the families described in this chapter, children have been exposed to these traditions of usage from early childhood. Home prayer meetings are still conducted regularly and provide an additional site for oral Bible-reading events, and children are in attendance.[4] As Jennifer describes:

> I go to church, every Sunday, hear the word of God. I always tell my niece, my families, all family relations: "Go to church"... my mother always give a Bible reading and have little meeting in the house if she can't make it to church.

Mothers also commonly sing with their children in Ngaanyatjarra from the hymnal *Turlku Pirninya* at home. As Adina sings, following the words in the hymnal with her finger, the children, Nina and Rosina, observe her. Later, Nina sits by herself reading and singing songs memorised from *Turlku Pirninya*. These observations shed light on the significance of social practices, such as reading the Ngaanyatjarra-English *New Testament* and singing from the hymnal *Turlku Pirninya*, in the home domain. In these literacy events, anyone can participate, irrespective of literacy competence, either by decoding or by memorisation and oral recitation. The iterative experience of singing in church and at home, in both Ngaanyatjarra and English, embeds literacy events within the sensation of affective connectedness to family and community. Furthermore, these events signal how Ngaanyatjarra children are socialised into a particular kind of literacy practice that differs from what is found in most Western middle-class homes.

In Western mainstream contexts, everyday practices, such as bedtime reading (Heath, 1982b) and mealtime social interaction (Ochs & Shohet, 2006), perform overt and covert language and literacy socialisation functions. Whereas such domestic interactions tend not to be structured into Ngaanyatjarra social practice, as a *yarnangu* educator describes:

> Like *yarnangu* families, when they newborn and they start crawling and walking, parents don't teach them like things like reading and all that. Parents they teach them the other way, Aboriginal ways, going for *maku* (edible grub), goanna, all that. What we eat, what's right and what's wrong. But in whitefellaku way, *tjitji* little ones grow up they listen to their parents read them book, it's like *nyaapa*, bedtime stories but in Aboriginal way... there's no books, just keep the stories in their head, tell the stories, dreamtime story. Whitefellas are different they have the book there... But when Aboriginal kids go to preschool everything is new to them. Look like they're going into another world.

This factor notwithstanding, it can be concluded that in some Ngaanyatjarra families, primarily the 'mission families', the habit of reading has been transmitted to successive generations, and children are being 'apprenticed' in literacy through observation and 'guided participation' with mature community members (Rogoff *et al.*, 1993). It must also be noted, however, that literacy transmission is taking place in families where the encounter with literacy has been more recent. Louisa was a child when her family came out of the Gibson Desert in the 1960s. As Louisa notes:

> I read lot Bible, I read any chapter or any Prophet who wrote Bible... That's how I get my sense back from reading and all that... I don't know the hard word in the Bible... I read, trying to read it... But I pray and like read straight out. Read all the history in the Bible, New Testament, Old Testament.

Her daughter, Darleen, has acquired the habit of reading from her. Darleen describes how her 'favourite thing' is to 'read Bible with my mother'.

In summary, these recollections reveal how literacy practice in this newly literate community has been influenced by the limited availability of resources in the domestic domain. Nevertheless, literacy practices introduced by the mission have become taken-for-granted practice in some domestic settings. However, as I show in the next section, literacy in community and institutional domains tends to be rendered as a contested local practice.

Community Domains

In this community, the office is the locus of daily social interaction. It is the site where people see and hear community news and where other types of literacy practices are enacted. Office workers are able to access literacy resources, computers and fax machines to facilitate personal and collective administrative literacies. Clem is a community liaison officer; he reads and writes at work, drafts sports notices and sends personal faxes. Kayleen assists with the funeral notices and reads new notices, while posting them on the office noticeboard. Jacinta, like others, finds out what is going on by reading the notices on the wall: 'always read them when we go in... all those faxes on the wall'.

The notices are mostly written in English and fall into two main categories:

Information notices: Shire (road reports); Ngaanyatjarra Media (training); Ngaanyatjarra Health (visits from dentist, vaccinations, vet, audiologist); school notices; electoral notices; swimming pool rules; ads (job, car for sale); community information (phones, plumber, rubbish collection, tax); and government media releases.

Events notices: Meetings: Native Title (trips, mining negotiation and mining money distribution meetings), NPYWC: workshops; Land Management Unit meeting, cancellation and postponement notices; and Warburton community meetings. Funeral notices and faxes. Posters for: Christian Fellowship/Conventions; Sunday School; sports carnivals; Warburton Youth Arts Project events; visitors; film nights; music festivals and community barbecues.

The notices represent the framework of everyday sociocultural interaction, events and administrative business particular to the Ngaanyatjarra region. They also provide insights into how people use text in culturally meaningful, everyday community contexts, irrespective of literacy competence. Different modalities are activated for information dissemination: communication is mostly oral, although some adults decode text or graphic symbols, and the more literate mediate and reshape written notices into oral modes for those less literate. Revealed here are cultural instances embedded with social meaning and linked to each other as literacy events. Events in the community domain provide arenas for adults to assume literate roles and participate in literacy events in sporting practice, exhibitions, arts projects and so forth.

Sports practice as a literacy event

Around Easter, notices go up at the office announcing the Alice Springs 'Lightning Carnival', signalling the commencement of the winter sports season across Central Australia. Young fellas at Warburton begin football training, and young women begin softball training. Each afternoon, training takes place at the community sports oval, and the local band brings along amps and instruments to practise in the background. Warburton football and softball teams are the 'Tigers' and follow the yellow-and-black code of their counterparts, the 'Richmond Tigers' – an urban football team from the city of Melbourne. Football colours act as a symbol of community identity and permeate local iconography. This affinity with AFL teams on the other side of Australia also encourages *yarnangu* to read newspapers to keep up with the national scores. Kenny gets newspapers from the office:

> Kenny stands out because he wants to read the sports pages because he wants to know who's on the team, and who's not, for the AFL game. That's a big deal for him and he knows that newspapers are a source of information and he can read well enough so it's worth his while, because he could get the same info on TV.[5]

Sports carnivals are high mobility events that everyone wants to attend. Each weekend of the winter season, hundreds of people travel hundreds of kilometres to be at the game. Carnivals incorporate not only football and softball competitions, but also a range of social activities: catching up with relatives, talent quests, car raffles and the 'Battle of the Bands' music competitions. Older men also use the time to arrange ceremonial business. Men take football games seriously. Older men organise the competition programmes and draft the announcements that are sent as faxes from the office to communities all over the region. Nevertheless, details often change and are communicated more effectively by word of mouth. The men also organise the necessary tables, chairs, microphones, loudspeakers and the pens and pads to keep score on the day.

Team sports, such as softball, football and basketball, are usually mediated without non-Aboriginal support and are sites for 'situated learning' for young people. At a sports carnival in Warburton, the main event is the football game on the grass oval. Meanwhile, on a red dirt pitch nearby, strategically situated next to the children's playground, a group of young women organise a softball competition. Unlike football games, where older men take a high profile role, with softball: 'just the girls do it... we always do it when football festival and practise every Wednesday night'. Once enough girls have gathered to make two teams, decisions are quickly made about who will be the umpire, captains and players. Naomi and Leah are natural leaders, and they organise the games, tally the scores and look after the scoresheets over the three-day carnival. Leah claims that she learned to score by observing the strategies of older players and, in this way, was apprenticed by the previous cohort. Umpires and scorers know the rules of the game and integrate textual elements into their practice. Darleen writes the names down for her team, but needs assistance with spelling. In this collaborative environment, individuals with less literacy proficiency are assisted by others and save face. Once the game commences, players code-mix between English and Ngaanyatjarra and use role-differentiated registers to call out instructions and interact with spectators.

The winter sports season continues until the football grand final is played, and the winners return to their home community with victory trophies. As the heat of the summer advances, winter sports recede, and adolescents congregate once more around the swimming pool and play basketball late into the night. Across the Ngaanyatjarra Lands, summer signals a return to the annual ceremonial cycle of Law Business.

Arts practice as a literacy event

Whereas, in earlier times, memories of the past were recounted orally, now acrylic painting and exhibitions document social history, and oral narratives are presented in a written form. Over time, new iconographies have entered the expressive repertoires, evident not only in sand storytelling and graffiti, but also in the visual arts. Artists from the Warburton Arts Project have exhibited locally, nationally and internationally. Una expresses her pride in seeing family photos on exhibit at the local gallery:

> I went one day and had a look and there was my grandfather's story, going down to Laverton. That's in that Cultural Centre there… Ooooh, I was really proud to read about my grandfather… I was really happy to see that little story written down about my grandfather.

Art exhibitions are textually mediated events replete with catalogues, banners, posters, and t-shirts laden with text and symbols.[6] Narratives are rendered as gallery notes for tour guiding or arts education activities. Alphabetic text is incorporated into acrylic paintings, 'art glass', ceramics, film and, now, websites. Paintings are signed with names, initials, crosses or 'squiggles' (i.e. an iconic representation of a cursive signature). Textual messages are inscribed on acrylic canvases as icons and messages by older artists and by youth in the new arts and digital media practices at Warburton Youth Arts Project and Ngaanyatjarra Media, as I discuss in Chapter 7.[7]

Institutional Domains

Researchers note that literacy practices in Western society are patterned by social institutions: the school, the workplace, the church and so forth, and what counts as literacy is derived from the prescriptive agendas of these institutions (Luke, 1988). As a consequence, certain literacies become more dominant, visible and influential than others (Barton & Hamilton, 1998). In the Ngaanyatjarra context, institutional domains likewise pattern the more visible literacies, whereas the literacies associated with the administration of people's everyday lives are less visible and less supported. It is in these public domains that literacy practices are exposed to criticism, and adults tend to be measured against the standards of the 'dominant literacies' (Barton & Hamilton, 1998) favoured by institutions, and, hence, people are often perceived as illiterate or failing.

Using data gathered from English language and literacy assessments of 527 adults (aged 16–65), out of an estimated *permanent* population of some 1600 people (including children), I found that this sample could be divided into three categories (see Appendix). Firstly, a group of approximately 20%–30%, whom I call the 'visible literates' – predominantly adults who participate in roles and domains that require written communication and have incorporated literacy into social practice; an intermediate group (some 30%) – that is the less visible literates, who may use literacy for personal/functional purposes; and the final third of the adult population – essentially, non-literates, who do not use literacy in everyday life. In the Ngaanyatjarra world, it tends to be the more 'visible' literates who participate in public life, including the institutional domains of training, employment and community governance, while those less literate tend to hover on the periphery.

Literacy for training

Ngaanyatjarra Community College opened in Warburton as a Registered Training Organisation in 1996. However, the difficulty of providing training in this remote location led to its closure in 2007. Accredited training has since been provided by the health, environmental health, land management, media and education organisations operating in the Lands.[8] Literacy issues, in part, account for low retention in courses and few certificate completions. Qualifications, even if attained, are rarely used, and certificates are easily lost.

Jennifer works as an assistant teacher at the school and has undertaken teacher training. She is one of the more literate adults, yet struggles with the academic discourses encountered in training sites:

> I was doing some computers jobs and typing... I always ask them any of the hard words when they talk to me and when it's on the paper... I always ask them: "What's this word? Can you just make it a bit easier for me so I can understand." I always tell them if they give a big paper to me... this is a strange word I always tell them and point to that word: "What's this word here?"... I don't get shamed to ask. I always tell them: "What's this?" because I want to get learn more.

Assistant teachers have also acquired Ngaanyatjarra literacy in informal language workshops.[9] Notably, these workshops provide an opportunity for intensive reading and writing in English and the vernacular. Jennifer notes that 'we only do it in the workshop', as the home environment militates against the capacity for trainees to study, a theme I return to in Chapter 6. Mountney comments that:

> Adults who are training in vocational courses tend to do all their written work in class. They read Ngaanyatjarra materials that they need to read, some of them are reading a limited amount of English stuff to do with teaching practices and their writing is fairly limited... people who have taken on study programmes... read lecture notes and try to write assignments, but because they've had very limited practice with that, it's very difficult.[10]

In workshops, adults have an opportunity to develop specific school-like literacy practices. They gain an understanding of the differences between spoken and written text, develop reading-out-loud skills and question-and-answer routines around written text and draft and redraft Ngaanyatjarra texts.

Literacy for work

Most employment in the Ngaanyatjarra Lands has been under the Community Development Employment Projects scheme (CDEP), since its introduction in the late 1970s, as discussed in Chapter 4. CDEP employment is not contingent upon qualifications. A few salaried positions have existed, however, the formal written application process is often beyond the English literacy competence of most adults. Thus in effect, literacy plays a 'gatekeeping role' by acting as a barrier to employment. In Warburton, CDEP jobs have included unskilled tasks, such as rubbish collection, garden maintenance, collecting firewood, cleaning and work at the brickworks. Additionally, jobs at the clinic, cultural centre, arts project, women's centre or land management require varying degrees of literacy competence.

Many CDEP positions do not require literacy for tasks other than filling in timesheets or signing names for the receipt of wages. Some roles do, however, require literacy and numeracy competence, and the more visible literates can be found working in the office, playgroup or the school. As an office worker, Kayleen is adept at using the computer and organising CDEP pay:

> Add them up, put the money in payslips. Anthony helps, do it together... Giving cheques out, writing order for people and send their money away to other places when people ring for their money like in Kalgoorlie. People ring for their money and we send it, write it down and send it... on a order book.

When asked how she learned the skills for the job, she answers: 'I don't know, learn self', indicating the subtle way in which she has been mentored by a staff member through a process of informal training, observation and 'intent participation' (Rogoff et al., 2003). Her husband, Clifford, works at the Shire. He considers himself a good reader, although he says he has never had a job where he 'really needed to read or write'. Naomi works with Ngaanyatjarra Media and operates the community radio station. She reads out community announcements: 'somebody might send a fax to me... I say it in English, then Ngaanyatjarra, do it both ways' and also writes:

> ...especially on the videos we have to write all the Ngaanyatjarra stories... sometimes English, but the main one is the Ngaanyatjarra, we have to use that, 'cause that's the main one for the Ngaanyatjarra Media.

Maisie, with some non-Aboriginal assistance, has established a community playgroup with other local women. The playgroup workers have created a learning environment suffused with literate elements. Walls are covered with English number and alphabet posters. Handwritten charts explicate daily routines: storybook reading, picture talk and songs and rhymes in English and Ngaanyatjarra. Workers also write daily programmes, weekly timetables and shopping lists in English.

Literacy for governance

Meetings routinely punctuate the temporal rhythm of community life. Ngaanyatjarraku Shire Council meetings and, to a lesser extent, Ngaanyatjarra Council meetings are held with predictable regularity and tend to conform to the textually mediated discourse structures of Western meetings. George, Clem, Wesley and others in the leadership cohort are well-versed in meeting procedure through long-term participation in meetings, workshops and advisory committees since the 1970s. A female leadership has also developed under the Ngaanyatjarra Pitjantjatjara Yankunytjatjara Women's Council (NPYWC), where April, Una, Patricia, Dawn and other women have represented the needs of women and children over many years.[11] Una remarks:

> At meetings there were all sorts of things, to read they used to give us, hand out sheets... and I used to sit down, and read, read, read... I used to read them and understand it and explain to some of the ladies, some of them who don't know how to read.

April comments:

> That's what we got to read when we go for meetings... we got a lot of fax in and they send us a lot of books, like bulletin, and newsletter.

Although participants read meeting agendas, minutes and often reports, assistance is commonly needed to penetrate the discursive features of the bureaucratic language. As George explains:

> I can read, but there are some words, really hard, like government words that I still don't understand... Like, when we go to meetings like Council meeting, I want to keep a note of what's been said at the meeting, like write it down, but I haven't got pad or notebook or anything like that.

Another leader expresses his frustration when observing adults unable to 'read between the lines' or comprehend the unfamiliar knowledge and procedures inherent in bureaucratic discourse: 'still we get caught out when people use hard words and idioms when coming to talk about things, English is not our language'.

Administrative literacies

In literate Western families, administrative literacies and personal record-keeping are typically synchronised with domestic cultural practice and enacted by individuals at home. Adults take individual responsibility for filing and retrieving tax information and storing bank statements, birth certificates or educational qualifications for some future use. Conversely, in Warburton and other Ngaanyatjarra communities, the community office is the administrative hub that takes collective responsibility for receipt of mail, phone calls to banks, government departments and parole officers, filling in tax returns, registering births and deaths and even arranging funerals. Similarly, rent, electricity and other 'bills' are paid through the office as deductions on CDEP payslips. Important personal documents, such as training certificates, firearms licences, driver's licences, as well as tax file numbers and bank details, are filed in the office, rather than at home; in part, 'so the kids don't get them and tear them up'. As Una explains:

> I get them government ones, pension [letters]... I can read them... I give it to the office person: "Put it away in my file". They are all in the file there. I don't keep that at home, the kids might, you know?

Most administrative literacies are too complex for *yarnangu*, who lack the formal oral and written registers required for bureaucratic interactions, and assistance is required for official phone calls, form-filling and interpreting official correspondence. This highlights the reality that for some adults, signing their name is the extent of their everyday literacy practice.

Houses in Warburton do not have mailboxes, so all mail is received at the community office. Official mail from government departments accounts for most of the correspondence collected by individuals. Although addressed personally, these anonymous, abstract interjections from unknown senders and locations tend to be unrelated to everyday life. Some literates, like Jennifer, read them carefully:

> Always read when I get mail. I always check the number and all when I get a cheque, that it's right amount... If a strange paper I always give it to the advisor... Some hard words in it, I must ask them: "What is it?" Find out what it is. I am confident.

Similarly, when Leah receives letters from government departments, she reads them, and, like other young literates, she also mediates for those less able to understand the bureaucratic English. Tinpulya finds that she, too, is called upon to assist:

> Sometimes I help with that, some people get their letters. They can read, but they don't know how, they can't understand it. They can read, but

when they reading some people they don't think and read. So it's like the lips moving, but not the brain working.

Some adults discriminate between the various types of official correspondence:

This one's rubbish, chuck it away. But we all know that blue letter – licence suspension or fine notice, have a look to see how much.

For others, administrative literacies are dealt with in an ad hoc manner. Official mail is either not collected or thrown in the rubbish bin unread. Mostly, it doesn't matter that correspondence from debt collectors, banks and superannuation or insurance companies is not dealt with, but sometimes, there are consequences.

Written off – literacy, traffic infringements and prison

Not addressing traffic infringement, licence suspension and outstanding licence transfer-fee letters may, in fact, have dire consequences. Damian McLean, community development advisor at Warburton, explains how fine enforcement letters 'create a trap... for people who keep poor personal records and frequently change addresses', as they become 'enmeshed in a trap in the justice system that's designed almost perfectly to ensnare them'.[12] An individual who leaves unpaid fines for long enough, by not responding to correspondence from the Fines Enforcement Registry or the Department of Justice (or does not undertake fines enforcement procedures to clear the fines through community work), will eventually enter a formal breach process and possibly incur a period of incarceration.

Most adults are inadequately educated about the consequences of unpaid fines. They do not understand that abandoning a car in the bush with the number plates left on or buying and selling cars with no official transfer papers – then not reading infringement notices, not paying the ensuing fines and continuing to drive – can eventually result in imprisonment for driving under licence suspension.

Everyone takes for granted that people understand, but there is no specific education... All they really understand is that your licence can be suspended for unpaid fines and that you can go to jail for unpaid fines.[13]

A sheriff asserts that 'literacy issues start from the first court appearance as people don't understand what they read or what they agree to':

Personal record keeping skills is often an issue. In order to pay fines person needs to keep letters, but people lose letters. People are bombarded with so many bits of paper they don't know what to do with.

A policeman asserts that 'no-one can read and write':

We always explain the bail form to them and make sure they know when to come to court... but most of them just screw it up and throw it on the ground or later they find it screwed up in their jeans pocket.[14]

In one instance, a young woman received a letter telling her that she owed $10,000 in unpaid fines; however, she misread the letter and thought she had *won* $10,000.

Mobility and motor cars are integral to contemporary Ngaanyatjarra social and cultural practice and, unlike in the past, driving around the desert is now regulated by the state. Driver's licences are now required for driving on 'any road available and used by the public' (*Road Traffic Act* WA). This now pertains to the Great Central Road – the main arterial, linking Laverton with the Ngaanyatjarra communities and the Northern Territory. *Yarnangu* feel an intense spiritual and social connection to this road. The Laverton to Warburton section follows the *yiwarra* – the route that people traditionally walked from rockhole to rockhole, and the original track was cut in accordance with the rockholes traditionally used as a primary source of water. In addition, some families later had agency in constructing the Warburton to Warakurna section of the road. From the Ngaanyatjarra viewpoint, they own the road, because it is their country. From this perspective, they see that driving on this road should remain outside the domain of Western law.

The arrest rate for unlicensed driving is high. Young men, like Troy and Jake, have fallen into this trap. As Troy describes:

The cops came round and said: "You never pay this fine. So you got to do this one, this like six months". So I went in and done six months straight, for doing that fine thing... I been get letter, fine letter... when I was read it and I was thinking: "Oh couple of weeks I'll pay it". But I forgot. Then cops come looking around for me and he told me: "Oh, you didn't pay this fine so we have to arrest you".

As mentioned above, the consequence of administrative illiteracy can be incarceration. However, *yarnangu* see only the unfairness of the white justice system and interpret incarceration for fines and traffic offences as *kunpu-*

kunpu palyara – 'doing it for nothing'. Silas, who also works for the Department of Justice, explains:

> That's why people use that word all the time: "No, I'm in here for nothing. *Kunpu-kunpu*, they picking on me for nothing". … But that person must have done something. He or she must have done something like never paid the fine, but they don't understand and they use that word *kunpu-kunpu*… but they don't know the back side of that thing, they don't know, background, what's going on. They don't know… or can't understand.

Jake reflects on this problem:

> Some boys they were in prison and on court time they don't understand what the judge telling them, they get sentence or go in prison, they get their months… they keep on ringing up to the shop, worrying about their children, wife. They keep going in prison.

It is evident that a significant number of Ngaanyatjarra men are typically spending part of their youth in prison – the 'inside world'.[15] Unfortunately, prison has become an all-too-common aspect of contemporary life. As indicated in the following vignette, where a father from the Ngaanyatjarra Lands was overheard saying to his son: 'Everybody has to go to jail sometime, so get up and go to court'.[16] One young man describes how he 'grew up in prison':

> Been going up and down… I come out from prison and do silly things, you know… No good, no life in jail. No families… Just like you're finished, same like nothing, you're looking and look like ghosts walking around, no families.

At the same time, prison (and juvenile detention) exists as an under-recognised site for ongoing education and training for adults from remote communities (Parliament of Australia, 2011). Accordingly, men who have spent periods of time incarcerated in institutions often have considerably better literacy and numeracy skills than their peers. As exemplified by Troy, who reflects on his recent learning in prison with a sense of pride:

> I was proud… doing English and all that, was good… I was learning about doing all that before… cause it was good. I wasn't worrying.

When he was younger, Kenny took advantage of the courses offered:

> Put my name up there, then we done a bricklaying course like that, done a welding in the school... That one lady she was working there, she seen me. "Ah you doing things good and quick and you know... we'll give you this tutoring, literacy".

Unfortunately, there is little articulation between prison education and community life. Certificates are issued, however the onus is on ex-prisoners to store them, in the unlikely event that they may mean something in the future.

> They do all those schooling there those boys from out here. Can do it there, quiet and sober, when you're wearing the greens... When those blokes leave, so excited to leave and come home. They can take all their work and certificates with them, but they so excited to go home they just run out and leave it in their cells or somewhere.

For most young men, credentials have little relevance, as Kenny admits: 'I brought a paper like this for the college but I threw it away, somewhere in the bush there'. Jake also recalls getting a 'certificate':

> Yeah, they told me: "Oh you can take it home, show your mother, families"... Threw it away in the bin in Kalgoorlie when I got out.

It can be argued that prison provides a new normative frame in which individuals are separated from familiar surroundings and able to take on the attributes of the new environment, including participation in education and employment. However, such individual practices generally cannot be maintained once young people return to the self-regulated community environment.

Conclusion

As noted in the Introduction, the definition of what constitutes literacy has been broadened by anthropologists and sociolinguists to affirm what can be accomplished with different literacies in various contexts, rather than what is deficient. Importantly, scholars highlight the strengths of diverse language and literacy socialisation contexts. In this chapter, I have described how Ngaanyatjarra children are socialised into the cultural processes and social and linguistic practices of the group through observing and participating in family and community activities (Rogoff *et al.*, 1993). I have shown, also, that Warburton is a literate community, in the sense that oral and literate strategies are used to decode, interpret and produce texts. Yet, there is a disjuncture between domestic practice and institutional literacy requirements. Additionally, the academic genres of literacy required for higher study have not been attained. In these respects, most children are not socialised into the particular type (Duff, 2008) of language and literacy practices that researchers view as antecedent to successful literacy acquisition at school (Wells, 1985) – that is, children are not acquiring the solitary literacy practices typically found in literate middle-class families, nor the dyadic oral and literate skills that match the kind of adult-child interactions used in schools (Cazden, 1988; Heath, 1982b; Heath, 1983; Snow & Ferguson, 1977). They are, however, acquiring the shared, communal or 'polyadic' oral and literate practices that match Ngaanyatjarra sociality. Such practices have been transmitted from the older generation, who acquired a template for alphabetic literacy practice in the mission. The affective significance of this tradition of usage derives from historically specific times, places and experiences, as I elaborate in subsequent chapters. Furthermore, adults in public roles are participating in textually mediated events and discourses that straddle the boundary between domestic and community domains, enabling youngsters in these families to see literate practice as elemental to everyday life. Children in these families are being socialised into literate habits, attitudes and modes as normative practice, albeit in a manner that differs from a Western frame. It is to the conditions and circumstances of the early encounter with Anglo-Australian settler society that I now turn, in order to understand the evolution of the historically produced norms and practices of the Ngaanyatjarra and the socially constructed nature of literacy in this context.

Notes

(1) The term 'code-mixing' indicates that interlocutors may not be aware of mixing languages, and the vernacular has become 'mixed and/or simplified' (AIATSIS/FAT-SIL, 2005: 28). 'Code-switching' 'typically involves bilinguals who know both languages, but choose to alternate between them' (AIATSIS/FATSIL, 2005: 85).
(2) Elizabeth Ellis – interview, 22 January 2004.
(3) Fay Paget – interview, 22 May 2004.
(4) Jan Mountney estimates that 100 adults in the 40-plus age group engage in public reading from Scripture (oral decoding with varying levels of proficiency in comprehension), whereas only some 20 adults are able to use word-attack skills, in order to independently read and comprehend the Ngaanyatjarra *New Testament*. Public reading may originate from the early practice of memorising and reciting Scripture or rote-learning catechism, enabling the less literate to enact literate behaviours. Similarly, non-literate Afro-American elders assist their grandchildren

to read Scripture by activating memorised oral 'reading' strategies (Dorsey-Gaines & Garnett, 1996).

(5) Youth Development Officer – interview, 1 March 2004.

(6) Catalogues include: Plant & Viegas (2002); Proctor & Viegas (1990); Turner (2003); Warburton Arts Project (1993: 702); Warburton Arts Project (1999); Wilurarra Creative (2010). Paintings and objects are lodged in the Warburton Community Arts Collection.

(7) Artworks incorporating textual elements created by Ngaanyatjarra artists include: *Right way to have a kurri* (Margaret Davies, 1992), and *All the early days rockholes* (Elizabeth Holland and Christine West, 2001) and *Sandhills and Signature* (Pulpuru Davies, 2004). Also a series of paintings by June Richards where text covers the canvas including: *We were at the mission and we used to paint differently* and *Only one thousand dollars* (June Richards, 2007). Artists from Warburton Youth Arts Project have also created artworks with text, including: *Those people getting filmed. They didn't know what that little box was* (Delvina Lawson, 2007), *You the girl* (Kresna Cameron, 2006) and *No I never* (Kresna Cameron, 2007).

(8) The Ngaanyatjarra Council has been the umbrella organisation for a number of service delivery organisations, including: Ngaanyatjarra Health Services; Ngaanyatjarra Land and Culture Unit; Ngaanyatjarra Community College; and Ngaanyatjarra Media, through which nationally accredited training has been provided within the Ngaanyatjarra Lands up to Certificate IV level.

(9) Assistant teachers tend to be unqualified and are known nationally as Aboriginal Education Workers (AEWs) or, more recently, Aboriginal and Islander Education Officers (AIEOs).

(10) Jan Mountney – interview, 3 March 2004.

(11) Ngaanyatjarra Pitjantjatjara Yankunytjatjara Women's Council (NPYWC) was formed in 1980. It grew out of the South Australian Pitjantjatjara Land Rights Struggle in the late 1970s and still provides a decision-making forum and service delivery function for women across the NPY lands in the cross-border region of WA, NT and SA, particularly in the areas of health, education, cultural, arts and social services.

(12) McLean – interview, 9 September 2004. Damian McLean commenced work in the Ngaanyatjarra Lands in 1982 and has been community development advisor at Warburton community for many years. He is also Shire President of the Shire of Ngaanyatjarraku.

(13) Sheriff, Kalgoorlie – phone interview, August 2004.

(14) Warburton Police (personal communication, August 2004).

(15) Nationally, Indigenous men have higher levels of contact with the criminal justice system at an earlier age than their non-Indigenous peers (Ogilvie & Van Zyl, 2001; Putt *et al.*, 2005). Based on population data (Brooks & Kral, 2007), of the 500 young people in the 15–29 age group, 23 males were in prison (Brooks, 2011b: 192).

(16) Sheriff, Kalgoorlie – phone interview, August 2004.

Part 2
New Figured Worlds

For the Ngaanyatjarra, their most fundamental ontological premises derive from the *tjukurrpa* – the 'Dreaming' or the 'Law'. The temporal unfolding of new conceptions of 'being-in-the-world' has played out against this overarching cultural schema. Earlier, I introduced the concept of the 'figured world' (Clammer *et al.*, 2004) as embracing a system of meaning, comprising historically produced norms and practices, as well as individual sense-making, as one 'figures' one's self into a new world of interpretation. A 'figured world' embraces the 'socially produced, culturally constituted activities', whereby people come to conceptually and materially produce and perform new understandings of self or identities (Holland *et al.*, 1998: 40–41). I use the schema *New Figured Worlds* in Part 2 to shift from the present to the past. I consider that any examination of contemporary Ngaanyatjarra identity, in relation to attitudes, habits and dispositions, associated with language, literacy and learning, must acknowledge the culturally constructed and historically produced nature of social practices. Hence, any understanding of the ideology and culture of current practices must be underpinned by an analysis of the socio-historical circumstances of the new figured worlds that have shaped the Ngaanyatjarra worldview in the post-contact period. How people participate in new social processes, including the production of their lives, work and relationships, thus depends, in part, 'on the changing historical circumstances that have shaped and do shape the ongoing social world they inhabit' (Holland & Lave, 2009: 1).

I begin Chapter 3, 'Mission Time: Adapting to the New', by examining how the early history of the mission at Mt Margaret formed the particular circumstances of the mission at Warburton Ranges. I introduce the first generation to enter, and be schooled at, the missions at Mt Margaret, Warburton Ranges and Cosmo Newbery. In Chapter 4, 'Everything was Different because of the Changing', I counterpoint the experiences of the next generation, as they came of age, under the changing conditions of the assimilation era in the 1950s and 1960s and self-determination in the 1970s. Chapter 5, 'The Cultural Production of Literate Identities', traces how the Ngaanyatjarra took hold of literacy in Ngaanyatjarra and English and started to use it for social and political purposes.

3 'Mission Time': Adapting to the New

Mt Margaret Mission

Only some 30 years after European settlement, Aboriginal people in the Eastern Goldfields – over 500 kilometres west of Ngaanyatjarra country, across harsh desert terrain – were considered to be the 'most degraded' in the state of Western Australia (Milnes, 1987: 151). After the discovery of gold in 1893, the 'Goldfields' quickly opened up to white occupation. Mining settlements at Kalgoorlie, Leonora, Laverton and Wiluna grew into townships, and conditions for Aboriginal people rapidly deteriorated (Howitt, 1990; Stanton, 1990). After reaching its peak around 1904, the gold rush went into decline. Pastoral development followed in its wake, alongside government offers of cheap land leases. The influx of Europeans and the resulting loss of access to traditional food sources saw local Aboriginal groups living on the fringes of European settlements or gravitating to the ration depots established for 'indigent' or 'destitute' Aborigines (Rajkowski, 1995). Auber O. Neville assumed the role of Chief Protector of Aborigines in 1915. This led to a worsening of conditions for Aborigines in all settled areas of the state of Western Australia, including the Goldfields (Milnes, 1987). Under Neville's exacting administration, Aboriginal people were so well protected that they virtually became 'prisoners in their own land, denied even the most basic right to control their own lives or the lives of their children' (Maushart, [1993] 2003: 333).

In 1921, a mission station was established at Mt Margaret, some 30 kilometres from Laverton, under Rodolphe S. Schenk from the United Aborigines Missions (UAM). This mission was to provide a refuge from the adverse conditions of the Goldfields. By 1935, the UAM was the largest missionary society in Western Australia and the only mission group in the Goldfields for some time (Biskup, 1973). The UAM had a reputation for establishing stations in situations so financially impossible that other missions refused to go there (Marks, 1960). Consequently, Mt Margaret (and subsequent UAM mission stations at Warburton Ranges and Cosmo

Newbery) relied heavily on financial support from church and other societies to maintain them.

Schooling at Mt Margaret

Schenk believed that 'the best future for Aboriginal people lay in their education and vocational training, and ultimately in their conversion to Christianity' (Stanton, 1990: 220). Significantly, the UAM was to play an important role in providing education for Aboriginal people in the Goldfields, when state education was not an option (Milnes, 1987).[1] By 1940, Western Australia was the only Australian state where the Education Department did not provide teachers for Aboriginal reserves, missions or settlements (Milnes, 1987: 272). It was not until the passing of the Education Act in 1945 that the state government displayed its intent to educate its Aboriginal population.

The first school for Aborigines in the Eastern Goldfields opened at Mt Margaret Mission in October 1926. Mt Margaret was viewed as a model mission settlement, distinguished from many other missions because of its achievements in literacy and numeracy (Stanton, 1988; Stanton, 1990). Educational achievements were attributed to Mary Montgomery Bennett, who, although untrained, was considered an 'outstanding aboriginal educator' (Biskup, 1973: 133) and ran the school from 1932 until 1941. Schenk and Bennett publicised the high standards achieved in literacy and numeracy (Bennett, 1935; Schenk, 1936), with the intention of garnering public support and proving that Aboriginal people were 'capable of being educated' (Morgan, 1986: 209).

According to anthropologist Adolphus P. Elkin, Schenk was extremely fundamentalist and regarded all Aboriginal custom and belief as works of darkness (Elkin, 1979: 310). Schenk's fundamentalism also underpinned his commitment to education, and drew on the 'Protestant impulse towards literacy' and his promotion of literacy for social mobility (Graff, 1987: 251).[2] Schenk departed from UAM policy by promoting secular education, not just the 'God is good, God is love' approach, typical of UAM missionaries (Milnes, 1987). He believed that 'the native who could read and understand the Bible stood a better chance of becoming and remaining a firm Christian than one who was illiterate' (Marks, 1960: 86). Schenk also cultivated an orientation to literacy, where Christianity provided the locus for textually mediated social activity. At the same time, he was driven by humanitarian ideals, believing that if Aboriginal people are not educated, 'they will always need others to speak for them' (Morgan, 1986: 138). Schenk's, and Bennett's, attitude to education and literacy was influenced by the post-World War I humanitarian campaign for the advancement of Aboriginal people, in which they played a significant role. Bennett was both an educator and writer (Bennett, 1930) and was involved in a lobbying network that supported the national Aborigines' Protection Society and the international Anti-Slavery Society (Holland, 2005; Paisley, 2005). Ideas encountered in these organisations no doubt shaped their expectations of the role of literacy and schooling for the progress and development of Aboriginal people. Bennett was also a friend of Charles and Phyllis Duguid, who established a mission at Ernabella in the north-west of South Australia in 1937 in a bid to preserve and protect the Pitjantjatjara people of the Central Reserve.[3] Bennett and the Duguids were allies in the campaign for the advancement of Aboriginal people throughout the 1930s and 1940s (Holland, 2005). Like Schenk, Bennett emphasised education, alongside employment, 'as the key to self-dependence and hence to assimilation based on rights' (Paisley, 2005: 74). Their emphasis on adult training for employment in the wage-labour market drew on the belief that with training, Aboriginal people, no matter what their descent, could attain the capacities of citizenship. These philosophies embraced the Mt Margaret community, until Schenk's retirement in 1953, and were to influence the UAM missions at Warburton Ranges and Cosmo Newbery.

Literacy learning: Schooling as 'civiliser' and colonial tool

For the last two centuries, conceptions of the value of learning to read and write have been intertwined with post-Enlightenment 'liberal' social theories and the 'expectations of the role of literacy and schooling in socioeconomic development, social order, and individual progress' (Graff, 1987: 3). For a long time, literacy learning was not necessarily 'a formal, distinct or institutionalized activity' or an event synonymous with childhood or youth (Graff, 1987: 237). The 16th-century Reformation most strikingly linked literacy learning to religious practice. This constituted the 'first great literacy campaign in the history of the West, with its social legacies of individual literacy as a powerful social and moral force' (Graff, [1982] 1994: 157). The 18th-century Enlightenment consolidated the ideological underpinnings for 'modern' and 'liberal' reforms of popular schooling. With the introduction of compulsory schooling in England and the United States by the late 1800s, schooling, in effect, institutionalised literacy learning (Graff, 1987: 261). During the 19th century, the new middle-class promoted literacy as the basis of moral order (Collins, 1995: 82) and schooling became a socialising agent (Graff, 1987: 263–275). Education promoters and social reformers instilled the moral bases of literacy, particularly in children of the poor, in order to avert idleness, pauperism and immorality (Graff, 1987: 261–264). The spread of the ideals of liberal democracy and capitalism pushed people towards functional literacy skills, and literacy became tied to social and economic development. Literacy also came to represent emancipation and enlightenment with the political mobilisation of the working class. This led to the demand for access to literacy as a right and the later rise of popular literacy movements among the poor and disenfranchised (Freire, [1970] 1993; Hoggart, 1957).

When colonisation was at its height in the late 1800s and early 1900s, Western schooling was utilised to 'civilise' the peoples of the colonies and progress the evolutionary process. Within the Western philosophy of 'linear, progressive or evolutionary change', illiteracy signified that the training required for civilization and progress remained 'incomplete' (Graff, 1987: 323). Colonial education was central to empire building, in order to instil Christian values and morality among newly colonised Indigenous peoples. Underpinning the proselytising impulse was the belief that through literacy, societies could traverse the 'great divide' and develop from 'darkness to light' or from 'primitive to civilised' (Riemer, 2008; Rogoff, 2003). Christian moral certainty paradigmatically influenced early attitudes to Aboriginal society and provided the intellectual and philosophical backdrop to colonial and missionary models of education. Moreover, these attitudes continue to underpin the perceived relationship between literacy, modernity and progress today. While it is commonly asserted that literacy has been imposed upon Indigenous peoples by missionaries or by representatives of the state to allow previously preliterate groups to 'see the light' and begin the linear progression towards civilisation and modernisation, this perspective does not take account of the complexity of diverse contexts, nor the agency of individual members of the receiving culture, as will be shown in this, and later, chapters.

Learning to Work

In addition to schooling at Mt Margaret Mission, Schenk emphasised 'learning to work' as a prerequisite for integration into wider Australian society. After initially offering food for free, Schenk adopted a 'no work, no food' policy, where workers were paid cash on a piecework basis for craftwork and carpentry, as well as labour from sandalwood pulling and dingo-scalp collection (Milnes, 1987; Marks, 1960). In 1925, the West

Australian government introduced a system to protect the sheep industry from marauding dogs, with the Vermin Board paying a bounty for collected scalps (Morgan, 1986). Trading dingo scalps was a crucial source of income at Mt Margaret (and later at Warburton Ranges), especially as, by 1928, Mt Margaret had become the central rationing station for the district, attracting large numbers of Aboriginal people.[4] With a growing population to support, Schenk's philosophy was underpinned by necessity, as the Mission was not in receipt of any government subsidies other than rations and could not rely on regular financial support from the UAM. Schenk also sought to ensure that men who had trained as shearers and station hands could seek work on local pastoral stations and be paid reasonable wages (Marks, 1960). Notably, Schenk's business dealings with Aboriginal workers were textually mediated – he used written job and payment records, believing that non-readers would seek out literates to assist and check payments (Milnes, 1987). In 1930, 23 Mt Margaret men found mustering work and were the first Aboriginal men in the Goldfields 'to be paid, one pound a week and keep' for pastoral work (Morgan, 1986: 120).

Valcie was born on Cosmo Newbery Station in 1930 and grew up in the bush with her mother. Serendipitously, in 1934, Valcie and her family sighted the missionaries as they passed through Cosmo Newbery on their journey to establish the new UAM mission station at Warburton Ranges. Valcie's white father was a returned soldier, who held the Cosmo Newbery pastoral lease. At that time, Commissioner Neville was allowing some children of mixed descent to remain at Mt Margaret, rather than send them to the dreaded Moore River Settlement.[5] Valcie was taken away from her mother by Neville's 'protectors' in 1939 and placed in the Graham Home at Mt Margaret Mission.

Valcie recalls that Mt Margaret was a good school.

...because the government was against the Aboriginal children being taught, going to school... It was only two hours school every day because so many children. And they weren't paid, but they just taught the children... It was a good education because they was teaching us something no-one else wanted to teach us. I stayed at the Home there. We had to help, over fifty girls in the Home. We had to do washing, ironing, mending, scrub the floor on our hands and knees, there were no mops or anything that time.

Around 1950, Valcie married a Mt Margaret man – one of the early workers at Glenorn Station, where they lived for the next 20 years.

My husband took me away to a station... He was from Mt Margaret too, he went to school there. He went up to about Grade 3.

Mt Margaret had given him the confidence to go out and seek work in the European world, but as an Aboriginal station worker, he constantly had to 'prove himself equal to the white man'. Valcie lives once more at Cosmo Newbery – now one of the Ngaanyatjarra Lands communities – with her children, grandchildren and great grandchildren.

The policies at Mt Margaret contrasted sharply with conditions for Aboriginal workers in the rest of Western Australia. Under the *Aborigines Act 1905* (WA), Aboriginal labour was controlled, in an effort to develop and expand the pastoral industry. The Chief Protector had the right to remove Aboriginal adults to any district or institution, and only adults under an 'employment permit' were exempt from these removal powers (Jebb, 2002: 77). At this time, any municipality could be declared 'out of bounds for all *natives* except those in employment', and a local police protector was empowered to 'order any *native* out of town' (Rowley, [1970] 1972: 68 [emphasis in original]). Anthropologist John Stanton points out that pastoralists in the Goldfields had the support of the Aborigines Department in securing permits for the employment of Aborigines. In return, the Department subsidised workers during the summer 'lay-off' season. Pastoralists were thus 'absolved' from having to provide for their workforce all year round, making the cost of Aboriginal labour very low (Stanton, 1988: 293). Schenk's humanitarian ideals compelled him to criticise the practices of the pastoralists. In turn, they complained that Schenk was influencing Aborigines in his demands for better conditions and attracting them to Mt Margaret with the 'promise of cash wages' at a time when few Aboriginal stockmen were receiving such remuneration in the Goldfields (Stanton, 1988: 293).

In due course, Schenk's lobbying for improved Aboriginal employment conditions was to exacerbate an already declining relationship with Commissioner Neville (Biskup, 1973: 132). Initially, a 'spirit of cooperation' had existed between Neville and the UAM, however, the rapid growth of the UAM strained matters and was exacerbated by Neville's antipathy to Schenk's policies. Public criticism of Neville's administration in relation to the desperate situation of Aborigines grew and finally led to the 1934 *Western Australian Royal Commission into the Status and Conditions of Aborigines*, led by Commissioner M.D. Moseley (Attwood, 2003; Paisley, 2005). Schenk and Bennett further alienated Neville during the Royal Commission by explaining that Mt Margaret people had high expectations of employment conditions and that conditions at Glenorn Station were unacceptable: 'the workers objected to being fed on the woodheap... being sworn at like dogs by the overseer; and after doing good work some were refused wages' (Morgan, 1986: 163–164). The Moseley Royal Commission paved the way for the introduction of the *Native Administration Act* in 1936, under which Neville was renamed Commissioner of Native Affairs and remained head of the new Department of Native Affairs (DNA) until 1940. Although enacted to *protect* Aboriginal people, the 1936 Act succeeded in further eroding individual rights, as the Commissioner had ultimate control over marriage, employment, education and place of residence (Morgan, 1986: 209). Neville also became the legal guardian of all 'native' children, whether illegitimate or legitimate, until they reached the age of 21 and had the right to remove children from their families (Haebich, [1988] 1992; Biskup, 1973).

Under Neville's 'protectionist' policy, Aboriginal people were separated into groups according to caste criteria. Full-blood people were categorised into three tiers: 'detribalised' and living near towns; 'semi-tribalised' and living on pastoral stations; and 'uncivilised' and living in a 'tribal state' (Jebb, 2002: 161). Neville considered that 'tribal or uncivilised natives' should be left alone, safeguarded in their tribal areas, therefore, education was not necessary, nor was it necessary 'to disturb their social state by attempts at Christianity'.[6] A 1937 Commonwealth and State Ministers Conference on Aboriginal Welfare had agreed that 'full-blood natives' should be educated to a 'white standard', *only* if 'detribalised'.[7] For 'detribalised' Aborigines, citizenship was the goal, and they were progressively offered 'citizen rights' through tutelage and selective exemptions (Rowse, 2005: 5). The *Native (Citizenship Rights) Act*, introduced in 1944, gave Aborigines the right to apply for a certificate of citizenship, 'provided that they were adult, literate, of industrious habits and good behaviour, and completely severed from tribal or communal associations' (Bolton, 1981: 151). Accordingly, an Exemption Certificate (exempting an individual from the 1936 Act) could be attained, thus removing education, employment and town residence restrictions (Stanton, 1988: 298).

After his visit to the Goldfields in the 1930s, Elkin lobbied to formalise a 'buffer zone' around the West Australian section of the Central Australian Aboriginal Reserve (initially established in the 1920s and encompassing the border region of the Northern Territory, South Australia and Western Australia).[8] This was to restrict access by non-Aboriginals and, hence, preserve and protect 'tribal' Aborigines of this region. At the time, it was assumed that full-blood tribal people, such as the Ngaanyatjarra, would remain in reserves that afforded continuing preservation and protection during their assumed transition to inevitable extinction. The declaration of the West Australian section of Aboriginal Reserve was consistent with Neville's determination to 'protect' full-bloods by leaving them alone. However, it ran counter Schenk's emerging plans to expand the UAM. In 1937, Schenk asked the DNA for permission to open a new mission on Cosmo Newbery pastoral station, some 90 kilometres east of Laverton, but Neville refused (Biskup, 1973: 139). Ironically, in 1941, Cosmo Newbery was established as a DNA ration depot, apparently, to 'thwart Schenk's "imperialist" designs' (Biskup, 1973: 185). The 'feeding depot' was ostensibly established to provide rations, but also to prevent 'bush natives from the Warburton Range area advancing further into civilisation and becoming useless hangers on around the goldfield towns and railways'.[9] When the UAM expanded its evangelising even further east into the Central Reserve, this was contrary to Neville's wishes.[10]

In sum, therefore, it was the policy of caste criteria *and* the conflict between Neville and Schenk that underpinned the circumstances that led to the establishment of a UAM mission at Warburton Ranges in 1934.

Warburton Ranges Mission

Up to this point, the full-blood Ngaanyatjarra and Ngaatjatjarra people of the Great Sandy, Great Victoria and Gibson deserts had remained virtually unaffected by the protectionist policy that had had such a deleterious impact on Aboriginal life in the Eastern Goldfields. The Central Australian Aboriginal Reserve provided them with a form of protection from outside incursions for longer than was the case in most other parts of Australia. Even their kin – the Pitjantjatjara in the South Australian sector of the Aboriginal Reserve – had greater exposure to the negative impact of doggers, prospectors and pastoralists, due to their proximity to the camel and rail routes north from Adelaide to Alice Springs. By this time, explorers, prospectors and doggers had made only occasional ventures into Ngaanyatjarra and Ngaatjatjarra country, as had parties of anthropological, scientific and geological surveyors (Gara, 2003).[11] These incursions notwithstanding, remoteness protected the Ngaanyatjarra from the more profound ravages of the colonial encounter.

Although temporary movement of Ngaanyatjarra people westward for ceremonies had been commonplace, the lure of the 'new world', exacerbated by periods of intense drought, accounted for new waves of migration. Droughts in the 1920s, late 1930s and mid-1950s brought many starving people out of the desert and into the ration depots, mission and towns of the Goldfields. Free railroad travel for Aborigines after 1925 led to some drifting further down the line to Kalgoorlie.[12] Desert people ventured west, because they wanted to 'see for themselves where flour, tea and sugar was coming from' and others to escape *warrmarla* attacks. Some also walked west seeking employment on sheep stations, especially during the years when employers competed for Aboriginal labour to fill positions vacated by Europeans conscripted during World War II (Milnes, 1987: 271). Some families remained in the Goldfields, where curiosity with European life led to an unintentional reliance on the materiality of European life (Sackett, 1978a). The establishment of Warburton Ranges Mission slowed the westerly drift, it did not, however, halt the movement altogether and a pattern of serial migration into the Laverton region developed (Brooks, 2002a; Stanton, 1983). The long trek west, either by foot or by camel – a journey of some 600 kilometres – took about six weeks (Plant & Viegas, 2002). After World War II, a direct cutline track to Laverton was constructed, reducing the trip to around 10 days. This, and a camel track between Warburton and Ernabella – a distance of some 500 kilometres, remained the only tracks in the region until 1957. It has been conjectured by Brooks that had the missionaries not arrived when they did, establishing Warburton Ranges Mission as an 'anchor point', it was likely that, by the 1950s, the desert would have been emptied with migration both west and east (Brooks, 2002a: 5).

Few Ngaanyatjarra actually settled in the Mission in its rudimentary beginnings, the majority still roamed in the 'hinterland' – the vast desert expanse between Warburton Ranges Mission in the west and Ernabella Mission in the east. These two isolated desert missions represented the pivotal spatial end points between which the nomadic existence of pre-contact times was maintained. Unlike Aboriginal groups in regions closer to white settlement, the gradual and benign nature of the encounter not only protected, but, to a certain degree, also enabled Ngaanyatjarra, Ngaatjatjarra and Pitjantjatjara people – who maintained their primary attachment to the country between the two missions – to deal with the frontier encounter on their own terms. These missions, as outposts of settler society, sought to build positive relationships with Aboriginal people, uniquely framed around learning and literacy, where Aboriginal people acquired a particular, albeit atypical, understanding of the ways of Anglo-European society.

The Schooling Imperative

In 1933, the Ngaanyatjarra families camping within the vicinity of *Mirlirrtjarra* (Elder Creek), near the Warburton Ranges, encountered a small group of *malikitja* or 'strangers'. UAM missionaries, William Wade and Fred

Figure 3.1 Early construction at Warburton Ranges Mission 1934
© Ngarnmanytjatja Archive, Ngaanyatjarra Council

Jackson, had traversed some 600 kilometres into the desert on this initial exploratory camel trip from Mt Margaret. Among the group, at what came to be known as 'Old Well', were Katherine and Arthur's father and his two wives; Rosie's father, Horace; and Mary and Harold's father and his two wives (see Table 1 in the Introduction). Una's father was a child when he witnessed 'Mr Wade' coming along with the camels calling out, *'yamatji muku-muku'* (gentle friend), and handing out sweets to the children. A year later, Wade, accompanied by his wife, Iris, and missionary, Harry Lupton, returned to establish the Warburton Ranges Mission. Importantly, Will Wade was already known and accepted by Aboriginal groups in the Western Desert, so few were fearful of him (Williams, 1998: 26).[13] Unlike Schenk, he was to show a more benevolent approach to local customs, and he tolerated the use of Ngaanyatjarra language.

One of the first acts, in the missionary tradition, was the establishment of a school. The school at Old Well was run by untrained teachers Iris Wade – who, before her marriage, had run a home for 'half-castes' in South Australia (Williams, 1998) – and Ethel Lupton – who had worked with M.M. Bennett at Mt Margaret, before transferring to Warburton in 1935 (Milnes, 1987). The early aims of the missionaries were 'to preach the gospel, to check polygamy and cruel customs in regard to young men in their corroborees' and to help 'stop degrading contacts with whites'.[14] In effect, however, life in the early days 'was so bogged down by the difficulty of establishing the essentials of life that the real work of making disciples was being neglected'.[15] In 1936, the Mission was moved from the flood-prone

Table 3.1 Estimated population at Warburton Ranges and Cosmo Newbery
1936–1973

| | Warburton Ranges | | Cosmo Newbery | |
	Estimated population	Children under 16 and attending school	Estimated population	Children under 16 and attending school
1936	---	22		
1937	300	20		
1940	---	43		
1944	403	---		
1945	370 adults	50		
1947	---	16		
1948	120–150	27		
1949	402	45		
1950	500 – 700	87		
1951	---	80		
1952	---	---		
1953	---	---		
1954	---	---		
1955	250	55		
1956	---	75		
1957	198	83		
1958	---	104		
1959	300–350	---		
1961	400	120	12	16
1962	450	122	16	---
1963	450	100	16	12
1964	450	86	45	15
1965	450	100	25	14
1966	378	101	25	13
1967	454	118	40	9
1968	435	118	43	17
1969	401	120	54	14
1970	417	136	46	18
1971	400	104	63	22
1972	408	104	50	20
1973	435	120	75	26

Key --- (data not available)[24]

Elder Creek to a permanent site on higher ground (and the present location of the Warburton community). Here, the missionaries built the 'Baker Home' to house the first generation of school boys and girls, and they turned their attention to the children 'for a deeper Christian impression will be left on them than on their parents'.[16]

At this early stage, Wade was reporting in the *United Aborigines Messenger*, 'the readiness with which the natives are leaving their children in the care of the missionaries and already 22 were at the Mission'.[17] By 1937, 10 boys and 10 girls under 16 were attending school daily.[18] Evangelising in English went hand-in-hand with rote learning and repetition: '[t]hey are learning texts of scripture, and one girl can repeat fifteen from memory'.[19] By 1937, 'eighteen scholars', aged from four-and-a-half to twelve, were learning to read and write 'with astonishing speed', and after only two months' tuition, 'these little ones can read any three-lettered word quite well' and 'are equally good at figures'. This gave the missionaries,

> ...ground for great hopes for the future... that, being able to read the Word of God, their lives may be transformed by the Holy Spirit, and with a real burning love for Christ they shall go forth and preach the glorious Gospel message to their own people in their own tongue.[20]

In 1947, the Mission expressed the view that the children's work was 'going ahead splendidly'.[21] However, a contrary government report suggests that tuition consisted of teaching the children to 'thank Jesus for the slops they receive and sing hymns in school'.[22] Little is known of the teaching methodology used by the untrained missionary teachers. It can, however, be assumed that they carried with them the Mt Margaret philosophy of high expectations of the 'educability' of Aboriginal people:

> If you have the time and patience there is nothing the native child cannot be taught. The work done at Mt Margaret is evidence of this.[23]

Table 3.1 is a compilation of the very few records of population numbers at the Mission between 1936 and 1973, when the Mission closed. As noted in the Introduction, it has been speculated that in the classical past, there were some 2000 people widely dispersed over a large area (Brooks & Shaw, 2003: 2–3). In 1954, the Department of Native Affairs estimated that across the extensive remote regions of Western Australia, approximately 6000 Aboriginal people were still living a nomadic life.[25]

Table 3.1 indicates the number of children recorded at Warburton Ranges and Cosmo Newbery missions, although the length of time spent in school is a matter for speculation. Scant evidence indicates that children were quite old when they commenced school, stayed intermittently and spent only the morning in lessons.[26] A 1947 DNA inspection report notes that children stayed for 'an average of three weeks and go bush for several months'.[27] A pattern that was to continue for at least the following decade:

> [A]n attempt is being made to give them a standard primary education when there is absolutely nothing in their prospective lives as adults to which this education can be applied. Just how successful is that attempt is open to question when it is known that they are dismissed into the bush for nearly three of the summer months each year.[28]

According to one teacher, the school operated on an *ad hoc* basis', where 'everybody had a go' and it was only after 1950 that it began to operate more consistently.[29] This aligns with the 1948 government decision to subsidise missions based on the requirement that they teach the '3 Rs' up to the age of at least 14 and provide some form of vocational training (Marks, 1960: 95–96). At this time, the teachers, Dora Cotterill and Edna Nash, were using a curriculum borrowed from Mt Margaret (Milnes, 1987). Despite additional teaching staff and increased hours of schooling, a 1951 DNA inspection found 80 children, aged four to 14, in a 'small hall' with poor quality teaching:

> At present the whole responsibility is carried by Mrs Nash, an untrained 'natural' teacher, who by sheer determination and natural ability and with the help of correspondence lessons… has hammered out a curriculum and evolved methods which are producing some results… These children have had about 18 months continuous schooling. For the first twelve months, they averaged about 1½ hours daily; latterly have been attending three hours daily. Six older girls and four older boys attend during the afternoon only. There are about 30 children in the six–nine group who are not able to attend school because of staff shortages… The only reading book available is Witcomb and Tombs Readers, which deal with objects and situations completely outside the range of experience of these children.[30]

Nevertheless, the UAM portrayed a positive picture, as indicated in a 1951 *Messenger*:

> On looking back to their effort of twelve months ago, we realised what splendid progress they had made with their schoolwork throughout the

year, and how much credit was due to those who, for love of the Saviour, had so patiently sought to teach our native girls and boys.[31]

In 1952, the timber school was replaced by a stone building that served as both school and church:

> Word has been received from the Warburton Ranges of the opening of the new school building to accommodate probably seventy children, all the work of the missionaries and their native helpers, built principally of stone taken from the locality... The school is furnished by desks made by Mr. Sam Mollenhauer, and they are so highly appraised that he has received encouragement to make more.[32]

By 1956, the school was still 'by no means adequate'. Many children were not commencing 'until they are ten or so years old' and completing school at about Grade Four standard (Grayden, 1957: 26–27). Grayden also noted that: 'if a good season occurs the parents are likely to take the child away from the Mission' for 'one or two years or more'. The school was also periodically left without teachers, and the dormitories and classrooms remained overcrowded.[33] In retrospect, for the mission generation, their 'limited' experience of schooling often amounted to less than three years (Green, 1983: 35). Significantly, this learning was taking place in a strange and almost incomprehensible linguistic and cultural setting. A number of the narratives in this chapter and the next indicate that *yarnangu* 'didn't know what was going on' when they were left in the school. With this factor and such short periods of instruction, it is hard to imagine that children in the mission time learned to read or write much at all. Nevertheless, as will be demonstrated, these experiences introduced the European concepts of schooling and literacy.

Mary, born in 1935, was one of the first children left in the Baker Home. Her father was in the group that made contact with missionaries Wade and Jackson at Mirlirrtjarra in 1933. Mary, Horace and Harold are siblings from the one father and different mothers. Mary recalls seeing her family only when they came in to the mission to exchange 'skintatja, papa skin' (dingo scalps) for mirrka (food). In the summer, they would collect her and take her to the bush. Mary remembers schoolwork every morning in the 'timber house', then when the bell rang at dinnertime, returning to the Home for lunch. Chores (washing the plates and washing clothes) took up half the day. Mary's memories of schooling are positive:

I was writing good way. I used to read. Lovely schoolteacher, Mrs Cotterill used to learn us and Mrs Nash long time ago when we little girl Mrs Mitchell used to look after us in the school...

Mary married Jack and had eight children, who went to school in Warburton and the Eastern Goldfields.

Katherine, born in 1938, *was also one of the first to be left in the Home. Her father was also in the group at Mirlirrtjarra in 1933.*

I didn't even see my mother, that's why my father brought me in to the mission. It was Baker Home. *Walykumunu* (really good). It was really strictly one, not allowed to go out, not allowed to swear or anything, we have to get the biggest, biggest hiding, strap, *ngarltutjarra* (poor thing).

At school, Katherine recalls reading and writing in the morning, then:

...we do like sewing, and that. Sometimes when we finish school we go out and when the meetings on for ladies, we go and looks after the babies.

She also remembers doing other chores:

Before we get up in the morning, before we have breakfast we have to wash ourselves and go out and do work in the morning at staff*ku ngurra*... Go out and wash the dishes, sweep the floor, clean the kitchen out, then go back to breakfast, and then go along to school.

After Katherine finished school, she remained in the Home until she married. She worked first as a domestic for the missionaries, then in the dining room, making breakfast for the next generation of school children.

Arthur was born around 1949. *He is Katherine's younger brother and was left in the Baker Home when he was about nine years old. He recalls that period as a 'hard time':*

My parents, they didn't want to let me go. I liked walking around travelling with my parents... The government want children to go to school to learn. So they explain about all that and made us to stay. It was a good Home but we still loved our mother and father and we wanted to be with them. And that's another part where you are all jammed in like, and you're forced to stay not to go. That was hard too for us, but we gradually learnt what the missionaries looking after us told us. Some other people say the missionaries were better [good] for nothing, but in a way we get learn. But that time it was different, you know, different from today… some of us got learnt properly how to read and write, and get to know how talking. At school they taught us a lot of things, like Bible, all those things, they sounded strange to us, see. At that time I was growing and knowing, "Oh yeah?" But *we didn't know what was up there or down here*, and all that, we was slowly learning.

At school, he remembers pencils, exercise books and storybooks:

…with stories like Waltzing Matilda, Once a Jolly Swagman, that man there, those sort of book. So when we was learning that way, well, we think we're gonna see that Jolly Swagman. But it was story, you know, we liked it.

While Arthur was in the Home, his family camped outside the mission. His father worked on the new track to Laverton and construction work inside the mission:

We used to see our parents go down helping, bringing the slabs and cracking it and levelling, starting to build. So we seen that school go up. School and it was a church too, you know, where people worshipped.

Arthur also remembers people working in the hospital, store and 'some ladies worked at the Home… they wash clothes'.

At the Christmas holiday time we go out. Go out and our parents bring us back to school, not on the right time but, you know… Bring us any-time they coming back this way. Walking and they bring us Home here.

Ultimately, Arthur recalls that,

…it was really hard for me, like you can only talk when your parents are down, there, see. But that's when they, when whitefellas was looking after us… and we think it's, well to me, almost forgetting about your mother, and like learning what the white people do. So we had to.

The translation mob like old Mr Douglas was here and he got older ones to write down all the language. So at that time I used to see my parents doing it too… Wilf Douglas, he used to do it at the school there or at his place where he lived. He used to get like Silas' father, and Jack doing that.

In 1961, Arthur left school and was sent to Pedlar's Hostel in Esperance.

Joshua was born in 1937.[34]

[W]hen I was a little boy… my mother and father… asked the missionary if they could look after me and they said: "Yes, we'll look after him". I remember my mother said to me, said to that *piranypa* (white people), in language she said: "*Yuwa, tjitji ngaanya kanyila purlkala nyawa*". That means: "Look after this little boy and see how he gets on". She said that, I still remember that.

We didn't have any papers and all that before, or pencil… I didn't know what was going on but I was only small. Then as I grew, a bit older, I knew what I was doing then… Education went better then, better and better. I got to the stage where I was learning school and other things… All the missionaries, they helped each other to get these books, books, and pads and pencil and all that, we got better and better. So we knew what we were doing… we learnt about *Katungkatjanya* side (Jesus)… that's what the missionary came out for.

But all the time we kept on going out bush, meet up with people… from the bush, some was still living, and they never seen a white bloke… no clothes… no blanket… nothing to carry around… just a spear and a fire and… woman had that *piti* (coolamon)… we don't live in one place, only in soak with a water there… so when we went for holiday, we stayed there… we don't bother about coming into the mission, just sit down there… learn things out there… that's when I was still little… so I had two ways of living.

In 1956, when Joshua was 16, he left Warburton for vocational training in the Eastern Goldfields.

Rosie was born in 1941. *Her father was also in the first group to make contact with missionaries in 1933 at Mirlirrtjarra. She was later left in the Baker Home:*

It was *walykumunu* (really good). We play outside, go bush, come back. When we heard a bell ringing we run, *pitjaku, kulilku*: "Hey, ringing the bell". And *kukurralkulatju* bath*ku* first, bath*ku*, mayi*ku* (we'd run for the bath first, then food)… Sunday we used to have Sunday School *turlku*.

Hear about Mama God, Jesusku *tjukurrpa*, story, *yuwa* every Sunday afternoon, *mungangka* and go back Home *kunkunarriku* (in the evening we go back to the Home and go to sleep).

Christmastime we used to get a *nyaapa*, race*imankunpayilatju*, *yurralku*, get a prize, present*pa mantjilku* (we'd do races and get a prize, get a present). And after that, after Christmas we used to go bush, must be couple of weeks *nyinarrayilkuuuuuuu* (stay for a loooooong time), come back home. Bush*palatju nyinapayi* we used to go bush *kukaku*, come back... *Marlaku pitjaku* Home-*ngka tjarrpaku, tirtu kanyilpayilanyatju* and school*kulatju pitjapayi* (We returned to the Home and they kept us for a long time and we'd go to school).

Walykumunu missionary-*ya*, (They were really good, all the missionaries)... *Nyinapayilatju* happyone*pa*, happy *Mama* God*ngalatju kulilpayi kulilpayi*, when we was little girl *kulilpayilanga* Jesus*nga tirtu* (we were happy listening to all the stories about God and Jesus)...Missionary used to give us little flour, flour little*leonepa*. Tea and sugar, *mayi* Sunday *nintilpayi* (We'd go out bush to get meat. Missionary would give us a little flour. On Sunday we'd get tea, sugar and food).

*Rosie finished school in 1954 and travelled out to Cosmo, Laverton and Kalgoorlie with her family. After she returned, she married **Harold (b. 1934)**, who trained to be a preacher and worked for Western Mining collecting copper in the 1960s. Rosie and Harold had seven children, including Carmel (b. 1963), Eileen (b. 1967) and Pamela (b. 1976).*

Dormitory schooling: Coercion or agency?

Why did families in the early days of the Warburton Ranges Mission leave their children to be cared for by these emissaries from an alien cultural world? A bad drought in the 1930s may have initially attracted large numbers into the Mission, with an expectation that food could be obtained. In correspondence from the Minister for Native Welfare in 1940, allegations were made that 'native children are retained at the mission as a means of securing the services of the parents in obtaining dog scalps'.[35] Given the scarcity of resources in the early days, this allegation may have had some veracity, and coercion may account for why some families left their children, although evidence of parental resistance has been noted (Plant, 1995).[36]

Silas perceives that when families left their children in the Home in exchange for food, the missionaries 'stepped in to look after the children' and to keep them 'safe'. Arthur recalls tales of 'warrmarla time', when revenge killings were still feared, and children were left with the missionaries 'to stay safe', as he explains:

> Before it was really hard for our families to settle, like to sit down in one rockhole... [if] they stay at the rockhole, homeland, well there's trouble, maybe trouble coming up from another tribes... it was really hard to be with our parents all the time, see. That's why you know, at the same time missionaries came... all that warrmarla business you know from another tribes come in, like revenge, payback and they go back. So really hard for like when we was small, they can't carry us and run, they wanna be free, just pick up what they need.

Arthur understands that the revenge party retribution lessened after the arrival of the Mission:

> Oh it went down a bit when the missionaries came, and when old Mr Wade showed about that cross, about that two man on the side, they understand a little bit, that time.

Survival in the desert depended upon the ability to traverse vast distances by foot, often in extreme heat with little food and water. This was hampered if a mother had to carry more than one young child. Mary believes that her family was happy to leave her in the Home in the 1940s: 'they been putting us in the Home, they don't want to carry long way, walk around, he got another one, my sister'. Molly also says her family was 'happy' to bring her into the Home. Her narrative provides an insight into how some families acted as cultural brokers, by sharing the symbols of the new world and encouraging relatives in the bush to bring their children into school.

Molly was born in 1940. *Her older sister was the first wife to one of the senior men in the group to first encounter the missionaries at Old Well in 1933.*

> We used to live round the bush when I was a little girl growing up... We used to travel to Giles [Weather Station] and back, my father used to travel around, any places... Then we came to the mission. One of our sisters, was living here... I didn't know I had a sister here. But one lady always used to go there with a little bit of clothes for her families, Harold's mother. She brought us back, she told us: "Come back home, come back. *Tjitji pirni* (many children) schooling there". They was happy, I don't know, I can't think what they was thinking. They just

brought us and left us in the Home. I must have been just 10 years old then. Old man, my old uncle he came over and said: "This girl want to go in the school". So they put me in. It was new, we used to sleep on iron bed. I think I felt alright, we had friends there. We had Mary there... our family, that's why I wasn't worried, they was in school there, those big girls. My brother was in the Home too... and my cousin... they was in school. Big mob of them... I was happy because we had a lot of family was in the Home... I had my little niece there... she was in school with her sister... Big family, I know them.

Although the dormitory experience was strange and new, as Molly describes, children were not socially isolated. In fact, they were interacting with relatives in a way that cemented social relatedness between horizontal, generational family groupings. In addition, families camped nearby the Home, and the children were returned to families for a lengthy period each summer.

Reciprocity and exchange

In his study of social relatedness among a neighbouring group – the Pintupi – Fred Myers emphasises the sentiment *kanyininpa* – 'looking after' or 'caring for' (expressed in Ngaanyatjarra as *kanyilku* or *miranykanyilku*) – as a core value in the framework of social relatedness and one embedded with an inherent expectation of reciprocated exchange (Myers, 1986; Myers, 2002). Drawing on Myers' analytical paradigm, it may be surmised that a certain trust must have developed during the initial interaction with the missionaries, especially as the Wades brought with them a sympathetic disposition, unlike many other first-contact and mission encounters.

By drawing on Sahlins' proposition that '[p]eople act upon circumstances according to their own cultural presuppositions... [and] sediment new functional values on old categories' (Sahlins, 1981: 67–68) and interpreting the encounter through the Ngaanyatjarra cultural frame of social relatedness (that is, within the traditional norms of reciprocity, requiring the sociocultural obligation to look after people), it can be speculated that the Ngaanyatjarra comprehended the missionaries' actions as *miranykanyilku* – that is, grounded within the social norms of 'looking after' the children. This framework would also have allowed *yarnangu* to overcome, to some extent, their distrust of the *malikitja* – 'strangers' – as highlighted in the following event. As mentioned earlier, the Mission moved to a permanent location in 1936. It was, however, situated on an important sacred site, along the *marlu* (kangaroo) dreaming track, passing through Warburton. Brooks discusses this incident (Brooks, 2011a), describing how the missionaries 'asked' the old men to show them a good site and even though they 'agonised' over the decision, because it was 'serious country', permission was ultimately granted. In other words, Ngaanyatjarra families tolerated the presence of these strangers on their country, as an act of reciprocity in the exchange relationship. Notably, the *marlu tjina* – 'incident' – also illustrates how, at this time, the senior Law men maintained spatial authority in this dynamic new social context, a point that will be returned to in later chapters.

In summary, it is evident that there was both reciprocity and agency in the early mission encounter. Some Ngaanyatjarra were strategically arming their children with a new form of knowledge so they could adapt to the inevitable coming of the new world. It has been suggested, by the son of an early missionary, that the Ngaanyatjarra wanted to embolden their children with sufficient information to deal with the changes that they knew were coming.[37] Similarly, Brooks suggests that families, in fact, took advantage of the missionaries to train their children to be the 'intermediaries' with Europeans.[38] Joshua describes it thus: 'we learn us about God, and how to live in the future'. Silas reiterates this point, saying that his father, Horace, advised him, as the younger generation, to take advantage of what the missionaries were offering, as 'one day we're gonna be finished and you got to stand up on your own two feet'.

Building a Christian Work Ethic

As noted earlier, Warburton Ranges Mission was established contrary to Commissioner Neville's wishes, and his punitive response was to deny financial support to the fledgling mission. The Mission was thus left to its own resources and had to be self-sufficient.[39] Although the Mission received funds donated in response to the good news stories in the *United Aborigines Messenger*, the trading of rations in exchange for dingo scalps was a critical early endeavour. Dingo scalps were taken to Laverton Shire several times a year, and the small bounty paid for each scalp went towards purchasing mission supplies (Mollenhauer, 2002). This enabled the Mission to exploit the bounty system to stay afloat financially. It also utilised the agentive participation of *yarnangu* in collecting *papa minyarra* (dingo scalps) in exchange for rations – a factor that enticed desert-dwelling families into the Mission, but also enabled them to maintain their hunter-gatherer existence. When scalps were brought into the Mission, a portion of the rations were distributed – in 1947, payment for a scalp was 10lb flour, ½ lb sugar, ½ lb tea and a pair of trousers or a dress.[40] The balance was, however, received only after a gospel lesson.[41] This confluence of mutual interests was a unique event in frontier history (Brooks, 2002d). The government wanted to pay to protect pastoral stations from marauding dogs; the missionaries who acted as intermediaries could thus sell the scalps to the government and obtain much-needed funds; and *yarnangu* who were desirous of food and new material objects were prepared to enter into an exchange relationship, albeit in exchange for evangelisation.

Insufficient food was a perennial problem at the Mission, and this led to an interdependent relationship between the missionaries and some *yarnangu*, illustrated by the ongoing mission reliance on hunted *kuka* (bush meat) to feed the children in the Home. With no government subsidies to assist with building the mission infrastructure, some adults in the early contact group provided labour in exchange for rations: they were trained as workers 'following along the well-tried and proven ways of Mr Schenk and his family at Mt Margaret' (Mollenhauer, 2002: 69). In the decade following 1947, men were employed hewing and carting stone for building, collecting firewood, well-sinking, fencing, making mud bricks and cutting a new road to Laverton. Pastoral work initially had a high profile, with the raising of goats for milk and meat and sheep for meat and wool for sale. Meanwhile, women engaged in typically female tasks: spinning, crocheting, knitting and sewing clothes to sell in stores, preparing meals, baking bread and sewing and mending clothes in the Home.[42] Once the first generation of schoolgirls reached adolescence, they were encouraged to work. Molly recalls being told to look after the babies at the weekly ladies' meeting, where women did craft and sewing, sang 'choruses' and listened to a 'simple message'[43]:

> All the ladies used to come to the meetings because, because you know why? Because there's a scone... They make a lot of scones for the ladies meeting where they sing, learn, same way, they preach, the missionary ladies preach.

At this time, Katherine was working as a domestic in a missionary's house, and young women with dormitory training, like Mary and Rosie, were working in the first hospital – an old house transported from Laverton in 1953.

Conflicting Values and Practices

By the 1950s, the Mission was reportedly 'influencing' some 500 to 700 Aboriginal people in the Central Reserve area (see Table 3.1), with the aim

Figure 3.2 Older girls from the Baker Home, Warburton Ranges Mission 1952
© Ngarnmanytjatja Archive, Ngaanyatjarra Council

of uplifting them 'to take their place as citizens of Australia, through evangelisation, education and the establishment of local industry by the natives for their own benefit'.[44] In reality, by the 1950s, two socio-spatial worlds had emerged. In one small group, were those who were 'accepted' by the missionaries, leaving the majority 'still in the bush'. The imbibing of Western values and practices by some Ngaanyatjarra led to a widening gap between them and those groups who remained in the desert hinterland or camped outside the mission compound when visiting their children or bringing in dingo scalps.

Silas was born in 1951. Silas' grandfather first made contact with the missionaries Wade and Jackson at Mirlirrtjarra in 1933.

My family, my mother especially was working for the mission like washing clothes for the missionaries, and working in the kitchen, cooking bread and doing this and that... And my father used to work for the mission, like going out getting them stores, when they used to go out like on a truck from Warburton to Laverton... Because the missionaries in that time they wanted an Aboriginal person to work for them, so they got my parents to work.

Silas went to school at Warburton:

[Then] I did one year in Wongutha Farm, Esperance. I was teenager. I wanted to get learn but I get twist off, twist off by some young fellas calling me to go to work in the stations... At Wongutha Farm we used to do like jack of all trades, like building, carpentry, saddlery, learning further more education like going to highschool there.

Silas later worked on stations in the Eastern Goldfields.

Silas conveys how some families would 'hunt for their living', while his family participated in the new exchange relationship, by getting food from 'rashing out' – that is, in exchange for rations, otherwise described as 'working for their living'. He states that 'in that time, the people who want to work for their living, they was accepted':

My family was a little bit different from the people who lived round the mission compound, when they was still in the *wiltja* and still in the bush. My family was a little bit different because they was accepted by the missionaries.

Silas' father, Horace (born 1932), had grown up in the Home and later became one of the first Ngaanyatjarra preachers. Horace was the first to wed in a Christian ceremony at the Mission in 1950. By 1951, Horace and his family were living in a cottage – also the first on the Mission to do so – although older relatives preferred to remain in the camp outside the Mission. Mary married Jack in the second Christian marriage ceremony. However, she considers that the missionaries 'forced her to get married':

When my mother and father been gone that ways and that missionary been give me to that man, Jack. I said: *"Wiya,* I don't want him". "Oh you gotta get married to him". *Yuwa,* he was saying that. That missionary used to look after us in the Baker Home. I said *wiya* (no)... the missionary got sorry for Jack because he had hard job doing everything, building house.

Men like Horace, Harold and Jack took on the role of intermediaries between the missionaries and the majority nomads who occupied the other social space outside the mission compound. Rosie recalls how:

Jack, Harold's brother Horace, every Sunday they tell a story to the people. They come from the camp they hear about the Lord Jesus and get you know, ticket, little ticket from the missionary for *mirrka* [food]. We used to get a ticket and get a *mirrka* and go back *ngurraku* [to camp].

Murray Wells, whose father was a missionary at Warburton, suggests that most people used to go to church for the rations afterwards: 'each person who went to church was given a little square token usually cut out of lino as they walked out, which was exchanged at the store after the service for flour, tea, sugar and jam' (Wells, 2002: 53).[45] In this way, those who took on the role of intermediaries were complicit in reinforcing a system where food was received in exchange for evangelisation. Conversely, they also freed the majority Ngaanyatjarra to maintain traditional social, cultural and linguistic practices, distanced from the Christianising influence of the missionaries.

Families who interacted directly with the missionaries were acquiring some of the cultural and linguistic practices of the Anglo-Australian strangers within the new 'social space' (Bourdieu, 1989) of the mission. In other words, they were constructing a new social identity that carried with it a new kind of symbolic power. Adults in this group also took on English first names. This signified an overt appropriation of the introduced symbolic system – that is, a cultural marker that publicly redefined the way that one perceived oneself and related to others. Significantly, the older men in these families were the *ngurrara* (the people with rights to the country) for the Warburton area. This gave them the cultural authority to make decisions for that country and to interact with visitors. Brooks has suggested that this positioning in the new social order gave them a head start in developing their role as the intermediaries between the missionaries and the nomadic families from more distant locations, who were also strangers to this country and so kept a respectful distance. Nevertheless, the camp, that is the social space outside the mission, remained the source of much power and authority and represented the domain in which most meaningful social life occurred (Brooks, 2011a).

To sum up, even though some individuals worked hard to acquire new social and linguistic practices in the Mission to arm their offspring with knowledge and information to deal the new Western world, it was not without conflict and identity struggle. As Silas reflects: 'my family, my father especially was a tribal, tribal leader, but he balance his Law in a private way… two ways, *yarnangu* Law strong and Christian ways'. George also emphasises that:

The missionaries they knew that we had our own culture but... they never interfered with the culture, cultural side. They did what they came out to do, tell the Good News, but people still had their ceremony business and all. Because old people like Jack used to work, stop in the mission and Silas' old man, some old people who finished now, they used to work together and help... but they never interfered with the Law side.

Nevertheless, even though traditional Law was not eroded, 'cultural conflict and identity split' were acutely felt (Brooks, 2002d: 80).

Changing socialisation patterns

Inevitably, sites of conflict and resistance developed between traditional values and introduced practices that emphasised countervailing moral values. Spear fights were a feature of daily life and the cause of many fights – represented in the *Messenger* as 'Satanic resistance to spread of the Gospel' – centred on the Mission's determination to protect girls from

Figure 3.3 Outside Warburton Ranges Mission compound fence 1950s
© Ngarnmanytjatja Archive, Ngaanyatjarra Council

polygynous marriages with older men.[46] The girls' dormitory lay within the fenced compound, and the missionaries locked the teenage girls in at night to 'protect' them from the advances of older men (Plant, 1995: 273):

> Girls of about 15 years and upwards being subjected to tribal laws, are the cause of dissension between the missionaries and the camp natives. To counteract the natives' demands for the older girls, the missionaries have surrounded the whole of the girls' home block with a seven-foot-high fence ring-lock stock fencing. It would not deter anyone determined to enter the compound and serves mainly to irritate the natives, who compare it indignantly with the goat yard… The Mission policy for these girls appears to be to oppose tribal marriage practice and encourage them to marry young men raised in the Mission Homes.[47]

The 'mission generation' was the first to experience the institutionalised durative aggregation of mixed gender, same-age cohorts under the new moral authority of Europeans. This would lead some young women to challenge traditional behaviour norms, especially the ceremonial obligation from birth that required the fulfilment of betrothals and the traditional practice of polygyny.

Una was born in 1951. *Una and Maisie (b. 1947) have the same grandfather. Her family was camping around Elder Creek in 1933 when Will Wade made the first camel trip. Una's father recalled this event, because he was admonished by his father for taking sweets from strangers. Una's father started school after the mission moved from Old Well:*

> They been schooling here… They used to have a shed, he told me all that story. They used to have them little board thing [slate] and they used to draw like people and animals, and they used to count them… he never wrote anything, only drawed.

When Una was a child, she was placed in the Baker Home:

> I was born here that's why they been put me in the Home… They used to wait for truck to bring food in. But not much, you know, they was sort of waiting. There was plenty of kangaroos and all that. But it must have been a little bit hard for them… people used to come out, that's first thing in the morning because the mission had to give the gun out to bring some meat for the mission. So they get lucky sometimes and bring some *kuka* back, *yuwa*, that's for lunch.

Una was happy in the Home, but remembers getting 'the strap' for running away:

> There was lots and lots of children from everywhere, we was all put in the school... some of them were put in the Home, but they didn't like it so they ran away to their parents... I was learning how to read and write.

Initially, her family maintained a nomadic life:

> Sometimes they come and visit us, you know, outside the fence. They used to come sit down and talk: "Are you right?" And we always say: "Yeah we right". ... But they was outside, they used to come and see us when they come in to get some ration... they used to come in and get food and go out. Holidays we go out and we get blanket, one each and we go out. All our families come and wait for us and they take us out.
>
> There was a lot of older people working with the mission in the early days. My father used to go out and get some stones to build around all these places here... They used to have houses like that built for the dormitory and for the schoolteachers.
>
> We used to go out. Like my father and mother used to like going that way to Cosmo and they used to come and take us to Cosmo, walking, not by car. They used to walk and stay there for little while and come back because my grandfather went down to Cosmo, staying there... my aunty was there, my father's brothers... they were already in Laverton.

After 1953, Una's family shifted to Cosmo. Una briefly went to school, then joined her family on a station outside Laverton:

> When I must have been around 13 or 14 we went out that way to Bandya Station then and my father used to work with his brother over there. They used to go out, I used to see them really early in the morning, they go out on the horse till five and come back.

In 1953, Cosmo Newbery Settlement, still a viable pastoral station, was finally handed over to the UAM by the West Australian government.[48] Families who were 'accepted' by the Mission were encouraged to shift there 'to do their work with the mission mob there'. This relieved the tension caused by overcrowding at Warburton and provided a staging post for goods and *yarnangu* travelling in and out for ceremonial Business.[49] Importantly, the distance between Cosmo and Warburton, and the proximity to the Christianising influence of Mt Margaret, were exploited by the missionaries, in an effort to separate young girls from the advances of older men. As Molly's nephew, Clem, recalls:

> The missionaries don't want them to get married a bit earlier, some of them was taken to Cosmo where they was able to, even my young aunt-ie, my mother's young sister [Molly] went over there. They were teached in the white man's way, in other words in the Western world.

Molly suggests that she and some other girls chose to go to Cosmo to escape the pursuit of older men:

> My mother and father and all the families I left them behind in Warburton. They wasn't happy but I put my foot down and said: "No, I'm going". They said: "You've gotta stop". And I said: "No, I've made up my mind, I want to go". I was frightened for the man who chase me round all the time.

Cosmo was also used as a training centre for adolescents, especially for boys drifting westwards from Warburton.[50] As Molly describes:

> About seven of us girls went there staying, learning to do housework, cleaning, cooking. Seeing as no schoolhouse was there we used to go to mission for ride, Mt Margaret for ride and we went to Bible study there for about two weeks.

Similarly, Maisie's narrative highlights the contestation around diverging socialisation practices. She tells how the missionaries set her sights on aspirations outside the traditional paradigm. However, her family intervened and gave her to her promised husband. Maisie married a traditional elder and returned to Ngaanyatjarra country. So powerful was this new socialisation, however, that to this day, Maisie regrets her thwarted aspirations. Such assertions of individuality represent early challenges to the Ngaanyatjarra status quo and the indisputable authority of the senior Law men. They also signal the sociocultural changes that were to come, most especially, the commencement of a new developmental trajectory for youth, oriented towards Western values and aspirations – a theme I return to later.

Maisie was born in 1947. *Una and Maisie have the same grandfather. During the 1950s, Maisie's father was working in and around Laverton:*

> First when I was at Laverton mum and dad take up hunting, and in those days didn't have much food, only ration, bush tucker like kangaroo, goanna. Father used to go do watering the garden at the clinic in Laverton... Station person come and they go out work muster the sheep... she do her part of the job by cooking... He wanted to do that job because that's the only way to get food.

In the meantime, Maisie was left in the Home at Mt Margaret Mission:

> Like Christmas holidays, the missionaries say to us: "Alright, you children have to wait for your mum and dad to come and pick you, pack all your things ready". ...They came in their early days car... and my uncle came and pick us up... took us to Laverton... When the school started, went back to Mt Margaret... At Mt Margaret Mission we are taught to speak English, talk English all the time.

As a teenager, Maisie was sent to Kurrawang Mission and attended Eastern Goldfields High School in Kalgoorlie. After finishing school, a missionary invited her to Melbourne.

> I had my things packed up but didn't went... mum and dad gave me away... Life were different because we didn't had much work but we have to go get married, that's the only way, go live with the man, 'cause there wasn't no job for a woman like me... In those days only job you can get was going out and helping husband mustering sheep and cooking, that's all job, and housework.

After Maisie married, she returned to Warburton and has worked as a childcare worker for many years.

Conclusion

At Mt Margaret, Schenk's unique emphasis on education, vocational training and employment was to give Aboriginal people 'a high degree of independence unparalleled elsewhere' in Western Australia (Biskup, 1973: 132). This was a significant factor in the process of social re-formation under the unfolding conditions at Mt Margaret, Cosmo Newbery and Warburton that has shaped the 'historical production of persons in practice' (Holland

& Lave, 2009: 1). Through the missionaries, the causality of the new world was explained and a template for social relations with Europeans was set. In retrospect, the continuity of the Wades (who were to remain at Warburton Ranges Mission until 1958) and other missionaries was to prove an important factor in the benign nature of the encounter with Anglo-Australian settler society, as the mission protected the Ngaanyatjarra from the extreme consequences of colonisation. The missionaries sought to establish positive relationships with *yarnangu* and the adversity of the context created mutual dependency. Mission schooling had social meaning, and Christian symbolism and sentiment resonated within an existing meaning system. In the space of a generation, profound changes took place. Within which time, some Ngaanyatjarra acquired new social, cultural and linguistic repertoires and were able to communicate in English, to a certain extent, and, likewise, acquired basic alphabetic literacy skills or at least had developed a sense of being literate.

Importantly, the intervention of the mission allowed people to pace their adaptation to settler society. To a certain extent, there was reciprocity in the early encounter and agency in the process of change and adaptation. There was also autonomy, in part, because of remoteness and because the majority Ngaanyatjarra populace remained connected to country, kin and ceremonial practice for longer than in other regions. Still now, *yarnangu* are appreciative of these factors and compare themselves to those who were taken away and 'lost their identity'. As Silas comments: 'that's why they talk about the "stolen generation"… it's a sad story and that's why they live in that in-between and they angry'.[51] Nevertheless, by the 1950s, significant changes in Aboriginal policy at a national level were to impact profoundly on this isolated and insulated mission and everything would be different 'because of the changing'. It is to the impact of the interventions and intrusions of the state – beginning in the assimilation era of the 1950s and 1960s – that the discussion now turns.

Notes

(1) The *1871 Elementary Education Act* had 'theoretically' provided education for all West Australian Aboriginal children residing within a three-mile radius of a state school, however, this was never properly implemented, leaving Aboriginal students excluded from state schools well into the 1930s. The *1905 Aborigines Act* made Aboriginal education the responsibility of the Aborigines Department (Haebich, [1988] 1992). Aware that they had a 'statutory responsibility to educate Aboriginal children', the Department admitted that it was 'powerless to do very much', due to lack of finances (Western Australian Government (1936) *Annual Report of the Chief Protector of Aborigines for the Year Ended 30th June 1935*. Perth: WA Government.).

(2) The 16th-century Protestant Reformation most strikingly linked literacy to religious practice and was influenced by the Calvinist Puritan emphasis on universal schooling (Graff, [1982] 1994). The Protestant and Calvinist influence in Europe and America helped promote the link between social mobility and literacy (Graff, 1987). The UAM had its roots in groups that had evolved out of 17th- and 18th-century German Protestantism, English Calvinist Puritanism and the mystical pietism of Bohemia and Moravia and opened missions in Australia in the 19th century. After 1940, the Methodists and Congregationalists withdrew their support for the UAM, leaving only the fundamentalist organisations, supported mainly by the Baptists, Church of Christ and Brethren churches (Edwards, 1999; McDonald, 2001).

(3) Ernabella Mission was established in the north-west of South Australia in 1937 by Charles Duguid, under the Australian Presbyterian Board of Missions. The missionaries had a relatively congenial relationship with the Pitjantjatjara and believed in education and training. A school commenced in 1940, and a grammatical description of Pitjantjatjara was published to support the school programme (Hilliard, 1968; Trudinger, 1943).

(4) *Annual Report of the Chief Protector of Aborigines* (1928: 6).

(5) Institutions such as Moore River and Carrolup Native Settlements embodied Neville's policy of removing children from families, thus assisting in the inevitable absorption of 'mixed blood' or 'half-caste' children into European society (Haebich, [1988] 1992: 182–191). Children sent to Moore River generally never saw their families again (Maushart, [1993] 2003; Neville, 1947).

(6) *Annual Report of the Commissioner of Native Affairs* (1945: 8).

(7) *Annual Report of the Commissioner of Native Affairs* (1937: 3–4).

(8) In 1920, the WA government gazetted an area of WA (including the Warburton and Rawlinson Ranges). In 1921, the SA government set aside an area in the north-west of SA, as did the Commonwealth government in the south-western corner of the NT. These three 'reserves' formed the Central Australian Aboriginal Reserves, with a total area of about 170,000 sq. km. Administration of the WA section of the reserves was handed over to Ngaanyatjarra Council on a leasehold system in 1988.

(9) WA SRO Acc 903 901/40 – Cosmo Newbery Native Station. *Acting CNA C.L. McBeath to the Hon.* MNA, 5 September 1947.

(10) WA SRO Acc 993 1220/61 17/762 – *From CNW to MNW summary of history of Warburton Ranges Mission*.

(11) The first explorer in the Warburton area was William Gosse in 1873, followed by Ernest Giles, 1873–1874 (Giles, [1899] 1995), Forrest in 1874, Tietkins in 1891 and Carnegie in the 1870s (Carnegie, [1898] 1982). Surveyors Talbot and Clarke came through in 1916, and in 1931, government surveyors Paine and Barclay traversed a route from Laverton to Warburton (Mollenhauer, 2002). Harry Lasseter made prospecting trips into the Peterman Ranges between 1897 and 1931. A trip from Laverton to Warburton by Michael Terry and his survey team in 1932 is remembered as the first sighting of a motor vehicle in the region. In 1935, anthropologist Norman Tindale surveyed and photographed people near the Warburton Ranges.

(12) WA SRO Acc 1733 511/42 – *Warburton Ranges Mission native matters (May 1946) Officer in Charge at Cosmo to CNA.*

(13) William Wade, a cockney Londoner, spent his early days as a sailor, prior to his conversion to the Salvation Army. He migrated to Australia in 1924. In 1926, he and R.M. Williams (the iconic Australian adventurer) explored the desert region of SA

and WA by camel, in order to become acquainted with the Aboriginal population for the Australian missions (Williams, 1998).

(14) *United Aborigines Messenger* (May 1935: 3).

(15) *United Aborigines Messenger* (October/November 1991: 10).

(16) *United Aborigines Messenger* (November 1938); *United Aborigines Messenger* (September 1940); *United Aborigines Messenger* (May 1948: 12).

(17) The *United Aborigines Messenger* newsletter was the 'organ' of the UAM. It was used to disseminate claims of achievement and success from UAM missions throughout Australia and assist in raising finances.

(18) *Annual Report of the Chief Protector of Aborigines* (1936: 17); WA SRO Acc 993 1220/61 *17/762 – From CNW to MNW summary of history of Warburton Ranges Mission.*

(19) *United Aborigines Messenger* (June 1936: 10).

(20) *United Aborigines Messenger* (February 1937: 9).

(21) *United Aborigines Messenger* (April 1941: 11); *United Aborigines Messenger* (January 1947: 11).

(22) WA SRO Acc 1419 23-7-3 – *Missions UAM Mission Warburton Ranges. Reports Annual Inspection,* 22 July 1947 (Report from Constable Anderson re. annual inspection of Warburton Ranges).

(23) *United Aborigines Messenger* (June 1935: 3).

(24) Sources for Table 3.1: *Report of the Chief Protector of Aborigines* (1936); *Annual Reports Commissioner of Native Affairs* (1937, 1944, 1945, 1949, 1950, 1954); *Annual Reports Commissioner of Native Welfare* (1961, 1962, 1963, 1964, 1965, 1966, 1967, 1968, 1969, 1970, 1971, 1972); *Annual Report AAPA and ALT* (1972, 1973); *United Aborigines Messenger* (September 1940, February 1948, May 1956, February 1965, September 1973); WA SRO Acc 1733 511/42 – *Warburton Ranges Mission native matters July 1947 Memo from Bisley Inspector of Natives to DCNA;* WA SRO Acc 1733 511/42 – *Warburton Ranges Mission native matters, 30 May 1950, CNA to D/Director of Rationing;* WA SRO Acc 1419 23-7-3 – *Missions UAM Mission Reports Annual Inspection 4 December 1951 McLarty (District Officer Central) to A/DoNA Kalgoorlie re report on Warburton Ranges Mission;* WA SRO Acc 1419 23-7-3 – *Missions: UAM Mission (Reports Annual Inspection June 1954–June 1955 Annual Report from UAM to DNA re. Warburton Ranges Mission);* WA SRO Acc 993 360/56 – *Warburton Ranges Matters (April-May 1957 H. Moorhouse Survey Report of the Warburton District);* WA SRO Acc 993 360/56– *Warburton Ranges Matters 4 March 1957 Sanitation Inspection Report Warburton Ranges;* WA SRO Acc 993 360/56 – *Warburton Ranges Matters 18 December 1958 ADO Eastern Goldfields report on Inspection of WR Mission;* WA SRO Acc1419 – *23-7-3 15/162 letter from CNW to Federal Secretary UAM;* UAM, March 1973, NTU Files – *Cosmo Newbery Annual Report* (Berndt & Berndt, 1959; Grayden, 1957).

(25) *Annual Report Commissioner of Native Affairs* (1954: 60).

(26) *United Aborigines Messenger* (May 1948: 12).

(27) WA SRO Acc 1419 23-7-3 – *Missions UAM Mission Warburton Ranges. Reports Annual Inspection 22/7/47 (Report from Constable Anderson re. annual inspection of Warburton Ranges).*

(28) *Annual Report Commissioner of Native Welfare* (1957: 135).

(29) Interview with Dora Cotterill (née Quinn) and P. Milnes Leonora (1981) cited in Milnes (1987: 379).

(30) Annual Report CNA 1950; WA SRO Acc 1733 511/42 – *Warburton Ranges Mission native matters (1942–1956) Oct 27–Nov 10 1951 Report A/D CNA and A/DOC Annual Inspection Report re. Warburton Ranges Mission.*

(31) *United Aborigines Messenger* (March 1951: 9).

(32) *United Aborigines Messenger* (April 1952: 7).

(33) *United Aborigines Messenger* (May 1957: 8); WA SRO Acc 993 360/56 – *Warburton Ranges Matters 18/12/58 ADO Eastern Goldfields Inspection report Warburton Ranges Mission.*

(34) Information on 'Joshua' (a pseudonym) is taken primarily from Warburton Arts Project (1993, 42–50).

(35) WA SRO, Acc 1674 73/5, Central Australian Reserve 17614, Letter to the Aboriginal Advisory Committee from the Minister for Native Welfare, 27 January 1940, quoted in Plant (1995).

(36) Vicki Plant, Ngaanyatjarra Council Native Title Unit historian.

(37) P. Gurrier-Jones – interview, October 2004.

(38) David Brooks (personal communication, March 2005).

(39) WA SRO ACC 993 1220/61 17/762 – *From CNW to MNW summary of history of Warburton Ranges mission.*

(40) WA SRO Acc 1733 511/42 – *Warburton Ranges Mission native matters 21/4/48 Bisley to CNA re. visit to Warburton 1947.*

(41) WA SRO Acc 1733 511/42 – *Warburton Ranges Mission native matters 21/4/48 Bisley to CNA re. visit to Warburton 1947.*

(42) WA SRO Acc 1419 23-7-3 – *Missions UAM Mission Warburton Ranges, Reports Annual Inspection 10/8/56, Superintendent to ADO Abridged Report on year's work ending 1956; United Aborigines Messenger* (October/November 1991: 10–11).

(43) *United Aborigines Messenger* (May 1948: 12).

(44) *Annual Report of the Commissioner of Native Affairs* (1950: 29).

(45) Murray Wells lived at Warburton Ranges Mission as a child (1956–1961), then at Mt Margaret Mission. His father drove the mission truck back and forth to Laverton to collect supplies. Wells returned to Warburton in 1974 to work in the bilingual education programme. After teaching at Blackstone for five years, he left the Education Department and worked as environmental health worker trainer, until he retired in 2006.

(46) *United Aborigines Messenger* (August 1959: 10); *United Aborigines Messenger* (September 1956: 9).

(47) Extract from Memo from Commissioner of Native Welfare to Minister of Native Welfare, 21 March 1957 – UAM Files, NTU Archive, Ngaanyatjarra Council.

(48) *Annual Report of the Commissioner of Native Affairs* (1952).

(49) *United Aborigines Messenger* (February 1954: 8); Stanton (1990: 221, 298); *Annual Report Commissioner of Native Affairs* (1953: 1).

(50) *Annual Report of the Commissioner of Native Welfare* (1955).

(51) Only one 'stolen generation' narrative is linked to the Ngaanyatjarra region (Powell & Kennedy, 2005). See Human Rights and Equal Opportunity Commission (1997); Read (1981), for accounts of the 'stolen generation'.

4 Everything was Different because of the Changing

'Native Welfare Time': Literacy and the State Narrative of Advancement

With an 'illiterate' and 'alienated' Aboriginal population, Aboriginal affairs in Western Australia were in a dire state when Stanley G. Middleton was appointed Commissioner of Native Affairs (1948–1962).[1] The introduction of the 1954 *Native Welfare Act* (WA) ushered in new freedoms for Aborigines, under the renamed the Department of Native Welfare (DNW). The Act, a cornerstone of Middleton's new social welfare policy, was amended in 1963 to remove the last restrictions that regulated Aboriginal life. To achieve social assimilation, Middleton was to reform policy, by dismantling legal restrictions applying only to Aborigines and bringing them 'fully into the scope of all governmental welfare benefits available to other Australians' (Schapper, 1970: 59). From the 1950s to the early 1970s, Aboriginal policy in Western Australia mirrored the national 'assimilation' policy, initiated under the federal Liberal government, led by Prime Minister Robert Menzies (1951–1963) (Haebich, 2005; Rowse, 1998).

Tutored assimilation

Under the reforming influence of Middleton, better educational opportunities for Aborigines prevailed, and literacy was inextricably linked to 'social development'.[2] A process of 'tutored assimilation through stages of monitored training' was implemented to bring Aboriginal people up to a 'satisfactory social standard' to enable assimilation (Haebich, 2005: 202; Rowley, 1972: 323). In fact, education became the platform for the state narrative of advancement that underpinned assimilation. By 1960, a special section in the Education Department had been established to deal specifically with Aboriginal education, and an explicit assimilation agenda was implemented across the state.[3] The DNW aimed to have all Aboriginal children receiving educational benefits of some type. Technical schools, agricultural schools, pastoral training and apprenticeships were established by the DNW, in tandem with a residential hostel system, supported by the Education Department *and* the missions (see Figure 2 in the Introduction).[4] The aim was to 'raise academic standards' and 'open wider employment opportunities' for Aborigines who, otherwise, would have 'remained illiterate'.[5] Aboriginal people were to be trained to become 'effective members of the nation', where employment and, ultimately, citizenship were the goals (Rowse, 1998: 8).

Middleton's decision to subsidise missions led to the establishment of 11 new missions in the Goldfields between 1948 and 1955, thus removing the dominance of the UAM.[6] Wongutha Mission Training Farm was established near Esperance in 1954.[7] In 1961, the Australian Aborigines Evangelical Mission (AAEM) opened a hostel in Esperance (operated by Mr and Mrs I.S. Pedlar) for boys undertaking agricultural training, as well as a hostel at nearby Condingup for graduate trainee workers.[8] The DNW and the Education Department opened the 'Boulder Working Youths' Hostel' in Kalgoorlie (also managed by the Pedlars and AAEM) to cater for young working men.[9] According to the DNW, after a two-year course, graduates would remain at the hostels to be employed on local pastoral stations for Award rates of pay.[10] Concurrently, Fairhaven Hostel in Esperance accommodated females attending secondary school, who were also assisted in finding employment, primarily as domestics. By the late 1960s, an additional eight hostels had been established in regional centres across the state so that all Aboriginal children aged from six to fifteen could attend local schools (Long, 1969: 25). A further two government hostels were established in the Goldfields, with the aim of ensuring that no child in the DNW Eastern Division was living under conditions 'too poor' to attend school. Nabberu Hostel opened in Leonora in 1967 and, lastly, Nindeebai Hostel in 1970 in Kalgoorlie.[11]

In the rhetoric of the time, hostels were instrumental in inculcating values to assist 'social development' by socialising adolescents into European habits and systems that would counter the social, cultural and linguistic 'deficiencies' of the Aboriginal home environment (Miller, 1966; Makin, 1977). According to a 1971 DNW account, the young women at Fairhaven made 'remarkable strides in self-advancement'.[12]

> Every girl is now able to obtain employment and live as an independent citizen. Several have married and have set up good homes, some in Esperance.[13]

While the young men at Pedlar's:

...have acquired the work habit, save hard and have ambitions about owning their own place one day. Regular employment, good housing and a sense of belonging to a district that regards Aborigines as useful and wanted citizens will, we hope, fall naturally into place...[14]

Conversely, critics at the time argued that the 'typical hostel situation... can no more provide experiences and skills for home-making, independence, and integration than could a prison' (Schapper, 1970: 36).

Initial policy reform was focused on youth, however, by the mid-1960s, the DNW considered that the progress of Aboriginal children was 'continually foundering upon the indifference and even hostility of illiterate or non-literate parents' (Long, 1969: 25). An Adult Native Education Scheme commenced in 1965 to train adults for citizenship and to stimulate parents' interest in their children's education, with 30 centres across Western Australia, including Laverton, Leonora and Warburton. The aim of the scheme was to 'develop literacy and community obligations and to assist the native people in their assimilation into our western culture'.[15] Critics, nonetheless, found 'most' adult literacy classes 'farcical and wasteful' (Schapper, 1970: 99). I return to this point in Chapter 5 by contrasting this approach to adult literacy with the enthusiasm for literacy in English and the vernacular at Warburton Ranges Mission around the same period.

The 'Native Welfare' generation at Warburton Ranges Mission

Up to the mid-1950s, remoteness had protected Warburton Ranges Mission and the Ngaanyatjarra, Ngaatjatjarra and Pitjatjantjara people of the Central Reserves from the 'tight bureaucratic system of written accountability', 'surveillance' and 'paternalistic control' of the Department of Native Welfare (Haebich, 2005: 207), leaving them 'ungoverned' (O'Malley, 1994) by state instrumentalities for longer than in other regions. It is in 'Native Welfare time', however, that interventions and intrusions from outsiders, including regular inspections by government officials, commenced.

In 1957, after decades of government neglect and public invisibility, a visit by W.L. Grayden, Independent Liberal MLA in the West Australian Parliament, sparked what became known as the 'Warburton controversy'. It was facilitated, in part, by the young journalist Rupert Murdoch, who threw the isolated Mission into the media spotlight for the first time. As a consequence, the Ngaanyatjarra became unwitting protagonists in the film *Manslaughter: The Warburton Range Film*, made by Grayden to 'expose' the 'plight' of desert people in the national fight for Aboriginal rights (Grayden,

1957; Grayden, 2002; McGrath & Brooks, 2010).[16] Between 1957 and 1964, the Gunbarrel Highway and other access tracks through South Australia and Western Australia were graded by surveyor Len Beadell (Beadell, 1967), enabling access to the newly erected Giles Meteorological Station (near what is now Warakurna community). The 'weather station' was built in 1956 to support the Atomic Weapons Research Establishment's 'Blue Streak' rocket-testing programme. The construction of new roads was to allow an even greater number of visitors to the area, including scientists, surveyors, anthropologists and mining exploration companies. Additionally, a DNW district office opened in Warburton in 1966.[17]

It is in 'Native Welfare time' that the Ngaanyatjarra began to reconfigure their collective identity in relation to a broader sociocultural space, prompted by the realisation that the boundaries of the known world expanded way beyond anything previously conceptualised. In classical times, whatever was known about other people or places was known through people's own experiences or stories related by others. It is in this time that the infiltration of 'depersonalised sources of information' (Kulick & Stroud, 1993: 24) – that is, decontextualised or objective knowledge originating from the Western world – commenced. Concomitantly, challenges to the indisputable authority of senior Law men and the traditional status quo increased and visits to the Goldfields became more frequent. This combination of factors incrementally led to a diminished sense of socio-spatial control, the consequences of which I discuss in Chapter 6. By the end of this era, the Native Welfare generation would experience an unprecedented encounter with the state that would leave virtually every individual identified by the bureaucracy. Furthermore, the state would question the future viability of the Mission and determine that young people be led away from Warburton Ranges for training and, ultimately, employment in the mainstream labour market.

Education for what?

In 1951, the Education Department finally agreed to second staff to mission schools, with the cost debited to the DNA (Biskup, 1973). It was not until 1956, however, that the first qualified government teachers arrived at Warburton 'Special Native School' (Green, 1983: 15–16). State intervention in education provision at Warburton commenced, with Middleton's assertion that Aboriginal people must become 'an economic asset, instead of a financial burden, to the state':

The missionaries at Ernabella in South Australia and at Warburton Range in Western Australia, are now educating large numbers of native children and evangelising many young people and adults, and the question arises as to how they can utilise this knowledge and training without some form of employment that will condition their minds economically to the impact of a white civilisation that, with the increasing population of Australia, is bound to come sooner or later.[18]

In 1956, Middleton affirmed the right, in accordance with Article 26 of the Declaration of Human Rights, of all Aboriginal children to have an education, including those at Warburton. He also questioned the outcome, once Warburton children had completed their primary education.[19] This opened up a debate on the purpose of education in the Ngaanyatjarra region that remains as unresolved today as it was in the 1950s.

By 1962, the Minister for Native Welfare was asserting that, despite all the money that had been spent on education at Warburton, there was little to show for it, and the resumption of nomadic life was likely. He considered it necessary to expose young people to 'civilised areas' and to 'lift them up' by giving them 'at least a handyman type of training for the boys – those with aptitude something better – and for the girls, domestic science and home crafts'.[20] At the same time, government officials and the UAM concluded that that there was no need for 'emergency measures' regarding sending children away, as they 'would not benefit from secondary education due to the low standard already reached in primary education'.[21] By 1964, however, the Warburton principal had raised four students up to the standard required to enter high school. From then, until the mid-1970s, a significant number of adolescents were sent to the hostels in the Goldfields.[22] Even though the duration for many was short, this represents a notable level of secondary education and training for what is now the current middle-aged to older generation.

In 1956, when Joshua was 16, he was the first to go to Wongutha Mission Training Farm near Esperance for vocational training:

When I went to Wongutha Farm I learnt more, which I didn't know here in the mission... When I got to Laverton, I was surprised to see roads like that because I never seen one yet before... [I was] learning about farm husbandry... And I came away from Esperance, got a job there in Woolabar Station... After two months I went back to Kalgoorlie, and had a job carting wood. I got sick of it... I went to Laverton... for about three weeks... policeman and Welfare at that time you know, they like to see youngfellas working... everybody had to work... Soon my aunty come around from Bandya Station... she said: "Oh. You want to come along?"...went station, really worked hard... not like blokes now, they don't know what axe is... from Laverton I went to Cosmo... I went out there working... But at that time people not allowed to, young blokes... government didn't want them to hang around... in town, in Laverton, even the police say: "Lock them up until they, till the shearing and all that over, and we'll let you out".

In 1957, Joshua returned to Warburton. He later worked as a Patrol Officer, bringing the last of the desert dwellers into the mission. In 1967, following training at the School of Mines laboratory in Kalgoorlie, he was employed full-time as a laboratory assistant for Western Mining Company. Joshua was also the longest-serving chairman of the Ngaanyatjarra Council and, later, director. Joshua's first wife was Rosie's sister. His second wife is Dawn (b. 1958). They have five children, including Naomi (b. 1978) and Leah (b. 1981). In 2001, Joshua was awarded the Order of Australia for his leadership of the Ngaanyatjarra people.

Education participation: Coercion or agency?

In the last chapter, I explored why families left their children in the care of the missionaries in the Baker Home in the early days of Warburton Ranges Mission. I emphasised that there was both reciprocity and agency in the early mission encounter and this enabled the development of a relationship of trust. By the 1960s, however, a new era had commenced. A significant change came with the closure of the dormitory in 1961, when some 120 school children were placed back in the care of families. At this time, around 400 people were living in *wiltja*, or windbreak constructions, made of branches or sheets of iron, in camps with no sanitary or ablution facilities and little firewood.[23] The UAM continued to provide a dining room, and children walked into the Mission for ablutions, clean clothes and meals five days a week while attending school.[24] According to Neville Green – a teacher at Warburton in 1966 – parents began to accept school as a government institution, however, 'the relevance of Western education was never established', and the school was dependent on the dining room to attract children from the camp (Green, 1983: 16).

Simultaneously, pressure was placed on parents to send their adolescent children to the Eastern Goldfields for schooling. Although Joshua had gone to Wongutha Farm as early as 1956, the majority were sent to Esperance and other locations after 1964. The girls boarded at Fairhaven Hostel and the boys at Pedlar's, while others were sent to Kurrawang Mission and bussed daily to Eastern Goldfields High School in Kalgoorlie. Green considers that there was 'uneasiness among parents but no-one really knew how to oppose such a decision, other than by a retreat to the bush', and 'teachers and missionaries assured the parents that their children would be safe' (Green, 1983: 17). Wells comments that he didn't think that families *chose* to send the kids away to school', rather 'it was the mission influence and the expectation by agencies like Native Welfare'.[25] As Clem recalls:

> They organised that, they got all the forms in the school... they done all that because missionaries were like parents was, we had not only the parents from when we was born, but also we had missionaries, then we had Native Welfare.

It has also been suggested that Warburton adolescents were inculcated with the notion that returning to Warburton would be a backward step in the prevailing atmosphere of advancement (Kral & Ward, 2000: 28). Ngaanyatjarra people's own memories of the hostel experience are, in general, positive. As one middle-aged woman recollects:

> I went to Esperance, high school for one and half years, living at Fairhaven Hostel then work experience, I used to look after a little boy, housework, when parents at work, in town, going out for day working by myself then coming back. Lots of girls doing that, some used to go out to work for the week then come back at the end of the week to hostel. Learnt about work, being with whitefellas, good experience.

Despite positive recollections, the coercive aspect of Native Welfare policy is also indicated in Clem's narrative.

Molly's older sister's son, **Clem, was born in 1953***. His father was in the group that had first contact with the missionaries at Elder Creek in 1933.*

> My mother died when I was a baby. I was taken care of by my grandparents and I lived only a short life in the bush... In that time it was very hard, we usually get frightened for white people, especially us... In 1959 I went to the mission school... I think I was the last boy who entered that Home, Boys Home. I used to read Dick and Dora, and learn a little spell. The missionaries used to help us how to pronounce English words. I thought it was a good fun learning this, in school, learning things from them... *I didn't know what was going on,* but it was good and I always looked forward to come to school... because there were a lot of friends there.

We used to stop in the dormitory... Then Native Welfare told us it was all going to be changed. That was in 1960, 1961 and we used to go camp now. But our parents used to help us come to school because missionaries always tell them: "Oh, you got to tell them kids to come to school"... But I loved to go to school... I pick it up how to read and write.

When Clem was about 11, he was taken to join his family in Laverton, who had walked out earlier.

My grandparents, they went there because their family was there. Also my grandfather and my grandmother's daughter was there, she was married out there. So I went down there... that's when I heard all these Aboriginal kids talk strong English. So I was able to speak that, when I started to speak what I learn at Warburton I was able to be level with children over there... I was able to communicate with them, express myself freely. I was able to mix in with lot of Aboriginal children, white children, half-caste children. My reading was [level], because I was doing spelling, the most important we had was spelling in Warburton School, I was doing a lot of spellings and I was able to write it out.

Around 1966, when Clem was 12, he was transferred to Kurrawang Mission.

When I first went there they give us an exam, which level we gonna go in. 1H, 1A, 1E, 1J, like that. Most of my Aboriginal boys and girls that I went to school with they all went into 1J, they was all Aboriginal. But I was a bit smarter than they were and I was put into the [higher] class where there was all the white children... My parents used to catch a mail truck, down from Laverton to see us in Kalgoorlie... I was going to stay there but the Native Welfare, he talked me into agreeing to his terms... He talked me into going to Wongutha Farm... I was to do the 2nd Year high school, but Native Welfare came and picked me up and took me.

I had dreams of being a builder and I had dreams of doing this and that. That was in 1967. So I went down there... I didn't like it. I was getting taught about the farming but I didn't want to do it, so I ran away... I wanted to go to school more, learn to write more, all just like university things... But at that time full blood Aborigines wasn't given the privilege to go on to further education. Only half-caste were given that privilege. And I thought: "Oh well, all my dark people they were stockmens". So I went and became a stockman. I was still 14, it was sad. So I wandered around, then went to the station... I worked on Bandya Station, Glenorn and Jidamia near Kalgoorlie.

Prior to European contact, strangers and venturing into unknown territory were feared. Time was mostly spent in the company of kin, moving within relatively predictable socio-spatial parameters. As suggested earlier, sufficient trust must have developed between the Ngaanyatjarra and the missionaries for *yarnangu* to have confidence in the missionaries' assurances that their children would be safe in the country of strangers. Furthermore, fears were assuaged, because the hostels were often managed by 'familiar' Christians. The experience of isolation was also ameliorated, because adolescents tended to reside with same-age, often kin, groupings. By taking a Bourdieuan perspective, it can be suggested that the *habitus* of the mission was replicated in the social space of the hostels. Hostel life represented a 'world of commonsense' (Bourdieu, 1989: 19) with spatially relocated, but familiar, practices. In this respect, the hostel experience mirrored the practices at the mission, as families entrusted their children into the care of the extended Christian community in the Goldfields.

George affirms this. While he is aware that Native Welfare controlled the movement of children, he also highlights agency in the exchange: parents recognised that children would learn skills to negotiate the new world 'on their behalf':

My parents they was really happy for me going to school, going to learn the language so I can talk to white people, to talk English, they used to tell me, my parents. So when in time they need help I can talk on their behalf and I been doing that when I been in school, talking with my family when Native Welfare come around... They been a bit worried when we been away, but they know we was in good care. We stayed in hostels and they used to come around and visit us on the weekends. Native Welfare, they put us in, but when we went to the hostel we had like missionary people there to look after us, go to church every Sunday. My parents they been working here in the mission, so they was really happy.

Nevertheless, there was ambivalence. Silas acknowledges that the missionaries 'wanted to give us hope to go forward into towns and cities and get a good job on that level... to grow up to be a good citizen'. However, others, like Clem, remember only paternalistic control: 'you're dictated to by missionaries from the word go, you're told to put a trousers on, shirt on, this is the way you got to dress, you got to eat this food, you got to eat that and it has continued on till this day'. Ultimately, however, immersion in this Anglo-European environment exposed Ngaanyatjarra youth to a broader range of Western social, oral and literate practices than would otherwise have been experienced at Warburton Ranges Mission. As George remarks:

> I wasn't taken away for years and years like some other people, they been stolen from their family, taken away and never went back. It was different with me, I just went for school, learning and came back to be with my families… all of us here been sent away for school, missionary time, we did our job, we learn, then we came back here.

As will be discussed below, most young adults were later to return to their home in the Western Desert in the 1970s, during the era of self-determination.

George was born in the desert in 1956. *His father's family walked out 'Laverton way', and his mother's family had gone east to Haasts Bluff and Papunya. His mother's father had five wives, and his grandmother was the youngest one and she came 'Warburton way'.*

> They used to bring all the dingo skin, they used to sell'em and get all the *mirrka* and go out again. They got flour, tea, sugar, tin of meat… My older sister went in the Home then, and they spent more time here… I never went to school here, I was about two years, one and a half, something like that… my father used to work for the missionary, looking after the sheep and goats. We had some people coming from Laverton for ceremony and my father found out he had families that way, that one he been looking for. So that's when we start travelling that way, that's when my father been seen his brother, Jim's old man… my father's oldest brother.

> We moved from here in '58… then the families moved that way first and we went behind. With the camel we walk… we put our swag on the camel then we walk… Lot of families travelling that same time. The family stayed in Cosmo for a couple of years, my old man been working round there, looking after the sheeps. Cosmo was mission, cattle, growing vegetables there, garden, school. But I wasn't going to school then I was just doing kindergarten, preschool. I went to Laverton when I was about five, start going to school then around 1962.

George's family lived on the Laverton reserve for about four years. His father was 'carting wood for Native Welfare', and his older sister worked at Laverton hospital.

We lived in the *wiltja*. In that time it was big, biggest mob there... Life was hard for my family when I was little... We had to go to school in the 1960s, compulsory schooling, Native Welfare would check.

Around 1967, Native Welfare sent the children to Nabberu Hostel. The family followed and camped on the Leonora reserve.

Leonora School had more white kids than Laverton... Mostly the kids who been living there had their parents working on stations... It was good, go to school every day, night time we used to do our homework, boss set up little night class where they do a homework with kids... school was good.

George recalls 1968 as the year he won an award from Leonora School for 'best in the class' and was rewarded with a train trip to Perth.

I stayed there about 1968, 1969, then 1970 I went to Kurrawang another school, Christian Home... going to the old high school in Kalgoorlie. I was about 14 then... I think the Native Welfare decided.

Meanwhile, his family remained in Leonora,

...because I had a young brother and sister in Nabberu Hostel, so they was there looking after them. They would go out to stop with the families on the weekends, then they go back to the school, go back to the hostel.

In 1971, George was sent to Mogumber Agricultural College.

When Native Welfare tell me I got to go to school and my parents they support that Native Welfare. It make me sad when I go away from the family, but now look back it helped me so I can read and write and talk... During school holiday I used to come back from Mogumber, they used to send me on the plane straight to Leonora, spend time with my family, then I go back. That time my family was in station near Leonora, Glenorn Station.

In 1972, George was sent to Esperance.

We had like a hostel out on the farm called Condingup. That was owned by the Pedlar's, so out on the farm, instead of going back to Esperance we stayed in that little block of land we had from mission.

In 1973, George commenced an apprenticeship in boiler-making and lived at Mt Yorkine hostel in Perth. He later continued his apprenticeship in Kalgoorlie. By then, his family had returned to Warburton. George followed soon after.

That's when I went through the ceremony and got man then, 1973, late 1973. And I still went to work around the station when I go back to Yundamindra, and work sometimes when I go back into town. Then when they start working here [in Warburton]… Like mustering cattle, I built the stockyard here… planting trees, sometime I work in the garage, old workshop. People still lived in *wiltja* right round the area… Mr Howell, when I came back he was boss, for a short time till that government took over then… People start working then and they used to get money. Lot of money. Like before mission time they used to get not much, you know.

About that time I was working everywhere, round Northern Territory too… Then I travel to Papunya with my mother's family for work there, on the building, they build a big hospital there, 1974, 1975. Because I had a work experience, my time, I went in another country. But I spoke good English, they let me in because I could understand them, spoke good English. And I asked for a job and they said yes, and they even give me room to stay in the quarters with the workers, white workers.

As will be shown, over subsequent years, George was to play a significant leadership role in the Ngaanyatjarra region.

Jim was born in 1953. *Jim's father and George's father had the same mother.*

My mother when she was little she came in here, Warburton and went to mission school here, Old Well… I remember her writing her name. I think about where she got learn? She must have got learned in the Home here, in old mission schooling. She used to tell a story, Bible story to us, from a book… must be from the picture, I think.

My grandmother left them here and she went to town too. When my mother grew up she chased my grandmother behind. I don't know why they went Laverton way, they must be want to find out what's happening on that side way.

Jim's mother and father met in Cosmo Newbery. His father had walked out from the desert many years earlier and had no schooling. Jim had eight siblings. Three of his sisters went to school in Laverton and two siblings in Mt Margaret.

My father didn't want me to go in the Home... so I have to stay with the family, different stations, following my father around until I was old enough to go to school, they brought me back to Laverton.

Jim started school in Laverton in 1959.

They had a reserve there, native reserve, from the reserve we used to go to school... We stayed at that school for maybe two or three years then my father started working in Leonora. He wanted us to go to Leonora to be close to where he was working, so we was schooling in Leonora. Then when he was working in Laverton district, we were sent back to Laverton, like that keep going.

Around 1967, the family shifted to Cosmo Newbery Mission.

From that we changed into a mission style education, got a bit different. Had a whole year there, then had to go to Wongutha Farm in Esperance, Welfare organised that I think. They let the family know they'll pick us up and take us and put us on the train... then on the bus to Wongutha Farm and we stayed there, training for one year round 1968. Training we done like farm work doing fences, and mechanic too, we learned how to shear the sheep, train, training for carpentry, building. And we had to go to Esperance for school, junior high school in Esperance, then come back and do training, must be two days every week.

Well, I came back for holiday this side, Laverton, but went working on the station. From there I went back to Esperance, not Wongutha but Esperance in town, Pedlar's Hostel they call it, where all the boys go... I came to Kalgoorlie hanging round in the streets, walking round. And I thought to myself: "Oh I'll have to get a job". So I went into another hostel in Kalgoorlie, working boys hostel. So when you go in you just get your own room and you get your meal and all there. So I stayed there and I got a job, I worked at the mine, Kalgoorlie mine... That bloke was finding job for us, he was looking in the paper... He was from the Welfare I think.

So I got a job in the mine, I used to look after eight big engines... Used to start from one engine, right up to eight, knock off time, then go home. I had to keep it running good... They just asked me if I know English and if I read... that was all. Working there I got a certificate to work in any mine in Western Australia. Got paid every weekend. Stayed must be four, six month. There was some other boys was there too, from this side. They was all getting homesick and I was thinking, well I must be join them and come home too. I wanted to stay and work, same time I was thinking about my family too. From Laverton they moved away and they was here [Warburton], around 1970, 1971, 1972. Then I worked at Laverton at Wonganarra went it first started. I was building, making slabs, footpath slabs, some new houses coming up so we had to help with the houses too.

Around this time, Jim returned to Warburton, but found that 'no work was round', until the mission was handed over to the government and turned into a settlement around 1973. So he took off again, moving with the [Law] Business and seeking work once more in the Goldfields and further afield.

From that time I went away in 1974, yeah. We went on the ceremony and I went to Wiluna... Murchison way. No-one from here. I was travelling, working on different stations then, around Meekathara. Then I went up north, Kimberley way, come back.

After Jim returned to Warburton around 1977, he married and, later, had two sons.

That time we started working now. Helping get things built, hospital... Them old people... telling the people to start work 'cause there's all these new things coming. And this mission gonna finish and this change, *they keep changing all the time.*

Jim stayed in Warburton then, working in the office and managing the community music recording studio.

'Testing time'– the last wave out of the desert

In 1954, the DNA was estimating that around 6000 'nomad natives' were 'beyond the confines of civilisation' in remote regions of Western Australia.[26] This population included the last of the Pintupi and Ngaatjatjarra, who came out of the Gibson Desert – north-west of Warburton – and the Rawlinson Ranges – around the NT border to the east – during the 'testing time'. At this time, the Commonwealth government, in cooperation with Great Britain, had established a programme of testing long-range missiles to be fired from Woomera in South Australia in a trajectory north-west across the Central Aboriginal Reserves. Over several years, the last of the desert groups were visited in their country by Native Patrol Officers from the NT

Administration, the Atomic Weapons Research Establishment and the DNW. This coincided with movement into settlements at Papunya in the Northern Territory, Jigalong in Western Australia (Long, 1964) and Warburton between 1957 and 1966, as well as a terrible drought between 1960 and 1966. Historian Pam McGrath (2010) suggests that, despite suggestions that the desert was to be 'cleared out' (Davenport *et al.*, 2005), the Rawlinson Range people retained significant autonomy by maintaining a pattern of returning to their country around Giles weather station (Dousset, 2002; McGrath, 2010). This autonomy was facilitated, in part, by the ongoing economic exchange associated with dingo scalp collection, well into the 1960s.[27] Joshua worked with the Native Patrol Officers, making contact with the last of the desert dwellers:

So I end up going round to Jupiter Well, Kintore... Tjukurla... Kiwir-rkura... we seen a lot of people there, naked people, *ngarltutjarra* (poor things), still in the bush, didn't know anything about anything... they never seen a motor car, or *piranpa* (whitefellas) or *mayi* (flour) or any-thing... They had a *tjukurrpa* alright, big *tjukurrpa*. They was travelling around *kata* (head) full of *tjukurrpa*... So I started working with them, Native Welfare, from Western Australia and Northern Territory.

Joshua assisted in bringing a number of the last families into the Mission:

Another day in the morning we went to Gary Junction then I took Windy Corner... as we were driving along we seen a fire going up... got closer to Taltiwarra we seen Darren and his family... He was only a little boy... so we stayed with them, for a day, two days, gave them *mayi*, flour... Everybody was taken in, from their *ngurra* (country), leaving everything behind... then I went out to Patjarr again... that's when they was doing a film, I was there.

Darren was born in the Gibson Desert in 1956.

I was about six or five when we been all come here, mission. We all come here, all families. We was staying at, just near that airstrip, that's only flat, we was camp I don't know nothing at that time. I was sitting down and they tell me: "You wanna go school?" So I come here, I was schooling little bit, not much. My mother's sister she went Wiluna way, so we wanna go. I don't know I had a families that way, I just followed them old people... we went towards Wiluna, my families... We was walking... two months... we got a lift there... got to Mt Margaret

Mission. Camped there and got another ride, got to Leonora, stayed there and we start walking again. And all my families they was still in Warburton, I was the first bloke that followed them old mans... When I got to Wiluna they told me: "Oh you got a families here, your mother's side families". ...So I been stayed there.

I never been go to school, I got a job, Desert Farm. I was planting a lot of rockmelons, orange, mandarin, all sort of plant. From there my sister, she told me: "Oh you want to come station?" I went to one of them station, from there working, mustering sheep. Pay cash... In Desert Farm they was giving us same pay, cash. Good money, enough money for me... Oh I been drink too much... I went to old prison Geraldton, two month. Then I went another two months and I went across to one prison just out of Perth.

I come back Warburton 1980... Bit changed to me when I come here. Like buildings and school, hospital and all them airstrip... I been come here when they had a really tiny tin house, no floor... They was working. They was mustering too, they had a lot of bullocks. Mechanic, collecting wood, all that. They give me a job. First I was carting wood, got a different job plumbing... There was heap of jobs here.

Darren married Eileen (b.1967), and they have one son and two grandchildren.

The 'Gibson Desert Mob'

Once in the Mission, the newcomers from the desert experienced Western food, 'government clothes' and schooling for the first time:

We can't understand what this white people come, we a bit scared... First time to start the food from the white people like apple, orange and like tin-a-meat and all tinned stuff. So we get learn slowly. When we been get into mission so we get more learn, so we get used to it.

The traditionally oriented habits and dispositions of this group contrasted starkly with the accrued social or symbolic capital of the mission-acculturated generation. The 'Gibson Desert mob' were rendered outsiders, yet their temporal proximity with pre-contact practices imbued them with greater Law- or *tjukurrpa*-affiliated 'cultural capital' (Bourdieu, 1989). Some families remained at Warburton, where life was beset with the difficulties of adjustment:

This group has from the time of their first arrival at Warburton played something of the part of a measuring stick for the other residents... the local people, who by this time had been *in situ* for more than thirty years, were quite antagonistic to the newcomers. Having made adjustments, some of them painful, to the whitefellas expectations and way of life, it must have been uncomfortable, not to say undermining, to be confronted with what amounted to a vision of one's own past. (Brooks, 2002d: 77)

A pattern of teasing and marginalisation commenced, although this has largely been ameliorated by intermarriage between family groups. Darren, Mick, Kenny and Louisa experienced this transition as children. As Louisa describes:

I went into school, but didn't understand what was going on... it was fun, but I didn't even really recognise it was school. I didn't know that was the right place to learn, you know, for me. I didn't had no ideas about that. I just went along.

Other families made the long trek west by foot or on the monthly Laverton-Warburton run in the ex-army truck obtained by the Mission in the 1960s to carry stores and mail (de Graaf, 1968: 11–13). Once in town, the 'Gibson Desert mob' gravitated towards the town reserves and reconnected with relatives in Laverton, Leonora, Wiluna or Jigalong.

'If you don't go to school, Welfare will send you away' – life on the reserves

Under Commissioner Middleton's 'family welfare' policy, the government was persuaded to give up Aboriginal settlements, such as Moore River and Carrolup, in the hope that 'moral and political pressures would establish Aborigines in the towns' to assimilate as members of the town community (Rowley, [1970] 1972: 55). Paradoxically, this policy gave rise to the growth of reserves on the edge of centres like Kalgoorlie, Leonora and Laverton. Once the *Native (Citizenship Rights) Act* Exemption Certificate was abolished in 1961 there were no longer any prohibited areas. This dramatically 'altered the lives of Goldfields Aborigines' (Morgan, 1986: 268–269). The lifting of legal restrictions on towns meant that schools, hospital services, employment and housing became available to *all* Aborigines. A whole new range of educational and employment opportunities opened up, as people were now free to reside wherever they wished (Stanton, 1988: 298). As adults at Mt

Margaret Mission took advantage of the new freedoms and moved to urban centres in search of employment, desert people from further west drifted into Mt Margaret and congregated on the emerging 'town reserves' in Laverton and Leonora seeking employment (Stanton, 1983; Stanton, 1988). Some families on reserves maintained family routines and had agency in the manner in which they negotiated the newly imposed expectations of education and employment. Others, however, were less able to adjust to the effects of alcohol and the new living conditions and struggled to meet the state-imposed standards of parenting.

Patricia grew up at Cosmo Newbery. When her father found work at the mine at Mt Windarra Nickel Project, the family shifted to the Laverton reserve:

> We used to stay in the camp and go to school, Laverton District School... stayed there for must be two years or three... And we didn't have no houses at that time, never had a house to go to school, just from the camp.

Jim's father was doing seasonal mustering, while the family camped at the Laverton reserve:

> We went to school every day... If you don't go to school Welfare will send you away somewhere, must be down somewhere in the mission home somewhere, Kurrawang or Norseman.

Others recall the police, working for Native Welfare, picking up children who ran away from school and taking them to Nabberu Hostel.[28] George's family moved to the Leonora reserve, after Native Welfare shifted the children to Nabberu Hostel:

> My parents used to go out working on station and do odd jobs. I was still in primary in 1967... Native Welfare shift us kids first and family was back in Laverton. So they shift because of us... they were doing little bit odd jobs and sometimes travelling to Wiluna, going to stations.

Historian Anna Haebich suggests that the hostels were also established for those children deemed by state authorities to be 'neglected' (Haebich, 2005: 212). For some, hostel life offered a reprieve from the drinking on the reserves. Louisa was taken to Nabberu Hostel, as was Kenny, who recalls his parents 'drinking right through', when at the Laverton reserve.

Louisa was born in 1959.

I was born in the bush round Patjarr, roaming around when I was small, when about five came to Warburton... Came here and started going to school... but only stopped here for a little while... then I went to Laverton... I didn't know Laverton was a town, old town. First time I saw a town... I went to Laverton school, my grandmother took me there, she looked after me and put me in the school... I didn't learn to read until I was at Leonora School.

Native Welfare, that's the time they found out, telling us to go to Leonora, to Nabberu Hostel, Leonora School... Two years there. Then family keep on shifting, so we have to go because parents was moving to Wiluna. Then we got to Wiluna and I stayed there, they said we going to Karalundi then.[29] Big mob families they just came here, some walking in here... for [Law] Business... they was introducing everyone, crying to each other... They was remembering...

I was running amok, used to drink when too young. Welfare found me and said: "Oh take this girl back to school, Kalgoorlie". They took me back to Kalgoorlie then, ended up over there then. Stopped at Nindeebai for few years at Project Centre. At 20 I been working, world was just like free it was. Came back to Warburton, training as nurse. Then working YMCA... Then back to Laverton, I keep on going little bit drink, drink side, come back. Or keep going to Leonora, stay with my other families... Come back here. Used to do bits and pieces to get money. It was getting up to CDEP. Now I got NAATI Certificate for Interpreting. Darwin for leadership course... governance and all that, capacity. It was good. I learn anything.

Louisa lives in Warburton and has six children, including Jake (b. 1983) and Darleen (b. 1987), and numerous grandchildren.

Kenny was born in 1972. *His father is Darren's older brother.*

My family they come from somewhere around Patjarr area in the 1960s. They came here first to Warburton then started making their way down that way looking for job... I stayed here [Warburton], but I never go to school... We was trying to go to school, but they was keep on, like teasing. Every day just walk around here... mainly I went to school up that way, Laverton, Mt Margaret, Wiluna. My father, mother working round there, station in Leonora. Weebo, Tarmoola, Glenorn, round there. I used to go school there when I was a little boy in Leonora, stayed in the hostel there… We was stopping in the reserve… They been drinking, they been alcoholic, them mob.

The family shifted to Wiluna to join other Gibson Desert families.

I went in high school when I was 14, started at Wiluna… I kept going right up to 16… When I tried going the next year, the school said: "No, you're right, you can stop, go home… don't worry about coming to school". They was working at Desert Gold… and my mother worked in Emu Farm. They keep doing that, like that now, work, alcoholics go to the pub, get the money, go straight to the pub. I didn't wanted to stay there much more, all cousin mob they came back this way so I thought I'd follow them… So I kept going to Tjukurla… Tjukurla was just starting '88. I stayed two or three years in Tjukurla… I was building that garage, driving tractor… Then came back this way to go up to Patjarr. We all moved back then, whole lot…

Kenny now lives in Warburton. He has worked with the Shire Sport and recreation officer and is now an environmental health worker. Kenny wants to be a Council leader in the future.

Education for Unemployment

The move 'from rations to cash'[30]

Western Desert society represents a kin-based social economy founded upon the rule-bound, sanctified nature of reciprocity and exchange embedded in social relationships and ritual. In classical times, social transactions were enacted through the trading and the exchange of weapons or utensils, the ritual exchange of objects after the completion of funeral ceremonies or bestowals of meat from a man to his future in-laws. When people came into the missions, they encountered a new exchange relationship constructed specifically to discourage what was termed at the time 'pauperism'. The distribution of rations was underpinned by the desire to inculcate Aboriginal people into 'earning' rations, thus reinforcing an 'ethical relationship between effort and reward' (Rowse, 1998: 40–41). At Warburton, *yarnangu* soon learned that rations were not given, but earned as payment for dingo scalps or work done around the Mission. As a 'reward for effort', workers received a 'chit' – a piece of paper marked with the number of hours worked – an abstract representation of cash. The chit could then be exchanged for rations, blankets or second-hand clothes at the mission store. Nevertheless, the 'reward for effort' relationship had the potential to be confusing, as churchgoers were also rewarded with a similar token that was also exchanged for rations, as noted earlier.

After Middleton's appointment in 1948, subsidisation at Warburton Mission commenced. Instructions were issued for the rationing of 'indigent natives' on the understanding that 'the issue of rations to able bodied natives will be dependent on the first consideration that employment is not available'.[31] The UAM reported that,

Natives are not permitted to come and just sit around the mission all day in the hopes of cadging food or eating up the earnings of those who work, but are sent out hunting and encouraged to live their normal bush lives… the indigents are rationed on Mondays and the Child endowment goods are distributed for the camp children on Thursdays… there are 27 boys and 34 girls in the Homes with 60 children in the camp making a total of 121 for whom we receive Child endowment.[32]

Despite their best intentions, even with subsidies, the Mission's capacity to provide rations, in exchange for labour, was limited, primarily because rationing alone was insufficient to support the numbers reported at the Mission.

Meanwhile, families who had walked out to the Goldfields, adapted to the altered circumstances. Significantly, they learned that, 'like whitefellas you got to go out and work for yourself'. As Valcie recalls:

Even bush people, they right… all working on stations and only rations for real old people in those days… no Social Security, no nothing. If you don't work you don't have anything. You don't have sit-down money or anything. And money wasn't good in those days, but whatever money, look after it, spend it right.

Valcie's son, Wesley, concurs:

They had to work for a living because there was no such thing as the dole… After the ration depot finished, well they got to go and work for their own money. Then they had to go and work station and that was part of learning and they still kept on learning on the job. Got to understand the white man, understand the white man boss.

Clifford also heard stories from his family:

I think they learned just to work, look after yourself, put food on the table... the people who camped around the mission they were sort of cared for... people who worked down that way Cosmo, round Laverton, stations, Leonora... they had to work or else they wouldn't get nothing coming in. They learnt that habit. They had to work.

Clifford was born in 1968. *His mother was born around Warburton Ranges and never had much schooling. In her teens, she ran away from a traditional marriage at Warburton and lived at Cosmo from 1955 to 1963.*

All them mob, they was down Cosmo, Laverton. Dad was born in Leonora. He went to school in Mt Margaret, they met in Laverton. He never had much schooling either, just basic, Grades 3, 4... from the early ages he just went on stations.

Clifford grew up at Cosmo.

I went to school Laverton. I was moving between Laverton, Cosmo, Laverton, Cosmo, Mt Margaret because my parents they was working on stations all the time. They was out at Laverton Downs, out at Bandya, back to Banjawan Station, back to Leonora area. If they was in the Leonora area we'd go to Mt Margaret stay with relatives there... I'd go and stay with relatives at Cosmo when they was at another station or we'd all be there together.

We had to go to school all the time. I think it was in their upbringing you know, they thought it was right... We got sent to Norseman stayed at the Norseman Mission... three years I done there, finished about 15, 16. Then I went to Wongutha, had a year up there. Well there was school, school then just working, farm work. Basic yeah, three Rs. When I left there I came back to Cosmo. Stayed there for a while, worked on the station... long time ago, in '86, '87. From there I went into town and I got a job at Windarra nickel mine... I just walked in and asked: "Can you give me a job?" and they said: "Yeah, come back on this day". I was Trade Assistant in the workshop.

A while later, he shifted to Tjirrkarli and married Kayleen (b. 1972). Kayleen went to school in Warburton, then the Project Centre in Esperance. After she returned to Warburton, she worked at the store and clinic. Kayleen now works in the community office, and Clifford is an employee at the Shire of Ngaanyatjarraku.

Access to social security

The rationale for assimilation was based on an ideology of 'modernisation' that linked 'general economic prosperity to the completion of the Indigenous "progression" to waged citizenship' (Rowse, 1998: 210). The programme of 'tutored assimilation' was expected to bring Aboriginal people to a standard warranting receipt of cash wages for the employed and welfare benefits for the unemployed, based on the assumption that they adopted the family form and household structure of 'normal' Australians (Rowse, 1998: 117). The residential hostel and adolescent training programme was established to enhance literacy and social development and 'to raise aborigines to the highest level of employment'.[33]

The Department of Native Welfare is well aware that lack of regular work is one of the major factors working against assimilation. Regular, satisfying and remunerative employment nearly always leads to an improvement in all other aspects essential to assimilation – housing, hygiene, education and social acceptability generally… In the long term, most faith is being placed in the education of Aboriginal children, not only in primary schools but to higher levels in secondary schools. But the problem of finding employment for youths and adults has to be faced today so that the task of assimilation can go forward. (Department of Native Welfare, 1967: 27)

However, for the training to be effective, 'rations would eventually have to be replaced by cash' (Rowse, 1998: 170). The official goal of assimilation thus necessitated equality of access to social security benefits and inclusion in normal industrial awards as 'indisputable entitlements' (Rowse, 1998: 114). However, the 'effects of access to money… as a basic force in social change' were not taken into consideration at the time (Rowley, 1972: 322).

During the Second World War, a number of important changes had been made to social services laws in Australia. 'Detribalised' Aborigines became eligible for child endowment under the *Commonwealth Child Endowment Act, 1941*. In the following year, this was extended to missions and government institutions (Sanders, 1986). In 1944, the *Unemployment and Sickness Benefit Act* was applied to all Aborigines, provided that they were considered by the Department of Social Services (DSS) to be of sufficient 'character, standard of intelligence and social development' (Sanders, 1986: 93). It was not until 1959, however, that amendments to the *Commonwealth Social Services Act* finally allowed 'nomadic' Aborigines independent access to child endowment and the pension. These social security reforms were based on the DSS 'principle' that if an Aborigine demonstrated his 'ability to handle money wisely and to manage his own affairs', then payments could be paid directly to him, *or* the mission would receive the payments and give out part of the pension to the individual in the form of a 'pocket money' payment (Sanders, 1986: 99). The distribution of social service benefits set the stage for the formation of an administrative identity – unmediated by social relatedness – in accord with the bureaucratic requirements of the state.

The formation of an administrative identity

Most of the 31 children who came into the Baker Home in the 1930s and early 1940s were registered with Ngaanyatjarra names.[34] Once in the dormitory, most were allocated English first names. Adults who engaged in direct interactions with missionaries also started to take on English first names. After 1959, identity requirements for social security eligibility were formalised by the state – proof of residence, date of birth, naming and signatures were required – and by 1961, the registering of Aboriginal births and deaths also became compulsory (Jebb, 2002: 260). Family surnames were acquired in Warburton between 1955 and 1958, in accordance with a 1954 DNW circular, advising that 'where possible English surnames should be used' (Powell & Kennedy, 2005: 34–36). At Warburton, surnames were applied somewhat haphazardly: some family members received different surnames, a few men were named after their wives, and older people were arbitrarily placed in family groups, irrespective of relatedness – factors that became clear after the first population census in Warburton in 1966.[35] Nevertheless, in its attempt to assimilate Aboriginal people into European institutionalised norms, the social security system was never able to cope with aspects of Aboriginal sociality, like traditional marriages (i.e. marriages not registered at law) and polygynous marriages (Sanders, 1986).

Pension and child endowment cheques, written out to an individual's newly acquired surname, were sent to the mission superintendent. The receipt of a portion in the form of pocket money (with the remaining proportion allocated in rations) required a verification mark – a signature (the phonographic code for the new oral vocative) or an 'X' (a legally valid stylised mark). The rest of the money was kept by the mission. Wells suggests that during the 1960s, the subsidies were the means by which the mission kept operating.[36] It was thus in the mission's economic interest to promote the acquisition of English nomenclatures, as only schoolchildren with English names could be claimed under the Act and subsidised by the DNW.[37] Warburton Mission continued receiving government subsidies to provide three meals a day for some 100 school children and stores for pensioners well into the 1960s.[38] By this time, food bought from the store using minimal cash from limited poorly paid employment or pocket money from child endowment or pensions had become a significant part of the diet. A small-scale mining venture with Western Mining Corporation commenced at Warburton in the 1960s. This generated some optimism regarding a potential 'mining boom' that never came to fruition. The closure of the dormitory in 1961 coincided with a drought and contributed to the cessation of earlier self-reliant nomadic foraging patterns (Plant, 1995). Mark de Graaf, principal at Warburton School (1962–1963), describes a miserable picture of around 400 adults subsisting on meagre resources, with hungry parents 'begging' for food from children fed in the dining room (de Graaf, 1968: 136).

By 1965, Warburton had become a community of discontent, with people 'fighting, quarrelling, stealing, threatening', broken down equipment, lack of staff and a lack of economy.[39] The UAM was urging the DNW to take more responsibility for the community.[40] The future of Aborigines in the Central Reserves area was investigated and the mission difficulties acknowledged by the DNW.[41] An inquiry into economic development recommended that for the Warburton people still living in windbreaks 'to make change' and adapt to a future life 'similar to any other Australian community', they would need special assistance in 'education, housing, hygiene, training, and employment'.[42] Significantly, the payment of full cash social service benefits directly to individuals commenced at Warburton only in 1971, despite amendments to the *Commonwealth Social Services Act* in 1959.[43] The real turning point, in terms of economic independence, came with the election of the federal Labor government in 1972. It is important at this juncture to highlight the rapidly changing circumstances at this time, as the Ngaanyatjarra moved from the localised paternalistic control of the mission and state control under Native Welfare to the onset of a new federal policy era of self-determination, only a short while later. Under the self-managing ethos of self-determination, *yarnangu* would suddenly be required to manage not only their personal affairs, but also the affairs of the community as a whole, as I discuss later.

The expectation of employment

As noted earlier, the employment context in the Goldfields was unusual. Mt Margaret Mission had created high expectations, regarding employment conditions for Aboriginal pastoral workers, and had established a reputation for instilling confidence and producing leaders (Marks, 1960). This is portrayed in Wesley's account of his father's working experience at Glenorn Station:

He left the mission home and he went and worked on a station, Glenorn Station. And when he went there... the blokes teaching him and seeing what a good worker he is and make him a windmill man, he was in charge of the windmills. And they have him sitting outside and they provide him with a feed, but he sit outside because he's Aboriginal so he can't sit inside. But he didn't care, he's still working, working hard. The blokes trust him and end up he getting all the young fellas from Mission Home working, they all go and work under him. Just to prove to that white man that he can work as hard as him and he can have the skills to be able to do whatever. So then he started teaching all the young boys from Mt Margaret Home... He tell the boss there that there's a good source of employment, young people you can employ, from this place. So they all started getting skills from working round stations. And then eventually he moves inside and eats at the table with them. But that's proving the point that he can do it. And that's what happened to a lot of Aboriginal people, you know, they put the effort into proving that they can do it, because they had to or they'd be left in the scrap heap.

It is also reinforced in Marlon's narrative:

I went to school in the 1950s, only had six or seven years schooling... In that space of time I was taught everything you know and when I went out to work: "Where you went to school?" they asked me. "Mt Margaret". Squatters and managers said: "You know how to work better than the rest of the people". I said: "Yeah, lot of these people they come straight in from the bush, they don't have that education, they was never shown". Now that I had that little bit I can come out into the world and get any type of job.

These experiences notwithstanding, the assimilationist expectation of 'advancement' through education did not correlate with the complex, contradictory and changing employment context emerging both in Warburton and in the Goldfields.

In 1957, Ronald and Catherine Berndt conducted an anthropological survey of the Central Reserves-Goldfields region (Berndt & Berndt, 1957). They asserted that 'not enough' employment was available in the whole Warburton-Laverton-Leonora-Kalgoorlie region, and the problem of employment for Aborigines was 'a vital one, complementary to that of education' (Berndt & Berndt, 1957: 7). By the 1960s, the UAM was being told that it must empty the desert missions and 'get people into the Goldfields where they will get employment' (Douglas, 1978: 113).

Meanwhile, the Commissioner considered it 'fatal' for Warburton people to come west, unless they were sufficiently 'advanced' to be absorbed into employment.[44] Despite the ambiguity of the situation, the training of work-ready young adults was still advocated.[45]

Earlier, I focused on the adolescents who were sent to the residential hostels in the Eastern Goldfields for further education. Attention is now turned to the young adults, who, once their training was complete, remained at the hostels that catered for young working men and women and were assisted in finding employment as pastoral workers and domestics. As Haebich notes, these young adults were, in fact, compelled by the state to participate in the hostel training and employment programme:

> While the summary removal of unemployed Aboriginal adults was repealed in the *Native Welfare Act 1954*, the Act retained the commissioner's authority to remove Aboriginal children as their legal guardian. These provisions were not repealed until 1963, and the department retained until 1972 the duty of providing for the "custody, maintenance and education of the children of natives" and "the control, care and education of natives in native institutions". (Haebich, 2005: 205)

In effect, this cohort remained under the control of the Native Welfare Department until 1972. Moreover, their employment was procured by DNW or a hostel manager, and wages were controlled by an intermediary. Additionally, if young adults were found *not* working, they could be picked up by the police (acting for the DNW) and taken to a station, in much the same manner as truant children were forcibly taken to schools or hostels. Arthur recalls: 'it was really strict at that time, the government, Native Welfare sent us to Pedlar's'. Importantly, the employment context described here did not form part of the open labour market. Yet, in 1963, the Native Welfare Department opportunistically reported that Pedlar's Hostel accounted for a 'rise' in Aboriginal employment in the region.[46]

George was a working boy at Condingup training farm outside Esperance in 1972 and recalls being paid only when he returned to Pedlar's. Jim was in a bit of trouble as a young man, and, instead of going to prison, he was sent to Pedlar's:

> That time I was bit young and got in trouble and the court sent me over there. So I stayed there for nearly two years, till I turn 18... instead of going to prison I had to go there and work... Yeah, like they called it "state ward", till you were 18... Go there and the bloke who run the hostel he found a job for us on a farm. I stayed there for must be year and a half... Managing the farm job, working hand on the farm,

shearing, mustering sheep... They paid the hostel manager and the hostel manager paid us... every Friday, they pay us. Manager take money for board.

Arthur further acknowledges, 'my way was forced, like, just the job part... that's why I got that habit'.

When they were young men, Marlon, Arthur and Silas all worked together on stations. Importantly, their narratives also evoke agency, in the manner in which they negotiated their working relationships, sometimes even walking away from stations if the conditions were too 'rough', as Marlon describes:

Go out work hard all day from five to midnight, low money, not enough sleep, bad food, rude manager, swearing. Go out work till shirt and trousers break, shoes break, no wash, can't go to shop to get new clothes, worked till clothes fall off your back.

Arthur continues:

I been around every stations, and you see grumpy man... station owner, we didn't like that man, so we moved around till we, till I can see this is a kind man he look after Aboriginal people. So I stayed at this one station ten or eleven miles south of Laverton... and that station owner he looked after us because he teach me, teaching me the right way... So I kept working.

Nevertheless, to this day, a perception remains in the Ngaanyatjarra collective memory that ample employment was available in the Goldfields. Wesley recalls that even for those 'not that educated', there was plenty of work in town: 'Laverton Hospital was full of young Aboriginal people working, as was the Shire, now a battle to find one'. Then, as Arthur says, *everything was different 'because of the changing'*:

The wool price went down, not enough meat, bullocks and things, this is around Laverton, that time used to be no rain, no grass, stations all went down. And mining mob came that time. When I was still working there, mining mob came around... they were buying the land and the station owners all got out then. That time it was really hard.

Marlon was born in the bush around 1942. *He remembers his family collecting 'papa minyarra' dingo scalps to trade for bags of flour from Mr Wade. Around that time, it was 'desperate times' in the drought. People started wondering why others* *were heading west. Some, like Marlon's family, followed their tracks. They walked to Cosmo Newbery Settlement when it was a 'rough place' with 'forced labour and floggings' under Superintendent Donegan.*

All from Ranges they went that way too. All went that way too much fight at Ranges I think, especially when they lose a loved one, don't want to look at the memory.

In 1954, after Cosmo Newbery Settlement was handed over to the UAM, children old enough to attend primary school were transferred to Mt Margaret Mission, and Marlon was put in the Graham Home.[47]

I don't remember school, everything was new to me, *I didn't know what I was doing there*, what they put me in the Home for? It felt like in a cage, you know you put a bird in the cage. I didn't know what I was doing in there, how can I get out of that? I was locked up... All the things what they do in the mission time you don't see that today.

In the 1960s, Marlon was at Pedlar's Hostel:

Just working there, didn't think it was training, lot of young fellas... Worked on 10 or 11 stations round the Goldfields, working as a team with other blokes, not on your own, doing the mustering. In those days cheap labour, Aboriginal blokes, so long as you got your boots and your clothes that's all you need. Worked hard, in heat and rainy days, on weekends, not like today.

Around 1968, Marlon started at Yundamindra Station near Laverton, regarded by Aboriginal workers as a 'good station'. He stayed there for many years as head stockman and overseer. He returned to Cosmo around 1974 so that his eldest son could go to school.

I didn't want him to go to Mt Margaret in the Home like me. Cosmo had more freedom see, I had to hang onto my kid, I wanted to look after my son the way I wanted to look after him and bring him up the way I wanted to bring him up. Mission was still there at Cosmo, better there because closer to my area. Plenty of work in Cosmo, I was a leading hand, still stock cattle sheep for about 12 or 14 years... till my kids all grown up.

Marlon later worked in Laverton as a police aide and at Mt Windarra mine. He also worked at Docker River. He moved to Tjirrkarli around 1983 with his wife, April, and the family, where he was Chairman for many years. Marlon was also a strong leader on Ngaanyatjarra Council and ATSIC Regional Council.

Everything was Different

Prior to the 1960s, Aboriginal people in Australia were virtually excluded from formal participation in national political developments. Following the 1967 Commonwealth referendum for constitutional change, Aboriginal people were finally constituted as part of the national populace (Attwood, 2003). As noted earlier, the 1963 amendments to the *Native Welfare Act* removed many of the last restrictive regulations pertaining to Aboriginal people in Western Australia. Unfortunately, however, the new freedoms also coincided with an increasing dearth of employment opportunities, the growth of sedentarisation on the reserves and the lifting of alcohol restrictions.

Before the late 1960s, Aboriginal labour had operated on a permit system, whereby the supply of rations, clothing, blankets and medicines, and the cash payment of wages was 'a matter between local employers and the Aborigines' (Rowley, [1970] 1972: 257). In December 1968, the *Federal Pastoral Industry Award* determined that all Aborigines employed in the pastoral industry Australia-wide should receive equal wages for equal work. In Western Australia, however, the new provisions did not apply to full-blood Aborigines employed as station hands, *unless* they held a full Certificate of Citizenship under the *Native (Citizenship Rights) Act* (Jebb, 2002).

> The core of any discussion about "equality" rests on the premise that a worker will have access to basic and award wages as well as access to full unemployment benefit when unemployed. The exclusion of Aboriginal workers, primarily in the pastoral industry, in the Eastern Goldfields from these basic rights exposed an inherent contradiction in the DNW policy. Without economic equality the chance of achieving Middleton's dream of integration was minimised. (Rowley, 1972: 251)

Ironically, from 1969, the rural economy in Western Australia entered an unforeseen decline: wool prices plummeted, and poor seasons and wheat quotas drove many farmers into difficulties (Burnside, 1979; Bolton, 1981). At the same time, increased mechanisation was introduced to reduce labour costs. This led to reduced employment in the Eastern Goldfields, as pastoral stations closed up or were taken over by mining companies, coupled with an 'intractable set of problems' at centres, such as Wiluna, Laverton and Leonora, exacerbated by access to alcohol (Burnside, 1979: 262).

Unemployment benefits: The beginning of 'free money'

By the end of the 1960s, declining employment prospects and the 'ineradicable proportion of structurally "unemployed" men' (Rowse, 1998: 138) had brought the question of Aboriginal eligibility for Unemployment Benefits (UB) to a head. At this time, Aboriginal people were caught in a vicious cycle: lack of employment was exacerbated by the inability to qualify for UB and by the DNW trying to rid their offices of rationees (Rowley, [1970] 1972; Jebb, 2002). In addition, diminishing Aboriginal employment options were intersecting with the growing confusion among welfare officers regarding Aboriginal people's eligibility for UB. By 1965, the UAM was reporting that families were reluctant to stay at the missions:

> ...lack of employment, the need to be in work to get Social Benefits for unemployed, and the practice of Native Welfare issuing rations to children of parents who are indigent, ie between the working age and old age pension; all has a bearing on keeping them on the reserve at Laverton.[48]

It was only after 1972 that a newly elected federal Labor government, under Prime Minister Gough Whitlam, declared that 'all Aborigines should be paid award wages when in employment and should otherwise be eligible for the full range of social security payments, including UB' (Sanders, 1986: 285). Rowse suggests that at this time, with the advent of many new cash sources (wages, UB and other social service benefits), there was 'a propensity' for Aboriginal people to be unable to distinguish between the source and purpose of various cash pathways (Rowse, 1998: 179).

With the introduction of UB, Ngaanyatjarra people had their first experience of 'free money' or 'sit down'. Many did not welcome it, as Wesley's sister, Helen, emphasises: 'it didn't seem right to get the dole when you were capable of working'. Jim concurs:

> I never been on that... it's not good, for me   in that time my father told me that I'm old enough to work now: "You got to work for your own living". I think that money, that sit-down money made them give away all them jobs. Over there getting free money, why not sit down?

Arthur sums up the growing confusion at that time:

> I don't know why, but the changes came in, like you don't have to work and you still got the money coming in, all those sort of changes came, changed it around.

As Marlon reflects:

> I got used to working and supporting my family, got good money… I buggared it when I came here, to Tjirrkarli about 1983, now I got no money. Came here and watched my family drinking and I started drinking too. From that time to today they made a big mess with "sit down" – the government policy when they first gave "sit down"… the damage they done. Before we had to work to keep the family going, that's what we were taught. When we came back to Warburton: don't work, you don't have to, everyone said you don't have to worry about it now. And we got Unemployment Benefit. That was "government time" and a "you give me this" attitude started and went right through, like: "If they ask for things then I can too". So we all got into this habit of sitting down, lining up, waiting for the money. Now they say: "Why you all sitting down?" But it was their stupid idea in the first place, the government policy, that caused so many people to sit down and loaf and put their hand out. I changed too from hard working six to four, to getting the free money, no sweat at all… Now the government, all jumping up and down, saying we're lazy.

April was born in 1955. *April, Patricia and Jennifer have the one grandfather. When missionaries arrived at Warburton in the 1930s, April's father (born 1925) was too old for school. April's mother (born 1940) was in the Baker Home. April was also at school in Warburton, until the family shifted to Cosmo Newbery Mission in the mid-1960s, where her father was a preacher. April, along with Wesley, Patricia and Una, continued in the new government school at Cosmo.*

> In 1970 I went to Kalgoorlie, Eastern Goldfields High School. We sort of had a little classroom where a few of us Aboriginal children go… We were living at Nindeebai Hostel with other children from Warburton and Cosmo… I was in the low class… must be because we wasn't, you know, understanding of what they was doing… but that was a lower class, you know, right down the bottom, because I wasn't learning… At Nindeebai we had extra teaching… Wednesday and Thursday nights… extra, homework classes.

I stayed in Kalgoorlie, that Nindeebai Hostel for two and a half years then I moved to Fairhaven Hostel, Esperance. I left school, but I just went down there for work. I been working in a motel like ordinary domestic job doing washing, washing dishes all day… the people who were looking after us at the hostel they give us a job… I been working on the farm too, but housework mainly.

I was doing a little bit of work in the shop in Cosmo in 1973. Then Mr Cotterill [missionary at Cosmo Newbery] got me another job, I was working Leonora Hospital, you know like cleaning up… It was a bit frightening for me first. Especially when I was living over Leonora there was lot of drunks, just got their thing, you know, Citizen Rights, and the people sometimes annoy you for money… I knew some people there, like girls I went to school with, they was working there at the hospital… It was alright living over there, but I was a bit homesick… So I came back to Cosmo… they was looking for Aboriginal Education Worker, so I started working in the school, for three years.[49]

Soon after, April and Marlon married and went to live in Laverton where Marlon was a police aide… but 'too many drunks gave him a hard time', so he returned to Cosmo. Around April 1983, Marlon and their children moved to Tjirrkarli.

But we had no school there so I start up for school, in a little shed… Mainly I was teaching numbers and writing, and a little bit of reading because they used to bring books down from Warburton School.

Later, April worked as an Aboriginal health worker for many years.

I'm on the Health Advisory Committee, Women's Council… I'm still working, I like working, my husband keep on saying: "Hey you wanna leave this job and stay at home?" And I say: "No!"

April and Marlon have now retired to a small outstation. Their children remain in Tjirrkarli, and their son has followed in his father's footsteps as community chairman.

'Painted with the same brush' – alcohol and its effects

When the *Native (Citizenship Rights) Act* was repealed in 1971, West Australian Aborigines finally gained full citizenship rights *and* alcohol restrictions were lifted (Fletcher, 1992: 1). The ramifications of unrestricted access to alcohol had a dire effect on the towns of Wiluna, Leonora and Laverton, as well as Mt Margaret, Cosmo Newbery and Warburton (Sackett, 1977). European – Aboriginal relations deteriorated and alcohol-related violence, arrests and incarceration increased.[50]

The removal of the remaining restrictions on alcohol impacted profoundly on the social development strategy and the outcomes of tutored assimilation. Some Ngaanyatjarra perceive that, as a consequence, they were no longer seen as potential workers, irrespective of their education or work experience. April considers that as alcohol took over, education was undermined:

> When them young girls, young men came home after being away for two or three years... learning a lot of things, work and everything, reading, writing, and all that... They came back and sort of went down, drinking. Teaching them to drink, instead of teaching them to go out to the station or get a job in small towns like Laverton, Leonora. From that time, you know the ones I went to school with they went down... instead of going up and learning different things... they all drinking... which wasn't right, should have been all working, there was a lot of jobs there... When I was still going to school I used to see a lot of young ladies come back from Kurrawang, Esperance and they work in the hospital, work in the Welfare office, work in the shop, they had jobs everywhere.

Wesley suggests that all Aboriginal people in the Goldfields were 'painted with the same brush'. April attests to this:

> Citizen Rights come in, that just went down, wasn't good... We had no encouragement you know... they don't look at fullbloods... not encourage the fullbloods... they had that feeling all the time in small towns like Wiluna, Leonora, Kalgoorlie or Laverton.

Wesley asserts that, prior to this, non-Aboriginal people had been 'building up relationships' with Aboriginal people, but non-restrictive drinking rights and the introduction of 'money for nothing' led to negative stereotyping that continues up to this day. Ngaanyatjarra leaders lament on how things might have been different, had it not been for *everything changing*.

To sum up, ultimately, the expectations of assimilation, education and employment under Native Welfare were unrealistic and based on an increasingly outmoded paradigm that did not correlate with the rapidly changing socio-economic circumstances of the late 1960s and early 1970s.

The federal government implementation of award wages when in employment, otherwise eligibility for the full range of social security payments, including UB, contributed to high unemployment (Sanders 1986). Yet the assimilationist policy of social development had placed the onus on individuals to take responsibility for their own advancement and tried to separate young people from the influence of families. Tutored assimilation attempted to develop a social orientation away from the Aboriginal family and forge individuated hopes and aspirations linked to the Western world, but social-relatedness and connection to country were to prove a more powerful force. Sir Paul Hasluck, one of the architects of assimilation, later had misgivings about this individualist approach, reflecting that 'we did not see clearly the ways in which the individual is bound by membership of a family or a group'.[51] Anthropologist Charles Rowley concluded that the causal factors in the process of social change were not properly considered, as it was assumed at the time that schooling was 'the main factor in social change' (Rowley, 1972: 322).

This ideology is evident in George's narrative. He explains how even when living on the Laverton reserve, his parents always told him to go to school, in the belief, he says, 'that there would be jobs at the end'. So it was for many Ngaanyatjarra. Despite education, training, employment experience and a 'work ethic', articulation into a market-based cash economy was hampered by insurmountable barriers. These included: no labour market in the desert, diminishing employment prospects in the Goldfields, alcohol *and* the introduction of social services benefits or 'money for nothing'. In other words, education aspirations and expectations of mainstream employment were curtailed by political and economic factors beyond the individual control or comprehension, of most Ngaanyatjarra.

'Government Time': Self-Determining Practices and the Assertion of Control

The election of a federal Labor government, under Prime Minister Gough Whitlam (1972–1975), saw the introduction of much-needed social reforms across the Australian political spectrum in attitudes to race, language and cultural identity. A policy of self-determination saw Indigenous people gaining rights in the areas of governance, employment, education, language and land rights. Equal opportunity now hinged upon their self-managing capacity. Indigenous policy was developed at a national level, under the federal Department of Aboriginal Affairs (DAA). Change had already commenced in Western Australia when the state Labor government, elected in 1971, prioritised the dismantling of most of the remaining legislation that had treated Aborigines differently from other members of the community. The functions of the Native Welfare Department were now absorbed by the new Department of Community Welfare (DCW) and the Aboriginal Affairs Planning Authority (AAPA) (Bolton, 1981: 167).

When the new things came in

From the 1970s, the social and political landscape across the Goldfields and the newly emerging 'Ngaanyatjarra Lands' was dramatically transformed. Ngaanyatjarra communities, although in Western Australia, were serviced by Commonwealth DAA from Alice Springs until 1987, when Kalgoorlie DAA took over the central desert region (Fletcher, 1992). In 1989, the functions of DAA were taken over by the Commonwealth Aboriginal and Torres Strait Islander Commission (ATSIC), giving *yarnangu* unprecedented political self-representation through the ATSIC Western Desert Regional Council. The UAM relinquished control of Warburton Ranges Mission between 1972 and 1973. As they were no longer the administrative backbone of the community, the remaining missionaries turned their attention to language work. Warburton Community was incorporated in 1973; AAPA and the DCW took on the administration of the community. The first 'community advisor' was appointed. Self-determination ushered in the opportunity for Ngaanyatjarra people to re-form and collectively use their acquired skills and practices to construct a new community of interest within which to assert agentive control.

Warburton in the 1970s is remembered by *yarnangu* as 'lots of people, new things, new buildings', as new physical structures began to replace the rundown mission infrastructure.[52] Simultaneously, the transition to government administration corresponded with growing community unrest. Where mobility had previously allowed for dispersal, the intensive aggregation (without the release of tension enabled by dispersal) of extended family and more distant classificatory kin tended to amplify disharmony between groups from different 'country'. In 1972, DAA promised *yarnangu* housing within six months, however, by 1974, only staff housing had been erected (Douglas, 1978). The lack of work and a 'surplus' of UB or 'free money', combined with unrestricted access to alcohol, aggravated law and order problems (Green, 1976). Warburton was considered a 'squalid' place: 'like a dustbowl, full of drunks, with spearfights almost daily'.[53] Eventually, these combined factors led to a so-called 'rampage of destruction' in 1975 (Douglas, 1978). Matters continued to deteriorate to such an extent that, in 1980, Warburton was declared the most troubled Aboriginal community in

Australia by the federal Minister for Aboriginal Affairs (Blacket, 1997: 150). Community infrastructure remained tenuous throughout the 1980s, exacerbated by poor water and sanitary conditions in the camps and the constant demand for firewood. Alcohol and petrol sniffing-related violence, incarceration and deaths ravaged the community. Damian McLean recalls that period:

> Petrol sniffing would generate a lot of tense arguments, it was a very tense, very violent sort of place... A lot of them just sniffed themselves into oblivion, what's around now [2000s] is better than what was around then. Through the Lands over that period I think it was 29 deaths, but around Warburton it would have been about 18 to 22, from the early 1980s through to the early 1990s, young men predominantly. There were always people dying, people going off into sorry camps, abandoning houses, continually things like this were going on, like this all the time, it was inevitable that you weren't going to get any consistency in anything.[54]

Unemployment and the inception of CDEP

Around this time, Ngaanyatjarra adolescents from the hostels, disillusioned by being unable to find employment in the Goldfields, were drifting back to Warburton.

> These are young people who feel unwanted in White society and so return to their own community only to find they do not have the tools with which to demonstrate the new skills they have learned... nor do they have a means of livelihood except finding methods of extracting pension money from elders... Generally speaking, neither parents nor children can see any real purpose in White Australian education. (Douglas, 1978: 117)

Around this time, Warburton had 500 on UB, and McLean recalls:

> No-one would receive any pay for weeks then suddenly people would receive a big cheque in backpay and people would take it and go into town and blow it... Child endowment was a mess too as it was irregularly paid. At that time the office in Warburton had no doors, no windows, experiencing the breakdown of everything.

With few training or employment opportunities available in Warburton, many young adults who had returned from the Goldfields moved on to the new government settlements in the Northern Territory and South Australia, recently established in reaction to the displacement of Aboriginal people, after the awarding of equal wages in 1968. George recalls that it was:

> Different from here, went over there working [in 1968] when they start the new settlement in Docker River, even Amata. Some like from Docker River been going to school in the mission here... they shift back to Docker River from Warburton and they help build that place up too. And over in Amata way, like from South Australia way... they grow up here, been to school here, been to Pedlar's too, so they know. They went back to South Australia side, they build up their communities like Irrunytju, Mt Davies, Kalka.

Around 1969, Docker River helped resource *yarnangu* camping around Giles, Wingellina and Blackstone (see Figure 1 in the Introduction). This enabled Ngaatjatjarra families to return to country near the Rawlinson Ranges and, later, establish an outstation at Tjukurla. When anthropologist Nicolas Peterson visited the Central Reserve in 1970, he found that at Warburton, 'there was neither money available to pay people nor projects for them to work on' (Peterson, 1977: 138–140). Whereas, at Docker River, Aboriginal workers were paid under the NT 'Training Allowance', instituted to assist in the employment of Aboriginal workers in capital works' programmes in the new government settlements (Rowse, 1998: 172–178).

Such short-term initiatives did not, however, resolve the primary conundrum: Aboriginal settlements in remote Australia did not form part of the open labour market. The federal Community Development Employment Projects scheme (CDEP) was thus initiated to meet the unusual requirements of bush communities.[55] In 1977, it was recommended that the Ngaanyatjarra communities at Warburton, Wingellina, Blackstone, Giles and Jameson be included in the 'experimental phase' of CDEP (Coombs, 1977) – a scheme that subsequently expanded across the national Indigenous sector and is currently being disbanded, as I discuss in the Conclusion. This early model was 'not simply a means of providing employment as a source of a minimum cash income, but a training exercise in self-management and increasing independence' to enable Aborigines to do work chosen by the community to strengthen economic independence and local quality of life (Coombs, 1977: 1–2).[56]

> The scheme is based on the provision of funds for employment projects approximately equivalent to the total unemployment benefits that would be payable should all eligible Aborigines apply for such benefits. It has enabled the communities concerned to plan projects for their di-

rect benefit and has removed the socially debilitating effect of "sit down" money.[57]

At Warburton, CDEP (and the attached on-costs) was the primary factor in the stabilisation of the community, as it enabled the establishment of an office and administrative assistance. CDEP was also integral in providing the economic foundation to support the establishment of the new outstation communities. In 1975, seed-funding was made available by the federal government for basic facilities, and non-Aboriginal community advisors were employed to assist people in setting up the new communities. Regional political support was initially provided by the Pitjantjatjara Council (then the Ngaanyatjarra Pitjantjatjara Yankunytjatjara Council), until the formation of a separate Ngaanyatjarra Council in 1981.[58]

'Homeland Time' – Outstations and the Return to Country

Affiliation to traditional country was the main factor that drove the outstation movement, with the older generation determining the location of new communities. The four new communities of Wingellina (*Irrunytju*), Blackstone (*Papulankutja*), Jameson (*Mantamaru*) and Giles (*Warakurna*), in effect covered what had previously been the hinterland, that is, 'the huge, previously uncatered-for region between Amata in the east and Warburton in the west' (Brooks, 2002a: 10).

The outstation movement was the magnet that attracted Ngaanyatjarra and Pitjantjatjara people, who had earlier drifted west to the Goldfields and east to Ernabella Mission (and later Amata and Docker River), back to their traditional homelands on the West Australian side (see Table 4.1). After 1972, Cosmo Newbery passed from UAM to AAPA jurisdiction and remained a functional pastoral station.[59] With little employment and drinkers travelling regularly between Laverton and Warburton, conditions at Cosmo deteriorated.[60] Eventually, resolution came when Cosmo was handed over to DAA in 1979.[61] Nevertheless, DAA withdrew funding in the mid-1980s, and many residents decamped to the new outstation at Tjirrkarli. Cosmo Newbery lay dormant, until Wesley's family returned in 1989 and re-established a viable community.

Wesley was born in 1961. That same year his family left Glenorn Station (where his father had worked for many decades), and the family first went to live at Cosmo Newbery Mission. At Cosmo, his father worked on the new training and trading

Table 4.1 Estimated population of Ngaanyatjarra Lands 1972–1983

	Warburton	Cosmo Newbery	Wingellina	Warakurna	Jameson	Blackstone	Total population
1972	408	70	–	–	–	–	478
1973	435	65	51	–	–	–	551
1974	438	75	16	31	–	–	560
1975	251	62	70	165	120	155	823
1976	273	68	94	201	110	166	912
1977	350	53	85	97	126	134	845
1978	350	68	85	97	126	134	860
1979	230	26	120	150	210	100	836
1980	400	130	110	100	180	100	1020
1981	400	80	130	200	210	100	1120
1982	573	62	130	102	222	104	1193
1983	453	72	133	147	102	91	998

Sources: Annual Report DNW 1972; Annual Reports AAPA and ALT 1973–1983

station established by the UAM. At that time, Cosmo was a thriving pastoral proposition supplying meat to Warburton Mission, as well as an orchard and vegetable garden. When Wesley's father was at Cosmo, he itinerated as a Christian leader in the Goldfields and Mt Margaret. Wesley commenced his schooling at Cosmo. The family later moved to Mt Margaret, where Wesley's father was manager. His father was also on the Laverton Shire Council and, from 1973, Chairman of Wongutha Wonganarra Aboriginal Council in Laverton – an early initiative in Aboriginal self-management. A secondary school had recently opened in Laverton, because of the employment openings at nearby Mt Windarra mine, enabling Wesley to complete Year 10 and continue on to Perth for further education. After finishing school, Wesley returned to Laverton and worked at Wongatha Wonganarra. He then travelled around NSW, before returning to work at Mt Windarra mine for five years. He was later store manager at Mt Margaret Community. In 1989, Wesley's family decided to re-establish Cosmo Newbery community. With no government support, the family had to rebuild the community from scratch. They opened a store and a petrol station and reinvested the profits in the community. Initially, there was no school. Wesley's wife, who had been an Aboriginal Education Worker at Mt Margaret, started a school for the small group of children in a run-down house. They were assisted with resources from Mt Margaret and ran distance education classes, until an Education Department school opened. In 1990, the community came under Ngaanyatjarra Council and Warburton community provided financial assistance. Wesley has been a strong leader for the Ngaanyatjarra people on the Council, especially in education and Native Title. His children and grandchildren continue to live at Cosmo. His sister, **Helen, was born in 1955** *and went to school at Cosmo, Mt Margaret, and later, Perth. After studying at Kalgoorlie Technical College, Helen worked as a nursing assistant at Leonora and Laverton hospitals and also at Wongutha Wonganarra in Laverton. She now operates the store at Cosmo.*

Finally, around 1990, the 'Gibson Desert mob' – many of whom were living and working in Wiluna – heard that an outstation was to be established at Patjarr, in their traditional country north of Warburton. Despite the ravages of alcohol and social fragmentation, many in this group had worked on stations and under the self-managing ethos of the Ngangganawili Community Council and the new CDEP projects at Desert Farm and Emu Farm (Sackett, 1977; Sackett, 1990).[62] They returned with confidence and skills:

> [Being away] made us more savvy to working with whitefellas, speaking English and being more vocal, you don't sit back, you get up and do things. And because we've been away from country it makes us more stronger about going back to our lands and looking after country.[63]

Ultimately, the homelands movement relieved the pressure of overcrowding in Warburton and fulfilled the desire for greater autonomy and control. The location of the new communities was driven by *yarnangu*. In some cases, the determination to return to the country was so great that people shifted without adequate resources or assistance from non-Aboriginal staff. Accordingly, they were required to take on roles and responsibilities and 'were able to go that extra step'.[64]

Some adults returned from the Goldfields with a new 'habitus': a familiarity with European practices, English language and a 'literate orientation', and also a sense of themselves as workers:

> They are people that have sort of been leading lights in their communi-ties and in the area like Teacher Aides, Health Workers and Council Chair people. They would have had that foundation from school here but that was built on by their experiences away from their communities. They saw a bit more of the outside world. They had a greater opportunity than what exists today when they did come back to sort of participate in more meaningful work in the community.[65]

Wesley reflects on the process:

> You go and work for white man and they speak to you in their language
> and you get to understand and you keep picking it all up. You can under-
> stand the whole system... But they did spend a lot of time learning be-
> fore they had to take responsibility.

Marlon and April shifted from Cosmo to Tjirrkarli around 1983:

> We set this place up... come here with no school, no house, nothing we
> had to go and look for food. We started with nothing... we had to fight
> hard for a school. We was left behind. But we got it going.

Self-determination is recalled as a period when *yarnangu* were integral to the
community building process, irrespective of English language and literacy
competence. Employment participation, at this time, was perceived as
greater than under the mission. *Yarnangu* were employed in the offices,
stores and schools. Their skills matched the requirements of the time. The
perception was that people worked together to make it happen, 'whitefella
staff were like family', and there was an idealism associated with what
could be achieved.[66]

Education and self-determination

Self-determination thrust *yarnangu* into a new social environment;
while still based on a collective notion of Aboriginal sociality, people were
now required to exercise unprecedented responsibility for their own affairs.
Schooling had hitherto been linked to paternalistic control, then, with
virtually no prior experience, families were expected to compel their children
to attend school and undertake the training that would lead to self-
management outcomes. Ironically, this changed social context was coupled
with a growing realisation that schooling was not going to deliver the
outcomes needed to fulfil employment and self-management aspirations.

By the late 1960s, it was found that few Aboriginal children in the DNW
Eastern Division had the academic ability to undertake conventional high
school courses.[67] Students from Warburton still in the residential hostels
were channelled into the 'Special Projects Schools' (Kral & Ward, 2000: 31).
As Wesley reflects:

> The sad thing about Nindeebai is they might have been thinking they
> were going to school, but... they didn't go to a proper school, I think
> Project School was more just physical learning, welding or something.

Progressively, Warburton teenagers began to resist being sent away and 'established a reputation for being aggressive and unco-operative' (Green, 1983: 112).

By the mid-1970s, the 'ultimate futility' of the hostel education programme was sensed: 'most go for the sake of the experience rather than any ultimate opportunity that might be offered'.[68]

> [T]here is an increasing dissatisfaction with the practice of sending secondary age children away from Warburton for their "high school" or equivalent education. Parents, and more particularly the old people feel this is wrong... relatives express constant concern about the welfare of their children, and become so agitated about them that once they have them home for term breaks, they are reluctant to allow children to return for succeeding terms... Children become homesick and despondent to the point of manifesting antisocial attitudes aimed at drawing upon themselves the negative attention necessary to cause authorities to send them back to Warburton.[69]

By the 1980s, the 'project centres' had closed, and the Education Department no longer supported sending adolescents away.[70] The few Ngaanyatjarra students still boarding at Nindeebai Hostel were 'forced' to go into the normal stream at Eastern Goldfields High School, but were unable to cope.[71] Meanwhile, in the Ngaanyatjarra Lands, rudimentary education facilities had been established at the new outstation communities, albeit with minimal Education Department funding. Education staff attributed poor school results to truancy and mobility between Warburton and the outstations.[72]

Jennifer was born in 1966. Her family was a 'Christian family' at Warburton Ranges Mission. Jennifer went to school at Warburton during the 1970s: 'I used to like school because I wanted to get learn so I can be a boss'. Then, like many of her cohort, she was sent to the Eastern Goldfields. She boarded at Nindeebai Hostel in Kalgoorlie and went to school at the Project Centre for one year. Jennifer has now been working at Warburton School as an Assistant Teacher for many years. She is literate in both English and Ngaanyatjarra. She would like to learn more about teaching and has enrolled in a teacher training course.

Bilingual education

The ideology of multiculturalism/multilingualism that arose in the 1970s, in response to national social and political changes, led to much-needed education and language policy reform. In 1972, a national campaign was launched to promote Aboriginal language education for children (Hoogenraad, 2001). Bilingual education was introduced into a number of government and non-government schools in the Northern Territory, South Australia and Western Australia (Hartman & Henderson, 1994; Simpson *et al.*, 2009). A pilot Bilingual Education Programme was introduced at Warburton School in 1974, in tandem with an Aboriginal Teacher Aide training scheme (Glass, 1973). Unfortunately, the Warburton bilingual programme was short-lived and had ceased by 1980, although some Ngaanyatjarra literacy teaching has continued off and on since.

From the mid-1980s, the Education Department implemented a post-primary programme in the Lands' schools (Kral & Ward, 2000). This paved the way for increased teacher numbers and drove the provision of permanent school buildings and teacher housing in the new communities. It also led to high teacher turnover and decreased social relations between the schools and the community (NLLIA, 1996). Some families have subsequently returned to the practice of sending teenagers away for residential secondary schooling outside the Lands. Nevertheless, despite many attempts to reinvigorate schooling over the intervening years, a despondency remains regarding the purpose of schooling, and the 'weak linkages between schooling and the meaningful occupation of young people' are not being resolved (NLLIA [Vol. 2], 1996: 139).

Conclusion

Thus far, in Part 2, I have explored the post-contact 'figured world' by studying the interrelationship between local, state and national arrangements, practices and expectations, in order to understand how the Ngaanyatjarra have participated in new social processes and responded to the changing circumstances and conditions of 'political-economic and cultural-historical conjuncture' that have shaped 'local practice' (Holland & Lave, 2009). I have shown how some Ngaanyatjarra were paradigmatically 'habitualised' into the schooling and work practices encountered on missions and stations. Once the state introduced incomprehensible waves of policy change, however, *yarnangu* began to experience a diminishing sense of certainty, predictability and control that has continued up to the present day.

Examining these changes from a socio-historical perspective allows us to retrospectively question whether schooling, and, concomitantly, literacy, has enabled the Ngaanyatjarra to realise the goal of employment in the market economy within the space of a few generations. The answer, evidently, is no. However, the problem here lies with the expectation (as intimated earlier by Rowley) that schooling is the main factor in social change. In pondering this question, the spotlight is thrown on to another important issue: have Ngaanyatjarra families transmitted schooling as a meaningful cultural process to successive generations? I consider that, paradoxically, the post-contact experiences of this one remote group have, in fact, contributed to disillusionment regarding the purpose of schooling, primarily because literacy has not been the enabling factor, the employment prerequisite, promoted by church and state ideology. On the other hand, the negative consequences of rapid social change notwithstanding, the conditions of the Ngaanyatjarra post-contact experiences, starting with Schenk's unique approach at Mt Margaret Mission through to the mission at Warburton, combined with the unfolding experiences in the Goldfields, have contributed to the historical production of a resilient collective identity, able to adapt to change and deal with the vicissitudes of the ontological shift to modernity.

In the next chapter, I separate literacy from schooling by considering the shift from oral to literate ways of being. I examine how Ngaanytajarra adults have acquired and used literacy for their own social and cultural purposes. I explore the evolution of a politicised Ngaanyatjarra collective, able to deal with the contingencies of the era. I show also how *yarnangu* were instrumental in establishing their own communities and creating a governance structure that transformed the quality of life for the broad community of interest. Importantly, their children were able to observe the strength and agency of parents and grandparents, who, with varying levels of education and literacy, built the community infrastructure and asserted leadership.

Notes

(1) *Annual Report Commissioner of Native Welfare* (1971).
(2) Middleton's reforms followed the survey on Aboriginal affairs by Resident Magistrate F.E.A. Bateman in 1947 and the release of the *Bateman Report* in 1948 (Bateman, 1948; Biskup, 1973; Bolton, 1981).
(3) *Annual Report Commissioner of Native Welfare* (1960: 30).
(4) *Annual Report Commissioner of Native Welfare* (1966: 28).
(5) *Annual Report Commissioner of Native Welfare* (1972).
(6) In 1942, the Federal Aborigines Missions Board of the Churches of Christ opened a children's mission at Norseman. After 1948, the Australian Aborigines Evangelical Mission established a mission at Cundeelee, followed by Kurrawang Native Mission, established by Brethren Assemblies of Australia (1952). In 1954, Moore River Settlement was handed over to the Methodist Overseas Missionary Society and renamed Mogumber Mission (later Mogumber Agricultural College), and Seventh Day Adventists opened Karalundi Mission near Meekatharra, followed by a mission in Wiluna in 1955 (Biskup, 1973; Milnes, 1987; Rowley, [1970] 1972).

(7) Wongutha Mission Training Farm was established by R.W. Schenk, son of Rodolphe Schenk, as an agricultural training school for boys of post-primary school standard, providing a two-year course in farm practices and basic school subjects. Training of girls commenced in 1962 (Liddelow, 1979).

(8) *DNW Newsletter,* Vol. 1, No. 5 (August 1968: 44).

(9) *DNW Newsletter,* Vol. 1, No. 6 (December 1968: 55).

(10) *Department of Native Welfare (DNW) Newsletter* 1: 2 (August 1967: 27).

(11) *Annual Report Commissioner of Native Welfare* (1966: 27); *DNW Newsletter* 1: 9 (January 1971: 47).

(12) *DNW Newsletter* 2: 2 (Christmas 1971: 46–7).

(13) *DNW Newsletter* 1: 4, (March 1968: 33).

(14) *DNW Newsletter* 1: 4 (March 1968: 17).

(15) *DNW Newsletter* 1: 2 (August 1967: 35).

(16) In 1956, W.L. Grayden secured the creation of a Select Committee of the Legislative Assembly to inquire into the plight of people in the Central Reserves, in relation to the British government's atomic bomb programme at Maralinga (Attwood, 2003: 149–151). After visiting Warburton Ranges Mission, he raised the alarm (Western Australia Parliament, 1956). The 1957 surveys of the Central Reserves-Goldfields region, by Ronald and Catherine Berndt, arose out of the 'Warburton controversy'. They found Grayden's account of undernourishment and social breakdown in the Warburton Ranges area to be an exaggeration (see, also, Brooks, 2011a; McGrath, 2004). The 1957 attempt to pass the 'First Bill for Citizenship Rights' in WA arose out of the Warburton controversy, as an attempt to counter the unfavourable publicity provoked by the 'Warburton Controversy' that mirrored the growing unease in Australia, concerning the treatment of Aboriginal people (Berndt & Berndt, 1959: 3).

(17) *United Aborigines Messenger* (October 1966: 5); *Annual Report CNW* (1966: 27).

(18) WA SRO Acc 5296 321/74, 13 December 1951 – *From CNA Middleton to the Undersecretary for Mines.*

(19) WA SRO Acc 1733 511/42 – *Warburton Ranges Mission native matters (1942–1956) 27/9/56 letter from Middleton CNW to Editor United Aborigines Messenger.*

(20) WA SRO Acc 993 1220/61, 18 July 1962 – *Notes from meeting between MNW, CNW and UAM.*

(21) Report of the trip to Warburton Ranges, 14 to 21 September 1962: UAM Files – NTU Archives, Ngaanyatjarra Council

(22) In earlier research (Kral & Ward, 2000), findings from 100 interviews with Ngaanyatjarra adults indicate that approximately 60–70% of the middle-aged cohort self-describe as having participated in the hostel programme. In Appendix 1, data from the 2004 Ngaanyatjarra Council CDEP Skills Audit indicate that of the 119 interviewees (CDEP recipients only) in the 41–61 year age group, 42% claim to have had no post-primary schooling.

(23) WA SRO Acc 1419 23-7-315/162 – *Letter from CNW to Federal Secretary UAM.*

(24) WA SRO Acc 993 1220/61 – *Warburton Ranges Mission, general correspondence Nov. 61 Johnson Welfare Inspector's report*; Report on nutrition at Warburton Ranges July 1972 – NTU Files, Ngaanyatjarra Council.

(25) Wells – interview, 1 April 2004.

(26) *Annual Report Commissioner of Native Affairs* (1954: 60).

(27) Some of the last images of hunter-gatherer life in the Australian desert were taken by Grayden in 1953 (Grayden, 2002), Native Patrol Officers (McGrath, 2010) and Ian Dunlop and the Commonwealth Film Unit (Dunlop, 1966–1970) in the 1960s.

(28) Elizabeth Ellis (personal communication, April 2004).

(29) Seventh Day Adventists established a school at Karalundi Mission near Meekatharra, WA, in 1954, for children from pastoral stations (Biskup, 1973: 254). Karalundi closed in the early 1970s. It was later re-established as a Christian boarding school. Families in the 'Gibson Desert mob' continue the tradition of sending their adolescent children to Karalundi for schooling.

(30) Title adapted from Rowse (1998: 112).

(31) WA SRO Acc 1733 511/42 – *Warburton Ranges Mission native matters 30 May 1950 CNA to D/Director of Rationing.*

(32) WA SRO Acc 1419 23-7-3 Missions UAM Mission Warburton Ranges – *Reports Annual Inspection June 1954–June 1955 Annual Report from UAM to DNA re. Warburton.*

(33) WA SRO Acc 1419 EG 23-1 18 August 1954 – *ADO Eastern Goldfields to Superintendent Cosmo Newbery Native Mission.*

(34) This information was obtained from Norma McLean – one of the original group of children in the Baker Home in the 1930s. She had kept a photocopied record of this list in a bag over many years.

(35) Glass and Hackett (personal communication, September 2005).

(36) Wells – Interview, 1 April 2004.

(37) WA SRO Acc 993 1220/61 – *General correspondence Dec. 61: Report on inspection of Warburton Ranges Mission re. pension and family allowance.*

(38) *United Aborigines Messenger* (February 1965: 6).

(39) *United Aborigines Messenger* (February 1965: 6).

(40) WA SRO Acc 1733 66/65 – *Warburton Ranges Native Matters April 1965. Correspondence: UAM Federal Secretary to CNW.*

(41) WA SRO Acc 1733 66/65 – *Warburton Ranges Native Matters June 1965. Correspondence: CNW to MNW.*

(42) WA SRO Acc 1733 66/65 – *Warburton Ranges Native Matters Report Superintendent of Economic Development to CNW 1965.*

(43) *Annual Report Commissioner of Native Welfare* (30 June 1971).

(44) WA SRO ACC 993 1220/61 17/762 – *From CNW to MNW summary of history of Warburton Ranges Mission.*

(45) WA SRO Acc 1733 300/64 – *Employment Survey (Central Reserve and the Eastern Division, including Esperance and Kalgoorlie).*

(46) *Annual Report Commissioner of Native Welfare* (1963: 36).

(47) *Annual Report Commissioner of Native Welfare* (1955: 27).

(48) UAM Western Desert Report presented to the Federal Conference Melbourne, April 1965, by District Superintendent, Keith R. Morgan – UAM Files, NTU Archives, Ngaanyatjarra Council.

(49) Claude and, later, Dora Cotterill (nee Quinn) were at Warburton, then Cosmo Newbery missions from 1947.

(50) This culminated in a serious incident near Laverton between police and Warburton men travelling to Wiluna for ceremonial Business. Known as the 'Skull Creek affair', it was of such severity that it led to the Laverton Royal Commission (Western Australia Parliament, 1976, Woenne, 1980).

(51) Sir Paul Hasluck was Commonwealth Minister for Territories under Robert Menzies' federal Liberal Government (1951–63) and a key architect of the assimilation policy (Rowse, 1998, 2005a).

(52) *United Aborigines Messenger* (December 1976: 16–19).

(53) Fay Paget (personal communication, April 2004).

(54) McLean – interview, 9 September 2004.

(55) *Hansard* 'Aboriginal Employment' (1977: 1921).

(56) Another of the original CDEP projects was initiated at Wiluna 'Desert Farm' and 'Emu Farm' to improve the socio-economic aspects of community life, reduce the damaging effect of alcohol, increase training and develop general employment skills and assist community members to manage their own affairs (*Annual Report AAPA and ALT*, 1977). See, also, Sackett (1990).

(57) *Annual Report AAPA and ALT* (1978: 9).

(58) In 1976, the Ngaanyatjarra, Pitjantjatjara and Yankunytjatjara people formed the Pitjantjatjara Council. It was agreed that membership was available to all, irrespective of state borders. On 4 November 1981, the Pitjantjatjara received freehold title to over 102, 630 sq. km of their traditional lands under the *Pitjantjatjara Land Rights Act (1981)* (Toyne & Vachon, 1984).

(59) The UAM withdrew from Mt Margaret in 1976, and ownership was transferred to former mission residents under the Aboriginal Movement for Outback Survival Inc. (AMOS). Mt Margaret has continued operating, having attracted a new community (including a group from the Gibson Desert and their descendants) to fill the vacuum left by the original inhabitants (Stanton, 1983; Stanton, 1990).

(60) *United Aborigines Messenger* (June 1979: 9).

(61) *United Aborigines Messenger* (July/August 1980: 14).

(62) *Annual Report AAPA and ALT* (1976: 9).

(63) Elizabeth Ellis (personal communication, April 2004).

(64) Wells – Interview, 1 April 2004.

(65) Wells – Interview, 1 April 2004.

(66) Dorothy Hackett (personal communication, 2004).

(67) *Annual Report Commissioner of Native Welfare* (1967: 27). By the 1960s, secondary education had expanded across Australia, and educational qualifications based on recognised certification had become a national issue (Milnes, 1987: 347). This was to erect an insurmountable barrier to Aboriginal students, especially those from remote communities. Academic standards now determined procedure through the school years. Nevertheless, in 1963, a new Education Department regulation stipulated that normal practice was to maintain chronological, rather than scholastic, promotion between grade levels, with all 13 year olds to be transferred to high school, irrespective of academic performance (Milnes, 1987: 399).

(68) School Policy Warburton Ranges 1974 – Ngaanyatjarra Council archives: Education File.

(69) School Policy Warburton Ranges 1974 – Ngaanyatjarra Council archives: Education File.

(70) Concern regarding the project classes was addressed in the 1984 *Beazley Report*. The Report found conflicting evidence on the relevance and adequacy of the 'project' classes. On the one hand, they were perceived to provide practical skills; on the other hand, they were seen as 'dumping grounds', with students given no opportunity to work on the mainstream Achievement Certificate curriculum (Beazley, 1984: 334–335).

(71) Wells – interview, 1 April 2004.

(72) Warburton Ranges Special Aboriginal School: School Policy 1979 – Ngaanyatjarra Council archives: Education File.

5 The Cultural Production of Literate Identities

Prior to contact with European society Western Desert people used a complex of communication forms and semiotic systems to convey meaning; through language, sign, gesture and gaze, special speech styles and registers, non-verbal communication and the iconic representations found in body painting, carved designs and sand drawings.[1] These relevant meaning-making systems were deployed in the manipulation of the symbols, and the resources, of the known world within a sociocultural system of complexity, subtlety and capacity for innovation. The first exposure to Western symbols and alphabetic script may have been the initials and dates carved by early explorers and doggers on trees and rocks. As time went by the strange signifying system used by Europeans was echoed in the symbols encountered on the introduced objects of Western material culture (alphabetic script on food boxes, tobacco tins, hessian sacks and so forth) and later in Bibles and school-books. With the arrival of the missionaries the mapping of the new world onto an existing system of meaning-making symbols commenced. This drove an inexorable shift in the cultural patterning of interactions that led to altered discourse practices and communication forms. It also paved the way for the emergence of textually mediated roles and identities.

In this chapter I begin by tracing the introduction of literacy in Ngaanyatjarra. I also draw attention to the shift from oral to literate habits, and ways of thinking and acting, in order to highlight the implications of the short history of literacy for this recently preliterate group. In this light, I focus on the manner in which *yarnangu* have taken up literate strategies in English and Ngaanyatjarra for their own sociocultural purposes within the space of two generations.

From Oral to Literate: Changing Modes of Communication

The taken for granted nature of literacy in Western society (and English literacy in Anglo-European countries) and its primacy in everyday life, masks its complexity (Graff 1987; Graff [1982] 1994). In general, little account is taken of how literacy has evolved over many centuries in many societies, from its origins in oral traditions through the transformation of social and cultural practices, and the invention and adaptation of the material resources and technologies that support the particularities of Western literacy. Yet, we in the West still cannot claim to have achieved universal literacy.

In Britain and Western Europe the cultural shift from 'memory to written record' took place over more than two centuries. Michael Clanchy's study (1979) of the Norman introduction of literacy to medieval England (1066–1307) charts the shift from oral to literate habits and ways of thinking and acting. He explicates how the shift from trusting memory and the spoken word, above the written word, and from 'habitually memorizing things' to writing them down, was a *gradual* process that took time to develop (Clanchy 1979: 3). Following on, the introduction of the printing press to England in 1476 encouraged the spread of literacy and language standardisation, and print gradually began replacing the oral aspects and memory arts of scribal culture (Graff 1987; Eisenstein 1985). Despite significant change, England remained neither a 'wholly literate' nor a 'wholly illiterate' society for a long time (Schofield 1968: 312–313). In fact, until the end of the sixteenth century the term 'literate' was not used as a marker of self-identity, but as 'a descriptor to dichotomize the population into literates who could read in the vernacular languages and illiterates who could not' (Heath 1991: 4). Until at least the mid-nineteenth century rote repetition and oral reading dominated classrooms and attention to meaning was neglected, so students were not learning to read well (Graff 1987: 326–327). At this time in the United States, being 'literate' meant the ability to sign one's name or an X to legal documents, as well as the 'ability to read and recite memorized passages, not necessarily with comprehension' (Rogoff 2003: 260–261).

Literacy, Christianity and Adults at Warburton Ranges Mission

Early exposure to textually mediated practice at Warburton included listening and singing to the Word of God, in a manner reminiscent of the oral, often collective, events that typified the early development of literacy in Western society (Clanchy, 1979: 214–220). Soon after their arrival, the missionaries attempted to communicate the Scriptures in English, using Gospel pictures to explain 'the good news of God's grace and love to these needy and benighted souls'.[2] Even though early interactions were assisted by intermediaries who had spent time in the Goldfields (Brooks, 2011a; Morgan, 1986), a profound language gap existed. Until the 1950s, textually mediated interactions were primarily in English. This followed the English language model, set by R.S. Schenk at Mt Margaret Mission. Virtually no linguistic or educational attention was paid to the mother tongue, Ngaanyatjarra, until 1952, when a new direction in UAM language policy commenced. UAM linguist Wilf Douglas aimed to 'break the barrier of unknown speech'.[3] His work on Ngaanyatjarra was the first serious study of the language (Douglas, 1955). By 1957, Douglas had compiled the first grammatical analysis of Ngaanyatjarra and devised Roman alphabet orthography, based on the Pitjantjatjara orthography developed at Ernabella Mission (Trudinger, 1943).[4]

Horace, Jack and Harold, whom I introduced earlier, were among the group that Douglas first worked with to trial the vernacular 'Gospel recordings' in 1953:

The messages recorded on the tape were also written on paper, so that in the days following we were able to select extracts for use in meetings, and for introducing visiting natives to the Gospel. A few small portions

Figure 5.1 Christian meeting, Warburton Ranges Mission 1939
© Ngarnmanytjatja Archive, Ngaanyatjarra Council

of Scripture... were translated, and many opportunities were given to read these to the people. It was indeed a privilege and joy to be able to read God's Word to the older folk, in a language they understood. Even the children could barely contain themselves when a new portion was read to them in the familiar terms of the camp speech.[5]

After this initial success, the teaching of vernacular reading commenced with the cohort of young women who were soon to leave the Baker Home, including Katherine, April's mother, Patricia's mother and Clifford's aunt:

> The girls made rapid progress, and immediately started teaching the younger girls to read. By the end of five weeks they could read the five basic Primers, which had introduced them to their complete alphabet, and were able also to write simple sentences in their own language. The Primers were designed with a view to giving the young people a clearer understanding of English, also, and contained a simple English-Wangka dictionary.[6]

According to an account in the *Messenger* in 1957, 'amazing results' were achieved: young people who have been taught to read 'now read to their own folk'; boys learned to read in a month, and girls from the Home, now married, taught their husbands to read.[7] Moreover, teenage girls were soon able 'to write short stories in their own language, after five weeks, of one hour each day'.[8] Reading primers, entitled *Wangka* (language or talk), were prepared as the first vernacular reading materials available in the Mission and remained the main introductory readers until 1969 (Glass, 2000). These events were significant, as *yarnangu* were able to see their mother tongue – a language previously only heard and spoken – signified in a written form for the first time. This, in turn, led to the realisation that meaning could be exchanged in written, as well as spoken, text, and communication became 'imbued with a sense of permanence' (Engelke, 2009: 161).

Adult literacy and the Aboriginal church

The new vernacular outlook within the UAM was coupled with a move to establish 'self-supporting, self-governing, self-propagating Aboriginal churches'.[9] In 1957, Douglas established the Western Desert Bible School and Translation Centre in Kalgoorlie (renamed the UAM Language Department in 1958). Bible study schools operated under the guidance of Douglas and his wife, Beth. In an early Bible study school in 1957, men from Cosmo Newbery and Warburton travelled to Mt Margaret. Classes involved exegetical studies of the 'Old Testament, New Testament, Bible Teachings, Christian Service (Witnessing, Sermon Preparation, Art and Music)', as well as vernacular literacy and the memorisation of Scripture. The Warburton men were given separate classes, in which they did Scripture translation and compiled a small book of hymns and choruses.[10] Horace was one of the first preachers to participate in Bible school classes, later improving his Ngaanyatjarra reading through translation work with missionary Noel Blyth. The drive to establish an Aboriginal church continued throughout the 1960s. Preachers were sent for training to Gnowangerup Bible Training Institute (GBTI) in south-western Western Australia, and Harold briefly undertook evangelist training at the Australian Inland Mission Bible College in NSW.

The Aboriginal church gained momentum once graduates from GBTI began itinerating. By the 1960s, *yarnangu* were participating in textually mediated Christian practice, within a web of connections that extended across the Goldfields. The UAM Mission at Cosmo Newbery was an important site with Christian Endeavour activities for children, regular ladies prayer meetings and services led by local church leaders. Wesley's father and April's father itinerated with workers at nearby stations, and trips were made to Laverton and Leonora 'to contact the people in the towns and native reserves'.[11] Meanwhile, the UAM Language Department was producing reading material for dissemination across the Goldfields:

> From Kalgoorlie we send out English literature to a growing number of aboriginal and part-aboriginal readers. It is not easy to find good literature in English simple enough to meet the needs of some of the people... But what we are sending out is increasing the desire to read on the part of the people, and we trust that more and more literature of the right type will become available as Christians and missionaries become conscious of the value of the printed page. (Douglas & Douglas, 1964: 54)

Gospel Centres were established in Leonora and Laverton for the distribution of Christian materials.[12]

> Literature... puts into the hands of the ordinary missionary a valuable means of communication, instruction and propagation of the Gospel. It also assists the local church leaders and teachers... Over all, the trend is to consolidate the effectiveness of Gospel outreach in its many forms. Not only so – here is an effective means of making newly-literates more literate, and opens new doors of economic opportunity.[13]

The above quote reveals the overriding concern, in the 1960s, regarding the perceived relationship between literacy, modernity and progress. The commencement of vernacular literacy inflamed the already extant ideological rift between church and state (as mentioned in Chapter 3). That is, between the Christian desire to provide the written Word of God to adults in their own vernacular and the new state narrative of advancement through schooling and literacy in English. Assimilationist rhetoric inextricably linked literacy to schooling and the state's desire for individuals to progress towards citizenship and participation in the labour market economy. On the other hand, the UAM embraced adult literacy as an extension of social relatedness, attached to meaningful practice, often in contexts not visible to the state, albeit for the ultimate goal of Christian conversion.

In the 1960s, Native Welfare policy was that English be spoken 'in all dealings with native children'. Missionaries using the 'native dialect' were 'requested to discourage this practice':[14]

> While it is desirable that the Missionaries learn to converse understandably with the natives they profess to enlighten they must be brought to realise that if the natives are to make their way in a white man's world it is essential that they be given a good command of English… very little can be gained by attempting to make tribal natives literate in their own language.[15]

Meanwhile, the UAM argued that 'the ability to read in the vernacular will be one of the greatest incentives and helps to the reading and mastery of English'.[16] Moreover, it was even suggested that the Lord had 'revealed methods which enable "primitive" folk to become "literate" in comparatively short time', and the 'greatest incentive to learn to read is the desire to read the Bible in the mother tongue'. The missionaries believed that unless they gave people 'Scriptures in their own speech', they were 'doomed to failure'.[17] This approach drew on the Protestant tradition, where the meaning of God's message is in the *written text*.

As noted in Chapter 3, the 16th-century Protestant Reformation most strikingly linked literacy to religious practice (Graff, [1982] 1994). Harvey Graff postulates that in the wake of the Reformation in Sweden, 'near-universal levels of literacy were achieved rapidly and permanently', without the 'concomitant development of formal schooling or economic or cultural development that demanded functional or practical employment of literacy'. A 'home and church education model' was fashioned to train a 'literate' population (Graff, [1982] 1994: 159; Kapitzke, 1995; Strauss, 1978). However, as Graff points out, the Reformist educational process of rote memorisation of the alphabet and catechism left many 'less than fluently literate'; even so, some 'effect' of literacy must have 'taken hold' (Graff, 1987: 141). Similarly, in later colonial contexts, Christian missionaries (often influenced by the Protestant tradition, in relation to preaching the Word of God in the vernacular) shaped the literate world for preliterate groups, as in Africa (Harries, 1994; Prinsloo, 1995) and also Papua New Guinea, where the link between literacy and the church remains strong, with few uses for literacy outside schooling and the Christian domain (Kulick, 1992; Kulick & Stroud, 1993; Schieffelin, 2002; Schieffelin, 2007). On Nukulaelae, in Polynesia, no social arena is as 'suffused with literacy' as religion (Besnier, 1995: 116). In Alaska, literacy was introduced in Cyrillic through the Russian Orthodox Church, concomitant with the development of specialised Indigenous leadership roles within the church (Reder & Green, 1983; Reder & Wikelund, 1993).

A church of the people

In 1966, the UAM declared that the church was 'no longer a mission church, but the church of the people'.[18] Large Christian conventions, organised solely by Aboriginal Christians, became an annual event at Mt Margaret (Stanton, 1990: 221). Conventions provided opportunities for preachers to hone their skills and demonstrate leadership, and youngsters observed these practices.

Initially, at Warburton, church leaders relied on Bible story pictures. As Molly recalls, the 'Good News' was shared using Gospel pictures:

They used to have a Christian picture that's all, all the picture. One person stand up with all the picture, lift him up another page, another page... whitefella got to be there and a dark bloke is there, like that.

Services and Sunday School were held in camps with hymn-singing and a prayer led by family members:

Aboriginal teachers used to hold their own class... We used to have our own Bible School. The training they gave us, we used to teach, if you want a speaker for next week, well, you go and pick that speaker yourself they can speak on Sunday. Training, running their own things.

In the process of becoming church leaders, local preachers were acquiring new speech events and performance modes in the oral delivery of sermons at church services (c.f. Schieffelin, 2002). At first, the church leaders were

Figure 5.2 Christian meeting, Warburton Ranges Mission 1960s
© Ngarnmanytjatja Archive, Ngaanyatjarra Council

illiterate and this fuelled the missionaries' 'urgency to have God's word in their own language so they may have spiritual food to feed upon, that they may be able to fully understand the wonderful message of God's salvation to them'.[19] Herbert Howell (who commenced as a teacher at Cosmo Newbery in the 1960s) suggests that, over time, preachers displayed varying degrees of English competence[20]:

> Writing was not called for. Some were able to read English but not write in it. Others could not speak nor read nor write English. Leadership roles did not call upon English literacy very heavily if at all. A small number of men could read English and did so in church services from the Bible.

In due course, however, continues Howell, reading in Ngaanyatjarra became 'almost an essential skill'. Thus, literacy became integral to the church leadership role.

Una returned to Warburton from the Goldfields around 1966. She recalls observing her mother learning to read Ngaanyatjarra:

I used to go round and sit down and listen to the older people… and I was thinking to myself: "Oh that's too hard, I can't do that"… But that was my language. I used to come and sit down when the older people were talking to Miss Hackett and Miss Glass… my mother used little books like *kapi, waru, mirrka* all that. She used to take little papers like this home and I used to sit down and say: *"wa-ru, mirr-ka, ka-pi"*. Then I got interested. They used to have a little Bible and songbook, then I used to learn, learn, learn.

When I left school I used to read all sorts of, any sort of books I see on the ground. Sometimes we get Reader's Digest… or sometimes they come second-hand and I used to read them… We used to stay long way and we used to sit down home, nothing to do and I used to sit down and read, anything what I see.

Una's motivation grew. She participated in the DNW Adult Native Education classes and worked with Glass and Hackett, translating the New and Old Testament, and contributed to the development of Ngaanyatjarra dictionaries. Una is one of the more skilled literates and has 'authored' a number of published stories. She says translation work is hard:

Got to use your brains, only special people can do it. Need to get young people learning how to do it, some do… but not enough to pass on the skill. Got to really understand English and how to speak good Ngaanyatjarra.

Una knows that her fluency in English has given her a special skill as an interpreter.

People came to talk for housing: "Yes, we want more houses to be built"… I used to help talk for my father, you know, if any other white man came asking questions about: "You like this?"… I learnt how to, you know, just stand up and talk to people like a government man… And that's how I used to talk strongly for my people. I used to read them, those books. I used to sit down slowly and read them… by myself, without anyone reading it for me… I wanted to do that so I can learn more… It was really important for me to do that because I was thinking to myself: "Oh one day I might speak to, like, when I get up for any other meeting, you know".

Una has also represented the needs of women and children:

We didn't know there was a Woman's Council there for us. And then I heard: "Oh there's a meeting out that way, for only women". So I always used to get up and talk for all the Warburton women. At meetings there were all sorts of things, to read they used to give us... and I used to sit down, and read, read, read... I used to read them and understand it and explain some of the ladies, some of them who don't know how to read.

Una is aware that she hasn't had much schooling, yet everyone thinks she went to high school: 'Whenever I go out I stand up, and I talk to them, and they think: Oh this woman she knows English'.

A literacy campaign

After some initial success with male preachers at Warburton, a broader adult vernacular 'literacy campaign' commenced with the arrival of missionary linguists, Amee Glass and Dorothy Hackett, in 1963. In retrospect, Glass and Hackett acknowledge that they did not find the keen interest in literacy that they had hoped for:

...there is a problem here as those who had grown up in the Home at the Mission and had been to school where they were taught in English, preferred the services in English. They seem to think it is a step back to learn to read and write in their own language.[21]

After the UAM relinquished control of Warburton Ranges Mission in 1973, Glass, Hackett, Howell and his wife, Lorraine, remained in the community and focused their attention on Scripture translation, teaching literacy and providing language services to non-Aboriginal staff. They also itinerated and distributed Christian reading materials to the new outstation communities.[22] Glass concentrated on teaching semi-literate and illiterate adults, although she concludes that 'few of the illiterates made any significant progress' (Glass, 2000: 3). Nevertheless, during the annual Bible Schools, observers noted the 'growing demand' for adult literacy and the 'astounding' number of children attending holiday Bible schools.[23] Interestingly, a contemporaneous report from the school notes the difficulty that teachers were having in promoting the value of literacy:

Reading has to be recognised for the important skill that it is, and especially in the light of the developing situation at Warburton. Unfortunately, reading, for various reasons, does not seem to be integrated into the thinking of the children as being a worthwhile skill. Seldom is any in-depth attention paid to reading material. There is a tendency for children to look at books and magazines, skimming rapidly over the pages as they go. The article is then flung in the direction of the storage area, another book is grabbed, and the process repeats itself. This method, implying carelessness and lack of interest, denies comprehension opportunities.[24]

By 1982, doctrinal differences had arisen between the remaining missionaries at Warburton and the UAM. Douglas resigned, the UAM Language Department in Kalgoorlie ceased to operate and the Bible training section was transferred to GBTI. Glass and Hackett, along with the Howells, also resigned from the UAM and formed the Ngaanyatjarra Bible Project. Hackett and Glass moved to Alice Springs and have since published many Christian and secular vernacular texts, including dictionaries and the New Testament and part of the Old Testament.[25] Their continuity, alongside Summer Institute of Linguistics (SIL) linguist Jan Mountney, has been a significant factor in the development of adult vernacular literacy in this region.

That some older *yarnangu* 'took hold' of literacy (Ferguson, 1987) can, in part, be attributed to the missionaries' respectful, albeit proselytising, interest in Ngaanyatjarra language and culture and the fact that the human themes and narrative style of biblical discourse are meaningful and 'directly translatable' to Western Desert people (Rose, 2001: 75). Moreover, literacy made sense within the 'social space' (Bourdieu, 1989) of the Christian community – where knowing how to read acted as a symbolic, and real, marker of the passage into this new community. In the next section, I turn to events outside the Christian domain that engendered incipient literacy practices among the Ngaanyatjarra.

Literacy as an Emergent Social Practice

By the 1970s, only some 40 years after the initial exposure to literate practices, some Ngaanyatjarra started to use literacy for secular social *and* political purposes. Moreover, literate identities started to emerge, and cultural ways of using written language developed, as did innovative individual and collective approaches to textual communication.

In 1973, Glass attended a SIL workshop in Darwin.[26] Subsequently, in consultation with Douglas and a few Ngaanyatjarra literates, changes were made to the original Ngaanyatjarra orthography: the diacritics were removed and replaced by digraphs to represent the retroflex consonants and 'rr' was to be used to represent the alveolar flap/trill (Glass, 2000).[27] A year later, David, Clem's brother and another Warburton man attended a short 'Creative Writers Workshop' at SIL in Darwin. This event was acclaimed as 'a significant moment in literacy advancement' and the beginning of a 'literary movement'.[28] Prior to the workshop, these men could read and write only a little in English, yet, by the end, they were able to write 'imaginative stories of high quality' in Ngaanyatjarra:

> Surely here is the beginning of a body of literature written by the people and for the people... we as Christian missionaries should be teaching the people to produce and enjoy good literature for themselves, as well as encouraging them to read and enjoy the Book of books.[29]

David was born in 1946. *He was in the Baker Home and finished school in the early 1960s. At which time, he says, he was unable to read English.*

> I was looking at them, some people was working and I thought, well I better start working too... That was on mission time, I was putting in lights for the missionaries when we first built that mission power house there. We don't have a house at that time, we was on the *wiltja*. We used to camp long way, other side airstrip and all, we used to shift around.

David also worked in the old store and the bakery.

> From there, I heard that there was a new settlement in Docker River being put up. So I went there for work. Most of the people working at Docker River were from Warburton. One whitefella put me as the foreman, so I was putting up the stockyards for the bullocks, making fences.

After he returned to Warburton, David married Jane (b. 1956). He also commenced language work with Glass and Hackett:

> I couldn't even read my own language because, I was thinking: "How come? I should be reading my own language"... We went up to Darwin... Dorothy and Amee always teach us how to read through like *pa-pa, ma-ma*... and we got better and better... She give us a sort of paper like this and we had old *nyaapa*, what that computer? Typewriter, old typewriter... I was getting learn how to sort of be fast type writer... And that's the time we was making, writing a stories too, drawing and writing a story.

David has had a respected role as Ngaanyatjarra literate.

Secular vernacular literacy

Government approval for a pilot bilingual education programme at Warburton School in 1974 provided the catalyst for the production of locally focused secular texts – traditional stories and children's books – in Ngaanyatjarra (and English) (Glass, 1974). Simutaneously, Glass, Hackett and Wells supported an Aboriginal teacher training programme. The new Ngaanyatjarra primers *Nintirriwa-la Wangkaku* – designed using principles from the SIL Gudschinsky method (Gudschinsky, 1973) for teaching vernacular literacy to 'preliterate people' – were incorporated into the school curriculum (Glass, 1973: 8). Importantly, the bilingual programme provided a domain within the school where literate Ngaanyatjarra language speakers could be the 'experts'.

A bilingual community newsletter *'Warburtonngamartatji Tjukurrpa* – Warburton News' was established as an initiative of the newly formed AAPA community council to communicate information on the new agencies. At least 40 editions were produced between 1973–1980:

> When I worked on the community newspaper I used to get all the stories first, reading it into English, get it into my *kata* (in my head) and *kulilku* (think about it) and then follow the English line and translate it. Like that *palyalpayi* (that's how I did it). It was easy for me, I just picked it up quickly, self (*yungarra*). (Plant & Viegas, 2002: 59)

Information of local social and cultural interest could now be accessed in a textual mode. Notably, the newsletter reveals the growing concern among *yarnangu* regarding 'strangers' encroaching on their domain without permission and the confusing number of new white administrators and advisors:

> Why is it that we in this place keep getting a surprise when we see cars and Europeans and aeroplanes coming and going? I will tell you the news so that some of us won't be ignorant all the time. That's why we are writing this newspaper so that you will all be able to read it and know what is happening.[30]

The newsletter recorded the transformation of the community during 'government time'. As can be seen in Figure 5.3, a balanced representation of both English and Ngaanyatjarra is evident – a factor of great symbolic significance at the time. Other newsletters have since been initiated; however, print media has been superseded by digital communications.[31]

Patricia was born in 1963

> My father's family comes from Warburton area. My *kaparli* (grandmother) and *tjamu* (grandfather) was born in the bush somewhere near Warburton.

Warburtonngamartatji Tjukurrpa
Warburton News

Volume 4 No 7
Wednesday, November 21st, 1979

Hospitàlngamartatjiluya watjara -
Tjitja Adeletu, Ruthtju, Gilbylu, Mati
yirnalu puru Ruthtjuya mukurringkula
goodbykarralkitjalu yamatji pirnila.
Palunyaluya pirnipurlkaku nintirringu.
Puruyanyu pukurlpa nyinarranytja
ngurra ngaangka.

Hospital staff say -
Sisters Adele, Ruth, Gilby, Mati yirna
and Ruth would like to say goodbye to
all the friends we have made at Warburton.
We have learnt many things and are glad
that we have lived in Central Reserve
for a short while.

Mantingkaya pitjaku
Mr Neville Mellornya, Mr Douglasnga,
puru walypala kutjupanya pitjakuya
kutjupa Tjantingka. Nyangkaya
pirninyartu pitja miitingiku Manti
yunguntjarra. Nyangkalan pirninyartu
wangkaku tjuuku. Kaltaya Mr Mellornya
walypala pirninya marlaku yanku Cosmoku.

Coming on Monday
Mr Neville Mellor, Mr Douglas and another
man will come here next Sunday. They
want everyone to gather for a meeting on
Monday morning. We will all talk about
the store. Then Mr Mellor's group will
go back to Cosmo.

Jonathanngapula Kathynya
Kutjupa Mantingkalpipula Jonathantupula
Kathylu Kununarranya wantirra wati-
pitjangu. Palunyanyapula yurltutjarra
pitjaarni. Nyinakupula Mr and Mrs
Cotterillta palunyatjanu pitjaku
Warburtonku.

Jonathan and Kathy Bates
Last Monday Jonathan and Kathy Bates left
Kununarra. They are coming along by car.
They will stay with Mr and Mrs Cotterill
for a while then come here.

Purnu payipungkula
Communitylulatju tjimarri pirningka
payipungkulanytja purnu pirni
yarnangungkatja. Purulatju nintilku
manikitjalu Alice Springku puru
Perthku. Purulan manikaralpi purnu
pirninya payipungama yarnangungkatja.
Mary Machalu yininti payipungku.
Nyangka minyma pirniluya yininti
pirninya murtu-murtulku. Mary
Machalunyu purtu nyakupayi yinintiku.

Buying artefacts
The community has been spending a lot of
money buying artefacts from the people.
We also need to sell these artefacts in
Alice Springs and Perth so that we have
enough money to continue buying artefacts.
We especially need people at the artefact
store to work dividing seed necklaces
into shorter lengths and would appreciate
any help as we have orders for these and
Mary Macha has been waiting a long time
for these.

Figure 5.3 *Warburtonngamartatji Tjukurrpa – Warburton News*
Source: Warburtonngamartatji Tjukurrpa – Warburton News , Vol. 4 No.7
November 1979:1. Collection held by Amee Glass and Dorothy Hackett.

The missionaries was here already, but my nanna was in the bush, they came and met the missionary, Mr Wade... My father was born down the creek.

My mother's family is from somewhere round Blackstone way, my other *tjamu* comes from Blackstone area. My grandmother comes from around Warakurna. They met and they came through Warburton and heard that Mr Wade was here and they put my mother in the Home. Her parents was staying down in the bush, just coming down must be visit her, go back.

Patricia's mother (b. 1940) was in the Baker Home and learnt Ngaanyatjarra literacy from Wilf Douglas.

My father's family shifted to Cosmo in the early 1960s... working... fixing windmills, fence... My mother went down to Cosmo and they got married in a church... Stayed there for a long time... At Cosmo we lived in a house and spoke mainly English, but just sometimes Ngaanyatjarra.

The family moved to Laverton reserve when her father got a job at Mt Windarra mine.

Stayed there for must be two years or three. We have to take our homework and do it and we have to take it back the next day in the morning to the teacher... My friends that come down from Laverton, Aboriginal kids from the class, do home work all together and they help me out... sometimes my mother helped me.

Although there were no other books or papers in the camp, Patricia recalls her mother reading the Bible.

Then, must be 12 years of age I went to Kalgoorlie, Nindeebai Hostel... I wanted to go... Went to school at Project Centre. Do gardening, cooking. School, maths and all, reading, writing.

Later, the family returned to Warburton. After Patricia married, she moved to Warakurna, where she worked in the clinic and school. Patricia also started to learn Ngaanyatjarra literacy.

Miss Hackett and Miss Glass used to come down to Blackstone and I sit down with her and read Ngaanyatjarra... Then we start teaching, teaching Ngaanyatjarra in the school, must be two days a week. I went to do some translating in Alice Springs for Bible thing.

I want to work, because I like working you know, instead of sitting down, boring... I like working 'cause you can know how to read, read, write, fax papers through, photocopying, all that things. Get learn more... Can't just sit down and do nothing. It's important for people to work.

A few years ago, the family returned to Warburton. Patricia is a Ngaanyatjarra language worker and has been Chairwoman of NPYWC. Patricia's daughter, Lucy, was born in 1980 and her granddaughter, Shantoya, was born in 1998.

Letter-Writing as Social Practice

Letter-writing is considered by literacy researchers to be the perfect genre for personal or political expression, as 'complete command of reading and writing skills is not necessary for the effective assertion of agency through literacy' (Barton & Hall, 2000: 9). In the history of literacy, in many societies, letter-writing appears as a 'pivotal genre' that people readily 'latch onto' (Besnier, 1995: 16–17; Ahearn, 2001). Letters 'written in the style of speaking' have been elemental in emerging genres of writing in the Western world (Bazerman, 2000; Fairman, 2000). Researchers have highlighted the role of the scribe in mediating letter-writing (Clanchy, 1979; Graff, 1987; Kalman, 1999). Letter-writing has existed as a significant, yet largely invisible, social literacy practice in remote Aboriginal Australia,[32] partly because the ephemeral nature of letters has meant that examples of early correspondence have rarely been preserved. In the Ngaanyatjarra context, the continuity of relationships between *yarnangu* and certain staff has led to the unique preservation of corpora of letters, revealing the significance of letter-writing as an incipient social literacy practice in the Ngaanyatjarra context.

Early exposure to letter-writing can be traced back to the 'prayer letters' used by the UAM as a means of informing supporters in urban locations of their work and encouraging donations (Milnes, 1987: 164). Valcie recalls addressing 'about a thousand or more envelopes' to Prayer Partners at Mt Margaret in the 1940s:

We had to do the envelopes and we daren't write it crooked on the envelopes... We had to do it straight and good handwriting. And they had taught us to write properly in school, and with Mrs Schenk.

Later, while at Glenorn Station, Valcie recalls corresponding with her friends. As noted earlier, prior to 1954, towns were prohibited areas, and Aboriginal people were excluded from entering, unless under an employment permit. Assistance from non-Aboriginal intermediaries, like station managers or missionaries, was no doubt required to access the resources needed to write and post letters. Arthur recalls how he would get paper from the 'station man':

> I used to have my case, comics, books... I still had my letters, you know writing letter all the time... Had pencil, writing pad, envelopes, stamp...

He also wrote letters to his sister, Katherine, at Warburton 'all the time', and she replied only 'sometimes'! Molly also remembers writing letters while at Cosmo: 'we knew how to read and write there, we used to write like a letter, letter to our boyfriends, that's all... in Kurrawang'. Similarly, when April was working at Leonora hospital:

> I had nothing else to do so I used to lay down and read. We used to do a lot of readings, writing. I done a lot of writing... they used to write letters and I used to write back.

Jim says that at Pedlar's on the weekends, he 'read all the time, books, all kind of books [and] we write back home to family'. As an aside, a recurring theme among this cohort is that with few other distractions, letter-writing and reading were leisure-time activities.

Glass and Hackett have corresponded in Ngaanyatjarra with literates since the 1960s. Most of the letters discussed here are sourced from their corpus of some 110 letters (see Table 5.1). Their collection can be divided into two categories: 'letters of affect' and 'letters of advocacy'.

Letters of affect

Early letter-writing, for the Ngaanyatjarra, was inextricably linked to maintaining social relationships and realising sociocultural aspirations. As a new mode of communication, letter-writing was taken up by the Ngaanyatjarra at the intersection of specific events in time and place and as a consequence of certain preconditions. Firstly, separation from family (as students and workers or during periods of incarceration) exacerbated the desire to maintain social relatedness. Secondly, the urge to move back to traditional homelands necessitated the development of a new form of

Table 5.1 Letters – Corpus A

Sender	Recipient	No. of letters	Years	Language
Male prisoners	Glass and/or Hackett	7	1977–2003	English
Ngaanyatjarra people absent from home	Glass and/or Hackett	18	1965–1989	English
Ngaanyatjarra people absent from home	Glass and/or Hackett	28 (2 dictated)	1965–1990	Ngaanyatjarra
Young people away in hostels	Glass and/or Hackett	16	1965–1979	English
Young people away in hostels	Glass and/or Hackett	1	1970	Ngaanyatjarra
Ngaanyatjarra female, who had moved elsewhere	Glass and/or Hackett	15	1966–1988	English
Husband	Wife	1	1977	Ngaanyatjarra (dictated)
Ngaanyatjarra male	Aboriginal friend	1	1980	Ngaanyatjarra (dictated)
Family corpus:				
Daughter at Hostel	Glass and/or Hackett	1	1960s	English
Father in Warburton	Glass and/or Hackett	3	1971–1973	Ngaanyatjarra (dictated)
Father in Warburton	Daughter at Hostel	4	1972–1974	Ngaanyatjarra (dictated)
Father	Official letters to Government/Advisor	4	1973–1976	Ngaanyatjarra & English (dictated)
Official letters:				
Ngaanyatjarra people	Government: AAPA, DAA, etc.	10	1973–1975	Ngaanyatjarra or Ngaanyatjarra/English (dictated)
	Community Advisor	1	1975	Ngaanyatjarra & English (dictated)
	Editor, West Australian	1	May 1975	Ngaanyatjarra & English (dictated)

communication with outsiders. The circumstantial particularities of this era provided not only the motivation to communicate in a written form, but also access to the resources, the 'materiality' (Hall, 2000), that enabled this new social practice.

In pre-contact times, social interaction was primarily within the small family group, or band, and between kin-based relations. Relatedness to kin and country was, and remains, of foremost importance. For the Ngaanyatjarra, being away from family or country for extended periods causes a deep emotional and physical yearning for people and place. Such circumstances engender intense empathy for the emotional suffering of relatives who are alone or absent. This elicits the particularly Ngaanyatjarra emotion *ngarltu* ('compassion'), as in the term *ngarltutjarra* ('poor thing'), used for one whom one feels compassion for. Myers (1986) emphasises that in the Western Desert, the discourse of daily life is heavily nuanced with emotion or 'affect': compassion, melancholy, grief, happiness, shame and so forth. Affect, in Ngaanyatjarra, is expressed using oral and kinaesthetic repertoires. Body parts are an important 'category of metaphor' (Douglas, 1979) used in figurative speech and affective expressions and idioms, where the emotions of grief, anger and desire derive from the *tjuni* (stomach) or *lirri* (throat):

> *lirri kampaku* – to feel very angry (lit. throat burn)
> *lirri talan-talan(pa)* – to be angry (lit. throat hot)
> *lirri warurringku* – to become very angry (lit. throat become hot)
> *tjuni kaarr-kaarrarriku* – to become homesick (lit. stomach broken)
> *tjuni kartaly(pa)* – to feel bereaved, sad through losing a relative (lit. stomach broken)
> (Glass & Hackett, 2003)

Yearning for kin and country, arising from lengthy absences, was not unknown in pre-contact times: marriage sometimes separated kin, young novices travelled long distances with the *tjilkatja* (that is, when travelling to manhood ceremonies in a ceremonial party) and post-initiate young men travelled widely for lengthy periods. In the assimilation era, however, a new experience was encountered in the enforced separation of youth from kin and country. This situation engendered the desire for affective communication that, in the pre-telephone era, could only be undertaken in the written register. Thus, letter-writing emerged as a social practice to ameliorate feelings of *watjil-watjilpa* and *tjuni kaarr-kaarrarriku* ('loneliness' and 'homesickness'). Especially as, in the early years, the government supplied only one free travel permit per year, so mid-term school holidays were spent in the Goldfields, thus exacerbating the sense of longing for home.

Missions and hostels provided the institutional support for the enactment of letter-writing: a fixed address for mail to be received, material resources and literate Europeans to mediate the process. Between 1965 and 1979, Glass and Hackett received 17 'letters of affect' (one in Ngaanyatjarra and the rest in English) from adolescents in hostels. They also recollect schoolgirls asking for materials to correspond with relatives in the Goldfields. Una recalls writing to her uncle at Pedlar's Hostel:

> When I was down in Warburton here… he wrote letters back… I used to sit down and write and I used to think: "Oh what I got to put?" Then I used to sit down and write to friends.

Phyllis wrote to Glass and Hackett in English and Ngaanyatjarra from Fairhaven Hostel in 1972 and from GBTI the following year. Other writers sent family news, reported on events, talked of their Christian faith *and* communicated their homesickness.

Phyllis was born in 1954. *She grew up at Warburton Ranges Mission. In the late 1960s, when she was about 15 she learned to read with Glass and Hackett.*

> We all living in *wiltjas*… there was nothing on in Warburton, there was nothing to do and then we'd come over and learn to read, there were no DVDs or TVs or anything then… then the new things came in like TV.

From 1971, Phyllis boarded at Fairhaven Hostel for two years. She recalls that, at the time, she was one of the few young people who could read Ngaanyatjarra. Phyllis told the missionaries that her goal was to be a missionary. She recalls that she 'really wanted to be something'. So she went to GBTI for two years. Notably, Phyllis was the only female to undertake evangelist training. She married in 1975 and returned to the Lands. Phyllis later became one of the few Ngaayatjarra to undertake formal training in Alice Springs. She was enthusiastic about education and worked as an Aboriginal education worker for many years. She was especially committed to teaching Ngaanyatjarra in schools. Gradually, however, she 'lost heart', when she perceived that education was 'coming to nothing'. Phyllis then became one of the few trained senior Aboriginal health workers. Over the years, she has maintained her literacy skills in English and Ngaanyatjarra and remains a strong leader. She and her husband have both worked with Glass and Hackett on Bible translations. She has also written and translated a number of children's stories. Phyllis is an important role model for her granddaughter, Nina.

Table 5.1 includes letters from a father to his daughter, while she was at Fairhaven. Although the father was unschooled, he attained some rudimentary vernacular literacy proficiency as an adult. When he wanted to write to his daughter, however, Glass or Hackett acted as scribes: transcribing and, sometimes, translating his letters into English.[33]

July 1972
Are you well? I pray for you. Battery of company truck is flat. I have no money so you might send me some. Will you come in August? XXX has his daughter here and I want to have my daughter close. With all my heart I'm calling you back to your birthplace.

August 1972
Thanks for money. Are you still trusting in the Lord? The missionaries in Esperance have brought you up and we are only half your parents. XXX and his wife are truly parents to their child. My daughter is like an orphan. On Sunday we'll have a service at XX. God is Lord of all.

The summarised translated excerpts from the father's letters (above) are overt in their expression of cultural meaning and values: affective appeals for compassion and obligation, pain at the separation from kin, the significance of birthplace and the encoding of Christian practices.

'Letters of affect' also include letters to and from prisoners. Prisons are a context where the social value of text is enhanced, and letters represent the physical proof of connectedness to the outside world (c.f. Wilson, 2000). As discussed earlier, from the 1960s, increasing numbers of desert people, particularly men, were incarcerated for alcohol-related incidents. With imprisonment came a fixed address, access to resources and the support of literacy mediators. Howell recollects how letters in English, written to parents by young men in jail, were often brought to him to be read and translated.[34] Molly and Una recall a 'lot of letters' in the 1960s and 'no telephones'. Likewise, Jacinta recalls that when her husband was incarcerated in the 1980s, they wrote to each other, because there was no telephone at home. Telephones were introduced to Warburton and the other Ngaanyatjarra communities after 1990. This contributed to the demise of letter-writing as a significant social practice. Yet, as will be discussed later, video-conferencing, Facebook, Skype and mobile phone text messaging have taken over as new modes of communication for maintaining social relationships at a distance.

Literacy as a Political Strategy

As discussed in the previous chapter, the era of self-determination thrust Ngaanyatjarra people into an altered socio-political milieu, where adults were to experience the liberating surge of emotion associated with regaining control over events that mattered to them as a cultural group. It catalysed an assertion of agency, and literacy became embedded in broader social goals and cultural practices. As their social orientation started to shift beyond the local, the impetus for written communication became 'event-centred' (Besnier, 1995). Ngaanyatjarra adults began to use literate strategies to realise sociopolitical goals. 'Letters of advocacy' (incorporating both letters and petitions) thus emerged at the confluence of events that were both internal *and* external to the Ngaanyatjarra world and were utilised as a collective response to meet new ideological aspirations.[35]

Letters of advocacy

Significantly, an early literacy event was in direct response to a perceived cultural transgression. In 1936, when the Mission moved to its permanent location, permission to relocate had been negotiated with, and ultimately granted by, senior Ngaanyatjarra Law men. After the government took over the Mission in the 1970s, rundown infrastructure needed replacing; however, decisions regarding construction were not negotiated with traditional owners. In 1975, a new 'hospital' was to be built in Warburton, once again, on the *marlu tjina* 'kangaroo' dreaming track (mentioned in Chapter 3), giving rise to the fear that the site would be damaged by trench-digging. Ngaanyatjarra elders were outraged and a 'rampage of destruction' ensued (Douglas, 1978). In response, the construction company, Cooper and Oxley, departed. In May 1975, the *West Australian* newspaper reported 'Mass Spearings Feared at Warburton'. Warburton men responded by enlisting Hackett to act as scribe for a Letter to the Editor.[36] A paraphrased excerpt follows:

> *May 1975*
> Not upset nor want to fight. Didn't chase Cooper and Oxley away with spears. Had meeting and asked them to leave. Older men complained about digging up the sacred site, so we sent them away. We won't start more trouble.[37]

The disturbance led to the withdrawal of nursing staff and the school principal and non-Aboriginal teachers were transferred to other schools. Murray Wells remained at Warburton and, along with three Aboriginal teaching assistants, kept the bilingual programme going. Elders asserted political agency by sending a petition to the director of primary education in Western Australia. From a cultural perspective, this event foreshadows the decreasing capacity of the Ngaanyatjarra to assert socio-spatial control – a point returned to in Chapter 6.

The next major event to engender 'letters of advocacy' related to the outstation movement. 'Homeland time' was propelled by the strongly held desire to return to the country, and the Ngaanyatjarra took full advantage of the resources offered by the newly elected Whitlam Labor government. Letters, dictated to Glass or Hackett in Ngaanyatjarra by senior leaders, were sent to officials in DAA and AAPA requesting assistance, mostly requests for trucks, Land Rovers, bores or money. Once again, the depth of feeling for, and relatedness to, country is conveyed in the letters. As the following translated excerpts indicate:

November 1973
...We are asking to stay in our own country...

July 1974
...I want a bore at Jameson my own country. Have become an old man at Warburton...

September 1974
...Please come to see my home at Patjarr. Bring lots of landrovers...

May 1975
...This story is about my country. Aborigines and white men have been getting stone from my country. A bore needs to be put down...

In these instances, older people utilised letter-writing as a collective social practice. Most were unable to write independently, so Glass and Hackett acted as scribes. Glass recalls one old man wanting her to write a letter to an official, but he had no idea what writing letters was about, nor what he should put, and told her: 'just tell him my name'. The scribed letters captured the essence of the oral intent, and salutations and other features of the written genre were added. Once non-Aboriginal community advisors were appointed to assist in managing the new outstations, letters were sent by the community exhorting them to 'come quickly'. In one instance, Harold and two other men dictated a letter advocating the need for funds to help build a direct road from Warburton to Giles Weather Station near the newly established outstation at Warakurna. Families recall making the road without assistance, and progress updates were documented in the *Warburton News*, mentioned earlier.

Importantly, the letters discussed here were instrumental in achieving results, as indicated by the existence of the requested communities and roads today. In the space of less than 50 years, the Ngaanyatjarra (even those with minimal individual literacy competence) had embraced literate strategies. Moreover, they recognised the power of the written word in this highly charged ideological environment. As I discuss next, the Ngaanyatjarra continued to utilise oral and literate strategies that would transform their quality of life.

Literacy and Leadership

The 1970s mandated unprecedented Aboriginal participation in national political arenas. By the 1980s, even Aboriginal people in remote Australia were thrust into new forms of engagement with people and institutions beyond their community, and this led to 'an expansion of the forms of community with which Aboriginal people felt they could identify' (Myers, 2010: 112). Ngaanyatjarra leaders took up the challenge, locally and nationally, with the establishment of the Ngaanyatjarra Council, the Shire of Ngaanyatjarraku and, after 1989, self-representation through ATSIC – the new national Indigenous governance mechanism.

Jim was an ATSIC Regional Councillor for six years, from 1990 to 1996

I been away in that ATSIC time, meetings... working for education, adult education and all. That time I can see what's limiting that education. Some of our young kids, you know, late 1980s and 1990s, kids wasn't learning properly, can't speak good English. They can go back home and can talk language really good, but when it comes to talking English and writing, they can't even write their own name properly.

Education has remained important to Jim, and he has passed this ethos down to his two sons.

At home I would read, read like when my sons was little. And I used to tell them to go to school every day and they went to school every day. Then they went away to high school.

Jim sees that his sons need to be strong in the Law and learn leadership skills. His first son, Clarrie, was born in 1979.

Sometimes I take Clarrie to Council meeting so he can listen and learn so he can be [leader] next time. When all these people here all pass on young people got to take over and run the Council, talk for the people. They got to learn to talk up in public – what they call it? Public speaking.

Jim still lives in Warburton with his wife, two sons and grandchildren.

George reflects on this period with great eloquence. While acknowledging the difficulty of having been sent away for schooling, he considers that the experience empowered his cohort to be at the 'frontline', ready to take on the leadership challenges of the time:

> I think it was bad some way… but to look back now, I went away to learn something, so I got little bit both feelings… But if I didn't been send away I wouldn't be here now… Most of us my age, our parents worked with the missionaries, looking after the sheep, building the old house, getting the wood. We had to go out and train, work experience, mix up with the whitefellas, working together, then coming back home and doing it yourself… When we came back, we was all ready, those who been in Fairhaven, Pedlar's, we was ready because in that 1970s, that's when that change, when the government took over… All those who'd been sent away, we was start to be in the frontline, to start setting up the Council, working for Health, everything, getting the Shire and all, worrying about our own Land, for our roads, health, everything… in my time culture was still strong, it was still strong in that time when government took over… mostly I been away white side, whitefella side, then when I came back… I knew it, in my heart but I hadn't been through the Law, so I had to go through first then, learn the Aboriginal way, culture side.

As George points out, leadership in the Western Desert requires more than Anglo-European skills and competencies – it was essential that, as the young men returned, they attained the requisite cultural competencies. Anthropologist Annette Hamilton describes how, in the eastern Western Desert, if men evaded the manhood-making ceremonies by going away to work, even if they had grown to full adulthood, these uninitiated men would be considered children by older men (Hamilton, 1979: 185). Lee Sackett concurs (Sackett, 1977. 90) – to ignore or avoid the Law Business is, he states, socially isolating, as such an individual remains 'but a boy – incapable of having a voice in decision-making processes' in the eyes of the *watiya* (initiated men).

Rather than being weakened or fragmented by the assimilation era, some Ngaanyatjarra took advantage of the experience and strategically armed themselves with knowledge and skills that were to prove essential in the 1970s policy environment. George, Clem and Patricia, who had been away in the Goldfields, returned to Warburton with literate behaviours, as well as fluency and a broad lexical range in oral and written English. Contiguously, however, they were no longer fluent Ngaanyatjarra speakers. It was during the 1980s and 1990s, through participation in literacy lessons and assisting with Bible translations, that they regained oral fluency in Ngaanyatjarra. In addition, exegesis of Biblical passages for translation provided an intellectual framework for the analysis and discussion of written text that honed their discursive skills. Many in this cohort consolidated skills during the so-called Christian 'Crusades' that came to fruition in the emerging leadership arenas in the Ngaanyatjarra Council and the Shire of Ngaanyatjarraku.

Two narratives, in particular, exemplify the profound sociocultural and linguistic shifts taking place among the young adult generation at this time. I turn now to George and Clem, whose narratives depict the story of change in this era.

George returned to Warburton in 1973

I did learning to read the language… used to come round, sit down and read books… learning to read language then… from 1974 to 1976. It was hard for me because in language and I finding it a bit hard to make the sound. So Mr Howell, Miss Glass and Miss Hackett, they help me get all the sound right first… I didn't get any certificate, I just learning how to read.

He persevered, until his competence in Ngaanyatjarra literacy matched his English.

By the early 1980s when they translating the Bible I was one of the first to read that in the church… Reading Bible and looking after the church side here… Sometime I travel to other community tell the Good News.

In the 1980s, George developed his leadership skills.

I was living in Cosmo then… with my wife, we was newly married, we shift that way, with her family… I been working there training to be a manager, looking after Cosmo… DAA from Kalgoorlie, they was learning us… we used to go for course in Kalgoorlie with people from Coonana, Cundelee, Warburton… I came back to Warburton from Cosmo… After we left, Cosmo Newbery was finished, nobody lived there, finished… That's when I start get on the Council talking for land rights now, that's when we got the 99 year lease.

That's when I start travelling to Canberra, go to workshop with other Aboriginal people all over Australia, talking for land rights… Across the border in South Australia they been get their freehold, Northern Territory, and we trying to do the same. And that's when I got involved. Doing the talking… I go down to Perth, meeting, talk to the Minister… Also during that time I used to work for State Working Party, for petrol sniffing, work for AAPA in Perth… We did some books in Ngaanyatjarra language for young kids. That's when we used to have a lot of this one here [makes the hand-sign for petrol sniffing] too many young people passed away. And also drinking, people used to cart the drink every day. Till they made the by-laws… made it safe for the old people to live in peace… before that by-law it was really worse, people used to fight every night, kids had no sleep, somewhere around 1983, 1984, 1985.

George began working toward the establishment of the Shire of Ngaanyatjarraku.

I was really happy back home, still we had problems. Like when I got on the Council, all our roads never been done, even this one going up to Laverton. So Council decide to put some member from Council to go on the Shire, Wiluna Shire. That's when my uncle, he was the first one [to be elected on to Wiluna Shire]…

I was a member of the Executive of Ngaanyatjarra Council, that's when I got into Shire Council there on Wiluna side. Now I'm the longest Councillor still on Shire of Ngaanyatjarraku, longer than anybody else. Work is mainly roads, money for roads, budget, get letters from communities or other department letting us know they are coming to visit. Sometimes we have the local government Minister come out here. Minutes get sent to the office, get them. Read all the report from the staff who work for the Shire, their report we read. People elect me as a Chairman for Ngaanyatjarra Council, 1995 I think…

We was still a bit worried and people needed a strong bloke to work, lead the Council. Chairman from '95 to '99, four years. Before I became a Chairman I used to help Ngaanyatjarra Council… We said that the government gonna get hard when we get older, got to have some extra money so gonna start saving up so we start a Saving Plan.

All those things what I do I don't get paid. I been doing it for a long time. I do it for my land and for my people so we can live in a good place... To make things good to live in the community so people can be happy... I like to help people and make me feel good when I help somebody, people, like talking for the Shire to come up here... And with the Council, a lot of things I did with the Council. I feel really happy inside. And for young people too. *Yuwa.*

Clem also returned to Warburton in the 1970s

Well, I always speak English at that time. English was my main language I could hear because I went to school from Laverton onwards living with people who always speak English all the time, so I became English-speaking young man. So I came back Warburton, got married... I had to get to know who my families were. The brothers and sisters that I left behind and all the children I grew up with, see what they were doing... So it took me about... four years to speak my own language... I had to learn about hunting, learn how to hunt, learn how to live co-operative way and all that. Become an Aboriginal!

After all that knowledge I was getting in school I came back here and I seen most of the Aboriginals weren't given privilege to lean towards this Western way... I felt that I should do that work for my Aboriginal people... That money was there for Aboriginal people to help Aboriginal people, but it was the white people who helping Aboriginal all the time... Aboriginal people came in from the bush lived with the missionaries, then the missionaries finished and Native Welfare took it on. When Native Welfare finished, DAA was doing the thing. We were still having white people to help us and I thought during that time, I was saying Aboriginal people should be taught the ways of the Western world and so they can, with this knowledge they have, that trainings they have, they can run their own affairs... we came back from Wongutha Farm, from the highschools, ladies was sent to Fairhaven and we all came back to Warburton.

Ngaanyatjarra Council was just the starting point for us to be more independent, running things self... old people looked upon me to be an interpreter because I speak English because I know how to read and write. I started being a main figure in Docker River. I went there in 1970 just because we had more money. Once Australia changed for stockmen we can't get paid well, so we all went to South Australia and Northern Territory because we was getting more money than for working than in Warburton, Laverton, Leonora, all that. In Docker I was supervisor and I was appointed to be a Chairman of the community council.

The Christian 'Crusades'

A nascent Christian leadership had been nurtured by the UAM in the 1960s. By the 1970s, however, the declining influence of the Mission, coupled with the strain of community life and the detrimental effect of alcohol, contributed to an atmosphere that was open to outside influences. In the 1980s, an evangelical fervour spread like wildfire across the desert and an Aboriginal Christian leadership emerged (Blacket, 1997; Bos, 1988; Sackett, 1977; Stanton, 1988; Tonkinson, 1988). Ignited in 1981 by two visits from a Christian evangelical group from Elcho Island – an Aboriginal community in the far north of the Northern Territory, it catalysed a wave of Christian activity, and Ngaanyatjarra agency and leadership, known locally as the 'Christian Crusades'.

The 'Crusades' were a new form of Christian activity that ultimately led to the growth of a secular, political leadership. As McLean notes:

A lot of people made a decision that instead of getting bogged down in drinking and everything else they just moved out of that and went forward... It gave people experience of actually having a significant leadership role in a whole new paradigm.[38]

Hundreds of Aboriginal people participated in Christian meetings in Warburton, Laverton, Wiluna, Jigalong and beyond, with thousands gathering at meetings in Mt Margaret, Kalgoorlie and Perth. In 1982, the *West Australian* newspaper reported that 'purpose and calm have replaced violence and terror' at Warburton and this has happened 'entirely in the absence of white influence'.[39]

Glass and Hackett suggest that the genesis of the 'Crusades' leadership group can be sourced to the formation of skills at GBTI. Clem reflects on his own experience:

In 1971 I went to Bible College... Gnowangerup [GBTI] for two years. I was doing English... I was working differently on the spiritual side... They was training the Aboriginal to go back to learn about the Bible, teach them in a spiritual way. Reading, memorising, understanding. Interpret, talk about it and discuss it... we used to do our own writing, we got to learn like at the school... We gotta do that to write your own sermon down.

At GBTI, students acquired the 'habitus' – the oral, literate and social practices of Christian leadership – and replicated these modes during the Crusades. As Clem illustrates, once more:

> Well, Crusade was a time that's when you have to speak to people then. Make a speech, preaching, but you got to choose a right word to speak and all that. It was the Lord I was talking about, it was the Holy Spirit living. And full Aboriginal people going out to Mt Margaret, Leonora, all that. They were my brothers... and the music was electric guitars. We didn't know nothing about it so we just went along and we taught each other as we went right around to Perth, Geraldton. A lot of leadership, that time. I tell them the first thing we do is we got to be clean, bit different to the Aboriginal people today, we got to be, living like white way. But I wasn't thinking like a whitefella I was thinking about a missionary, who taught us to wash and be clean, at Gnowangerup you learn about that. You learn, you got to wash the floor, mop the floor, you got to polish the floor, make the beds. Wear neckties and shave. They teach you how to live, dress up properly and all that. I took that on... Wherever we went a lot of Aboriginal people joined up with us from Leonora, Kalgoorlie, Norseman.

Ultimately, the Crusades enabled the development of an Aboriginal leadership of sufficient strength to lead people out of the low ebb of the 1980s, described in Chapter 4. Importantly, the emergent leadership group was not imposed by an outside authority, nor did they challenge traditional authority structures. Younger men had always been excluded from positions of real power within the Law; however, this generation of young men – armed with Western knowledge, combined with adherence to traditional Law – formed a new power base. The approval of senior Law leaders, and their participation in evangelical meetings, diminished some of the residual conflict between Christianity and traditional religion. This was integral to the success of the young leaders and enabled them to speak with authority about certain issues. In sum, the nascent 'political' leadership group was not a challenge to the senior Law men, but a sanctioned requirement of the times, and their support enabled the agentive participation of young leaders in the secular political domain.[40]

Ngaanyatjarra Council

On 24 June 1980, a meeting was held at Warburton to form a Ngaanyatjarra-specific representative body. The five original member communities were Warburton, Warakurna, Blackstone, Jameson and

Wingellina. As a regional representative body, Ngaanyatjarra Council has effectively represented the now-11 communities for over 25 years. Like their Pitjantjatjara kin in South Australia, Ngaanyatjarra traditional owners sought inalienable freehold title over their land. In 1982, the Ngaanyatjarra Council organised a Land Rights convoy to Perth to present their views to the West Australian government. This consolidated a growing sense of united solidarity and political influence. The Ngaanyatjarra Council participated in the Seaman Inquiry into land rights for West Australian Aborigines, however, land rights' legislation was defeated in state parliament in 1984 (Fletcher, 1992). In November 1988, the Ngaanyatjarra people accepted 99-year leases. Maureen Tehan, legal advisor to the Pitjantjatjara Council and Ngaanyatjarra Council for a decade from 1984, suggests that this was a 'big thing', as they were the only Aboriginal group in Western Australia to gain 99-year leases.[41] Significantly, the Council had also implemented strategies to curtail the ravaging impact of alcohol and substance abuse. The passing of the *Aboriginal Communities Act 1979* (WA) allowed them to create bylaws (gazetted in July 1989) that resulted in a form of law and order on the Ngaanyatjarra Lands that has been critical to the success of the region (Staples & Cane, 2002: 21). Then, on 29 June 2005, Ngaanyatjarra Council gained a historic Native Title Determination – the largest in Australia – reached through negotiation, not litigation.[42]

Shire of Ngaanyatjarraku

Prior to 1984, the Ngaanyatjarra region was within the extensive Shire of Wiluna. However, at that time, local government systems monopolised resources in the western sector of the Shire. Furthermore, *because* they were not rate-paying property owners, the entire Ngaanyatjarra constituency in the eastern zone of the Shire was effectively disenfranchised (Fletcher, 1992: 1). Accordingly, municipal services, especially roads, were severely neglected in the Ngaanyatjarra region. In 1984, the *Local Government Act* was amended, giving the majority Aboriginal composition of the Shire the capacity to vote. At the time, Ngaanyatjarra voters had minimal experience of the electoral processes of liberal democracy. Nevertheless, in 1985, with a large voter turnout, the first Ngaanyatjarra representative on the Shire of Wiluna Council was elected, and this was a 'big event, a big victory'.[43] Following this success, and aware of the non-compulsory voting requirement in local government elections, the Ngaanyatjarra tactically used an electoral education campaign to increase voter participation. An Aboriginal majority was reached in the 1987 Wiluna Shire election: voting in two Ngaanyatjarra men and one Aboriginal representative from Wiluna (Fletcher, 1992).

By 1986, political recalcitrance, on the part of the minority non-Aboriginal Shire Councillors, made the Shire unworkable. At one meeting, the Aboriginal Councillors withdrew, the quorum was lost and a government commissioner was appointed to administer the Wiluna Shire. The next logical step was for the Ngaanyatjarra to create their local government area. A petition, signed by Ngaanyatjarra representatives, seeking to draw up new boundaries was sent to the state Minister for local government. In 1993, the first local government election for the new Shire of Ngaanyatjarraku was held, and eight Ngaanyatjarra Councillors were elected, unopposed.[44] The formation of the Shire of Ngaanyatjarraku symbolises the determination of Ngaanyatjarra people to have agency over local governance and service delivery. Most importantly, literate strategies were implemented to achieve political goals. A significant strategy was the 'petition' that, in effect, encoded their claim for real political representation within mainstream processes. By petitioning the Minister, the Ngaanyatjarra were fully aware that they were exploiting their relatively recently acquired rights as citizens. Tehan suggests that the creation of the Shire comprised 'highly sophisticated political moves', and Ngaanyatjarra leaders, like George, Joshua and others, understood these strategies and utilised them effectively.

Oral speech styles and the written register

As described thus far, the 1970s and 1980s significantly altered the nature of Ngaanyatjarra sociality. As Ngaanyatjarra people's sociocultural experiences broadened, an expanded range of rhetorical styles, speech events and a new performativity emerged. This led to new 'sociocultural dispositions' (Ochs, 1990: 292) and a shift in the manner in which traditional speech styles and registers were deployed. Here, I describe how new forms of social interaction influenced communicative practices.

During the Christian Crusades of the 1980s, large meetings were organised by *yarnangu*. This was a new type of speech event – one that engendered a new mode of public performance, where individuals were required to overcome their sociocultural propensity to *kurnta* (shame) in front of strangers and hone their rhetorical skills. Clem identifies how he assisted preachers in acquiring the evangelical mode of sermon preparation and performance:

I picked out a few people who I thought were like leaders and I taught them how to preach, taught them how speak, taught them how to make movements and look at people… How you dress… yeah I taught them all about it… I wrote sermons myself. And I told them if you fellas speak, you got to speak what you read from the Bible. Some of them, in my team they all went to Gnowerangup, then when that was finished they went to Perth.

Through participating in new monologic performance genres, like 'the sermon', this generation of young leaders acquired a repertoire of Western-style communicative practices that would prepare them for the new secular political arena they were to encounter.

In Western Desert society, emotions such as compassion (*ngarltu*) and shame (*kurnta*) 'constrain' the way in which social action is organised (Myers, 1986: 125). The term *kurnta*, glossed here as shame, shyness and respect, is manifest in a tendency to avoid focusing on the individual person and a reluctance to stand out or step forward in the company of strangers. Accordingly, strangers or visitors to a camp or community experience a certain degree of discomfort, or *kurnta*, and hover on the edges of social space, awaiting an invitation to enter. Introduced speech events, such as large gatherings or 'the meeting', ushered in a new rhetorical context, in which the Ngaanyatjarra had to learn how to employ 'straight talking' strategies that, at first, may have been a 'shock' or a linguistic transgression of the boundaries of normative social interaction. In the old days, *tjitirrpa watjalku* (indirect speech) was the preferred norm, as direct speech could be interpreted as a challenge – a risky rhetorical form in this kind of society. Direct speech – *tjukarurru watjalku* – is employed in situations requiring 'straight talking'. People frequently refer to 'straight talking' with an expectation that the talk will result in promises that will not be broken. Whereas indirect speech – *tjitirrpa(pa) watjalku* or *kiti-kiti watjalku* (speaking to the side) – employs subtle, highly metaphorical features and is typically used to deal with conflict in public. It is also deployed when individuals who stand in a constrained relationship need to communicate with one another and do so obliquely – *tjarlpa watjalku* – by speaking indirectly. In this constrained context, advice may be given in a polite manner, and the speech event incorporates morphological and lexical features, such as: the politeness suffix *-munta*, the particle *tjinguru* (maybe or perhaps) expressing uncertainty or even possibility, and the future tense form of the verb (e.g. *kulilku*), rather than the command form (e.g. *kulila*).

Still today, community meetings range across the oral-literate continuum, and communicative interactions between Ngaanyatjarra and European interlocutors may result in what Liberman terms 'strange discourse', full of ambiguity and imprecise understandings (Liberman, 1985: 176–178). Accordingly, cultural issues may override Western meeting procedure, and, if unresolved, family disputes may spark unexpected outbursts and pleas for compassion. In this highly charged rhetorical context, a skilled orator needs to utilise *tjitirrpa watjalku* (indirect speech) to defuse simmering tensions.

Distinctive features of Ngaanyatjarra speech style and register are evident, also, in the incipient literacy practices of the Ngaanyatjarra, as is the encoding of cultural meaning. It can be posited that some texts in the written register came to embody a form of communication that straddled the boundary between orality and literacy. In the following communicative event, textual, rather than oral, conventions are utilised, not for an audience of known kin, but for *malikitja* or 'strangers'. In a letter (see Figure 5.4a and 5.4b), dictated in Ngaanyatjarra, translated into English and sent to the Minister for Aboriginal Affairs in 1973, a request is made for services to support a new outstation. The recipient is unknown – a stranger. Thus, the relationship between interlocutors elicits the indirect register, indicating the respect and politeness typical of utterances with persons where social distance is required. This is represented by the use of specific politeness markers – the future tense verb ending *-ku*, the politeness suffix *-munta* and the particle *tjinguru* (maybe or perhaps):

Wanytjawara-munta tjunku ngurra?
When will you put homes?

Kalatju purtulatju tjapilku tjinguru.
Perhaps we will ask in vain.

Revealed, also, is the encoding of cultural meaning: the connection to country, the expression of *ngarltu* (compassion) and an emphasis on *miranykanyilku* (looking after people).

Literate Identities

For some Ngaanyatjarra, literacy has been a symbolic and real factor in the formation of new social identities, in a time of profound sociocultural change. New forms of Ngaanyatjarra personhood have been constructed around specific events located in time and place, as well as social relatedness associated with key individuals like Glass, Hackett and Howell. Certain experiences have shaped the roles that some Ngaanyatjarra have assumed. Throughout this volume, attention has been drawn to literates like Arthur, Una, April, Patricia, Jim, George, Clem and others; all of whom have taken on the role of scribes, readers, orators and interpreters on behalf of the collective. Their new embodied literate identities evolved out of the social and cultural forms they encountered and the practices of the Western world they engaged in. In some cases, they observed and acquired literate behaviours

Warburton Ranges,
P.M.B. Kalgoorlie 6431
November 19th 1973

Senator Cavanagh
Dept of Aboriginal Affairs,
P.O. Box 241,
Civic Square A.C.T. 2608

Dear Sir,
I want to talk about Blackstone. When will you put houses
and make it a place for all the pensioners to stay at the Settlement
of Blackstone?
We are waiting for George Bialobrodsky to put a bore down there.
Perhaps George will be able to do that before Christmas after he
has finished around Warburton.
Perhaps we will ask in vain. We are wanting to stay in our
own country. You say the word and quickly s end a house from Canberra
maybe. Perhaps the Government will help me and give me a Landrover
so that we can stay in our own country. We are waiting for a bore.
When a bore is put down we will go and live at Blackstone. Jackie
Forbes, Fred Forbes, Jimmy Benson, Yiwinti Smith, Dinny Smith,
Norman Lyons, Barry Bill and Mr Duncan. These are the ones who
always stayed at Blackstone.
Perhaps after Christmas you will send a caravan with medicine
to Blackstone for the children. For the children first of all send
a caravan and food for white women so that a sister can stay there
with her own food. And she will look after the children and give
them needles when they become sick.
We would like you to send a big truck to take the pensioners'
food from Warburton to Blackstone. And to send a caravan and a sister
to look after the children at Blackstone.
We have sent this to Mr Caranagh so that you can see about
Blackstone from Canberra. And so that you seeing from Canberra can
say.
We want to live at Blackstone in our own country. After we
have stayed here for a while and eaten Christmas we would like to
go to Blackstone.
First perhaps you will send a caravan and two sisters to
Blackstone to look after the children. Two sisters and their own
stores so that they can stay there all the time even over the
weekend.
First of all send a caravan and two sisters with food so
that they can stay there and give medicine to any sick people while
they are at Blackstone. And the two sisters at Blackstone can
send a radio message to Warburton to the Council and they will come
and get the sick person and take them to hospital at Warburton.
And when they are better take them back to Blackstone. When a child
becomes sick perhaps the mother and father also can be brought to
Warburton to be near the children and then taken back to Blackstone.
It would be good for two sisters to live at Blackstone and
give medicine and look after the sick.
Look for two sisters and when you can get them, send them to
Blackstone to give medicine to the children and men at Blackstone,
to live at Blackstone in a caravan and look after the sick.
When you are ready to send a house, send two sisters first
with a caravan and medicine to live at Blackstone.

Yours sincerely

Dinny Smith.

Figure 5.4a Letter sent to Department of Aboriginal Affairs, 1973. Collection held by
Amee Glass and Dorothy Hackett (English).

Warburten Ranges,
P.M.B. Kalgoorlie 6431
November 19th 1973

Senator Cavanagh,
Dept of Aboriginal Affairs,
P.O. Box 241,
Civic Square A.C.T. 2608

Blacksonekurna wangkakitja. Wanytjawara-munta tjunku ngurra.
Palunyatjanu tawunpa tjunku wati mapitjatjakuya Pensioners
pirninya nyinatjaku tawunta Blackstoneta?
        Kalatju kuwarripa waitumara puurumaratjaku kapi nganalu
Georgetju. Tjinguru before Christmas puurumalku Georgeulu
Warburtonta ngarnmanytju wiyaralpi.
        Kalatju purtulatju tjapilku tjinguru. Palunyatjanu
ngurrangkalatju nyinakitja mukurringkula. Watjala warrpungkulalpi
wiyala Canberralanguru tjinguru tawunpa. Tjingurutju kapamantu
helpumanuma ngankuku Landrover nintilku ngurrangka nyinatjaku.
Puukuletju nyakula. Puurumalku nyangka puungkalatju nyinaku
ngarnmanytju Blackstoneta. Jackie Forbes, Fred Forbes, Jimmy Benson,
Yiwinti Smith, Dinny Smith, Norman Lyons, Barry Hill, Mr Duncan.
Palunyanyaya Blackstonetat nykmapayi.
        Caravanpa tjinguru wiyalku medicinetjarra tjilku pirniku
after Christmas Blackstoneku. Tjitji pirniku Blackstoneku
caravanpa ngarnmanytju wiyalku mirrka mitjitjiku caravanpa
tjunkunyangka sister nyinatjaku storestjarra nyinatjaku mirrkatjarra
nyinatjaku. Kayi miranykanyinma pikarringkunyangka tjilturrunama.
Palunyangka tjitji pikarringkunyangka.
        Mukurringanyilatju mutuka purlkanya wiyaltjaku pensioner
pirniku mirrka katitjaku Warburtontanguru Partininytjarraku.
Kan caravanpa ngalyawiyalku sisterkamu tjitji miranykanyiltjaku
Blackstonetanguru.
        Mr Cavanaghlakutulatju wiyarnu nyuntulun nyakutjaku
Blackstone nga nyakutjaku nyuntulun Canberralanguru nyakulan w
watjaltjaku.
        Mukurringanyilatju Blackstoneta nyinakitja ngurra
yungarrangkalatju. Christmaspalatju nyinarra kuwarripa nyakula
ngalkulalatju Blackstoneku mapitjakitja.
        Ngarnmanytju caravanpa wiyalku sister kutjarra wiyalku
Blackstoneku nyinatjaku miranykanyiltjaku sister kutjarra puru
mirrka storestjarra nyinatjaku tjarntutjarra matron kutjarraku#
pulampa weekendpa nyinatjaku tirtu.
        Ngarnmanytju caravanpa ngalyawiyalku sister kutjarra
mirrkamarntu stores sister kutjarraku nyinatjaku, medicinepa
pikatjarra pirniku nintiltjaku blackstoneta nyinarranytjalu.
Ka sister kutjarralu Blackstoneta nyinarranytjalu Warburten ku
telephone ngalyawiyanma councilku ka kukurrakiku mantjira katiku
hospitalku Warburton Rangesku. Nyangka walykumunurringkunyangka
marlakulu makatiku Blackstoneku. Tjitji tjinguru pikarriku mama
ngunytjurtarra katiku hospitalku Warburtonta kanyilku makatiku
Blackstoneku.
        Sister kutjarralu ngula palya nyinaku Blackstoneta medicinepa
nintilku kanyilku miranykanyinma.
        Manyawa sister kutjarra mantjiralpi ngalyawiyala Blackstoneku,
Blackstoneta miranykanyiltjaku medicinepa nintiltjaku tjitji pirniku
wati pirniku Blackstoneta nyinarranytjalu, Blackstoneta nyinatjaku
caravantjarra nyinatjaku miranykahyiltjaku.
        ready tawunpa wiyalkitjalu sister kutjarra ngarnmanypa
ngalyawiyala caravantjarra medicinetjarra pitjala nyinatjaku
Blackseene ta.

Figure 5.4b Letter sent to Department of Aboriginal Affairs, 1973. Collection held by
Amee Glass and Dorothy Hackett (Ngaayatjarra).

from the previous generation; for others, they were the first in their family to become literate. I turn now to David and Silas, whose identities, roles and status in this speech community are inextricably linked to literacy.

David

David reads and, to a lesser extent, writes, predominantly in Ngaanyatjarra. He had minimal schooling: 'never did get *ninti purlka* (really knowledgeable) at the mission, not really, not me, left school at Grade 3'. As he says:

> I don't read the newspaper in English, only in Ngaanyatjarra I read... because I never went right through in the school.

David was one of the three men who attended the 1974 SIL workshop in Darwin, when the so-called Ngaanyatjarra 'literary movement' began. He has since contributed to Bible translation work, assisted in dictionary compilation and taught Ngaanyatjarra language to non-Aboriginal staff. In addition, David has authored collections of unpublished and published traditional stories (Glass & Newberry, [1979] 1990). David has the authority to communicate events and concerns using written, rather than oral, strategies. He weaves orality and cultural meanings into a writing style that is not separate from social circumstance as an autonomous process, but overtly tied to social relatedness.

David is the sole writer of the second corpus of letters shown in Table 5.2. Missives intended for a local audience are written or dictated in Ngaanyatjarra, whereas official letters intended for an English-speaking audience are mediated with a scribe. David reflects on his overtly literate practice: 'I'm the only one who does that. I think about what I want to say and I can explain it better writing than saying those words'.

David's writing reveals the influence of the oral tradition, with texts written predominantly in a style of speaking, inclusive of features that mirror Ngaanyatjarra speech styles and narrative discourse structure.[45] In a series of letters – dictated in English and scribed by a non-Aboriginal friend – David employs circumlocution to indirectly embed requests for work, money or cars, within oral 'travelling narrative' schemata (mentioned in Chapter 1). Glass (1980: 60–69) suggests that such 'journey' schemas in Ngaanyatjarra are typically organised around a 'departure phase', a 'transit phase' and an 'arrival phase', with each phase encoded and elaborated in predictable patterns of grammatical and lexical cohesion. David exploits the distance and indirectness of written language in this sequence of letters that

Table 5.2 Letters – Corpus B

Sender	Audience	No.	Content
David in Darwin, 1974	Amee Glass	1	Personal news
David in Warburton, 1975	Senator Cavanagh	1	Request for bore, truck and money for outstation
David	Pitjantjatjara Council	1	Claim for money, re: deceased relative
David	Ngaanyatjarra Community	1	Narrative history of Ngaanyatjarra Council
David	Community Advisor	1	Concern for petrol sniffers
David	ATSIC and Community Advisor	1	Letter, including work history and request for vehicle to do work
David's wife	Community Advisor	1	Work history and request for loan
David	Community Advisor	1	Support for wife's request and own request for work
David	Community Advisor	1	Request for vehicle to do work
David	Editor, Ngaanyatjarra News June 1998	1	Open letter, including work history and request for vehicle to do work
David	Notice to all staff, Warburton	1	Plea for respectful road use during Law Business
David	Lawyer	1	Compassion, re: son's circumstances in prison
David	Lawyer	1	Compassion, re: son's arrest
David	Police statement	1	Written statement, re: events around card game
David	Police	1	Request for return of gun and licence
David	General audience	3	Narrative histories, including requests for vehicles/money

travel through the journey schema by building upon what has come before, repeating what has already been said and recounting scenes from his working life, before arriving at his climax: the *indirect request*. In an early letter, he writes:

> This is what I'm writing about. To let you know that if you are getting a truck for that side, for the work, then this is what I'm thinking about. I can't be taking a load of people around in the back of the truck and telling them what to do. One work truck not enough. You should get a second hand Toyota for the supervisor so he can run around and check up on the work, giving advice. I'll be giving out different jobs to each people and they'll be getting busy on all those jobs. So, whoever doesn't work, then I'll know about it, and I can put their right hours. It won't be only one job, they'll get wood and chop it, and they'll go and get the sand for the garden and put it around the house, and get the rubbish and take it to the dump. So I'll be busy running around and that's what I'm asking for a second hand Toyota, to do that running round. Every night I've been thinking about that. Wouldn't be my Toyota, would be for the CDEP work.

Features of the traditional speech style – *yaarlpirri*, the early morning style of public rhetoric or oratory, mentioned in Chapter 2 – are also evident in the use of utterances which have the character of formal announcements. According to Liberman (1985: 4), *yaarlpirri* is a more formal version of ordinary discourse – an interactional system where comments are addressed to all persons present, the content is objectified and the public nature of the discourse minimises personal interests, as evident above. More letters and requests ensue; here, David uses recapitulation, or serial development of the topic, as a rhetorical device. When David's request is still not fulfilled, he writes a further letter to the community advisor:

> One more thing I want to tell you, if I'm still waiting for the truck... Another thing's in my mind too. You know those cars like you got for the office and like Tjirrkarli got for CDEP, I should run around checking the name with those sort of *yurltju* [sic] when they are working with the tip truck. It wont [sic] be easy when they are working. I'll make them work hard too. All kinds of jobs I'll be giving out. They'll be busy. I'll make it easy for you, you'll be in the office and I'll be looking after everything outside and they won't bother you. That's why it will be easy for you. That's why I went back on the CDEP so I can work hard

on this job. If I do get this job as foreman that means you can put me on the salary because I'll be working hard on this job.

In another instance, David is angered by staff insensitivity to rules concerning driving on roads during the Law Business, and he writes an open letter to all staff. For David, the situation is sufficiently extreme to warrant a public exhortation, written in English, aimed specifically at a non-Aboriginal audience. The text encodes features of the hortatory speech genre (Glass, 1980) – the admonitory mode often utilised in *yaarlpirri*. Hortatory texts are those that persuade, condemn, praise or complain (Goddard, 1990). In Ngaanyatjarra social interaction, direct criticisms are rare, and people strive not to embarrass each other in public; moreover, indirectness, congeniality and tolerance of aberrant behaviour are aspired to. Although the text admonishes inappropriate behaviour around Business time, it is also embedded with ambiguity and congeniality. Additionally, the grievance is addressed in public, rather than directed at individuals when it is later published in the local newsletter – the *Ngaanyatjarra News* – functioning, in this case, as 'publicly available discourse' (Liberman, 1985: 4).[46]

Another genre in David's repertoire is the 'legal statement', inclusive of letters to lawyers and police statements. David says he writes statements because he has a short memory: 'I might lose all the words what I was saying before, that's why I got to write it down before the police come and ask me all the questions'. In one example, the opening statement declares: 'This is what really happened'. His written recount acts as a mnemonic, reminiscent of Clanchy's (1979) account of the shift to trusting writing over the truth of the spoken word in 12th-century England. In this case, the paper acts as David's 'witness', indicating that he now considers written, rather than oral, communication to be more reliable, as he explains:

Just for the whitefella to think if I'm telling liar. I got to make sure on the paper, sort of witness, you know… just my witness so the police can find out, come and ask me and I'll say, in this letter, I'll just write it down so he can prove it, that was my writing and my story, so they can know, the police, they might come and ask me if I'm telling liar to them, but they can see this paper… they can prove it on the letter, on the piece of paper.

David's processes also illustrate, to draw on Clanchy once more, the 'shift' from habitually memorising information to writing it down.

Silas

Silas, like his father Horace before him, acts as a cultural broker, by playing a mediating role as a pastor and community leader.

> Sometimes I read newspapers, you know, what's going on in Australia or in the world, what's happening. And I tell my auntie or I tell my people, families in language then. It's very important to read the thing and tell the people in language what's going to happen. Like this problem we have if the money that the government people been giving it to the Aboriginal community and the government people been say that they been wasting a lot of money... And that's why I tell them sort of things to the people who don't understand... about what's happening like the government side... Because without I'm telling them, they don't know what's going on in the world. You know it's too hard and something might happen in Warburton or in the Ngaanyatjarra Land and they might say: "Why didn't people tell us?"

Silas is also a fine public orator and is often called on to deliver speeches at public events. Despite having no formal training, Silas assumed the role of pastor around 1991.

> Before I became a Christian I used to live a bit... outside a church. But I still had that teaching from when I was a kid. To become a pastor I dedicate my life and I made that promise with my Lord and I was accepted by the missionaries as like a pastor then. And I still balance that.

Silas has learned through observation, imitation and participation:

> I used to look at my father [Horace] and I used to look at the missionaries and I used to look at my uncle and I would sometimes ask my father, or ask my uncle which passage he been read... just learn by looking and learning from the way that person conduct that service.

Unlike his father, however, Silas utilises solitary literacy strategies to develop his expertise and has devised his own 'Bible Study' programme:

> I got the book home about how to be a successful pastor. I got that and that help me too, so I can be guided, guided by that doctrine... I got videos about like Jimmy Swaggart and I got video about Billy Graham.

I sit down and watch how they do it and I think: "Ah well, I'll try and preach this subject what this man been preach". But I wouldn't go on his way when he was preaching, but I'll change it... Because if you want to be a preacher, you got to be yourself... like I can't copy... But I can get a, like a feedback. But I can't be like Billy Graham or I can't be like Jimmy Swaggart, you know, I got to be myself.

Silas prepares his service at home: 'I make my preparation by reading my story first hand and I keep it in the section, which one can I read'. His practice includes writing notes (often from a book of prepared sermons) for telegraphic reference when delivering his oral sermon:

Sometime I write and keep it in a... in a column so I wouldn't forget... like a one page, then I look at it and I think, ah well, now I got to say this, I got to say that. So I don't have to, you know, like twist off. It's very important to go on that.

Every Sunday morning, Silas brings his notes to church, carefully organised inside a leather-bound wallet:

When I take the church service, some of my audience... can't hear much about English, so I preach in language too... I never been reading from the Ngaanyatjarra Bible but I been like translating out of my own, from the English Bible, and I translate it... I talk in language... I read, I read the Bible and I do the illustration, illustration by the explanation.

Most Sundays, by the time he arrives – attired in a white shirt, black pants, polished shoes and reading glasses – Clem and the Gospel band are already warming up. The band has been playing since the 1980s Crusades and still sing together at Sunday services and Christian conventions. Their singing attracts a small congregation, mainly older people, who gather on the grass in front of the church; larger gatherings are more common at funerals and Easter or Christmas conventions. People carry with them the English *Good News Bible*, the Ngaanyatjarra *New Testament* or the hymnbook, *Turlku Pirninya*. These publications, worked on over many years with Glass and Hackett, are emblematic as artefacts of spiritual and linguistic significance.

Services typically wend their way through a sermon, prayers and Scripture readings, and the congregation is invited to share a song or a testimonial. The stylised performance mode of Silas (and other preachers) incorporates reiterated formulaic phrases, Christian tropes and paralinguistic elements, such as hand waving during Gospel singing and the laying on of hands. Affective oral testimonies feature and testify to the transformative power of *Mama* God – a feature that can be traced back to the 1980s Crusades, when Christian practice became endowed with an evangelical aspect.

In this diglossic context, Silas deftly shifts between oral and written texts. He also switches register between spoken English, marked as a high speech variety, and his mediated use of Ngaanyatjarra, as 'phatic punctuation' (Kulick, 1992: 147):

> We can look back, we can think back to what happened in Warburton long time ago.
> We extremely conscious today that our lives are rapidly moving along and will soon be over.
> You know it'll soon be over you know, *wiyarriku, wiyarriku...*
>
> Where are we going?
>
> *Wanytjatja?*
> What is our purpose?
> *Nyaapa, nyaapaku palyala?*
> The Bible reminds us that God is gradually drawing us forward to the day when Jesus will return.
> Jesus *marlaku pitjaku.*

Silas announces a Hymn from *Turlku Pirninya*: 'Can we start with Number 22: *Tjiitjalu-rni kanyinma wartangka yitingka*' and continues:

> *Yuwa*, our reading this morning is from Luke Chapter 17. And the song we just sang is, you know, it means about them people who stood long distance and they watched Jesus, they watched Jesus going into the village... Let us pray:

> *Mama* God, you are the supreme God, you are the God from yesterday, today and forever more... And I pray for my people in the Ngaanyatjarra Land. I pray for my people right across this land of Australia... And I pray for the European people. I pray for the people who brought this Gospel out into Australia... and you know we can look back to the precious memories of the missionaries all this and that, at what they done here long time ago.[47]

As a pastor and leader, Silas seeks, as he puts it, to 'look over the horizon and beyond, to further himself beyond the horizon'. When he goes to Christian meetings outside the Ngaanyatjarra Lands, he says that people are surprised that he is Aboriginal. However, he tells them that he is not special; it is just that 'he has no *kurnta*'. Silas, in many ways, incarnates the complexity of contemporary Ngaanyatjarra identity. His oratorical style is inflected with a symbolic fusing of layers of cultural meaning: he compassionately links the mission past with the present and reaches out beyond the local, by 'embedding' Ngaanyatjarra people 'in an imagined larger community of persons' (Myers, 2010: 121), while simultaneously rendering an optimistic future 'imaginary' (Taylor, 2004).

Conclusion

The historical perspective, used in Part 2, brings to the fore the ideological frames that have created the habitus – the normative practices – associated with language and literacy in the Ngaanyatjarra lands today. I have considered how two prevailing ideologies – the Christian commitment to providing the written Word of God to adults in Ngaanyatjarra and the new state narrative of advancement through education in English – impacted on literacy development from the late 1950s to the early 1970s. The technology of reading and writing and the new practice of interpreting the world through written text arose concomitantly with the arrival of Christianity. It was through Scripture that adults were introduced to a deeper understanding of the concepts that accompanied the European vision of the world. As the primary 'textual artefact of literate participation' (Kapitzke, 1995: 54) over many decades, these texts have had a *particular* sociocultural influence. Literacy in the mission was imbued with a social purpose and cultural meaning, rather than advanced as a technical skill that would enhance employability in the labour market economy. This, in turn, has shaped the manner in which people have taken hold of literacy for cultural and political purposes and how they have integrated alphabetic literacy into their existing communicative repertoire. Christianity continues to manifest significant emblematic value, evident in the artefacts and tropes that regularly surface in oral discourse, Gospel songs and hymn composition. Moreover, these early imprints have shaped the concept of literacy still evident today, as discussed in Chapters 1 and 2.

It can be concluded that the mission and the state shared a similar goal in trying to create different types of persons using literacy (c.f. Makihara & Schieffelin, 2007). Yet, as I have shown in this chapter, a perseverant and independent Ngaanyatjarra identity and sense of place in the world was galvanised through the cumulative effect of political successes, where the Ngaanyatjarra used literacy for their own cultural and ideological purposes.

Significantly, during the 1970s and 1980s, it was young adults who were at the forefront of the innovations and changes outlined above. As will be shown in Chapter 7, it is the new youth generation who are, once again, utilising introduced technologies to extend and transform the cultural practices inherited from previous generations. They, in turn, are socialising the next generation.

Notes

(1) Jenny Green (personal communication, September 2010).
(2) *United Aborigines Messenger* (October 1973: 11).
(3) *United Aborigines Messenger* (May 1957: 12).
(4) For accounts of the early use of vernacular literacy in Aboriginal communities, see Edwards (1969, 1999); Ferguson (1987); Gale (1997); (Kral, 2000). For linguistic work on Western Desert dialects, see Trudinger (1943); Douglas (1955, 1964), followed by Glass and Hackett (1970); Glass (1980); Goddard (1983); Hansen and Hansen (1978).
(5) *United Aborigines Messenger* (March 1954: 9).
(6) *United Aborigines Messenger* (March 1954: 9).
(7) *United Aborigines Messenger* (May 1957: 12).
(8) *United Aborigines Messenger* (August 1958: 10).
(9) *United Aborigines Messenger* (August 1958: 10).
(10) *United Aborigines Messenger* (December 1957: 10).
(11) *United Aborigines Messenger* (November 1963: 18–19).
(12) *United Aborigines Messenger* (February 1965: 8); *United Aborigines' Messenger* (February/March 1968: 12–13).
(13) *United Aborigines' Messenger* (August 1968: 13).
(14) *Annual Report Commissioner of Native Welfare* (1957: 12).
(15) WA SRO Acc 1419 EG 23-1, 19 December 1956 – From DO-C McLarty to CNW, re: arguing against UAM teaching vernacular at Warburton Ranges.
(16) *United Aborigines Messenger* (March 1954: 9).
(17) *United Aborigines Messenger* (August 1958: 10).
(18) *United Aborigines Messenger* (October 1966: 5).
(19) *United Aborigines Messenger* (October 1966: 5).
(20) Herbert Howell – email interview, 2004. Herbert Howell was a teacher at Cosmo Newbery between 1963 and 1966 and, in 1971, was appointed superintendent at Warburton Ranges Mission. In 1978, he and his wife, Lorraine, moved to Warakurna community to establish a new ministry.
(21) *United Aborigines Messenger* (December 1964: 18).
(22) *United Aborigines Messenger* (September 1973); *United Aborigines Messenger* (March/April 1984).
(23) *United Aborigines Messenger* (February 1976: 10), *United Aborigines Messenger* (December 1976: 16–19).
(24) School Policy Warburton Ranges 1974 – NTU Archives: Education File.
(25) Hackett produced a series of 11 Christian Education books, and a number of Ngaanyatjarra writers, storytellers and illustrators have had their stories published through *Tjaa Yuti* Books (Books in our Language). Publications by Ngaanyatjarra authors include Butler (1993); Glass & Newberry ([1979] 1990); Richards (1997).

Other publications include Glass & Hackett (2003); Hackett (2004); Ngaanyatjarra Bible Project (1999, 2003, 2007), as well as Glass & Hackett ([1969] 1979); Glass (2006).

(26) The Summer Institute of Linguistics, funded by a consortium of Evangelical Protestant organisations, began in the USA in the 1930s (Collins & Blot, 2003), and missionary linguists continue studying unwritten Indigenous languages around the world and developing dictionaries and educational materials, as well as Bible translation.

(27) In other Western Desert dialects, the retroflex sounds are still represented by diacritics (l̲, n̲, t̲), as in Pitjantjatjara/Yankunytjatjara (Goddard, 1987) and Pintupi-Luritja (Heffernan & Heffernan, 2000).

(28) DAA Newsletter (WA) 1: 8, September 1974; *United Aborigines Messenger*, September 1974.

(29) *United Aborigines Messenger* (September 1974: 3).

(30) *Warburtonngamartatji Tjukurrpa – Warburton News* 2: 1, 25 June 1975.

(31) After 1996, the Ngaanyatjarra Council produced eight editions of the *Ngaanyatjarra News*.

(32) Early Aboriginal letter-writing includes examples from the south-east of Australia (Nelson *et al.*, 2002; van Toorn, 2006), as well as Killalpaninna (Austin, 1986; Cane & Gunson, 1986), Hermannsburg (Kral, 2000) and Ernabella (Hilliard, 1968; Goddard, 1990) missions.

(33) Glass and Hackett – interview, 8 May 2004.

(34) Howell – email interview, 2004.

(35) See other early examples of the use of petitions, Attwood (2003); Reid (1983); van Toorn (2006).

(36) Hackett (personal communication, May 2005).

(37) Letters from the personal collection of Glass and Hackett.

(38) McLean – interview, 9 September 2004.

(39) *West Australian*, 10 April 1982, cited in Blacket (1997: 196).

(40) McLean – interview, 9 September 2004.

(41) Tehan (personal communication, August 2005). Maureen Tehan was a lawyer at Pitjantjatjara Council from 1984 to 1991, then legal consultant to the Ngaanyatjarra Council from 1991 to 1994.

(42) The Claim covers some 188,000 sq. km of land, stretching from the Gibson and Great Victoria deserts through to the border with South Australia and the Northern Territory.

(43) Tehan (personal communication, August 2005).

(44) Tehan (personal communication, August 2005). The Shire encompasses nine Ngaanyatjarra communities and provides local government services over an area of some 159,948 sq. km. Cosmo Newbery falls within the boundaries of the Shire of Laverton and Kiwirrkura, within the Shire of East Pilbara.

(45) Many of these texts remain in the personal collections of Herbert Howell, Charlie Staples and Albie Viegas.

(46) *Ngaanyatjarra News* (June 1998: 17–18).

(47) The alternate typeface represents reading out loud from the text. It is transcribed from church services at Warburton on 25 April 2004 and 2 May 2004.

Part 3
Past, Present, Future

In Part 2, I considered how the encounter with Anglo-Australian settler society drove an inexorable shift in the cultural patterning of interactions that has shaped a new range of 'sociocultural dispositions' (Ochs, 1990), communication styles and textually mediated roles and identities, in Ngaanyatjarra society. In Part 3, Past, Present, Future, I further explore the implications of change for contemporary social practice and for language and literacy socialisation. I also address the manner in which the youth generation is building on the historically produced norms and practices detailed in Part 2, as well as embracing new systems of meaning as they move into a new world of interpretation. In Chapter 6, 'The Meaning of Things in Time and Space', I examine the spatio-temporal implications of the culturally and historically constituted everyday world (Holland & Lave, 2009). I trace the adaption to new forms of practice and consider the consequences of dwelling in the built environment, concomitant with the acquisition of the objects of Western consumer culture. I explore, also, the relationship between social space, social practice and the artefacts of literacy. In Chapter 7, 'You Fellas Grow Up in a Different World', I turn to the current generation of adolescents and young adults and discuss how new digital technologies are enabling agency in learning and fostering the development of multimodal literacies, as well as new forms of creative cultural production.

6 The Meaning of Things in Time and Space

The taken-for-granted nature, in Western society, of the long history of being and dwelling in the built environment, coupled with the almost imperceptible evolution of systems of meaning associated with 'things', masks their relatedness. Disguised, also, is how these elements factor in the development of a particular kind of language and literacy socialisation environment and the formation of particular types of persons or literate identities. Cultural practice results from the acquisition and transmission of the 'cultural tools', habits, routines, dispositions and attitudes of a cultural group, over successive generations. Children become culturally competent members of their own social and cultural group through socialisation into the 'cultural processes' of that group, and they acquire the linguistic and cognitive orientations of previous generations. Child development is, therefore, a process of socialisation or enculturation that is 'inextricably bound to the process of orienting oneself within systems of meaning' (Miller, 1996: 183). It is these factors that I address in this chapter, as I explore how the Ngaanyatjarra encounter with modernity has altered previously normative spatio-temporal practices, demanding a conceptual adjustment to the way that individuals dwell in space and how they interact with objects in domestic space. Importantly, these elements have implications for the kind of world that children are socialised into and the attitudes, dispositions and norms that are observed and absorbed long before children enter the classroom.

Altered Spatio-Temporal Practices

In classical times, Ngaanyatjarra life was oriented around the overarching taxonomic categories of the natural world and the sociality, values, norms and practices that allowed people to act coherently in that environment. There was, as Henri Lefebvre terms it, a 'concordance of time and space' (Lefebvre, [1974] 1991: 267). Temporal rhythms were aligned with the seasons, the cycles of the sun, moon and stars, ceremonial cycles and the interrelated patterns of hunting and gathering. The arrival of the Mission and the inseparable introduction of Christianity and a European cultural ontology set in train profound shifts in spatio-temporal orientation that have reshaped Ngaanyatjarra ways of being in the world. Mission life imposed a new socio-cultural framework and reconfigured previously normative temporal and spatial rhythms. In this process of re-socialisation, children acquired new names, a new language and new physical dispositions in the shift from nakedness to wearing clothes.

The temporal

Upon entering the Baker Home, children encountered dwellings that afforded shade, tasted strange foods, slept on beds and sat on chairs at tables. 'So we are seeing real changes', claimed the missionaries in 1948:

> ...our boys and girls are aiming for a higher standard of living than mere food and water... Education is closely allied to Evangelism, and it is said "Cleanliness is next to Godliness". We now have a bathroom for the children... Containing two showers and a 6ft galvanised bath, it has already given the boys and girls a sense of ownership and privacy unknown to the native in his camp socialism. To see the clean hands and faces, the tidy hair, as the places are filled at the meal tables, is to feel a sense of achievement. Another improvement is the manufacture of beds...[1]

Molly, who went into the Home around 1950, recalls the introduced routines:

> School, was a good school because we learnt to read and write and go there in time... We used to have a bath night time, go to sleep, get up, wash our faces, comb our hair, have breakfast, go to school... At Sunday school go sing hymns, pray and go out... I lived here for most of my life.

Significantly, the new social institutions of schooling, dormitory living and church altered temporal rhythms by introducing chronological time and a calendric cycle. Upon leaving their children in the Mission, families encountered temporal boundaries that hampered familial intimacy. The annual Christmas party signalled that families could collect their children and return to traditional country, only to 'come back two moon time' – that is, after a couple of months. Summer periods enabled families to return to traditional practices. This was a critical factor in the maintenance of ceremonial and physical links to kin and country and assisted in subverting the breakdown of family relationships in the mission encounter. Moreover, it provided an intensive, iterative context for language socialisation and acquisition of the oral narratives associated with place within multigenerational family groupings, as Molly articulates:

> Every year they used to pick us up for holidays every Christmas and take us away as far as Giles, and come back nearly winter time. We walk around and eat bush tucker all the time... They'd tell stories at night, they'd talk to one another loudly and we'd lie down and listen... It was a very good education for me, strong family, strong teaching, strong inside. They taught me a lot of things those old people... I sat down and listened. Every time they taught me... they showed me how to do it, I used to watch them... I think they learn a lot from their older people not from the whitefella, but from their parents... I listened to my old people and they taught us many things.

By the 1960s, the tradition of travelling by foot had transformed into a dependence on the missionaries transporting an increasingly sedentary population out to windmills in a 'big Austin truck' for the summer break, with additional rations supplied by the Mission.[2]

As noted in Part 2, certain families became affiliated with the Mission early on. Consequently, it was not only the children in the Home, but also the adults in these families who were habitualised into the introduced practices, habits and attitudes. Over time, they developed a reconstructed 'sense of one's place' (Goffman, 1956). In due course, the introduced temporal parameters became routine and influenced practice: with the seven-day week pivoting around Sunday – the 'Lord's day' and the flow of the day punctuated by the ringing of the bell announcing new routines. Christian rituals – Christmas, Easter, baptisms and weddings – created 'temporal frames' (Musharbash, 2003: 192) that became the new normative. The mission encounter, in fact, ushered in a whole new temporality, inextricably intertwined with what time means within Christianity (Engelke, 2009; Schieffelin, 2002). Christianity, Engelke asserts, is a 'religion defined by events in time'. A concomitant effect of Christianity's 'eventful nature', he continues, is that time operates 'linearly' and cultivates 'a certain kind of historical sensibility about the mechanics of the past, present and future' (Engelke, 2009: 156). This contrasts markedly with the concept of cyclical time experienced in classical Ngaanyatjarra society. The shift in notions of temporality can be illustrated linguistically. In the past, oral narratives were punctuated by a 'framework of spatial coordinates' (Myers, 1986: 54). Gradually, *yarnangu* began to recount narratives using temporal duration, by incorporating expressions such as 'mission time', 'station time', 'testing time' or 'government time'. Nowadays, the indices of Western chronological or calendric time are realised as taken-for-granted temporal markers in oral and written narratives.

Over time, metronomic cultural practices – measurable time, measurable development and performance, punctuality and a morality around how time should be spent (c.f. Young, 1988) – have, to some extent, become normative and are being transmitted to successive generations as taken-for-granted practice. The predictable chronologically regulated rhythms of school, work and church, coupled with the secure supply of food and water in the Mission and the arrival of electricity in 1962, led to the creation of a sector of the day that could be devoted to leisure. The tasks and chores of the hunter-gatherer life were no longer as time-consuming and no longer considered work. This introduced uncertainty around how time should be used. Everyday life now pivots around Western assumptions associated with how time should be spent and is a source of conflict. Schooling, training, employment and governance determine daily practice, as well as lifestream expectations. These institutional frames are controlled by the chronologically regulated parameters of the 'working week' and the 'nine to five' working day.

Nevertheless, despite decades of imposed Western temporal structures, unpredictable events regularly fracture this ordered rhythm. Irrespective of 'school-time', children commonly accompany adults to the store, the office, to work and meetings and on other cultural events and trips. Opportunistic travel to sorry camps, funerals or football or to visit relatives in locations hundreds of kilometres away is undertaken without a second thought, in spite of other commitments, the condition of cars or the availability of spare tyres or water. In an unplanned life, there is little need for diaries, calendars and other mnemonic tools necessary for keeping track of time. Furthermore, seasons continue to determine temporal rhythms. The long, hot summer equates with school holidays, fewer non-Aboriginal staff in the community and the time when much of the ceremonial Law Business takes place. For young people, summer means swimming in the community pool and playing basketball late into the evening. In winter, it is football or softball with days spent absent from school or work at sports carnivals in the home or other communities.

The spatial

Despite changes at a superficial level, spatial practice in Warburton, especially for older people, continues to operate at the intersection of diachronic and synchronic time. The synchronic town grid, imposed by the Mission and subsequent town planning, overlays the deeply felt 'spaces, rhythms or polarities' (Lefebvre, [1974] 1991: 164) of the diachronic relationship with country. Public space in Warburton is linked to the *marlu tjina* Dreaming track. Connection to this symbolic space is maintained by persistent cultural, collective belief systems, where oral and semiotic resources are associated with the rhythm of deep time relationships with country. Despite profound change, many contemporary practices are still shaped by deeply held cultural schemas and orientations. The underlying ideological framework that determines cultural practices and processes is predetermined by these socio-spatial factors.

Warburton, since its inception, has been the locus that has drawn people from all directions in the Western Desert. Large numbers camped in *wiltja* constructions in the vicinity of the Mission, until the homelands movement relieved the pressure of different groups living in close proximity. The transition over the last few decades from mobility and *wiltja* living to more stable residential patterns has thrown the generations together in bounded domestic spaces. This has exacerbated family tensions and challenged the boundaries of social etiquette, especially for those in avoidance relationships. Despite being 'all married in now', loyalties, jealousy, teasing and sometimes feuding between families derives, in part, from the intensive aggregation in one locale of families from different country. The pressure to maintain harmony between disparate family groupings can also lead to public explosions of anger or frustration, known colloquially as 'going off', 'getting wild' or 'tempered up'. *Nganyirri purlkanya* (short outbursts of violence) are a socially acceptable release of tension, after which relations return to normal. The swift resolution of conflict is a requirement of desert sociality, where grievances cannot be held on to for lengthy periods, as the maintenance of social harmony is vital to survival.

Continuity with the past is signified in housing located according to the cardinal directions that signal socio-spatial origins of family groups. As noted earlier, in the 1960s, when the last of the Gibson Desert families were brought into the Mission, they camped away from the community, across the creek bed in the *kayili* or 'north' camp:

We used to have to walk in the cold mornings, have a shower, have brekkie and go straight to school. We walked with a tin cut down with fire, that's how hard it was for us, we had no vehicle *wiyartu* (nothing). We were outsiders. Some people lived right close to the mission boundary, but our families had to live out that way because we had feeling for that country. Still like that now, you can see the houses built on different sides. Just a way of life. My family all comes from the north so live that side. But all married in now. It's our culture.[3]

Still today, these deeply felt socio-spatial distinctions are of prime concern, evident in dwellings clustered around 'Top End side', 'Mission Block side', 'Bottom End' and 'Laverton Road side'.[4] Linguists have noted that spatial orientation is key to understanding Aboriginal social and cultural processes and practices (Levinson, 1996; Wilkins, 2006). The manner in which the Ngaanyatjarra index their world reveals that space and place are prioritised – signified in the emphasis on deictic markers of spatial location that endure, in accord with cardinal directions – and are elaborated as identity markers in contemporary artwork, graffiti and song.

Contested local practice in the space between

The centrality and constancy of the *tjukurrpa*, deriving from a timeless past, is fundamental to the Ngaanyatjarra worldview and provides an enduring moral authority that lies outside individuals and underpins everyday life. Despite the permanency of this ontology, on a day-to-day level, the Ngaanyatjarra struggle with the changed power dynamic and the assumed authority of the state and non-Aboriginal value systems. In the 'space between' – as anthropologist Michael Taussig terms the 'space permeated by the colonial tension of mimesis and alterity' (Taussig, 1993: 78) – contested meanings and irreconcilable differences hover, and the loss of socio-spatial control is acutely felt.

Until the 1960s, people who roamed in the vast desert hinterland maintained a sense of autonomy. Senior Law men held unquestioned authority over the parameters of known space. In that dispersed social space, *yarnangu* could choose if, and when, to interact with Europeans. As described in Part 2, since that time, the extent of senior people's authority has largely been challenged, and socio-spatial control has been incrementally eroded. In contemporary community life, despite their numerical dominance and indisputable status as traditional landowners, Ngaanyatjarra ways of being have, in many ways, been relegated to the margins of the introduced institutions, and their capacity to shape public space has all but disappeared. Warburton has been transformed into a place like a 'town' – a process that commenced in the 1970s:

> *Yarnangu* would find that building was going on but they were never asked whether that building should happen. In Warburton the kangaroo dreaming goes right through and on numerous occasions, almost every time some big infrastructure program has gone on people have got upset

because they perceive that damage has been caused to that track. So lessons were never learnt... it's a bit of a sad tale at Warburton in terms of Aboriginal control. That's something that's been there since the outset and its never got any better. It's got worse in the sense that the ratio of staff is greater and so many staff coming who people don't know about and they suddenly find that it has mushroomed, all these other people here doing jobs.[5]

At its inception, the physical isolation of the Mission facilitated an intimacy between *yarnangu* and non-*yarnangu*. A milieu of interdependence and working together continued through the 1970s and into the 1980s.[6] Over time, however, non-Aboriginal people have assumed greater authority over the public space – an aspect played out in other Indigenous communities (Merlan, 1998; Trigger, 1992). A simmering resentment from some *yarnangu* against perceived non-Aboriginal authority is exacerbated by the discrepancy in living standards. Staff mostly occupy furnished, air-conditioned houses and drive big, new, work Toyotas. Conversely, *yarnangu* tend to live in sparsely furnished, non-air-conditioned houses and drive older cars or walk.[7] Furthermore, despite their temporary status, staff tend to hold the keys to buildings in the public space, leaving *yarnangu* with a sense of being 'locked out', literally, as well as figuratively.

Social theorist Anthony Giddens suggests that modernity has evolved concomitantly with an 'acceleration' of the idea that humans can 'control nature' (Giddens, 1991: 144). It can be speculated that modernity has wrought a schism in the Ngaanyatjarra worldview, by introducing the notion that individuals have 'choice' and 'control', rather than events being determined by the *tjukurrpa*. The immediate post-encounter generation took on the new world as a logical system within a cultural framework of non-change. In Chapter 4, I highlighted narratives emphasising how 'everything was different because of the changing'. These recounts reveal how *yarnangu* have felt increasingly powerless in their capacity to comprehend and control change, particularly in the Western institutional domains of education and employment. Rather than offering certain outcomes, these institutions have offered unpredictable and often incomprehensible shifting parameters and led to disillusionment associated with unfulfilled expectations. Clem sums up this dilemma:

They didn't give us the opportunity to make Aboriginal people advance towards advancement. There wasn't that possibility because... we still have to lean towards the European to help us with that. Some of us argued and argued and argued... in the 1970s... and I thought this was going to be the opportunity, we was going run our own affairs, run our own business to help the problems, like petrol sniffing and build a better facilities. You know, because we who came from the high school we knew things change for the future, so we thought, I thought, we were the people, we were the ones who was going to make it happen.

A sort of 'parallel universe' started to emerge after the initial optimism of self-determination faded. That is, when *yarnangu* were given unrealisable expectations of taking over jobs and controlling their communities. Aggrieved by this inexorable loss of socio-spatial control and the progressive devaluation and marginalisation of past practices and beliefs, the older generation has responded by distancing themselves from 'whitefellas'. The profound diminution of Ngaanyatjarra socio-spatial control, authority and autonomy has also led to humiliated cultural pride: 'government people and education say we are "no-hopers", but it's not true', says a community leader. Loss of socio-spatial control is manifest in contested local practice and ideological struggles, as I discuss in the next section.

Contested space: Child development and schooling

It is at the interface between traditional practice and accelerated modernity that the domains of child development and education are positioned as sites of conflict between cultural processes and introduced professional knowledge. As Holland and Lave assert, 'local struggles' are 'always part of larger historical, cultural, and political-economic struggles' (Holland & Lave, 2009: 3).

Schooling in the Ngaanyatjarra Lands is now assumed cultural practice, experienced as possessing an objective reality of its own, as 'an external and coercive fact' (Berger & Luckmann, [1966] 1975). Despite a legacy of unfulfilled expectations associated with what schooling promises to deliver, when asked, most Ngaanyatjarra affirm that schooling is important, in the belief that they are preparing their children for the future by sending them to school. As Jim illustrates: 'education is very important for young people, if you got no education you are nowhere, you'll go nowhere, you need that, it's very important for the future'. I would suggest, however, that some families are, in fact, taking on 'a mimetic form' (Bourdieu, [1980] 1990: 73) of constructed social practice when emphasising the importance of education in the 'space between'. In this contested space, schooling represents an *empty* practice, where rhetoric is disconnected from the lived reality (as indicated in the low school attendance rates).

Conceptualisations of schooling are, of course, drawn from Western cultural premises associated with child development and the ideal age timing for stages of learning. Prior to the late 19th century, in Western society, families were expected to take more responsibility for childcare and, moreover, to teach their children to read at home. At that time, the home and the workplace were less separated, so childcare took place side-by-side with learning through observing and participating in adult processes. This gave children the chance to observe and 'make sense of the mature roles of their community' (Rogoff, 2003: 130–140). With the introduction of compulsory schooling (in England and the United States) in the late 19th century, learning shifted from acquisition in a familial context embedded within community and church life to institutionalised learning. Industrialisation introduced the need for literacy for functional purposes (Graff, 1987; Clanchy, 1979) and in its 'drive to instruct, measure and prescribe the individual, the school jettisoned much of the learning in communities' (Heath, 1991: 4–5). Schooling became a 'socializing agent', aiding the 'inculcation of values' considered requirements for commercial, urban and industrial society' (Graff, 1987: 263–275). By the last quarter of the 20th century, however, critics in the developed world were pointing to the failure of schools 'to move large numbers of students beyond a minimal level of competence in literacy', and educators were chided for 'letting standards slide from past eras of mythical high achievement' (Heath, 1991, 4–5). Writers suggest that a moral panic arose, regarding the 20th-century 'literacy crisis' and the purported decline in literacy standards (Graff, 1987; Heath, 1991; Street, 1995). Heath posits that critics focus almost completely on schools, even though 'closer looks at the history of literacy in the industrialized nations of the West make it clear that developing a sense of being literate, rather than simply acquiring the rudimentary literacy skills of reading and writing, entailed far more than schools alone could give' (Heath, 1991: 5–6).

All over the world, modernity has institutionalised knowledge and professionalised expertise, and there is more regulation of everyday life than in previous generations. The increased regulation of everyday life in Western society represents a form of temporal control, not only as a strategy of interaction, but also as 'a medium of hierarchic power and governance' that grounds people and daily activity in the 'wider world order' (Munn, 1992: 109–110). In the Ngaanyatjarra region, and across remote Aboriginal Australia, a Western model of intervention by 'experts' (teachers, nurses, nutritionists and welfare workers) has been displacing the moral authority of the Aboriginal family to prescribe normative childrearing behaviours and practices. This is interpolated within a context where there is no cultural model for institutional intervention; one learns from one's elders and becomes knowledgeable through a different, culturally–grounded system. As Molly exemplifies:

> To be strong children have to learn the way of the land, in the land. Our Law, to be strong. That's what we're teaching our children. We teach them the way they taught us. Same way, not whitefella way.

In the Ngaanyatjarra Lands, non-Aboriginal educators tend to arrive with preconceptions and hegemonic discourses associated with learning and are, thus, imbued with the 'normativity' of formal education. This often precludes them from seeing the literacy and learning taking place outside school, a situation that is, as shown in Chapter 2, more nuanced than appears at first glance. Nevertheless, a school principal declares that 'reading and writing ability is *totally* dependent on school attendance' and another that:

> Sending kids to school is the most important thing, but adults are not interested in education. Education is not a priority for them and they don't care. They don't support the school. They say they care about education, but it's all words and no action as they don't send their kids to school.

Some teachers in the Ngaanyatjarra Lands attribute low academic performance to 'absenteeism, transience, lack of family and parental support and lack of discipline' (Goddard et al., 2005: 13). This is reinforced in public discourse, where an overarching frame of deficit is commonly attributed to learning in the Aboriginal home environment. As exemplified by commentators, who claim, for instance, that early schooling is 'concerned with overcoming elements absent in the home: peace and quiet, food, civility, reading skills, discussion, use of the English language and the work ethic' (Johns, 2006: 21), reminiscent of attitudes prevalent during the assimilation era, where it was hoped that 'social development' strategies would counter the social, cultural and linguistic 'deficiencies' of the Aboriginal home environment. Such attitudes serve as a backdrop to school – community relations.

Socio-spatial marginalisation and subordination has, in effect, consolidated a collective identification with an oppositional or antagonistic rejection of non-Aboriginal authority in its various guises – school principals, community advisors, store managers and so forth – when they do not build respectful, collaborative, working relationships with community members.

In this contested space, schooling is inevitably positioned as a site of enduring struggle, as families seek to re-assert control over their children's life trajectories. It can be conjectured that poor school attendance is, perhaps, a manifestation of families enacting their 'predisposition to reject authority' (Brooks & Shaw, 2003: 4), by counteracting the undermining of their moral authority as childrearing experts through assertions of agency and control in the 'space between'. As Rosina's grandmother illustrates:

> That principal is no good, driving around forcing kids to go to school… shouldn't be doing that, forcing [them] to go to school. Just because we're black… shouldn't be coming around and bossing us. White people think they are more clever just because we're black.

Through iterative exposure to expressions of resistance to institutional control, children are implicitly appropriating particular stances and attitudes to schooling. It is from this frame of diminished control in the public space that the nature of practice in the private or domestic domain is contrasted.

The Social Construction of Lived Space

Thus far, the spatio-temporal consequences of ontological change have been explored primarily from the perspective of altered spatio-temporal factors and interactions in the public space. In this section, the focus shifts to domestic space. Again, a practice approach is used to examine the relationship between dwelling and the reproduction of domestic socio-spatial practice. Practice theorists suggest that social practice produces and reproduces the meaning of space. As Bourdieu posits:

> Inhabited space – starting with the house – is the privileged site of the objectification of the generative schemes, and, through the divisions and hierarchies it establishes between things, between peoples and between practices, this materialized system of classification inculcates and constantly reinforces the principles of the classification which constitutes the arbitrariness of a culture. (Bourdieu, [1980] 1990: 76)

The manner in which habitus 'orients and naturalises' people's action in social space has been considered by theorists like William Hanks, who suggests that corporeal practices, the ways of inhabiting space and the ways that objects in space are used rest on 'an immense stock of social knowledge' (Hanks, 1990: 7). This knowledge may appear natural, but is, in fact, socially constructed (Levinson & Wilkins, 2006; Ochs, 1993). Accordingly, and importantly for my argument, the social construction of literate modes of interaction – that is, the habits and attitudes of time and space usage and the materiality required to enact literate processes (Heath, 1983; Purves & Jennings, 1991) – are synonymous with the built environment and the social construction of lived space, as I discuss later.

Like all societies, the Ngaanyatjarra developed a spatial code 'as a means of living in that space, of understanding it, and producing it' (Lefebvre, [1974] 1991: 47–48; Lawrence & Low, 1990; Robben, 1989). Generationally differentiated domestic practices, habits and routines emerged in the wake of sedentarisation – the slow shift to houses and the diffusion of the objects of Western consumer culture. In the 1950s, the missionaries used a card system to determine the level of 'sophistication' in Anglo-European customs to determine housing allocation.[8] This reinforced the social distance between the 'accepted' mission families and those still in the hinterland. When Silas was a child, his family was the first in the Mission to occupy a Western-style cottage with beds, a table and chairs. Concomitantly, they acquired the linguistic expressions of Anglo-European social etiquette that accompanied this new social space. As noted earlier, in 1961, when the dormitory closed, children were placed back in the care of families, when hundreds of people still occupied *wiltja* constructions. A 'reserve' (with toilets, showers and huts) was established outside the Mission boundary.[9] By the 1970s, only a few houses had been built, primarily for Western Mining Company workers, like Harold, as his daughter Carmel recalls:

> We had a lovely new house, "state house", built in 1973. We first lived in a little hut, like a one room tin house, then we shift to the "state house", there were only four here then. My father worked for Western Mining collecting copper. Other families had no houses, they were camped in *wiltjas* in the other reserve out near the old airport. The Gibson Desert, Docker River, Warakurna mob camped over the creek.

In the 1980s, most *yarnangu* were still living in temporary shelters in camps a long way out of town, and living conditions remained extremely poor. Petrol and alcohol-related deaths caused social disruption, grief and domestic instability. The frequent movement of large numbers of people into 'sorry camps' led to diminished social control and reduced capacity to nurture consistency in domestic routines. For most *yarnangu*, residing in houses did not become the norm until the 1990s. As a consequence, the generations who spent their formative years living in *wiltja* constructions were socialised into the socio-spatial orientation of a domestic environment, without the concomitant Western material artefacts. It has, therefore, only been the current young adult generation who has grown up in Western-style dwellings, in tandem with consumerism and the corresponding accumulation of material possessions. Having grown up in the built environment, youngsters are exhibiting altered social practices and corporeal dispositions as normative. In accord, a relationship between 'building-dwelling-thinking' (Musharbash, 2009) is developing.

Nevertheless, the Ngaanyatjarra construction of domestic lived space cannot be understood in isolation from the transformation of spatio-temporal practices, in accordance with regular principles and recurrent schemata. Insofar as social interaction has been propelled away from pre-established precepts or practices into the norms and routines of Western patterns of time and space usage, some sort of 'ordering function' or 'cultural schema' (Ortner, 1989) still operates. Rosie and Harold's granddaughter, Rosemary, describes how only two generations ago, families were:

> ...from all different places in the bush, rockholes... Hard life, they used to walk around in the hot heat. They used to carry the kids on their back and walk along, going place to place to the rockholes, camping at night and walking in the daytime.

Whereas now, Rosemary continues, families live 'all in the house, drinking water from the tap'. This quote is significant in the way that it emphasises the centrality of *kapi* (water) in Ngaanyatjarra secular and spiritual life. As touched on earlier, all Ngaanyatjarra people, even the young, maintain an underlying cultural propensity for *'tjukurrpa*-thinking' in everyday life. This is manifest in the way in which people interpret aspects of the world and conceive the links between people, country, events and phenomena 'through the lens of the *tjukurrpa*' (Brooks, 2011b), as identified here. Undoubtedly, over time, the values and dispositions of introduced domestic practice will be transmitted as habitus to the next generation, as many in the young adult generation are parents themselves. It is apparent that they are socialising their children into new domestic practices and space-ordering functions, as illustrated in the birthday party scenario described in Chapter 1.

Things in Space

In Western society, the interrelationship between social practice and how *inside* space is used is attributable to the long history of 'things in space', including the ordinary objects of daily life (Lefebvre, [1974] 1991:

116). Common-sense domestic, socio-spatial, corporeal and linguistic routines are implicitly assumed and derived from Western cultural history. In most Western 'middle-class' homes, normative assumptions are made about the ordering of domestic space and the use of material artefacts within that space. Accordingly, social meanings are sedimented in the routine actions of what Erving Goffman terms 'participation frameworks' (Goffman, 1981) associated with the things – the artefacts – of domestic space.

In classical times, *yarnangu* possessed few 'things' and the reproduction of everything in the known world was associated with the *tjukurrpa*. Moreover, the desert terrain provided them with everything that was needed for everyday life: water, food, medicine, implements and shelter. The meaning embedded in the material artefacts of the pre-contact world belonged to a different cultural schema:

> For every variety of food and item used by *yarnangu* (including implements, decorative and ceremonial paraphernalia, clothing items such as bark sandals, types of shelter such as the boughshed or *wiltja* and the windbreak or *yuu*) there was a sacred act of creation performed by a particular Being at a particular place. (Brooks, 2002c: 16–17)

These few secular and sacred possessions were produced from, and embedded in, the figured world of their use.[10] They were crafted by *yarnangu* for their own use, using only the materials available locally. Gradually, *yarnangu* adopted and accumulated the artefacts of Western culture – initially, objects such as axes, knives, blankets and billy cans (cf. Jones, 2007). Importantly, the integration of such objects into everyday practice happened concomitantly not only with the distancing of *yarnangu* from the origin stories of everyday objects, but also diminishing control over the modes of social and cultural production associated with the objects and the linguistic codes associated with their production and function.

The hunter-gatherer lifestyle was emblematic of 'efficiency' and 'opportunism' – and signified by minimal technology and few possessions – where having and holding on to knowledge was of greater importance than the possession of things. Opportunism insinuated itself deeply into the cultural psyche as an essential concomitant of survival: the mobility required to keep travelling across vast distances in search of food and water in times of drought or to flee the *warrmarla* revenge parties in times of perceived danger. As Western possessions were acquired, systems of portability were invented. In the early days, a *kaliki* (bag) – created using cloth or a *warntu* (a blanket folded, knotted and slung over the shoulder) – was used to carry a few personal possessions. As desert people acquired more possessions, the efficiency of the hunter-gatherer life was undermined. Moreover, people began to lose the mobility required to extract a living wholly from the desert (Brooks, 2011a). As the known world expanded, *yarnangu* acquired new perspectives. Moreover, the artefacts and actions of everyday life were ascribed with new meaning. Over time, they started to encode introduced *things* with new significance, and everyday performances were enacted in conjunction with the new artefacts of everyday life.

As Holland *et al.* (1998) suggest, artefacts are one means by which new 'figured worlds' are evoked, collectively developed, individually learned and made socially and personally powerful. In effect, new forms of personhood started to be constructed in response to objects. As noted earlier, Molly was in the first generation to be habitualised into introduced Western domestic practices. As an adolescent, she was at Cosmo Newbery Mission, where she and other young women were taught to 'save money' to 'buy things you want to move out to your own house' for a 'glory box' containing 'forks and knives and anything, cups, any plate and dish, tablecloth, tea towels'.

> [The missionaries] tell us you should have this, get ready. Like a mother, you know fuss over you, if you want to get married… Help you like that, she was like a mother to us. Helping us to get ready for anything you want.

Now, Molly says, she is 'really proud' of her daughter, who 'lives in her own house' and has 'her own things':

> They got their own fridge, frying pan, car, anything they can have, firewood of their own. That's got to be strong, that's how you make them strong to look after their own things.

Such a cultural shift in attitude to material culture is striking. Likewise, Una has incorporated Western-oriented values into her aspirations for her grandchildren and her sense of what she calls living like a 'proper person':

> I'd like to see my grandchildren having a good house and having a good *kurri* (spouse) to look after and working and happy family, like that… Little kids to go to school, important, very important thing is school… so they can learn more and more and more and they can get *ninti* (knowledgable)… They might start living like a proper person who might speak up: "We want new houses, we might build more and more houses, and maybe a big shop". Like that.

The desire for Western consumer goods has grown exponentially over recent decades, and the generational shift is palpable. In the 1990s, free-to-air TV was introduced, and images of Western material culture started to infiltrate households. Now, young people 'want houses because they've seen other people use them, and they've got TV, video and they want a stove to cook on... they're seeing it on TV and in all different places, so this sort of stuff starts to work its way through'.[11] Most houses, although sparsely furnished, typically have TVs, DVD players, fridges, washing machines and other accoutrements of modernity. Older *yarnangu*, like Wesley, comment that 'these young ones have got it too easy':

> Like nowadays it's easier to get from A to B, there's a lot more vehicles, they can be lazy, drive around, watch TV, watch video... do whatever they want to do, there's access to all that kind of things, white man things that came in. They don't really need to do much 'cause there's access to everything the outside world provides... TV, telephone. We only got TV in the last eight years.

Whereas, Wesley says, his generation went through an era 'where we had to fight for everything'.

Although the introduced objects of Western consumer culture have been incorporated into practice, they embody no comprehensible origin story, no recognisable mode of production and minimal associated cultural affective remembrance. This has led to what Pelto (Pelto, 1973) terms 'de-localization' or the growth of a dependency on non-local sources of production. In classical times, everything was known, and what was needed was generated from the known. It is now the global world that is intruding upon them, leading to an additional sense of diminished socio-spatial control. Globalisation and what Giddens terms 'the excavation of most traditional contexts of action' are altering 'the balance between tradition and modernity' (Giddens, 1994: 95), as I discuss in the next chapter.

Demand sharing and the social capacity to control 'things'

Bryan Pfaffenberger notes, in his discussion on the social anthropology of technology, that it cannot be assumed that 'a transferred artifact will succeed in bringing with it the ideological structure that produced it' (Pfaffenberger, 1992: 510) or the sociocultural practices that surround it. In other words, if the meaning embedded in material artefacts belongs to a different cultural schema and there is no comprehensible origin story, it is unlikely that relationships will build up around the artefacts. Furthermore, the adoption of certain artefacts does not necessarily imply the adoption of the system of logic that produced that artefact.

As commodities – *things* – became available in the Western Desert, a concordant set of assumed Western socio-spatial practices and attitudes (associated predominantly with looking after and protecting objects) did not necessarily develop. Hamilton notes that as materiality entered the Pitjantjatjara world in the 1970s, sociocultural reasons accounted for why adults struggled to maintain everyday objects (Hamilton, 1979: 111–113). She suggests that preventing children from doing things to everyday objects that fell outside the traditional framework of objects to be avoided (that is, *not* objects of a secret or sacred nature) was difficult to enact if it involved punishing another person's child or led to accusations of being 'ungenerous'. In relation to the 'free giving and getting' of secular objects, the assumption is that one does not deny access to others. The prioritisation and enhancement of social relationships through reciprocity and sharing stand in stark contrast to the Western perspective on the 'proper' care of material possessions (that is, as 'continuing assets' that must endure into the future). In the Ngaanyatjarra world, everyday life is still primarily orientated around the negotiation of relatedness. It is a social environment that privileges generosity and sharing. However, an orientation to 'demand sharing' (Peterson, 1993; Sansom, [1988] 1994) places pressure on an individual's social capacity to control social space and the storage of property. Cumulatively, these factors all impinge on an individual's capacity to enact literate practices in the domestic space – I return to this point later.

The cultural production of identity

In contemporary Western society, individual identity is inextricably linked to employment, income and the accumulation of material possessions in a consumer culture (Csikszentmihalyi & Rochberg-Halton, 1981). The symbolic power of money rests in the human effort required to earn it, in order to then spend it on consumer goods. This is dramatically lessened in a social economy where, as anthropologist Diane Austin-Broos notes, it is within the 'production of relatedness' that people access the goods of life (Austin-Broos, 2003: 129). This is affirmed by Myers, who suggests that the rapidity with which 'things' move through a network of relatives and friends in the Pintupi world indicates that 'objects are important as opportunities to say something about oneself, to give to others, or to share' (Myers, 1988: 17). That is, exchanges of objects represent 'a moment in the reproduction of shared identity' (Myers, 1988: 21), where shared identity is 'sustained' through the exchanges. From the Pintupi perspective, it can be perceived that people 'prefer to invest in people rather than things', and, that way, one's identity is 'transmitted through time' (Myers, 1988: 24). In other words, the Pintupi and, similarly, the Ngaanyatjarra prioritise a different form of accumulation – one that derives from investing in and increasing the social value of people, through caring for them as kin. This represents a very different worldview from the Western ontology, in which accumulated personal property constitutes one of the primary ways in which identity can be realised; where investment in objects is related to individual personhood and how time is spent. For *yarnangu*, life is made meaningful not through the accumulation of money and property, but through kinship and the ties that bind. In other words, *yarnangu* are living by a different cultural schema – one underpinned by the symbolic value and accumulated wealth of social relatedness. Cumulatively, all of the factors outlined above impinge on the relationship between space, artefacts *and* literacy practice.

Social Space and the Artefacts of Literacy

In most Western middle-class homes, everything, ideally, has its place, based on taken-for-granted sociocultural space-ordering rules – literacy artefacts are stored in cupboards or on bookshelves in particular ways, bills are pinned to pinboards, calendars are marked for upcoming events, personal administration is alphabetically indexed in filing cabinets, according to assumed systematic practice. Alphabetical ordering is used as a 'mediating structure' (Hutchins, 1996: 304) to facilitate categorisation, storage and retrieval. Such taken-for-granted literate practices are acquired through observation and habitual practice and have been passed down through the generations. The collocation of objects in domestic space hinges on a shared understanding of how the world is ordered and the relationship between objects, in much the same way that the collocation of semantic and grammatical categories in written text depends upon similarly shared schematic knowledge. As 'good readers read', they acquire the habit of textual collocation (i.e. a familiarity with English written discourse, where deictic expressions determine textual organisation, by maintaining the cohesion of anaphoric, cataphoric and exophoric chains of reference). Consequently, the habit of living in the built space also builds up socio-spatial typification, congruent interaction and corporeal dispositions. That is, as Berger and Luckmann posit, 'habitualized actions' become embedded as 'routines' or 'taken for granted actions' only when 'reciprocal typification of habitualised actions' build up through 'shared history' (Berger & Luckmann, 1975 [1966]: 70–85).

As discussed in Chapter 2, in Ngaanyatjarra sociality, irrespective of individual literacy competence, socio-spatial aspects militate against the capacity to enact literate modes at home. Although people succeed in holding on to a variety of small personal objects, such as money and keys secured on their person in wallets and pockets, and some *yarnangu* have retained certain personal items, such as photos, Bibles and hymn books, over many years, regulating the removal of larger objects in communal domestic space is difficult, as Mick relates:

> They break it all up when you have books and something like that... these kids here, when they go, they rip it all up... I lock all my spanners up inside. Spanners and screwdrivers, and wheel spanners and jacks. Put it all inside so people don't touch it, tyre and all. If you leave it in the back somebody come along and steal it, take off with it, they won't bring it back.

In fact, few *yarnangu* are able to experience locking the door and walking away from their home, secure in the feeling that when they return, everything will have remained as they left it.[12] Jacinta says, she would,

> ...love to have books, but people always come in there and take them. I'd like to keep them in my room, locked up. I got a lot of photos there, keep it in little basket, I keep it inside.

Jennifer tries keeping books at home:

> I keep it, but kids chucked it all out... Always keep my things private but they just go in there, chuck it away, make mess... I took some things to the house and I went to town and came back and I seen the things all over, just lying there... Must get a big cupboard or something with a lock.

Now, Jennifer's strategy is to store her personal papers at the community office: 'that way I can get it whenever I need it if anybody come and ask me, I just go there and grab it'. In this respect, the artefacts of literacy that go with houses are not building up. People cannot say: 'here's my phone bill, here's my rent, that's my letter box and that's my cheque book and that's where I store it all, and this is where I keep my calendar and diary to keep it all organised.'[13]

Furthermore, few houses have the furniture that literate processes and practices require: a bookshelf, a filing cabinet, a desk, a comfortable chair or a side lamp for bedtime reading. As Mihaly Csikszentmihalyi (1981: 59) points out, such domestic symbols are representative of 'settledness and affluence'. Such features cannot be attributed to most Ngaanyatjarra domestic contexts, where mobility and iterative relocations of domestic space impact on the capacity to enact home literacy practices. This is exemplified in the frequency of funerals and the swift movement to sorry camps in the home or another community, with families taking only bedding and essential possessions and often not returning to their old house, to avoid memories of the deceased. Under such conditions, gaining control over small personal goals in the domestic domain can lead to a feeling of control in the wider sense.

If you have increased control over your personal environment then your capacity to be an agent in the literacy experience is enhanced. That's a really big problem socially as there is nothing in the Ngaanyatjarra environment that empowers you to do that. Nothing… the chaos factor… no order… literacy is intermeshed with these aspects of the environment, housing, lifestyle, the expectation of literacy post-school, the formation of the supports to allow literacy to happen outside of school are inextricably linked to the social factors that allow literacy to happen, like storage, possessions, property. *It's not just knowing how to do it.* The isolated, solitary activity of reading a newspaper is chipped away at, not allowed to take place which is what newspaper reading or whatever is all about. All the aspects that literacy is hinged on are at war with the Ngaanyatjarra social reality, in so many ways it works against literacy.[14] [italics added]

Ultimately, the cultural practices and processes described above run counter to the tangential requirements of literacy – that is, individual ownership and the perceived need to look after and protect *things* and to conserve objects for future use. Moreover, these elements impact on socialisation practices, as children tend not to be socialised into the time and space rule-oriented boundaries that literacy practice demands. My argument is that the habit of living in built space builds up specific socio-spatial actions and congruent practices, in relation to the storage and use of the objects that are integral to literacy. The generations who spent their formative years living in *wiltjas* were socialised into the socio-spatial orientation of a domestic environment that was not conducive to the organisation of literacy artefacts and the enactment of home literacy practices. Now, we are beginning to see young people who have been socialised into living in the built environment exhibiting changed corporeal dispositions and habits, inclusive of literacy, as normative social practice, as I exemplify below.

Textual play

Unlike the older generation, Ngaanyatjarra adolescents display a corporeal confidence in the built environment. For them, the built environment provides a backdrop for the production of meaning and 'embodied action' (Goodwin, 2000). It is replete with spaces and surfaces that provide the 'co-ordinates' for social relationships and a 'structured sequence of settings' where social interactions can be enacted, encoded and decoded (Duranti, 1997: 321–323).

Everywhere in Warburton, every surface is daubed with the textual scribblings, patterns, icons and authorising marks of youth. Adolescents do not discriminate between surfaces, but interact with all materials of the built environment – brick, concrete, plastic, metal and paper – as surfaces to be filled with written expressions of self. Tags are smoked on to ceilings with cigarette lighters, rendered in marker pens on plastic bottles and in petrol on the bitumen road on sniffing nights, welded as initials on metal benches, drawn in dust on car windows and on refrigerator condensation, carved on trees, scrawled in charcoal on cement floors, etched on to skin as tattoos and traced in the sand during storytelling. Teenage girls spend extended leisure hours, long into the summer evenings, sitting around on the pavements chipping text into the concrete with the sharp end of a story wire; these peckings – redolent of traditional rock petroglyphs – become a permanent reminder of the moment. This rendering of symbols is transferred to other forms of compulsive scribbling and graffiti tagging, including the new multimodal expressions emblematic of contemporary youth culture at Warburton. Graffiti, in this context, is writing on the surfaces and in the spaces that young people inhabit and where they feel a sense of ownership. Rather than the negative connotations attributed to graffiti in some urban contexts, graffiti carries a different social meaning in a space where individuals do not have access to the material resources of literacy – a bedroom, a cupboard – where pen and paper can be stored. In this context, a wall is a space for inscription, exemplified also in the manner in which telephone numbers, until recently confined to the wall space around public phone boxes, are now scribbled on any available surface in the domestic space.

New technologies, new youth practices

Earlier, I referred to Pfaffenberger's notion that the adoption of certain artefacts does not necessarily imply the adoption of the system of logic that produced that artefact. However, as he elaborates further: '[n]ew resources are unlikely to be ignored if they can be woven into an existing or new activity system... to fulfill an essentially expressive function' (Pfaffenberger, 1992: 511). I finish this chapter by giving a further example of altered youth practices, in relation to the adoption of new technologies. Ngaanyatjarra youth are rapidly appropriating new digital technologies for their own sociocultural processes and purposes. As small mobile digital technologies – digital cameras, USB sticks, mp3 players and mobile phones – have become more affordable, *yarnangu* are purchasing these devices as individual everyday social objects. The size of these objects is important: most are small enough to fit into pockets and bras and can be slept with at night. In an environment predicated upon demand sharing, these are items of personal ownership that don't have to be shared. These technological artefacts are an extension of *yarnangu* sociality; they represent a medium of identity expression and a way of maintaining connectedness with others, and, as such, they are objects to be looked after for future use. Affective significance is embedded in these new artefacts. They make sense because they enable communication and the enriching of social relationships, albeit at a distance, thus illustrating that when the adaptability of material artefacts is immediately evident, new social practices emerge, corporeal dispositions alter and new resources are woven into an existing system to fulfil an essentially expressive function.

Conclusion

In this chapter, I have drawn attention to how successive generations have been socialised into different ways of being and dwelling. I show how socialisation contexts have been reshaped by the ideologies of the new institutional forms and practices, since first contact paved the way for the transformation of social processes. Previously normative socio-spatial practices have been reoriented around the built environment. It is in the embodied action of everyday routines and scenarios of domestic social interaction that the fundamentally different notions of 'temporal, spatial, and social ordering' (Ortner, 1984: 154) that underlie and organise Ngaanyatjarra society become apparent. These factors have clearly impacted on the acquisition of a coherent body of sociocultural knowledge and the associated practices, and this has implications for the socialisation of the next generation. Nevertheless, social practices are always in a state of flux and are responsive to changing historical circumstances. The conceptual and material aspects of figured worlds, and the artefacts through which they are evinced, are changing through innovation and use. Young people are the markers of social change, and new influences are shaping the multimodal literacy practices they engage in, as will be explored further in the following chapter.

Notes

(1) *United Aborigines Messenger* (May 1948: 12).
(2) *United Aborigines Messenger* (November 1962: 16).
(3) Daisy Ward – interview, 2000.
(4) A continuity of spatially relative orientations to 'country' is noted in the Australian anthropological literature (Hamilton, 1979; Merlan, 1998; Myers, 1986; Sansom, 1980).
(5) Brooks – interview, 15 August 2004.
(6) Hackett (personal communication, November 2004).
(7) The Ngaanyatjarra Lands have a number of long-term non-Aboriginal staff who have developed mutually satisfying working relationships which entail respect, high expectations of participation and complex discussions around concepts and tasks.
(8) David Brooks (personal communication, 2009).
(9) WA SRO Acc 1419 23-7-315/162 – *Letter from CNW to Federal Secretary UAM.*
(10) Everyday possessions included, for men, a spear and spear thrower and, for women, a foraging stick and a grindstone. Foodstuffs and water were carried in carved wooden bowls (*wirra* or *piti* resting on a carrying ring) balanced on a woman's head. Other items included genital coverings, bark sandals for traversing the hot ground in summer and wooden carved items, such as fighting clubs and shields, as well as *larra* (ceremonial carved wooden boards). Grindstones, because of their weight, were rare items of permanence left behind at rockholes as items to be returned to for future functionality.
(11) McLean – interview, 9 September 2004.
(12) Elizabeth Ellis (personal communication, July 2009).
(13) Damian McLean (personal communication, July 2009).
(14) McLean – interview, 9 September 2004.

7 You Fellas Grow Up in a Different World

Youth, coming-of-age in the Ngaanyatjarra communities, face complex competing language socialisation influences. The traditional developmental trajectory has altered, and young people have to 'figure out' new paradigms for new circumstances. This generation must balance the pressure of local sociocultural obligations and the expectation that they will follow in the footsteps of the older generation, with the pressure to participate in wider Australian society. They must simultaneously form life goals that are meaningful within their own sociocultural system and align with mainstream expectations. Yet, young people are also coming-of-age in an era where digital media forms part of the taken-for-granted social and cultural fabric of learning, leisure and communication. They are living in a digital, globalised world, where they must develop and share new understandings of what it means to participate in activities and relationships across linguistic, social and geographic time and space. This generation is connecting, communicating and learning through new media and imagining and constructing identities that are both tied to the past and stretch out to the future. To balance this complex of life goals and expectations, young people must acquire diverse linguistic and cultural practices, technological competencies and correspondingly hybrid identities.

Altered Developmental Trajectories

The encounter with modernity has led to a diminution of the rule-bound cultural processes and practices of the past and the inexorable erosion of the pre-contact maturation cycle. Prior to European colonisation, Western Desert society was 'strongly rule-bound, complementary, concrete, sanctified, inter-locking and predictable'. *Kurnta* (shame) operated as a form of regulatory control over young people, as did the authority of senior men. By contrast, the contemporary social world is perceived as 'open-ended, proliferating, seemingly rule-less and unpredictable' (Brooks & Shaw, 2003: 15).

Schooling introduced a lifespan division between childhood and adulthood that shaped a new social category – 'adolescence'.[1] The institutionalised proximity of mixed gender, age-graded cohorts led to the reshaping of traditional marriage patterns. Challenges to traditional marriage practices commenced with the mission-educated girls running away to seek same-age unions (but still 'right way', according to the section system). In the polygynous family groupings of the 1980s, a husband and, sometimes one, mostly two and often three, wives were still the norm, whereas the domestic environment now constitutes a dramatically different social arrangement, with only a few polygynous marriages among older people and a number of single mothers.[2] The stability of traditional marriage patterns ('promised' unions and polygyny) has been replaced by new forms of interpersonal relating: so-called 'love-way' relationships, multiple partners across the lifespan and relationships where alcohol or petrol sniffing may lead to domestic violence. Nevertheless, unions that violate the section system are still unusual, partnering is mostly 'proper way', with someone of the 'right skin' (see Figure 3 in the Introduction). As mentioned previously, generational moiety division – *tjirntulukultul(pa)* (sun side) and *ngumpalurrungkatja* (shade side) – remains central to the 'social and symbolic order' of Ngaanyatjarra life. The rules surrounding generational moiety interaction are strictly enforced and govern ceremonial activity and marriage rules. To marry 'wrong way' or *'yinyurrpa* way' (that is, to a person of the other generational moiety) represents the worst violation of rules relating to marriage partners. Such 'wrong way' marriages 'strain the rules of acceptability, particularly for the older generation' (Brooks, 2002b: 39–41).

The altered maturational cycle is placing greatest pressure on the identity formation processes of adolescent males. In the past, going through the stages of the Law was a time-consuming imperative for males. Young men who had been through the Law experienced a long period of pre-marriage independence, within which to test themselves and assert autonomy (Peterson, 2000). Now, young men are marrying at a younger age. Although going through the Law remains a significant cultural process, it is no longer sufficiently enduring or robust to provide the full complement of skills required for contemporary social paradigms or life circumstances. There is no longer a defined pathway clearly articulated, with the goals of later life for newly initiated young men to follow, leaving many young men in something of a 'social no-man's land' (Brooks, 2011b). Rapid social change has led to, what Brooks terms, the loss of a distinct and calibrated process of maturation and a socially specified set of activities to effectively occupy a person's time during the years between childhood and full adulthood.

Most importantly, the Western trajectory of institutional learning – schooling and vocational training – is not offering a substitute trajectory that makes sense within cultural paradigms. Under contemporary conditions, adolescent males tend to drop out of school after passing through initiation ceremonies around the age of 14. It is suggested by some researchers (Beresford & Omaji, 1996; Ogilvie & Van Zyl, 2001) that prison has become a replacement rite of passage into manhood. What is apparent, as noted in Chapter 2, is that prison is acting as a site for young men to test themselves, learn more and gain experience negotiating complex social interactions that parallels events in the traditional maturational cycle. By contrast, young women are maintaining a cultural logic in the process of identity formation that is inextricably linked to child-rearing and motherhood. This, however, also runs counter to the expectations of secondary schooling and leads to early school leaving. Ultimately, the divergence of the developmental trajectory of youth away from traditional cultural norms is placing pressure on the social fabric of Ngaanyatjarra society (Kral, 2010a).

With the loss of the time-consuming tasks and regulatory sanctions of the past, everyday life for young people is, by contrast, self-regulated. Moreover, minimal concentrated time is spent in institutional learning settings. Older people perceive that youngsters spend their time doing 'basically nothing', and 'play' has become the norm for how time is spent. Meanwhile, some young adults, like Adina, echo the work ethos inherited from the older generation: 'it's good for you to work for your own living instead of staying home and laying around'. Mary and Jack's grandson, Troy, was always told to go to school by his *ngunytju* (his mother's sister), who worked as an assistant teacher in the school for 20 years. Unusually, at 17, he was still at school:

> Then the Advisor came round and he told me: "Oh, you wanna sign your name for money, wages". Then I got a job. I was working at the Roadhouse, cleaning up, putting all the gardens... clean all the rubbish. Plant all the trees, it was good.

Troy describes how he wants to find a job: 'for money... get a big money then sit down for a while, buy a car, buy something like TV, and furnitures, tables, all that'.

To sum up, the social meanings still attached to the Ngaanyatjarra maturation period run counter to the requirements of Western institutional settings. It is assumed practice that, by 16, adolescents will have left school. Even adolescents as young as 12 are claiming: 'I'm too old for school and I've had enough'.[3] In 2006, it was found that approximately one-third of all 14 year olds, half of all 15 year olds and, 'essentially', no 16 year olds go to school; furthermore, only one-quarter of all 12 year olds had 'passable' attendance rates (Gordon, 2006: 6–7). Accordingly, youth have large amounts of discretionary leisure time to fill. Thus, conflicting parallel socialisation trajectories underpin the 'enduring struggles' and 'contested practice' (Holland & Lave, 2009) evident in both local discourse and national debate.

'Follow in our footsteps'

Older people emphasise the obligation that the young have to preserve and pass on Ngaanyatjarra identity and cultural processes to successive generations:

> We're holding the hopes for the children, we've got to give them hope... we got to teach them... our hope is our future, to know the country and to have strong leaders.[4]

But also they elaborate on young people's purported lack of education, work ethic and leadership potential:

> Young people today have no respect for elders. There is no discipline, they are stubborn people, can't listen to the parents... I'm really glad I got learn the hard way.

> It's just different because in our days we used to just work... Nowadays they just doing their own way. You know they sniffing, or doing something bad, throwing rocks at people or anywhere.

> They can't work or learn about anything... You know that's what we try to do to them, always telling them you should be learn, to be better than us. That's what I tell the young people, but no-one doing it... They got different ways I think, our way was, we was like forced, now it's a sort of free way for anyone to live now.

This leads to elders expressing frustration when they perceive young adults not following in their footsteps. However, the cultural logic of the gerontocracy works against young people contributing effectively, until they reach an appropriate stage in the maturational cycle. As Myers notes (1986: 246), for the broader Western Desert, 'putting oneself forward and taking responsibility' are 'important dimensions of an older man's identity... the privileges of full adulthood'. Ironically, however, in this case study, we see that the rebellious adolescents of the mission generation, who challenged the authority of the gerontocracy, are now the elders seeking to hold together tradition, as well as social cohesion.

It is clear that cultural transmission and socialisation patterns have been challenged. This may lead to negative outcomes, as outlined in earlier chapters. These factors notwithstanding, many young people are seeking experiences to fill the learning gap that institutions and, often, families seem unable to fill. They are becoming the self-appointed definers of new forms of cultural competence in groups that are configured around kin- and peer-affiliations, and, moreover, new technologies are leveraging a new space for learning and meaningful cultural production.

Performing themselves differently

The current youth generation is exploring and internalising, as anthropologist Francesca Merlan terms it, new and diverse 'intercultural arenas of social practice' (Merlan, 1998: 145) to forge an emerging identity not based on models reproduced within cultural memory, but on a synthesised multiplicity of influences. Places and strangers are no longer feared as they once were, and reprisals for cultural transgressions are less potent. Relationships are more overt, with public 'boyfriend-girlfriend' unions, single mothers and a discourse in the public space around previously private subjects. Over the generations, Ngaanyatjarra people have started to overcome their sociocultural disposition to *kurnta* and the manner in which this propensity organises communicative practices. Young people are able to deal with an increasingly complex range of intercultural social and linguistic interactions. Where earlier generations were more bounded by the parameters of ceremonial performance, successive generations have been observing and participating in an expanded range of Western performance genres. Exposure to TV, MTV and, now, YouTube has exposed youth to new performance repertoires, genres and forms of communication. This has extended the boundaries of possibility, and young people are now performing themselves differently from their elders. As positive images of youth culture are broadcast and circulated throughout the remote world, via remote Indigenous media organisations and Indigenous community television (ICTV), youth achievements are celebrated, allowing the spotlight to shine on individuals. This transformation of self is accepted and praised by the community.

As noted in Part 2, the older generation was adept at forming new internal structures by incorporating and manipulating new symbolic materials and resources into their existing meaning-making systems and communication modes. As signalled in Chapter 1, the youth generation is rapidly claiming new cultural forms and modes and adapting them for their own purposes. In reshaping their identities, they are indicating that they, too, are adroit in adapting to and incorporating change. This generation is representing what the future holds, rather than their parents or grandparents. From this perspective, they are providing new models for each other and for the children who will follow in their footsteps.

New Technologies, New Modes of Communication

The convergence of media technologies, with information and communications technologies (ICTs) made possible by digitisation over the last decade, has brought about profound changes in media and music production, communication and learning across the globe. The digital revolution has also penetrated the remote Ngaanyatjarra Lands, with the introduction of affordable, small, mobile digital technologies and the availability of the internet in communities, and now mobile telephones in Warburton. Ngaanyatjarra youth are part of 'digital culture'. This participation has, however, firm roots in a tradition of film, video and music production that has been evolving over recent decades. Prior to the 1970s, technology and media communications were virtually non-existent in most remote communities, including in the Ngaanyatjarra region. By the 1980s, however, a 'telecommunications revolution' (Hinkson, 2005) was well underway. This saw the genesis of Aboriginal media and music broadcasting and production in the desert.[5] Ngaanyatjarra Media was established as an Aboriginal-controlled remote media organisation in 1992. At that time, Aboriginal people were moving from the pre-television world – where communication was based substantially on face-to-face interaction, utilising a rich, multimodal oral and gestural repertoire (Michaels, 1986) – to increased exposure to broadcast television and a Western lifestyle. Ngaanyatjarra Media provided *yarnangu* with the opportunity to produce and broadcast radio and media that reflected their own worldview. Thus, despite the ubiquity of Western media images, young adults witnessed their elders using pre-digital media forms as a tool for language and culture maintenance.[6]

As touched on previously, with few resources in the domestic space, literacy and technology resources were previously available only in institutional spaces: the office, school or clinic. In these locations, ICT resources were expensive and typically mediated by non-Aboriginal intervention. In addition, the text-based applications typical of most office computers inhibited usage by *yarnangu* with low-level English literacy skills. While inequities in household-based access and participation exist, collective access has been enabled through the establishment of 'media centres' in some Ngaanyatjarra communities, in accordance with broadband, satellite or Wi-Fi availability (Featherstone, 2011). Here, young people have access to media and computer-based resources in the non-school hours. Young people are typically engaging with new media technologies, through film-making and music, in media centres, arts projects and online. Here, activities are public, yet privacy can be found for individual production and the safe storage of virtual and material artefacts. In addition, computers are becoming more common in the domestic space and are used to play and download music from iTunes on to mp3 players.

Warburton Youth Arts

The emergence of Warburton Youth Arts Project (WYAP) around 2004 coincided with the introduction of digital media technologies. It also built on the existing foundation of music and media broadcasting and production in the Lands. WYAP came into being at a time when attitudes to youth were at low ebb. Nationally, public and policy discourse was reiterating a pessimistic scenario regarding Aboriginal education and the future of youth in remote communities. Locally, leaders were expressing frustration that young adults were not 'following in their footsteps'. Elders, like Clem, were lamenting:

The world is changing the government is changing, we're crying out: who'll take on in our footsteps, who'll do that? We believe that only through education our people will survive.

Although a small group had commenced accredited media training with Ngaanyatjarra Media,[7] for most of the 60-odd 16–25 year olds in the youth arts cohort, film and graphics skills were attained through non-formal multimedia training workshops. Young people chose to participate because they wanted to learn. Mastery of computer-based multimedia skills came easily, as they experimented with digital stills and video cameras, planned storyboard sequences and edited films and slide shows in iMovie on the new Macintosh computers. The immediacy of the digital medium matched their creative energy, allowing multiple images to be shot and viewed, then surreptitiously deleted or downloaded for instant replay and communal repeat viewings. Public performances took place in community film nights and fashion parades throughout 2004 and in the 'Wilurarra Youth Arts Festival' in April 2005. Music recording, multimedia and arts workshops have continued and expanded, with regular festivals and exhibitions in Perth, Sydney and other regional centres. Young artists travel out to new places and extend their understanding of the world beyond Warburton. Following on, a younger cohort of adolescents has entered the renamed youth arts project: 'Wilurarra Creative'.[8]

New leadership pathways

Social relatedness underpins all interaction in the Ngaanyatjarra world and the youth arts project works within this cultural frame. Multigenerational involvement and support is integral to the process (cf Fietz, 2008). Approval from the gerontocracy is valued and sought. Elders, like Clem, have shifted their perspective and now express pride in young people:

> When I first seen that [films], I seen it in the hall. My daughter told me a little bit about it, she said: "Oh you gotta go and see that whole thing". So I went down there and that was really good... See them young people wanting to do things, because the world is changing, everything is changing, government changing and we can't change things, we're getting too old. But I'm sure you young people can get involved, so it makes me happy, you young people are doing really good. Doing something for yourselves, and not just for yourselves but also for your children and the people here. You getting a good name for the people... Gradually the people who run the government coming in here, they'll be seeing it and thinking: "Oh Warburton good". They'll be thinking differently now. They won't be thinking about sniffers, they won't be thinking about bad things, but thinking about good things, what's happening in Warburton. Well keep going. Like I said I'll support you all the way until I die!

At a meeting with WYAP in December 2004, Clem declared:

> You fellas grow up in a different world, in a different way. Not your mother and father way. It's important you can video it for other children.

At the same meeting, McLean told the young people:

> When all you mob went to school, you went to school in the early nineties and early twenties. In Warburton at that time there was a lot of sniffing and too many people drinking, there was a lot of violence and a lot of problems and all you people didn't get a lot of support when you went to school. Nobody made sure you went, nobody took much interest

in what you did in school. That was a difficult time to be a school kid. And a lot of people said: "Oh that mob, they missed out on school, anyway, we'll look to the next generation". And sort of wrote you guys off and said: "Can't fit you into education". Now with this youth arts project you guys…you're back into learning and you're back into doing things that are really important for you. And also really good for the kids who are coming behind to see you doing it, because they'll learn from that and they'll think: "Oh if they can do that, I can do that too". And it will give them confidence and they'll know that they can do it too.[9]

While it is evident that many in the current youth generation have missed out on schooling, it is also noticeable that the children of the leaders, described in Chapters 4 and 5, are emerging as the next generation of leaders, albeit in a different form. Importantly, it is arts-based and media organisations, like WYAP and Ngaanyatjarra Media, that are providing a learning environment for young people, especially those outside formal education, to acquire and hone new skills. At WYAP, Clarrie, Leah, Naomi and others have assumed leadership roles planning the exhibitions, fashion shows and book publications, as well as music festivals in conjunction with Ngaanyatjarra Media. As Silas notes, in a youth arts publication:

Young people have been taking up the challenge – learning and doing things for themselves. The young people are like the eyes for the old people seeing into the future… It's not up to someone else to show the way we are or control how we are seen. We are trying to do this ourselves in our own work. We are watching too. You can see the young people standing up for themselves, speaking out. Now is the right time for people to take notice. (Wilurarra Creative, 2010: 39)

Joshua and Dawn's daughter, **Naomi, was born in 1978.** *She was at school in Warburton in the 1980s. In 1992, she went to CAPS in Coolgardie for three years.[10] She finished school halfway through Year 10, because she wanted to return home to start work: 'cause I turned 16'. At that time, a small community radio room had just opened in Warburton, and Naomi was one of the first young media workers. She has since completed accredited media training. Through her role as a media worker, Naomi is emerging as a leader.*

I want to encourage all the teenagers, especially the girls, you know. Tell them not to sniff or run around. I like to do all that. Tell the young girls not to get married too young, you know. Just keep on doing what I tell them, that's what I want to do here in Ranges... It's hard sometimes because when you tell the girls, you know, some of them might think I'm joking, but I'm telling the truth. I want to do that.

Naomi's confidence and self-assurance is striking. Encouragement to do well at school, work hard and become a leader comes from her family. Her father Joshua was the long-time Chairman of the Ngaanyatjarra Council.

Dad always told me to work and live your own life, work for your own money and that's all. That's where all the advice from... he always tell me: "Oh Naomi, you keep on doing good things like me. Then one day, girls can easy do that, become a leader, you know, like a Chairwoman."

Naomi's sister, Leah, was born in 1981.

Both sides, mother and father born in the mission. They was schooling here and then they went to Esperance, schooling there and my father stayed there and got a job there in the Goldfields, mining. Then started in the ATSIC, then he came back this way... he had lots of jobs... Mother was working at the shop... They been working before, that's why I know how to work, do course. That why I learn from them, by watching them when I was little, been going school right through.

Leah went to school in Warburton, before going to CAPS in Coolgardie and Wongutha. Leah is now married and has one son. After training at the college in Warburton, she worked as a gallery guide, hairdresser and with the youth arts project. She now works at the cultural centre at the Shire. Leah says her family always encouraged her to learn to 'maybe run the community'. Leah likes working and considers Warburton a 'good and big place'.

It's got everything here... that's why they like it here so much, learning at the culture centre. And the young people they like working, training and all that. Make them busy in Warburton, instead of when they got nothing to do they start sniffing and all that, or start on the alcohol, going to town.

*Jim's eldest son, **Clarrie, was born in 1979.** He went to school in Warburton and also boarded at CAPS in Coolgardie and finished high school in Year 10. His younger brother also did secondary schooling at Coolgardie CAPS. Clarrie and his brother have worked with the Land Management Unit. Like his father, Clarrie is* *quietly taking on leadership responsibilities. He is captain of the football team, attends Ngaanyatjarra Council meetings and has been a leader in the youth arts project. Clarrie's passion is playing music and writing songs. He has a band with his brother and some of the other Warburton 'young fellas'. They have been playing music for many years, and their tracks have recently been released commercially on CDs produced by Ngaanyatjarra Media.*

Adaptive Learning

Informed by various theoretical strands from language socialisation and social learning theory, ethnographic research (Heath & McLaughlin, 1993; Heath & Smyth, 1999; McLaughlin *et al.*, 1994; Hull & Schultz, 2002) has recently focused on the potential that youth organisations have to support and stimulate non-formal, non-institutionalised learning, including literacy, in non-mainstream contexts. Writers suggest that arts-based projects provide a context for sustained learning that schools cannot match and are judged by youth themselves as desirable places to spend time. Researchers comment that adolescents look 'wholly different' when they find engagements that 'galvanize their natural strengths' (Damon, 1996: 469). Meanwhile, other research emphasises that digital technologies are enabling new kinds of agency in learning, allowing young people to take on the role of 'expert' (Barron, 2006: 198). David Buckingham suggests that much of the learning required for participation in online and computer mediated communication is carried out without explicit teaching:

> [I]t involves active exploration, "learning by doing", apprenticeship rather than direct instruction. Above all, it is profoundly social: it is a matter of collaboration and interaction with others, and of participation in a community of users. In learning with and through these media, young people are also learning how to learn. They are developing particular orientations toward information, particular methods of acquiring new knowledge and skills, and a sense of their own identities as learners. They are likely to experience a strong sense of their own autonomy, and of their right to make their own choices and to follow their own paths – however illusory this may ultimately be. In these domains, they are learning primarily by means of discovery, experimentation, and play, rather than by following external instructions and directions. (Buckingham, 2008: 17)

This 'discovery-based' approach to learning intersects with sociocultural learning theory (Lave & Wenger, 1991; Rogoff, 1990) that looks to everyday social practice in out-of-school settings for models of learning and engagement (Gee, 2004; Heath & McLaughlin, 1993; Hull & Schultz, 2002; Ito *et al.*, 2010). It also aligns with a growing literature that examines the relationship between online communication (Baron, 2008) and alphabetic reading and writing conventions and language use in new media settings (Crystal, 2008; Jones & Schieffelin, 2009; Thurlow & Mroczek, 2011).

In the Ngaanyatjarra Lands, young people are learning how to use and manipulate new technologies at an astounding rate. Much of this learning is taking place not in formal instructional settings, but through non-formal workshops and discovery-based learning in community-based learning environments, like the youth arts project and Ngaanyatjarra Media. Here, young learners are 'voluntarily developing expertise'[11]: they are learning by observation, trial-and-error experimentation, peer-to-peer teaching and everyday practice, because the activities and technologies are meaningful and relevant. Moreover, young people's developing ICT competence is defining a generational identity distinct from that of their elders, with new media representing a site where youth are exhibiting a technological expertise that far exceeds that of the older generation, as exemplified in the following vignette:

Phyllis tells a story about how her husband, Nina's grandfather, was given a laptop for work. He had it at home, but didn't know how to turn it on. Their granddaughter, Nina, who was eight years old by this time, was visiting. It was Nina who showed her grandfather how to use the computer. She had spent a lot of time watching young people use computers at WYAP and had played around with computers by herself. Phyllis laughs: 'Computer kids, they're different from us, they know'.

Learning new technologies

Playing, recording and performing contemporary music has been integral to Ngaanyatjarra culture for many decades. Numerous gospel and rock bands emerged during the 1980s and 1990s, however, few bands had used professional music recording studios, other than a small studio in Warburton, now the Wilurarra Creative youth arts studio. In late 2006, Ngaanyatarra Media introduced non-formal music recording workshops in a number of Ngaanyatjarra communities to teach local young musicians the GarageBand music recording program – free software available on the Mac iLife suite of applications (see Figure 7.1). Now, young musicians not only perform live at festivals, they have also woven new technologies into new forms of cultural production.

Figure 7.1 Youth musicians recording using GarageBand music recording software.
© Ngaanyatjarra Media

GarageBand recording took off with many of the aspiring young musicians across the region, including John and Nicholas:

> We learn music and computer. At first we didn't know how to do that music and computer. But he showed us and we looked, watched and learned. It was a little bit hard to learn. When we first started we couldn't work it out, we made lots of mistakes, but slowly we learned and now it's easy for us... Once we got used to it, it was right then. Started recording. He showed us a couple of times, a couple of days then we was doing it all by ourselves. He just let us do it. If we make a mistake we'll call him then he'll come. Then he'll show us, he'll keep showing us until we catch it all, you know. That's a good way of learning. That's a easy way of learning, like when people show you, when you practise, like when you do it, when someone show you and you do it again, and you do it, and try again and you'll get it, you'll catch it, like that. The more you practise the more you learn, like that.

After an initial demonstration by an expert mentor, Nicholas quickly developed his expertise. Soon, others were learning from him and from each other. According to John, Nicholas was already very skilled, but he never stood out from the crowd:

Nicholas is good at the computer because he's good at anything, like football and anything, but nobody saw it. With GarageBand Nicholas already knew he was clever, but other people didn't know he could learn so quick. He likes to fiddle around with things, touching everything, working it out.

After initially learning by observation and imitation, John and Nicholas also tried to learn more about GarageBand, by following written procedures:

We had the little GarageBand book, manual and we used to read it to work out what was what. We was looking at that, we didn't know. We were reading it, then we tried all the plugs, and we worked it out, how to save our work. At first we just turned off the computer and next day it was all gone.

In other words, they figured out what to do by trial-and-error experimentation. This tendency to experiment and try new things without formal training or reading the manual is consistent with Lave and Wenger's notion of situated learning (Lave & Wenger, 1991). By using the logic of the symbol system embedded in the GarageBand structure, in concert with action and embodied practice, they became, as Jean Lave states, 'learners who understand what they are learning', that is, 'active agents in the appropriation of knowledge' (Lave, 1990: 325).

Their experimentation represents an innovative reconstruction of moves through a set of sequenced relations between sound and symbol, utilising icon-based navigation. As they remark:

We record it on the computer, first we make the song right then we sing it. You press the red button that says record, press that. Then you record the voice. Then after when you finish you press stop. Then you can go back and listen to it. Press play. That's recorded there and you just listen to it. We'll practise a couple of times before we put it on, before we record it. If we're not happy we just leave it there or sometimes we just put it in the trash, just that track. Song, whole song sometimes or track. Or we just leave it if it don't turn out good.

Such 'visual/spatial thinking', states Pfaffenberger (1992: 508), is 'widespread in all technological activity systems, including today's high technology', especially the spatially-oriented and icon-based structure of the GarageBand program. The symbolic conventions used in these applications enable users – who, previously, would have avoided text-only procedures – to interpret, read and manipulate technology in socially relevant ways. In other words, young people are elaborating the spatial and symbolic dimensions of familiar communication modes and adapting them to new media activities. This is allowing, as linguist Charles Goodwin suggests, embodied actions to be 'assembled and understood through a process in which different kinds of sign phenomena', instantiated in 'diverse media' or 'semiotic fields', are 'juxtaposed in a way that enables them to mutually elaborate each other' (Goodwin, 2000: 1490). In this digital environment, learning a new procedure, performing technologically complex tasks and participating in new modes of cultural production can be mediated in ways that do not necessarily privilege alphabetic written systems. Participation is not contingent upon qualifications, or prior literacy or technological competence. Rather, it derives from a strong desire to read the symbols on the computer screen, in order to record the message embedded in the songs. These young men are fearless of technology, and this fearlessness is allowing them to stretch the boundaries of discovery, to find myriad ways of achieving the oral/aural outcome they have visualised in their mind, long before entering the recording studio.

Revealed here is the manner in which digital technologies are enabling new kinds of agency in learning and catalysing young people's imaginative capacities and how this technology is being used as a cultural tool. The generative principles of social and cultural reproduction are represented in youth media activities: what we are seeing is the *generative capacity* of the technological implements' (italics in original) (Sneath *et al.*, 2009: 18) and the capacity of these tools to enable users to experiment with new forms and layer symbolic structuring. Their innovation, their technological competence and their capacity to manipulate symbol systems, including alphabetic text, is allowing the young to imagine and create new ways of 'being', expressed not only in song, but also film and other multimodal productions.

John was born in 1985. *He is a Pitjantjatjara speaker.*

My grandfather (born 1937) and my grandmother they didn't go to school in the missionary days because they were adults, they didn't do reading and writing back in those days. They were still in the bush... My grandfather went to Ernabella and my grandmother went to Warburton Mission. Then they met up around the West Australian border. My mother grew up around here, Wingellina, round this area. My mother went to school in Wingellina, she done a bit of schooling, old school Wingellina, when she was a child. I don't see her reading and writing much because they probably went to school in *wiltja*, humpy and that. Not like a big house school, but just tin shed.

I went to school in Wingellina school, then I went to school in the Northern Territory. Katherine, I went to primary school there and came down to Alice Springs and went to high school, couple of years in high school and then came back out here to Wingellina.

John returned to Wingellina as an adult. He is a musician and works with Ngaanyatjarra Media.

The future for the band is like, we like to go out and play everywhere, play in different places, different towns, probably festivals, big festivals... In the future I like to see more things happening for young people and more stuff for them to use and more things for them to learn in Wingellina.

John lives with his partner Tinpulya and their two children in Wingellina.

Tinpulya was born in 1985. *She is a Pitjantjatjara speaker. Her grandmother's family came from country around the South Australian border. When her grandmother was young, she heard people saying: 'Oh, there's plenty feed in Ernabella, they giving it away, these whitefellas came in and they giving away mayi tjuṯa (food)'. Her family went into Ernabella mission. After another daughter was born at Ernabella, her grandparents thought: 'Oh this is where we're going to live forever, because plenty of food and water, mayi puḻkanya'.*

Slowly, they started learning a little bit of English... 'My grandparents also learnt reading and writing in Pitjantjatjara through Mr Trudinger, there were Bibles and Old Testaments'. Her mother started school, 'but it was just outside on table and chairs, no building'. Tinpulya says her mother is skilled in English, and when she was young, she worked in the clinic and the preschool. Tinpulya's father – a Yankunytjatjara man – also spoke good English.

I remember when I was little at the school I learned to read in English and at home Iearned reading in Pitjantjatjara because my father had a Bible and he was showing me how to pronounce it and how to read it... And my father had a talk with my teacher, so my father said: "I want you to take my daughter, only for one semester so she can go to primary school, so she can learn more, more English, read and write". And so

I did. But I was coming back to visit them, holidays. So only for two semesters I went. And then when I got a bit older like I was speaking the most English out of all my families. Like when talking to whitefellas I talk proper English, yeah. And as I was growing, like I was showing other people, other young girls, not to be like me, but for their future. So I was a bit role model for my community, for my school and class and for my friends.

Tinpulya completed four years at Wiltja Aboriginal boarding school in Adelaide,[12] then returned to Ernabella:

So I had to start back from Year 10 right up to Year 12 in Ernabella. I was doing Open Access College. That's a good way of learning because you feel happy, you're doing your Year 12 in the community around your family and friends and at home.

Tinpulya works at the Media Centre and uses her English/Pitjantjatjara literacy competence to assist with transcribing and translating recordings for locally produced music CDs and films.

Linguistic Creativity

Literacy research highlights the linguistically inventive 'system of social symbols' (Eckert, 1988: 186) and the proliferation of creative, everyday, non-standard uses of reading and writing that typify the adolescent age group (Camitta, 1993; Gilmore, 1986). In this section, I look at how young people have taken hold of new technologies and the manner in which they have engendered an explosion in creative multimodal literacies. I show how youth are incorporating cultural elements into oral, written and visual modes of representation and communication, and how linguistic texts are creatively interwoven into a range of expressive modalities, including music, song, film and graffiti.

International research (Hull, 2003; Hull & Stornaiuolo, 2010; Kress, 2010; Soep, 2006) suggests that fresh thinking about literacy has been ushered in by the arrival of digital technologies and the emergence of new social practices surrounding electronic media, digital film/photography and mobile-phone technology. Writers note that the uptake of informal forms of writing in online contexts is part of a broader set of social and cultural shifts in the status of printed and written communication (Ito *et al.*, 2010: 11). As James Gee suggests,

In the modern world, print literacy is not enough. People need to be literate in a great variety of different semiotic domains. If these domains involve print, people need the print bits, of course. However the vast majority of domains involve semiotic (symbolic, representational) resources besides print and some don't involve print resources at all. (Gee, 2003: 19)

An affordance of this change is the emergence of new forms of computer-mediated communication and the increasing prevalence of 'multimodal literacies' that draw on a variety of modalities: speech, writing, image, gesture and sound (Hull & Nelson, 2005; Kress & Van Leeuwen, 2001; Livingstone, 2002). An intertextual layering and blending of meaning, signs and symbols is typified in much new media production and interpretation and in the composition of multimodal texts, incorporating visual, oral, gestural and written modes of representation. This new approach is allowing us to reframe what is meant by literacy in a globalised world increasingly 'filled with digital artefacts and multiple modes and media available for communication across multiple symbolic systems' (Stornaiuolo et al., 2009: 384).

Digital technologies, as new tools of production, are enabling the generation, dissemination and decoding of multimodal texts. Digital practice incorporates the intuitive meta-textual skills of alphabetic literacy – standardised alphabetic symbols, left-to-right and top-to-bottom processing interacting with a pictographic symbol system. Here, users can engage with audio-visual media applications by using icon-based navigation, irrespective of alphabetic literacy competence. In addition, text can be integrated with image, sound, music and gesture to create digital artefacts in a manner that does not necessarily privilege alphabetic forms of signification. Ngaanyatjarra youth are embracing the 'symbol-rich, language-saturated, and technology-enhanced practices' that comprise global youth culture (Hull, 2003: 232). Online social networking through Facebook has recently gained popularity because it operates as a highly visual form of localised, parochial and socially meaningful interaction. In media centres, and even at home in communities with Wi Fi access, youth are uploading personal profiles, photos and films, using text and symbols in inventive ways, and writing, usually in English, about themselves and to each other. They are creating online family Facebook albums and using mobile-phone SMS as tools for maintaining sociality by taking 'delight in the generativity of texting conventions' and the 'infectious new forms' of textual play that these channels enable (Jones & Schieffelin, 2009: 1058).

Textual play

Evening is when the 'night prowlers', often the chronic non-school attenders, emerge. In the walking-around, night-time space, adolescents write their world as tags – initials, symbols or phrases – scrawled on a myriad of surfaces in the public domain. Adina's sister, Leanne, describes the night-time creativity of the gangways (gangs):

> They walk around all night with marker pens, if one person has marker pen they all ask: "Oh can I use it so I can write my name?" And they'll be writing their name. They'll ask that other person if they can borrow it so they can write their name all fancy styles, some they just write their friend's name and their boyfriend or girlfriend's name, or if they're from Warburton, so that they can let them know that it's that person.

In graffiti, relationships with kin, gangways and lovers are expressed in self-defined 'fancy writing', 'tricky writing', colluded coding and word games. 'Love-way' relationships (in the past, punishable with spearing in the leg) are now inscribed in the public space for all to see. Warnings are signalled for girls from other communities to read, and when 'they're enemies', girls erase each other's names. Such textual announcements can escalate into community brawls if individuals feel wronged or shamed in public.

Gangways invent and reinvent codes to disguise their identity; they write 'short way, tricky way so they can't read it, but us girls we can read it' – reminiscent of the 'short-way' secret language used by Pitjantjatjara female teenagers at Areyonga (Langlois, 2004) and the oral wordplay letter substitution strategies used by Ngaanyatjarra adults. As Leanne explains:

> So they'll be thinking hard who could this person would be? But that person won't show them how they do it. They'll be thinking hard: "Who's this person, they got a lovely fancy writing?" So they'll start copying that person.

Colluded codings are used when girls have boyfriends[13]:

OTLVS ALWAY WILL BE 4EVER

Or when girls are 'best friends':

◁ = *O3BF 4EVER* = ▷
O5B Friends

The individual self is also 'announced' (von Sturmer, 2002) as the *only one*, revealing, here, the assertion of individual personhood evident in contemporary iconography:

OAONLIE GIRL 4EVER and EVER OK-AY
1.A.ONLY IN 20T4 S.D.G.J
ONLY 1 4 NONE

In recent years, new styles of graffiti coding have emerged that resemble the shortcutting evident in mobile-phone and online text messaging[14]:

$$SS$$
ICU4URQT   ♥*s*
⊲*= SOQT =* ▷

This tendency to 'textual play' is repeated in other youth practices, where alphabetic text is only one form of representation within a whole range of semiotic systems and modalities that are used to index the world.

Multimodal practice often draws on traditional cultural elements, as epitomised in the multimodal enactment of narratives in *mirlpatjunku* (sand-story drawing). As noted in Chapter 1, young girls are familiar with the narrative schemata of *mirlpatjunku*, where symbolic and pictorial representations are integrated with spoken narrative and gesture in a 'coherent narrative whole' within a single 'frame' (Wilkins, 1997: 144). This familiarity is perhaps enabling youth to adapt to the creation of multimodal productions in the new digital environment. At WYAP, young people often engage in a form of textual play or habitual doodling while they work. These scribbled patterns, symbols, initials, socio-spatial signifiers, as well as personal names, names of family, friends or hip-hop musicians eventually find their way into multimedia productions. Young women, like Adina and Leanne, then need little assistance in reproducing graffiti-like texts, cartoons and drawings in applications like Photoshop Elements and iMovie.

Adina was born in 1982. *She grew up in Kalgoorlie and visited Warburton only now and then. She went to Eastern Goldfields High School and CAPS in Coolgardie. She says she was 'really brainy' at school and was put in a high class. She finished school in 1998, after completing Year 10. Adina returned to Warburton, after getting into a bit of trouble in Kalgoorlie. She is now married to George and Carmel's son and has one young daughter, Rosina. Prior to 2004, Adina took a number of*

Figure 7.2 Graffiti images, Warburton 2003-2006
Photos: Inge Kral. Layout: John Hughes

accredited training courses at the college in Warburton. She has participated in the youth arts project as a photographer, filmmaker, cartoonist and writer. She now works at the school. Adina is also the granddaughter of Clem's brother – one of the creative writers in the 'literary movement' of the 1970s. This is a source of great pride and inspiration for her.

Styling the New

Generationally differentiated arenas of social practice are changing the way in which Ngaanyatjarra youth are expressing themselves. Through their dress, gesture, visual symbolism and performative modes, young people are not replicating the past, but creating new forms. Remoteness no longer isolates them from wider culture influences. They are immersed in what Appadurai terms the 'global cultural flow' (Appadurai, 1996). In their productions, we are seeing deliberate and conscious linguistic switching or 'styling and crossing across social space and time' (Hill, 1999: 543; Alim *et al.*, 2009; Rampton, 1999). Through the incorporation of intercultural elements, young people are gleaning what they want from a myriad of sources and making it their own through symbol system interpretation, manipulation and production and forming 'semiotic reconstructions' (Pennycook, 2003: 527). They are identifying with images and speech styles of Afro-American hip-hop musicians and styling themselves accordingly. Adolescent girls are affixing photos from fashion magazines on to bedroom walls, identifying with these images and projecting this new self in fashion parades. Musicians are navigating between the local and the global and tuning into YouTube and the online world as observers and participants. Wider viewings of film productions at festivals, on television and online are forming a new kind of coalescence. Film and music clips are regularly uploaded on to the internet and through You Tube, and project websites reach out to a global audience. This is allowing young people to author a narrative that differs from that of the older generation and to have their trajectory and worldview validated in the public space. Such hybridity is now the new norm on a global level.

Nevertheless, despite these new dispositions, Ngaanyatjarra youth are still deeply rooted in their own cultural schema. In this generation, we are seeing continuities and transformations, as young adults hold on to their 'Ngaanyatjarra-ness', evident in the signs and symbols used by young people drawn from their propensity to '*tjukurrpa*-thinking', as pointed out earlier. Connection to kin and country and the enduring relationship between place and identity remain strong – for some young adults, the first contact their parents had with the Western world was in the 1960s, so the past is close. 'Symbolic condensations' (Munn, 1992: 114) of these connections are found in new expressive modes and forms of cultural production.

At Warburton in 2005, the youth arts group coined the term 'Stylie way – *Wilurarra* style' to embody the intertextuality of their new style and expressions of self through fashion, film and language. In this 'semiotic social space' (Gee, 2005), the term '*wilurarra*' (West) embodies polysemous,

Figure 7.3 Wilurarra Creative logo
© Wilurarra Creative

multilayered socio-spatial references: an intertextual blending of the cardinal direction 'west' – young people's geographical location, physically, in Western Australia, as well as their figurative location in modernity and the Western world, concomitant with hip-hop popular culture references. In a film about gesture and sign language (made for the *Wilurarra Stylie Film* DVD), the changing nature of communication is portrayed with young people blending new 'gangsta culture' hand signs with Ngaanyatjarra traditional sign language. The new 'stylie way' form, evident in young people's multimodal expressions, displays an overlapping of various semiotic systems. Oral language and non-verbal codes, such as gesture, gaze and hand signs, are integrated with symbols and gestures from contemporary, urban hip-hop culture. Elaborations are evident in contemporary iconography, including the new youth arts logo (see Figure 7.3).

Music and song: New forms, old themes

Songs are a unique textual space where the music is not notated, but collectively remembered 'in the mind', and the recorded song acts as a mnemonic. These oral texts are typically composed and sung in Ngaanyatjarra. Sometimes these oral texts are transcribed and translated into English for CD covers by young literates like Tinpulya.

Many songs incorporate recurrent cultural themes, conventions and schemas drawn from the traditional canon. Revealed in some songs is the 'encoding' of cultural meaning in the expression of *ngarltu* ('compassion') and an emphasis on *miranykanyilku* ('looking after' people) and empathy for individuals who are longing for country or kin.[15] Moral themes are also addressed in songs lexicalised around contemporary issues, where song represent a new form of 'publicly available discourse'. Traditional speech styles are appropriated and used to give a message. Songs that 'give a message' encode features of the hortatory speech genre; the admonitory mode often utilised in *yaarlpirri to* persuade, condemn, praise or complain (Goddard, 1990). As John declares, 'music is our way to give a strong message':

> It'll be stronger if it comes from like younger kids, younger people. So like the older people, you know, when they hear it they think: "Ah that's young ones telling us, singing these songs, telling us, singing this, saying this message on songs".

Musicians draw on a familiar speech style, by exhorting people to listen to their warnings about the dangers of drinking, smoking marijuana and sniffing petrol:

> We sing it in English, don't drink and drive, so when they driving somewhere, they might hear it and think it's a sign, must be telling me *mulapa* (true): "Don't drink and drive", it's a message. Lot of youngfellas passed away from all communities from going to town and drinking, that's why all the songs, you know.

In these new times, the sociolinguistic shift is palpable. Earlier, I mentioned how the adjective *tjukarurru* – 'straight' – is often used in terms of moral imperatives – that is, to denote the 'right way' of talking and behaving or fulfilling obligations and responsibilities. The quote above indicates the growing willingness for young people to discuss issues in public forums using 'straight talking' strategies, rather than circumlocution – the mode typically used to avoid direct criticism in public. The encoding of cultural values in song is further evident in the manner in which young people, like John and Nicholas, sing about their connection to country:

> ...looking after our sacred areas and waterholes and grandfathers' land. That's a strong message, like so younger generation can see that and listen to that and understand what the message is. We have responsibility for, like message and all that, singing and letting people know and like, getting the message out there.

These songs provide insights not only into the nature of youth language practices in times of rapid language shift (McCarty & Wyman, 2009), but also exist as a marker of shifting ideologies and identity formation processes in a time of change, as I show in the next section.

Shifting ideologies

As I suggest above, young people are negotiating concerns of sociocultural relevance through song, as a new type of storytelling practice. It is in songs that core cultural concepts are evident. A genre of songs about a 'man, woman or child alone/one' – 'wati kutju', 'kungka kutju' and 'tjitji kutju' – is highlighted in the contemporary canon. As discussed earlier, separation from kin and country engenders empathy for relatives who are alone or absent. As exemplified in the following Pitjantjatjara song:

Walytja tjutangku wantingu
Yangupala kutju nyinangi palunya
walytja tjutangku wantingu.
Paluru kutju nyinangi palunya walytja
tjutangku wantingu.
Paluru nyinara putu kuliningi,
putu mulapa kuliningi.
Palunya walytja tjutangku wantingu.

Family have gone away
One youngfella was sitting alone,
because his family had left him.
He was sitting alone because his family had left him.
He didn't know what to think,
still didn't know what to think.
All his family had left him.[16]

Although this genre is redolent of the theme of solitariness evident in *tjukurrpa* stories, it is also marked by the manner in which it differs from themes exploited by young Western songwriters.[17] In Western society, it is normative for young adults to strike out alone – that is, to leave one's 'home' place and to embark on an individual life trajectory, whereas, for Western Desert youth, different social meanings are attached to being 'one'.

In pre-contact times, immense social value was placed on social relatedness. The norm was for family members to be either within the broader collective for ceremonial gatherings or within a smaller band grouping, all within the parameter of attachments to particular country (Brooks, 2011a). In the absence of institutional authority, the Law provided a set of socially sanctioned norms of conduct or rules that governed behaviour in the broader moral community. Collective adherence to the rules of this social system was a necessity, and the system was held intact by the authority of the elders and by fear of far-away places and people. Even though self-reliance was fostered during the long period of pre-marriage independence, 'individualism', as a cultural concept, was unknown. In comparison, individualism and concerns with 'self' or 'selfhood' are concepts particular to Western culture. Western theories of human development have enshrined the moral concepts of 'individual rights' (Bourdieu & Passeron, [1977] 1990; Carrithers et al., 1985; Dumont, 1965). Importantly, the dominant Western ideology of individualism has imbued formal education with 'liberal assumptions' about the role of schooling, where successful life-course outcomes are tied to *individual* hard work and effort and the pursuit of credentials. By contrast, the individually-oriented construction of per-sonhood required for the Western school-to-work transition is not central to Ngaanyatjarra ways of being in the world.

Nevertheless, by examining socialisation practices and the ideologies that shape Western Desert society, one can identify that a transformation in the notion of selfhood has been taking place over the past few decades. Earlier, I looked at how the 'birthday party' is acting as a site for individual identity socialisation. I considered how naming and the bureaucratic requirements of the state impacted on the acquisition and transmission of individualised identity markers. I also signalled the manner in which the assertion of individual personhood is lexicalised in the iconography of youth graffiti. Yet, it is in youth cultural productions, such as songs, that the differences between Ngaanyatjarra and Western cultural processes and priorities are marked. Although shifting ideologies are evident, at this juncture, notions of collective Ngaanyatjarra personhood stand firmly at the intersection between tradition and modernity.

Conclusion

In this chapter, the adaptive learning strategies and behaviours evident in the current youth generation are foregrounded. I examine two local initiatives: Warburton Youth Arts Project and Ngaanyatjarra Media. I emphasise that where activities are tied to meaningful community projects, youth are engaging as the mediators and facilitators of multimodal productions in collaborative, intergenerational activities that positively affirm their contemporary Ngaanyatjarra or Pitjantjatjara identity. I show

how the affordances of new digital technologies are enabling new forms of cultural production, as well as multiple modes of communication and linguistic creativity. Young people are choosing to participate because these cultural production roles are in the domains of knowledge that matter to them – culture, arts, country and new technologies. In addition, they are merging the intercultural elements of Ngaanyatjarra language, gesture and style with global youth culture and English, thus forging and expressing new cultural perspectives, innovations and identities. Their productions illuminate the cultural practices and symbol structures in image and language that young people are using for identity formation. These young people are change agents, seeking to know more about the outside world, while simultaneously drawing on pre-existing knowledge from the local culture. These experiences are allowing young people to visualise themselves in positive, imagined futures (Kral, 2010b; Kral, 2011).

Notes

(1) Prior to the 20th century, 'adolescence', as a developmental period in Western culture, was unknown (James, 1993: 180). Adolescence as a concept appeared by the end of the 19th century, in tandem with the transformation from agricultural orientations to an urban industrial orientation (Rogoff, 2003: 171–174).

(2) McLean – interview, 9 September 2004.

(3) Principal – interview, 27 November 2004.

(4) Warburton community meeting – August 2004.

(5) The Central Australian Aboriginal Media Association (CAAMA), based in Alice Springs, was established as the first federally funded Aboriginal media association in 1979. After 1985, with the launch of the national AUSSAT satellite system by the Australian government, many remote Aboriginal communities were able to access broadcast television and radio for the first time. Observers saw the proposed launch of AUSSAT and the introduction of TV as a challenge to remote Indigenous culture (Michaels, 1986). These concerns, and the increasing demand for Aboriginal-controlled media during the 1980s (including Warlpiri Media at Yuendumu, EVTV at Ernabella and, later, Ngaanyatjarra Media), drove the establishment in 1987 of the Broadcasting in Remote Aboriginal Communities Scheme (BRACS), implemented by the federal DAA to equip remote communities with technology for local video and radio production and local retransmission (Rennie & Featherstone, 2008).

(6) Daniel Featherstone – interview, 13 April 2008.

(7) *Certificate III in Broadcasting (Remote Area Operations)* – a nationally accredited Training Package was delivered jointly by Ngaanyatjarra Media and Batchelor Institute of Indigenous Tertiary Education, Northern Territory.

(8) See http://wilurarra.com/ and http://www.youtube.com/watch?v=ppwAWKCn QuY&feature=channel

(9) Youth Arts meeting, Ngaanyatjarra College, Warburton, 13 December 2004.

(10) Christian Aboriginal Parent-directed Schools (CAPS) were established in 1981 in Coolgardie, Kurrawang and, later, Wongutha, in the previous location of Wongutha Mission Training Farm. The CAPS system was formed by concerned Aboriginal parents who had grown up at, or had links to, Mt Margaret Mission.

(11) S.B. Heath (personal communication, February 2010).

(12) The Wiltja programme for Indigenous students (initiated by the Pitjantjatjara Yankunytjatjara Education Committee in South Australia) is annexed to Woodville High School in Adelaide, South Australia.

(13) Graffiti was copied directly off surfaces and decoded as: OTLVS = Only Two LoVerS; O5B Friends = Only 5 Best Friends; 1.A.ONLY IN 20T4 S.D.G.J = One and only in 2004 So Don't Get Jealous.

(14) Decoded as: 'I see you for you are cute'; 'SS "loves" some one cutie'.

(15) Analysis of 101 songs recorded by young Western Desert musicians, 2003–2008.

(16) Lyrics by Chris Reid and Nathan Brown, from *Wati Kutju* CD Alunytjuru Band. © Ngaanyatjarra Media 2008.

(17) David Brooks (personal communication, October 2011).

Conclusion

In this book, ethnography has been used to address concerns associated with enculturation, cultural transmission and reproduction – refracted through the prism of changing social practice and the shifting modes of oral, literate and, now, technological communication. I have considered how the relational aspect of historical, social, cultural and ideological factors has impacted on, and influenced, language and literacy socialisation and learning in one community of practice, over a number of generations, in a time of profound culture change and language shift. By considering the relational complexity, I have sought to counter sweeping generalisations about youth, literacy and the role of schooling; leading to a nuanced account of changing social practices, the development of literacy and the cultural and historical production of literate identities in one remote Aboriginal setting. As I have emphasised throughout this volume, the learning trajectory of current and future generations is inextricably intertwined with a complex web of social, cultural, historical and institutional practices, processes, meanings, norms, ideologies, identities, settings and influences. Language socialisation builds on these 'different, overlapping and intersecting layers of experience' (Duff, 2008: xv) and frames young people's way of being in the social worlds in which they will live (Heath, 2008b). This complex web of language and literacy socialisation experiences factor significantly in determining how youth will engage and, indeed, succeed in schooling and other institutional domains across the life course. It is therefore imperative that we broaden our understanding of how and where indigenous youth are acquiring the knowledge, practices and dispositions required to function as competent members of social groups and cultural communities.

Changing Social Practice: The Ontological Shift

In this study, anthropology is the lens through which the adaptations that the Ngaanyatjarra have made, (over only a few generations, in the ontological shift to modernity – from a hunter-gatherer life, to a sedentary existence in the Mission and, later, the communities of the Ngaanyatjarra Lands) are viewed. Since first contact with Anglo-Australian settler society, the Ngaanyatjarra have incorporated extraordinary change, yet they have remained an essentially robust society. Without minimising the gravity of the colonial encounter and the detrimental consequences of change, as a group, the Ngaanyatjarra have exhibited reservoirs of resilience and a skillful capacity to adapt, transmit and elaborate their social practices and cultural processes. Their strength can be attributed to their unbroken connection to country and the continuity of their worldview, social practices, language and culture underpinned by the *tjukurrpa* – the Law – compounded by the fact that many Ngaanyatjarra have, to some extent, been able to assert agentive control in the creation of new ways of being and, ultimately, transformed identities in new 'figured worlds'. This has been achieved, in part, by being adept at taking on many European practices and institutional norms, albeit in a mimetic form in some domains. Nevertheless, as I have shown throughout this volume, each policy era: missionisation, assimilation, self-determination and, now, 'mainstreaming' (Altman, 2004) has put in place new externally imposed conditions and an illusion of certainty.

Mainstreaming: Everything different again

Anthony Giddens posits that identity is the 'creation of constancy over time, that very bringing of the past into conjunction with an anticipated future'. In all societies, he asserts, 'the maintenance of personal identity, and its connection to wider social identities' is 'a prime requisite of ontological security' (Giddens, 1994: 80). I would argue that in spite of the upheaval that the encounter with modernity has wrought, the Ngaanyatjarra collective sense of self and identity is strong and a distinctive cultural schema and worldview has been maintained. Nevertheless, ontological security has been challenged and undermined by the erosion of certainty linked to the constantly changing framework of institutional policies and practices and the ensuing disillusionment with unfulfilled expectations of what the future would hold.

In Chapter 4, I discussed how state intervention did not commence in the Ngaanyatjarra region until the 1950s. Over the ensuing decades, the state has incrementally assumed more and more responsibility for the delivery of government services and funding to the Ngaanyatjarra (and other remote Aboriginal communities) through its relevant state agencies in Western Australia, followed by the Commonwealth agencies DAA, ATSIC and the incumbent Department of Families, Housing, Community Services and Indigenous Affairs (FaHCSIA). Following the abolition of ATSIC in 2004, a new agenda, aimed at 'practical reconciliation', commenced across Indigenous Australia. A key platform has been the 'welfare reform agenda' (McClure, 2000), in tandem with the 2008 National Indigenous Reform Agreement.[1] Implemented to decrease welfare dependency by improving living standards in remote communities through 'mainstreaming' services, concomitant with 'closing the gap' in education and training provision to enable Indigenous people to move into the open labour market.[2] In this respect, all policy decisions are now made nationally or at a state level, irrespective of local conditions and opinions.

As a consequence, across the Indigenous sector, federal government policy and bureaucratic structures have altered to such an extent that localised and limited community autonomy now struggles in a web of bureaucracy (Palmer, 2005: 109). In the prevailing environment of top-down federal government bureaucratic control, small organisations, like the Ngaanyatjarra Council, are 'fragmented and under pressure and unable to fulfil an advocacy role amidst the pressure to understand and respond to the pace of change'.[3] Until recently, the overall administrative needs and service provision of the Ngaanyatjarra communities were met by the organisational structure of the Council.[4] Aboriginal leadership of the Council was strong; community participation at monthly meetings was high and outcomes tangible, giving *yarnangu* a sense of agency and security.[5] Importantly, for the argument I am making here, this enabled young people to observe their elders exerting effective leadership in local decision-making. The current top-down bureaucratic approach, oriented towards excluding Indigenous control over matters of local concern, has led to reduced community participation in local governance. In the Ngaanyatjarra region (and nationally), changes have included the devolution of the delivery of essential services to the state government, paving the way for a preponderance of intrusions by government bureaucrats and mainstream organisations, symbolised in the 'influx of new unknown and unknowable whitefellas in shiny white Toyotas'.[6] *Yarnangu*, as objects of, rather than agents in this change industry, are peripheral to the discourse.

The dismantling of CDEP

Indigenous public policy, in particular, the federal government's so-called 'welfare to work' agenda, is formulated against a backdrop of public commentary on 'dysfunction' and 'social collapse' in remote communities (Sullivan, 2010; Sutton, 2009). This discourse has construed CDEP as contributing to welfare dependency (Pearson, 2000; Spicer, 1997), irrespective of community development and management objectives, in locations like the Ngaanyatjarra Lands. Nationally, the phasing out of CDEP commenced in July 2009. Despite well-intentioned attempts to 'normalise' (Altman & Hinkson, 2007) service delivery to remote communities, in line with the mainstream, recent welfare 'reforms' have, ironically, led to increased uncertainty and confusion and, in the Ngaanyatjarra region, an elevated dependency on the welfare state. Anthropologist Patrick Sullivan suggests that the 'policy environment of the 1970s was in a similar state of uncertainty to the one we see today' (Sullivan, 2010: 1).

In Chapters 3 and 4, I discussed how a significant cohort of older Ngaanyatjarra was 'habitualized' (Berger & Luckmann, [1966] 1975) into the Western work practices on missions and stations. In a similar light, CDEP was perceived, locally, as 'working for your living'. Now, many adults previously engaged in community-oriented CDEP work are on NewStart 'unemployment benefits'. Until recently, CDEP enabled *yarnangu* to have agency in the improvement of their standard of living, allowing for discretion in how funds were distributed, benefiting all. Additionally, the loss of CDEP on-cost income is dismantling the viability of the Council by reducing their capacity to provide crucial services and depleting assets acquired, and systems developed, over the past few decades.[7] Outside 'providers', with no local knowledge, are taking over from the Council in the provision of, often inappropriate and unrealistic, training and employment pathways and goals.

Mainstreaming or marginalisation?

For the Ngaanyatjarra, their ontology, or 'way of being in the world', is marginal to mainstream Australia. Despite the permanency of *tjukurrpa* and their numerical dominance in their own country, on a day-to-day level, the Ngaanyatjarra struggle with the changed power dynamic and the assumed authority of the state and non-Aboriginal value systems. Everyday life is now more bureaucratised and subject to intrusions of the state, as well as national and global media, than ever before. It is at the intersection of local conditions and the bureaucratic requirements of the state that the growing marginalisation of the Ngaanyatjarra from authority over their own affairs is heightened.

The increasing complexity and volatility of the national policy environment is undermining pre-existing forms of collective local control. In addition, Ngaanyatjarra leaders are increasingly marginalised because they do not have the discursive oral and literate practices required to 'manage' communities and mediate the burgeoning requirements of the bureaucracy (Batty, 2005). Wesley, for instance, has extensive community management and governance experience, yet, he comments:

> The amount of reading I do every day to fulfil my role as Project Officer or Chairperson or Governing Committee member or Native Title or Education or whatever, the amount of paperwork that comes across my

desk is unbelievable and for me to keep up with all that I have to be capable of reading at a certain level. And with my experience, I went to what, Year 10? That's probably the minimum you'd need in this sort of situation... to be able to compete in this world, that is, with enough knowledge and confidence to be able to speak up. That's where we have a lot of [Ngaanyatjarra] people hiding in the bush back here and don't want to go out and speak up because it's, that confidence. A lot of our people rely on people telling them, like a lot of these mob will listen to and they'll trust everything that's said by any white person. They're not finding out themselves.

Furthermore, government policy, since the inception of the welfare reform agenda, has been predicated upon an expectation of *individual* English language and literacy competence:

This individual approach works best where the applicant has reasonable literacy and numeracy skills, viable use of English, adequate maintenance of personal records (i.e. income details, birth certificate, tax file information, rent accounts and essential services accounts), an understanding of Government programs and program delivery and a residential address for the receiving of relevant mail. To date, the lack of this individual capacity on the part of Ngaanyatjarra community members has been addressed by the Ngaanyatjarra communities pooling limited resources and capacity to represent themselves to Government and Government agencies. (Thurtell, 2003: 4–5)

Theorists (Gee, 1996; McDermott & Varenne, 1995; Ogbu, 1990; Varenne & McDermott, 1999) have examined how literacy, or illiteracy, can stem from the inclusion or exclusion of individuals or groups from societal power. It may be considered that many Ngaanyatjarra live in a separate domain, hence, their apparent nonchalant disregard for literate compliance with the nation state may, in fact, represent a deliberate assertion of their status as outsiders – marginalised from the mainstream and belonging to a different cultural schema. Nevertheless, it is undeniable that to deal more effectively with the demands of the state, the Ngaanyatjarra will need a complex array of English language and literacy skills and knowledge of bureaucratic systems. Not having the skills to deal with certain individual bureaucratic literacies can have dire consequences, including incarceration, as outlined in Chapter 2. However, as I indicated in Chapter 6, individual technical literacy competency can be undermined by social and cultural factors that run counter to the tangential requirements of literacy, including individual ownership, the perceived need to look after and protect *things* and to conserve objects for future use, as well as the time and space rule-oriented boundaries that literacy practice demands.

While giving credence to the serious argument that illiteracy may have negative personal consequences and preclude Ngaanyatjarra participation in their own governance and the mainstream labour market, it is not clear that pedagogy alone can provide the complex array of skills and knowledge required for future conditions. I discuss this conundrum by examining the complexity of literacy in the remote context, followed by a consideration of the consequences of altered socialisation processes and the need for new learning for new times.

Newly Literate or Failing?

Public policy discourse in Australia typically poses a singular developmental trajectory for 'successful' Indigenous youth futures, pivoting around institutional learning and employment in the 'real economy' (Pearson, 2000). Across Indigenous Australia, people are told: 'a job is the key to social and economic progress' and 'a job delivers self-esteem and the means to get ahead in life' (Commonwealth of Australia, 2008: 1). Moreover, literacy is promoted as the enabling factor that will give Indigenous people the opportunity to enter the labour market and reap the economic rewards. Paradoxically, a simultaneous narrative of educational failure has been played out in innumerable national reports and inquiries (Collins, 1999; Long *et al.*, 1999; MCEETYA, 2004). Currently, in this discourse, attention is focused on the failure of youth in remote Indigenous schools to meet national English literacy and numeracy benchmark standards.

Despite the work of many fine and dedicated educators in the Ngaanyatjarra Lands schools over the years, it is indisputable that students have not attained the academic preparation required to commence tertiary courses. Moreover, local vocational training also typically requires mediated English literacy support.[8] Nevertheless, this debate often does not take account of the social, cultural and historical correlates of literacy, and achievements are cast in Western terms only.I contend that a problem with the conception of literacy is evident in public and policy discourse. In particular, we have lost sight of the complexity of literacy in the remote context.

The Ngaanyatjarra case study sheds light on the important fact that the remote context must be viewed as newly literate. As I have shown, literacy cannot be understood independently of the social, cultural, political and historical forces that shape it, nor can it be analysed in isolation from the social practices that surround it and the ideological systems in which it is embedded. The acquisition, meaning and uses of literacy in the Ngaanyatjarra world have been precipitated by the intersection of social, cultural and historical circumstances and the conjuncture of church and state. The particularities of the Ngaanyatjarra experience have shaped literacy practices that are specific to that situation and context. The socio-historical conditions could not have been otherwise. In other words, the historical development of literacy in this region created the conditions that enabled the literacy practices documented here. In the newly literate Ngaanyatjarra context, what is remarkable is the extent to which alphabetic literacy has become a transmitted practice – a taken-for-granted cultural process among some individuals and in some families, particularly in families where the public roles and identities of individuals have been intertwined with literacy, where literacy artefacts and literate behaviours are permeating the space between public and domestic practice. I suggest, in fact, that the Ngaanyatjarra case study marks a benchmark for *normative* literacy practice *under such newly literate circumstances* – not when measured against mainstream standards that are incommensurate, but when compared with other *similar* situations. It does not, however, represent a replicable model for other remote communities, as the specificity of the circumstances and conditions negate this.

In newly literate circumstances, such as with the Ngaanyatjarra, a tension thus remains: trying to squeeze thousands of years of Western literacy evolution into a few generations will not achieve commensurability with mainstream benchmarks, while literacy remains a decontextualised technical skill. Literacy is, as Clancy (1979) illustrates, a gradual process. Furthermore, as Street emphasises (1984: 114) to 'eschew such gradualism' tends to lead to the failure of many literacy programmes, and, I would add, in the remote Indigenous context, that failure tends to be attributed to literacy learners themselves.

A 'literacy myth'

According to Harvey Graff (1979), Western education is imbued with a 'literacy myth'. In this myth, literacy is associated with ideological promises emblematic of modernity and progress and linked to economic growth and development (Collins, 1995; Street, 1995). Other researchers (Jessor et al., 1996; Rogoff, 2003; Serpell, 1993) have questioned the 'illusory' aspects of Western education and the idea of a linear cultural evolution based on the premise of a single developmental trajectory towards the same desirable end point. In his influential study of education and working-class students in

England, Paul Willis counters the 'common educational fallacy' that 'opportunities can be *made* by education, that upward mobility is basically a matter of individual push, that qualifications make their own openings' (Willis, 1977: 127 [emphasis in original]). Graff's notion of the 'literacy myth' resonates with what Australian researchers describe as the 'illusion' that the ideology of fair competition is neutral and where success or failure in the mainstream is dependent on individual hard work and effort (Falk, 2001; Smyth & Hattam, 2004). That is, the 'sequenced pathway' of the transition from school to work appears normal, but is, in fact, problematic, even in some mainstream contexts (Smyth & Hattam, 2004: 152). Importantly, this linear trajectory has even less relevance for Indigenous youth, where schools are teaching for labour market outcomes that do not exist in remote Australia.

A significant number of Ngaanyatjarra have participated in limited schooling, to varying degrees of success, over two, three and, even, four generations. Significantly, early education experiences made sense and provided the key actors with sufficient literacy and Western 'cultural capital' (Bourdieu, [1980] 1990; Bourdieu & Passeron, [1977] 1990) to be effective and confident agents at critical junctures in the slowly expanding encounter with the Western world. Over time, however, the expectations of what schooling could deliver were not fulfilled. Deep uncertainty now exists about what education *is actually for*, as the acquisition of literacy in the Ngaanyatjarra context has not correlated with improved socio-economic circumstances and employment. This raises the important question of finding new ways of setting young adults on meaningful learning trajectories in an environment where there is limited employment, yet a critical need for engagement in purposeful activity that will build the skills needed for 'successful' futures with, or without, employment.

A singular focus on pedagogy is linked to the well-intentioned belief among educators, researchers and policy-makers that if the right methodology is found, literacy learning will unfold. Significant amounts of time and money have been invested in implementing new literacy curricula and methodology, with each new version heralded as the panacea to the problem of Aboriginal illiteracy. However, assumptions that investment in literacy methodology will produce significantly improved literacy ability, and the associated Western 'middle-class' literate behaviours desired by policy-makers, need to be reassessed. In most mainstream English-speaking families, literacy builds on the long culture of literacy in Western society and the foundation of schooling. It incorporates interactive engagement and participation in other processes, practices and contexts that are meaningful and purposeful at an individual and community level, and there is a synergy between these processes. For literacy to take hold in the remote context, it must have meaning and purpose over the changing domains and practices that span a person's life, and this meaning and purpose must, in turn, be transmitted to the following generation.

The literacy myth noted above also hinges upon what Street terms the 'autonomous' model, where literacy is conceptualised in technical terms, independent of social context (Street, 1993b: 5). As Street contends, literacy in and of itself cannot promote social mobility or progress, as 'literacy practices are specific to the political and ideological context and their consequences vary situationally' (Street, 1995: 24). The problem with the autonomous model lies with the assumption that literacy learning is a 'straightforward skill-acquisition process that can be delivered in a carefully programmed way to large numbers of people in a short period of time, with roughly uniform or predictable outcomes' (Prinsloo, 1995: 458–459). Literacy learning is not a mono-linear process: it is multidirectional and erratic, incorporating formal instruction *and* informal acquisition, and the acquisition process is lifelong. Finally, as I note below, commentators generally *assume* a shared understanding of what literacy is, however, few have moved beyond a school-based deficit perspective on alphabetic literacy learning to notice the changing modes of literacy in the 'new media age' (Kress, 2003).

The assumed importance of literacy in English

Despite the early introduction of vernacular literacy and its purposeful application and diffusion, schools in the Ngaanyatjarra Lands, as in most other remote regions, now focus on the teaching of spoken and written English, with scant attention to the mother tongue. The continuing dominance of English as the language of literacy holds profound sociolinguistic implications. Literacy is not being learned in the vernacular, the first language, the mother tongue, the language of the inner voice – the language that is imbued with the concepts that form the psychic home where the core values of culture reside – but in a second language that many do not speak well and remain culturally distanced from. The actual and symbolic significance of language – and the connection between language, identity affirmation and belonging – in post-colonial minority language contexts, such as with the Ngaanyatjarra, cannot be emphasised enough. The marginalisation of Ngaanyatjarra language, in essence, signifies the symbolic marginalisation of Ngaanyatjarra culture and identity. For *yarnangu*, their language and culture signifies identity, belonging, heritage *and* difference.

Ngaanyatjarra people seek to maintain that difference – they do not want to be the same as Anglo-Australians.[9]

An Altered Language Socialisation Framework

In the 1970s, anthropologist Margaret Mead developed a theoretical model for considering notions of cultural transmission and change, based on three key forms: *postfigurative* (when the future repeats the past, change is slow and the old cannot conceive of any other future for their children, other than their own past lives); *cofigurative* (in which the present is the guide to future expectations); and *prefigurative* (for the kind of culture in which the elders have to learn from the children about experiences which they never had) (Mead, [1970] 1978: 13). In post-figurative and co-figurative cultures, socialisation is a clearly defined hierarchical and uni-linear process, involving the transfer of cultural values, norms, symbols and practices from the older to the younger generation. Mead emphasises ([1970] 1978: 17) that when there has been a profound break between the experiences of the old and the experiences of the young, cultural transmission and socialisation patterns are challenged. In societies undergoing rapid social change, such as with the Ngaanyatjarra, previously normative intergenerational roles and hierarchies are blurred. In this prefigurative context, the values, norms, knowledge and skills of the older generation are altering, and this is challenging pre-existing patterns for the succession of the generations.

The arrival of the missionaries at Warburton Ranges in the early 1930s, and the ensuing encounter with Anglo-Australian settler society, ushered in profound changes and impossible-to-imagine futures. Prior to this, the production and reproduction of linguistic forms were linked to a nomadic lifestyle, where language skills, strategies and attitudes were tied to a predictable framework of practice. Under the influence of the Mission and then Native Welfare, Ngaanyatjarra people's agency as parents was eroded. As a consequence, reduced sustained interactions between the young and the old began impacting on the intergenerational transmission of cultural learning – that is, the transfer of cultural values, norms, symbols and practices from the older to the younger generation. This has led to a profound shift in socialisation and learning processes within only a few generations: from observation and imitation and everyday social practice in the company of elders within a hunter-gatherer existence to a sedentary Western-oriented lifestyle pivoting around learning from experts within institutional frameworks.

As discussed in Chapter 2, successful engagement in schooling rests on the presupposition that individuals have had prior language or literacy socialisation of a particular type (Duff, 2008), in the home or community context. The particularities of the Ngaanyatjarra experience have shaped a repertoire of language and literacy practices that are specific to that situation and context. As I exemplified earlier, the 'church', and often vernacular, literacy practices that arose out of the Mission encounter have become conventionalised across the generations and are being reproduced as taken-for-granted practice in domestic contexts. Once they enter school, however, the message that many Ngaanyatjarra children are absorbing is that other genres and discourse styles are valued and prioritised and that they are failing to acquire the kind of literacy that leads to school success.

In Western society, social institutions and socially aspirant families provide specific guidelines concerning the role expectations and behaviours of children and adolescents (Burton *et al.*, 1996). Successful schooling is contingent upon an assumed and shared understanding of the 'normal biography', that is 'the clear and persistent pursuit of a credential' and the 'cultural logic' that follows (Smyth & Hattam, 2004: 145). Accordingly, youngsters are typically socialised into an individual trajectory of credentialisation, leading to some future maturation of abstract mainstream employment outcomes. It is in adolescence and young adulthood that speakers begin to encounter, to a substantial degree, the styles, registers and genres of discourse that advance negotiation, exchange, knowledge acquisition and skill build-up. These syntactic and discourse structures provide young speakers with the linguistic and conceptual tools to move toward mature adult roles. Facility in both receptive and productive oral and written language paves the way for academic achievement. Educators and parents carry an awareness that the language used in the years of schooling bears strong similarities to the communication needs of the workplace and in other mature adult roles.

School *is* an important site for the acquisition of language and literacy. However, in contexts where there is a disjuncture between the home and community, language and literacy practices, and the requirements of schooling, combined with contested local practice, schooling alone cannot provide all the language and literacy socialisation experiences required for mature adult communication needs. This is further complicated in contexts where adolescents are not spending sustained and durative learning time in institutional education. If Ngaanyatjarra and other remote Indigenous youth are to acquire the knowledge, skills, awareness and practices necessary to participate effectively in the mature roles in their own, and the wider, community, then attention will need to be paid not only to the provision of quality schooling, but also to language socialisation and learning as a lifelong process in contexts beyond institutions. As education anthropologists suggest, 'we must seek to expand educational spaces which might accommodate diverse models of the educated person' (Levinson *et al.*, 1996: 23). What is needed are 'inventive ways' of engaging learners in 'meaningful practices', by 'providing access to resources that enhance their participation, of opening their horizons so they can put themselves on learning trajectories they can identify with, and of involving them in actions, discussions and reflections that make a difference to the communities they value' (Wenger, 1998: 10).

In summary, prior forms of knowledge transmission and learning have been challenged by contemporary circumstances. The introduced Western trajectory of institutional learning, leading to labour market employment, does not yet offer a substitute developmental paradigm for Ngaanyatjarra youth. Nor does it match the economic reality of remote community life where employment options are limited and other social and cultural schemas underpin the practice of everyday life. Furthermore, introduced models of education, employment and governance have altered repeatedly, as have bureaucratic systems, so the young can no longer rely on life-course goals and markers transmitted from previous generations. Change is taking place with increasing velocity. Adolescents are experiencing far broader socialisation experiences than their forebears, and they can anticipate change. In a manner not unlike youth all over the world, they have entered the flow from the local to the global and are operating in a hybrid intercultural space. Contemporary living is giving them a vast repertoire of symbolic, textual and media resources to draw on in their construction of altered local practices, new forms of cultural production and a future-oriented narrative.

New Learning for New Times

Over recent years, a divide has grown between educationalists who see educational institutions as the primary site for learning and researchers who have developed a social theory of learning. Despite the generally accepted assumption that schooling is 'a more effective and advanced institution for educational transmission' (Lave & Wenger, 1991: 61), as I noted in the Introduction, theorists have drawn on anthropology and sociolinguistics to present a situated and social perspective that broadens learning beyond formal instruction, advancing the notion of learning and literacy as purposeful, context-specific and a socially organised practice. Assumptions about how and where learning should take place are being challenged by youth-media practices. Internationally, researchers have noted the shifting role of formal education and the heightened importance of voluntary informal learning, or 'apprenticeships', in young people's everyday lives, concordant with the global penetration of new digital technologies (Barron, 2006; Buckingham, 2008; Ito *et al.*, 2010). It can be suggested that Mead's concept of a prefigurative culture is exemplified in the new approaches to learning and the development of expertise outside institutional settings made possible by new digital technologies. New technologies are enabling the young to know more than their elders. It is the young who are 'prefiguratively' enculturating the old into the ways of modernity, while simultaneously providing new models for each other and for the children who will follow in their footsteps (Mead, [1970] 1978: 83).

Within the space of a decade, digital technologies have become embedded in everyday social life for Ngaanyatjarra youth. They are now a normative aspect of communication, maintaining sociality, cultural production *and* learning. In the last chapter, I exemplified how Ngaanyatjarra youth are displaying a desire to engage and learn, but not in institutional environments. Alternatively, many are seeking environments where they find the meaningful sociocultural engagement and effective learning that meets their needs and 'taking hold' of the linguistic affordances of new technologies. In a manner resembling the older generation, who engaged with the linguistic challenges of vernacular literacy described in Chapter 5, the youth generation is rapidly appropriating new skills and experimenting with new forms, thus indicating that they are adept at using literacies that are inherently multimodal. These young people are strategically arming themselves with the knowledge and tools required for new futures. The way in which they are claiming new cultural forms and modes and adapting them for their own purposes reveals much about their capacity for adaptation and change and symbol-system production and interpretation. The youth generation represents what the future holds, rather than their parents or grandparents. They are the ones rendering an optimistic future 'imaginary' (Taylor, 2004). From this perspective, they are providing new models for each other and for the children who will follow in their footsteps.

In Conclusion

Current policy debate encourages future education and employment 'choices and opportunities', by promoting outward mobility from remote communities into urban contexts. However, such outward aspirations may not be shared by community members and may lead to estrangement from belonging and place and the loss of a 'sense of one's place' (Bourdieu, 1989). For most young people, meaning in life for them and their children is inextricably linked to maintaining the connection to kin and country. As illustrated by Naomi:

I want to be happy because I still want work here in Ranges, not anywhere else. Just to be at home and work, that's where I want to be, keep
staying here and work. [Young people] want to stay home, not going
anywhere, town... Because that's their home, that's where they grew
up... That's their way of life.

Tinpulya concurs,

Well for me for the future, I would like to stay in *Anangu* community
and to make the community good, like make the community better and
better... I think for my future, what the future holds for me is more
good things and more interesting things and I'll just be patient and wait
and see, see where I'll end up. But for the future and for now I just want
to help people, young people and adults and old people. So yeah, that's
what I would like for my future, be happy all the time so long as I'm in
Anangu land.

Unlike the older generation, Ngaanyatjarra youth are socially and spatially
connected to digital culture. New technologies are opening the door to
young people's agentive participation in global culture (Hull & Stornaiuolo,
2010). Furthermore, networked communication is redefining time and space
practices (Lam, 2008). As John Seely Brown notes, digital technology lets
you live, learn and work in 'two spaces' (Seely Brown, 2002: 63). The
implications of technological change for conceptions of literacy, learning
and employment in the remote sector are enormous and yet to be harnessed.
The challenge for the Ngaanyatjarra, and other Indigenous societies, will,
however, lie not only in balancing the competing and sometimes conflicting
local, national and global ideological influences unleashed by networked
communication, but also in creating a space where diversity and difference
are valued – a space that gives valence to a plurality of norms, languages and
literacies and multiple pathways to learning.

Notes

(1)   Available at http://www.federalfinancialrelations.gov.au/content/national_agreements.
      aspx
(2)   In 2008, under the National Indigenous Reform Agreement, the Council of Australian
      Governments set specific targets for 'Closing the Gap', including halving the gap
      in reading, writing and numeracy achievements for Indigenous children within a
      decade (See http://www.facs.gov.au/sa/indigenous/progserv/ctg/Pages/targets.aspx).
(3)   Sophie Staughton (personal communication, July 2010).
(4)   The Ngaanyatjarra Council has been the umbrella organisation for various service
      delivery operations, including Ngaanyatjarra Health Services; Ngaanyatjarra Community

College; Ngaanyatjarra Services (Accounting and Financial Services; Building and Works); Ngaanyatjarra Air; Ngaanyatjarra Agency and Transport Services; Ngaanyatjarra Land and Culture Unit – a number of which have been disbanded in recent years.

(5) In 2004, former federal Minister for Aboriginal Affairs, Fred Chaney, described the Ngaanyatjarra Lands as 'the best administered Aboriginal communities in Australia' (Regional ABC Radio, – 9 September 2004).

(6) Sophie Staughton (personal communication, July 2010).

(7) These included the Ngaanyatjarra Council Savings Plan, conceived of in 1991 to cover funeral expenses, subsidies for old people and other essential community social programmes. Rent, electricity and other 'bills' have been paid as CDEP deductions under an internal income management system.

(8) Reviews include Goddard *et al.* (2000); Heslop (1998); Kerr (1989); Kerr *et al.* (2001); (Kral & Ward, 2000); NLLIA (1996); Tri-State Project (1990).

(9) Elizabeth Ellis (personal communication, June 2007).

Ngaanyatjarra Glossary

A glossary of words or phrases which are not self-explanatory within the text.

Ngaanyatjarra word or phrase	English translation
kapi	(1) water; (2) rain; (3) waterhole (noun)
kata	head
kuka	meat (noun)
kulilku	will listen
kunmarnarranya	name for someone who had a similar name to someone who died (proper noun)
kungka	girl (noun)
kurra	(1) bad/wrong way (2) also used as a slang expression, meaning 'fantastic'/'wow', depending on the context
kutju	one
marlaku pitjaku	will come back/will return
Mama Godku book	Bible (Father God's book)
marlu	kangaroo
minyma	woman
mirrka (syn. mayi)	food/vegetable food (noun)
munta	sorry (exclamation)
munta yuwa	oh yes (mhmm/indeed)
ngaanya	(1) here (2) this
ngarltutjarra	poor thing (exclamation)
ngayuku	mine/my
ngayuku tjamu	my grandson/grandfather
ngayukutju	my one only
ngurra	camp
ngurrpa-rna	ignorant + 1st person singular pronoun suffix
ninti	knowledgeable
ninti purlka	really knowledgeable (adjective)

Ngaanyatjarra word or phrase	English translation
nyaapa	(1) What? e.g. *nyaapaku palyala?* What [are we] doing it for? (2) thingumabob/whatyamacallit (noun)
piranpa	(1) white; (2) white person/whitefella/ non-Aboriginal
tjilkatja	accompanying a special boy travelling to manhood ceremonies in a ceremonial party (adverb)
tjina	(1) foot; (2) track (noun)
tjinguru	maybe
tjitji (Pitj); tjilku (Ngaa)	child (noun)
warntu	(1) blanket; (2) clothes (noun)
wanytjatja?	where?
warrmarla	'revenge parties'
waru	(1) fire; (2) firewood; (3) hot
wati	man
wiltja	(1) shade; (2) shelter (noun)
wilurarra	west (spatial adverb)
wiya/wiyartu	no/nothing
wiyarriku	it will be finished
yarnangu	(1) body; (2) person/people Nb *anangu* in Pitjantjatjara dialect.
yiwarra	track/road
yuwa	Yes
read*tamalpayi* (English loan word)	always reading (e.g. *yungarralu* read*tamalpayi* – he is always reading by himself)
Suffixes	
-ku	possessive or purposive nominal case ending, e.g. for, of belonging to
-lu	ergative ending for a nominal when it is the subject of a transitive sentence (i.e. doing the action), e.g. *papa-lu tjilku patjarnu* – the dog (subject) bit the child (object).

Ngaanyatjarra word or phrase	English translation
-nga	ending for name of person or place with word-final consonant, e.g. Fred-*nga*.
-nya	ending for name of person or place with word-final vowel, e.g. Barry-*nya* (i.e. subject of an intransitive sentence or object of a transitive sentence)
-pa	ending for nominals that are not names with word-final consonants, e.g. *marlany(pa)*, game*pa*
-ngka	locative nominal case ending (at, in, by), e.g. *ngurrangka* – in the camp; songbook*angka* – in the songbook

Source: Glass (2003)

Language Notes

Dialect names in the Western Desert have arisen out of lexical distinctions, plus the suffix -*tjarra* (Ngaanyatjarra)/-*tjara* (Pitj./Yank.), meaning 'having'. For example, Ngaanyatjarra is the language 'having' the word *ngaanya* for 'this'; Ngaatjatjarra is the language 'having' the word *ngaatja* for 'this'; and Pitjantjatjara is the language 'having' the word *pitjantja* for 'coming'.

Sound system and grammar

The sound system of Ngaanyatjarra/Ngaatjatjarra has six vowel sounds: three short vowels (a, i, u) and three long vowels (aa, ii, u). Three different kinds of l, n and t sounds (alveolar, dental and retroflex) are distinguished. The consonant sounds are:

stops	p	tj	t	rt	k
nasals	m	ny	n	rn	ng
l-sounds		ly	l	rl	
other	w	y	rr	r	

The retroflex sounds, rendered as rl, rn and rt in Ngaanyatjarra, are represented using diacritics (ḻ, ṉ, ṯ) in other Western Desert dialects (Goddard, 1987; Heffernan & Heffernan, 2000). In Ngaanyatjarra or Ngaatjatjarra (unlike the closely related dialects Pitjantjatjara or Yankunytjatjara), 'y' is placed in front of word-initial open vowels, e.g. *yuwa* – 'yes' (Ng.) and *uwa* – 'yes' (Pitj./Yank.). Word final consonants on nominals are unusual and commonly suffixed with –*pa*. Ngaanyatjarra employs suffixes to mark case relationships and bound or clitic pronouns (free pronouns are used less commonly). Some verbs also take prefixes, and there are four verb classes (-la; -0; -rra; -wa). There are two verb types, transitive and intransitive, with ergative marking on nouns. Ngaanyatjarra commonly employs enclitics for number marking on singular, dual and plural pronouns (Glass & Hackett, 2003; Howell, 1996).

Appendix
Literacy Assessments

In 2004, I assisted Ngaanyatjarra Council in conducting a skills audit of adult CDEP recipients. I was given permission to use data from 527 interviews of adults aged 16–65, out of an approximate permanent population of some 1600 people (including children). Assessments of English language, literacy and numeracy competence were conducted using the *National Reporting System* (NRS) (Coates *et al.*, 1995); a nationally recognised 'mechanism' for reporting outcomes of adult English language, literacy and numeracy programmes. The assessments provide a rare quantitative perspective on adult English literacy and numeracy competence in the remote context – the problematic nature of measuring literacy competence notwithstanding (Levine, 1998).

In the NRS system, literacy levels are as follows:

'*NRS 1*' indicates basic letter and number recognition skills and ability to read and write key words or simple sentences.

'*NRS 2*' indicates a 'functional' level of literacy competence: form filling and ability to read and write a short text on a familiar topic.

'*NRS 3*' indicates ability to read and write texts of some grammatical complexity, and comprehend and communicate relationships between ideas.

Table A.1 indicates *pre-test self-assessments*. In Warburton, 26% of adults perceive that they are able to read and write 'a lot' in English, with a slightly lower figure for the Ngaanyatjarra Lands as a whole.

Table A.1 Literacy self-assessment

Can you read/write?	ENGLISH		VERNACULAR	
	Warburton	Ngaanyatjarra Lands	Warburton	Ngaanyatjarra Lands
Nothing / A little	117 (74%)	415 (79%)	141 (91%)	465 (81%)
A lot	41 (26%)	111 (21%)	14 (9%)	47 (9%)
Not stated	1	1	4	15
Total #	159	527	159	527

Table A.2 is sorted into NRS *reading* assessments only. The data is approximate with interviewees' own perception of their reading competence, as noted in Table A.1., that is, 'NRS 2 and above' = 'a lot'. This indicates that most adults have a realistic sense of their own competence. It can also be concluded that the proficiency of young adults is commensurate with their elders. This suggests that older adults have not attained a higher level of literacy competence, contrary to anecdotal evidence.

Table A.2 NRS reading (Ngaanyatjarra Lands)

	Young (16–25 yrs)		Middle (26–40 yrs)		Old (41–61 yrs)	
	Government schooling in communities (1984–1993)		Government school at Warburton plus secondary hostels (1969–1983)		End of mission schooling and beginning of secondary hostels (1948–1968)	
NRS 1 and below	145	77%	168	80%	97	75%
NRS 2 and above	42	23%	41	20%	32	25%
Total # 527	187	100%	209	100%	129	100%

In Table A.3, assessments of young adult CDEP participants at Warburton indicate that competence in this subgroup is higher. This may be indicative of assessor reliability or that Warburton families have had a longer span for intergenerational literacy transmission to become evident.

Table A.3 NRS assessments (young adults – Warburton)

	Young adults (16–25 yrs)			
	NRS Reading only		NRS Overall (reading, writing and numeracy)	
NRS 1 and below	38	67%	40	70%
NRS 2 C and above	19	33%	17	30%
Total #:	57	100%	57	100%

Ngaanyatjarra and English

Data on vernacular literacy competence are difficult to obtain. Jan Mountney estimates that 8% of adults can read Ngaanyatjarra, which approximates with the self-assessments above (Table A.1). Her estimate correlates with the subjective data compiled by Amee Glass and Dorothy Hackett in 2004 (Table A.4).

Table A.4 Estimated Ngaanyatjarra and English adult literacy competence

Total #: 1015 Ngaanyatjarra speaking adults aged 15 plus

Illiterate	95	9.3%
Semi-literate in English	545	53.7%
Literate in English only	108	10.6%
Literate in Ngaanyatjarra only	11	1.1%
Literate in Ngaanyatjarra and English	90	8.9%
Literate in Ngaanyatjarra and semi-literate in English	64	6.3%
Total literate in Ngaanyatjarra	165	16.2%
Total literate in English	198	19.5%

References

Ahearn, L.M. (2001) Language and agency. *Annual Review of Anthropology* 30, 109–137.

AIATSIS/FATSIL (2005) *National Indigenous Languages Survey Report 2005*. Canberra: Commonwealth of Australia.

Alim, H.S., Ibrahim, A. and Pennycook, A. (2009) *Global Linguistic Flows: Hip Hop Cultures, Youth Identities, and the Politics of Language*. Abingdon and New York, NY: Routledge.

Altman, J. (2004) Practical reconciliation and the new mainstreaming: Will it make a difference to Indigenous Australians? *Dialogue (Academy of the Social Sciences in Australia)* 23 (2), 35–46.

Altman, J. and Hinkson, M. (eds) (2007) *Coercive Reconciliation: Stabilise, Normalise, Exit Aboriginal Australia*. North Carlton: Arena Publications.

Appadurai, A. (1986) *The Social Life of Things: Commodities in Cultural Perspective*. Cambridge: Cambridge University Press.

Appadurai, A. (1996) *Modernity at Large: Cultural Dimensions of Globalization*. Minneapolis, MI: University of Minnesota Press.

Attwood, B. (2003) *Rights for Aborigines*. Sydney: Allen & Unwin.

Austin, P. (1986) Diyari language postcards and Diyari literacy. *Aboriginal History* 10 (2), 175–192.

Austin-Broos, D. (2003) Places, practices, and things: The articulation of Arrernte kinship with welfare and work. *American Ethnologist* 30 (1), 118–135.

Austin-Broos, D. (2009) *Arrernte Present, Arrernte Past: Invasion, Violence, and Imagination in Indigenous Central Australia*. Chicago, IL: The University of Chicago Press.

Baron, N.S. (2008) *Always On: Language in an Online and Mobile World*. Oxford and New York, NY: Oxford University Press.

Barron, B. (2006) Interest and self-sustained learning as catalysts of development: A learning ecology framework. *Human Development* 49, 193–224.

Barton, D. and Hall, N. (eds) (2000) *Letter Writing as a Social Practice*. Amsterdam and Philadelphia, PA: John Benjamins Publishing.

Barton, D. and Hamilton, M. (1998) *Local Literacies: Reading and Writing in One Community*. London: Routledge.

Barton, D. and Hamilton, M. (2000) Literacy practices. In D. Barton, M. Hamilton and R. Ivanic (eds) *Situated Literacies: Reading and Writing in Context* (pp. 7–15). London: Routledge.

Barton, D., Hamilton, M. and Ivanic, R. (eds) (2000) *Situated Literacies: Reading and Writing in Context*. London: Routledge.

Barton, D. and Padmore, S. (1994) Roles, networks and values in everyday writing. In D. Graddol, J. Maybin and B. Stierer (eds) *Researching Language and Literacy in Social Context* (pp. 205–223). Clevedon: Multilingual Matters.

Bat, M. (2005) When you can't even buy a bedtime story. *Ngoonjook: A Journal of Australian Indigenous Issues* 27, 43–61.

Bateman, F.E.A. (1948) *Report on Survey of Native Affairs*. Perth: Western Australia Parliament.

Batty, P. (2005) Private politics, public strategies: White advisors and their Aboriginal subjects. *Oceania* 75 (3), 209–221.

Bauman, R. (1986) *Story, Performance and Event: Contextual Studies of Oral Narrative.* Cambridge: Cambridge University Press.

Bauman, R. and Briggs, C.L. (1990) Poetics and performance as critical perspectives on language and social life. *Annual Review of Anthropology* 19, 59–88.

Bavin, E. (1993) Language and culture: Socialisation in a Warlpiri community. In M. Walsh and C. Yallop (eds) *Language and Culture in Aboriginal Australia* (pp. 85–96). Canberra: Aboriginal Studies Press.

Bazerman, C. (2000) Letters and social grounding of differentiated genres. In D. Barton and N. Hall (eds) *Letter writing as a Social Practice* (pp. 15–29). Amsterdam and Philadelphia, PA: John Benjamins Publishing.

Beadell, L. (1967) *Too Long in the Bush.* Adelaide: Rigby Ltd.

Beadman, B. (2004) *Do Indigenous Youth Have a Dream?* Canberra: The Menzies Research Centre Ltd.

Beazley, K.E. (1984) *Education in Western Australia: Report of the Commission of Inquiry Appointed by the Minister for Education in Western Australia Under the Chairmanship of Mr K.E. Beazley, AO.* Perth: Government of Western Australia.

Bennett, M.M. (1930) *The Australian Aboriginal as a Human Being.* London: Alston Rivers.

Bennett, M.M. (1935) *Teaching the Aborigines: Data from Mount Margaret Mission W.A.* Perth: City and Suburban Print.

Beresford, Q. and Omaji, P. (1996) *Rites of Passage: Aboriginal Youth, Crime and Justice.* Perth: Fremantle Arts Centre Press.

Berger, P.L. and Luckmann, T. ([1966] 1975) *The Social Construction of Reality: A Treatise in the Sociology of Knowledge.* Harmondsworth: Penguin.

Berndt, C. and Berndt, R. (eds) (1980) *Aborigines of the West: Their Past and Present.* Perth: University of Western Australia Press.

Berndt, R. (1959) *Native Welfare in Western Australia since the 'Warburton Controversy' of 1957.* Perth: The University of Western Australia.

Berndt, R. and Berndt, C. (1957) *Summary Report: The University of Western Australia Anthropological Survey of the Eastern Goldfields, Warburton Ranges and Jigalong Regions.* Perth: The University of Western Australia.

Berndt, R. and Berndt, C. (1959) *Social Anthropological Survey of the Warburton, Blackstone and Rawlinson Ranges.* Perth: The University of Western Australia.

Besnier, N. (1995) *Literacy, Emotion, and Authority: Reading and Writing on a Polynesian Atoll.* Cambridge: Cambridge University Press.

Biskup, P. (1973) *Not Slaves, Not Citizens: The Aboriginal Problem in Western Australia 1898–1954.* St Lucia: University of Queensland Press.

Blacket, J. (1997) *Fire in the Outback: The Untold Story of the Aboriginal Revival Movement that Began on Elcho Island in 1979.* Sutherland: Albatross Books.

Bolton, G.C. (1981) Black and White after 1897. In C.T. Stannage (ed.) *A New History of Western Australia* (pp. 124–178). Perth: University of Western Australia Press.

Bos, R. (1988) The Dreaming and social change in Arnhem Land. In T. Swain and D.B. Rose (eds) *Aboriginal Australians and Christian Missions: Ethnographic and Historical Studies* (pp. 422–437). Adelaide: Australian Association for the Study of Religions, SACAE.

Bourdieu, P. (1977) *Outline of a Theory of Practice.* Cambridge: Cambridge University Press.

Bourdieu, P. (1989) Social space and symbolic power. *Sociological Theory* 7 (1), 14–25.

Bourdieu, P. ([1980] 1990) *The Logic of Practice.* Cambridge: Polity Press.

Bourdieu, P. and Passeron, J.C. ([1977] 1990) *Reproduction in Education, Society and Culture.* London: Sage Publications.

Brady, M. (1992) *Heavy Metal: The Social Meaning of Petrol Sniffing in Australia.* Canberra: Aboriginal Studies Press.

Brooks, D. (2002a) History of the Ngaanyatjarra Lands. In *Overview of Ngaanyatjarra People and Culture: Cultural Awareness Course Booklet* (pp. 2–11). Warburton: Ngaanyatjarra Community College.

Brooks, D. (2002b) Ngaanyatjarra kinship system. In *Overview of Ngaanyatjarra People and Culture: Cultural Awareness Course Booklet* (pp. 26–41). Warburton: Ngaanyatjarra Community College.

Brooks, D. (2002c) Understanding Ngaanyatjarra culture. In *Overview of Ngaanyatjarra People and Culture: Cultural Awareness Course Booklet* (pp. 12–25). Warburton: Ngaanyatjarra Community College.

Brooks, D. (2002d) What impact the Mission? In V. Plant and A. Viegas (eds) *Mission Time in Warburton: An Exhibition Exploring Aspects of the Warburton Mission History 1933–1973* (pp. 76–80). Warburton: Warburton Arts Project.

Brooks, D. (2011a) *Dreamings and Connections to Country among the Ngaanyatjarra and Pintupi of the Australian Western Desert.* Unpublished PhD thesis, Australian National University.

Brooks, D. (2011b) Organization within disorder: The present and future of young people in the Ngaanyatjarra Lands. In U. Eickelkamp (ed.) *Growing Up in Central Australia: New Anthropological Studies of Aboriginal Childhood and Adolescence* (pp. 183–212). Oxford: Berghahn Books.

Brooks, D. and Kral, I. (2007) *The Ngaanyatjarra Lands Population Study.* Unpublished report. Alice Springs: Ngaanyatjarra Council.

Brooks, D. and Shaw, G. (2003) *Men, Conflict and Violence in the Ngaanyatjarra Region: A Preliminary Anthropological Report.* Alice Springs: Ngaanyatjarra Health Service.

Buckingham, D. (2008) Introducing identity. In D. Buckingham (ed.) *Youth, Identity, and Digital Media* (pp. 1–22). Cambridge, MA: The MIT Press.

Burbank, V. (1988) *Aboriginal Adolescence: Maidenhood in an Australian Community.* New Brunswick, NJ: Rutgers University Press.

Burbank, V. (2006) From bedtime to on time: Why many Aboriginal people don't especially like participating in Western institutions. *Anthropological Forum* 16 (1), 3–20.

Burnside, D.G. (1979) The pastoral industry of the North-West, Kimberley and Goldfields. In G.H. Burvill (ed.) *Agriculture in Western Australia: 150 Years of Development and Achievement 1829–1979* (pp. 249–262). Nedlands: University of Western Australia Press.

Burton, L.M., Obeidallah, D.A. and Allison, K. (1996) Ethnographic insights on social context and adolescent development among inner-city African-American teens. In R. Jessor, A. Colby and R.A. Shweder (eds) *Ethnography and Human Development: Context and Meaning in Social Inquiry* (pp. 395–418). London and Chicago, IL: The University of Chicago Press.

Butler, M. (1993) *Piki-Piki Kurlunypa Marnkurrpa: The Three Little Pigs.* Alice Springs: Ngaanyatjarra Bible Project.

Camitta, M. (1993) Vernacular writing: varieties of literacy among Philadelphia high school students. In B.V. Street (ed.) *Cross-Cultural Approaches to Literacy* (pp. 228–246). Cambridge: Cambridge University Press.

Cane, G. and Gunson, N. (1986) Postcards: A source for Aboriginal biography. *Aboriginal History* 10 (2), 171–174.

Carnegie, D.W. ([1898] 1982) *Spinifex and Sand*. Perth: Hesperian Press.

Carrithers, M., Collins, S. and Lukes, S. (1985) *The Category of the Person: Anthropology, Philosophy, History*. Cambridge: Cambridge University Press.

Cazden, C. (1988) *Classroom Discourse*. London: Heinemann.

Clammer, J., Poirier, S. and Schwimmer, E. (2004) Introduction: the relevance of ontologies in anthropology – reflections on a new anthropological field. In J. Clammer, S. Poirier and E. Schwimmer (eds) *Figured Worlds: Ontological Obstacles in Intercultural Relations* (pp. 3–22). Toronto: University of Toronto Press.

Clanchy, M.T. (1979) *From Memory to Written Record: England 1066–1307*. London: Edward Arnold Publishers.

Cleary, V. (2005) Education and learning in an Aboriginal community. *The Centre for Independent Studies: Issue Analysis* 65, 1–16.

Coates, S., Fitzpatrick, L., McKenna, A. and Makin, A. (1995) *National Reporting System: A Mechanism for Reporting Outcomes of Adult English Language, Literacy and Numeracy Programs*. Melbourne: ANTA and DEET.

Cole, M. and Scribner, S. (1981) *The Psychology of Literacy*. Cambridge, MA: Harvard University Press.

Collins, B. (1999) *Learning Lessons: An Independent Review of Indigenous Education in the Northern Territory*. Darwin: Northern Territory Department of Education.

Collins, J. (1995) Literacy and literacies. *Annual Review of Anthropology* 24, 75–93.

Collins, J. and Blot, R.K. (2003) *Literacy and Literacies: Texts, Power and Identity*. Cambridge: Cambridge University Press.

Comaroff, J. (1985) *Body of Power, Spirit of Resistance: The Culture and History of a South African People*. Chicago, IL: University of Chicago Press.

Commonwealth of Australia (2008) *Increasing Indigenous Employment Opportunity: A Discussion Paper on Proposed Reforms to the CDEP and Indigenous Employment Programs 2008*. Canberra: Australian Government.

Cook-Gumperz, J. (1986a) Literacy and schooling: an unchanging equation? In J. Cook-Gumperz (ed.) *The Social Construction of Literacy* (pp. 16–44). Cambridge: Cambridge University Press.

Cook-Gumperz, J. (ed.) (1986b) *The Social Construction of Literacy*. London: Cambridge University Press.

Coombs, H.C. (1977) *The Application of CDEP in Aboriginal Communities in the Eastern Zone of Western Australia. CRES Working Paper – HCC/3: 1977*. Canberra: Australian National University.

Cope, B. and Kalantzis, M. (2000) *Multiliteracies: Literacy Learning and the Design of Social Futures*. South Melbourne: Macmillan.

Crystal, D. (2008) *Txtng: The Gr8 Db8*. Oxford: Oxford University Press.

Csikszentmihalyi, M. and Rochberg-Halton, E. (1981) *The Meaning of Things: Domestic Symbols and the Self*. Cambridge: Cambridge University Press.

Damon, W. (1996) Nature, second nature, and individual development: An ethnographic opportunity. In R. Jessor, A. Colby and R.A. Shweder (eds) *Ethnography and Human Development: Context and Meaning in Social Inquiry* (pp. 459–475). Chicago, IL: The University of Chicago Press.

Davenport, S., Johnson, P. and Yuwali (2005) *Cleared Out: First Contact in the Western Desert*. Canberra: Aboriginal Studies Press.

de Certeau, M. (1984) *The Practice of Everyday Life*. Berkeley, CA: University of California Press.

de Graaf, M. (1968) *The Ngadadara at Warburton Ranges*. Unpublished Teachers' Higher Certificate thesis. Perth: Teachers' Centre for Further Education.

deMarrais, K.B., Nelson, P.A. and Baker, J.H. (1992) Meaning in mud: Yup'ik Eskimo girls at play. *Anthropology and Education Quarterly* 23 (2), 120–144.

Department of Native Welfare (1967) *A Place in the Sun*. Perth: Department of Native Welfare.

Dorsey-Gaines, C. and Garnett, C.M. (1996) The role of the Black Church in growing up literate: Implications for literacy research. In D. Hicks (ed.) *Discourse, Learning and Schooling* (pp. 247–266). Cambridge: Cambridge University Press.

Douglas, W. (1976) Aboriginal categorisation of natural features (as illustrated in the Western Desert). *Aboriginal Child at School* 4 (5), 51–64.

Douglas, W. (1978) Evolution of a 'Rampage of Destruction' at Warburton Ranges. In M. C. Howard (ed.) *'Whitefella Business': Aborigines in Australian Politics* (pp. 105–124). Philadelphia, PA: Institute for the Study of Human Issues.

Douglas, W. and Douglas, B. (1964) *The Language They Know Best*. Adelaide: Aborigines' Friends' Association Annual Report.

Douglas, W.H. (1955) Phonology of the Australian Aboriginal language spoken at Ooldea, S.A. 1951–52. *Oceania* 25 (3), 216–229.

Douglas, W.H. (1964) *An Introduction to the Western Desert Language*. Sydney: University of Sydney.

Douglas, W.H. (1979) Communication: Aboriginal languages – an overview. In R.M. Berndt and C.H. Berndt (eds) *Aborigines of the West: Their Past and Present* (pp. 39–53). Perth: University of Western Australia Press.

Dousset, L. (1997) Naming and personal names of Ngaatjatjarra-speaking people, Western Desert: Some questions related to research. *Australian Aboriginal Studies* 2, 50–54.

Dousset, L. (2002) Politics and demography in a contact situation: The establishment of the Giles Meteorological Station in the Rawlinson Ranges. *Aboriginal History* 26, 1–22.

Dowley, C.W. (2000) *Through Silent Country*. Perth: Fremantle Arts Press.

Duff, P.A. (2008) Introduction. In P.A. Duff and N.H. Hornberger (eds) *Language Socialization (Vol. 8), Encyclopedia of Language and Education* (2nd edn) (pp. xiii-xix). New York, NY: Springer.

Dumont, L. (1965) The modern conception of the individual: Notes on its genesis and that of concomitant institutions. *Contributions to Indian Sociology* 8, 13–61.

Dunlop, I. (1966–70) *People of the Australian Western Desert*. Canberra: Australia Commonwealth Film Unit for the Australian Institute of Aboriginal Studies (film series).

Duranti, A. (1997) *Linguistic Anthropology*. Cambridge: Cambridge University Press.

Eckert, P. (1988) Adolescent social structure and the spread of the linguistic change. *Language in Society* 17, 183–207.

Edwards, W.H. (1969) Experience in the use of the vernacular as an introductory medium of Instruction. In S. Dunn and C. Tatz (eds) *Aborigines and Education* (pp. 272–288). Melbourne: Sun Books.

Edwards, W.H. (1999) *Moravian Aboriginal Missions in Australia*. Unpublished manuscript. Adelaide: Uniting Church Historical Society.

Eickelkamp, U. (2008) 'I don't talk story like that': On the social meaning of children's sand stories at Ernabella. In J. Simpson and G. Wigglesworth (eds) *Children's*

Language and Multilingualism: Indigenous Language Use at Home and School (pp. 78–99). London and New York, NY: Continuum.

Eickelkamp, U. (ed.) (2011a) *Growing Up in Central Australia: New Anthropological Studies of Aboriginal Childhood and Adolescence.* Oxford and New York, NY: Berghahn Books.

Eickelkamp, U. (2011b) Sand storytelling: Its social meaning in Anangu children's lives. In U. Eickelkamp (ed.) *Growing Up in Central Australia: New Anthropological Studies of Childhood and Adolescence* (pp. 103–130). Oxford and New York, NY: Berghahn Books.

Eisenstein, E.L. (1985) On the printing press as an agent of change. In D.R. Olson, N. Torrance and A. Hildyard (eds) *Literacy, Language and Learning: The Nature and Consequences of Reading and Writing* (pp. 19–33). Cambridge: Cambridge University Press.

Elkin, A.P. (1979) Aboriginal-European relations in Western Australia: An historical and personal record. In R. Berndt and C. Berndt (eds) *Aborigines of the West: Their Past and Present* (pp. 285–323). Perth: University of Western Australia Press.

Engelke, M. (2009) Reading and time: Two approaches to the materiality of Scripture. *Ethnos* 74 (2), 151–174.

Engestrom, Y. (1990) *Learning, Working and Imagining: Twelve Studies in Activity Theory.* Helsinki: Orienta-Konsultit.

Fairman, T. (2000) English pauper letters 1800–34, and the English language. In D. Barton and N. Hall (eds) *Letter Writing as a Social Practice* (pp. 63–82). Amsterdam and Philadelphia, PA: John Benjamins Publishing.

Falk, I. (2001) *Sleight of Hand: Job Myths, Literacy and Social Capital. CRLRA Discussion Paper D14/2001.* Hobart: University of Tasmania.

Featherstone, D. (2011) The Ngaanyatjarra Lands telecommunication project: A quest for broadband in the Western Desert. *Telecommunications Journal of Australia* 61 (1), 4.1–4.25.

Ferguson, C.A. (1987) Literacy in a hunting-gathering society: The case study of the Diyari. *Journal of Anthropological Research* 43 (Fall), 223–239.

Fietz, P. (2008) Socialisation and the shaping of youth identity at Docker River. In G. Robinson, U. Eickelkamp, J. Goodnow and I. Katz (eds) *Contexts of Child Development: Culture, Policy and Intervention* (pp. 49–58). Darwin: Charles Darwin University Press.

Fletcher, C. (1992) *Aboriginal Politics: Intergovernmental Relations.* Melbourne: Melbourne University Press.

Fogarty, W. (2010) *'Learning through Country': Competing Knowledge Systems and Place Based Pedagogy.* Unpublished PhD thesis. Canberra: The Australian National University.

Freire, P. ([1970] 1993) *Pedagogy of the Oppressed.* New York, NY: Continuum Books.

Gale, M.A. (1997) *Dhanum Djorra'wuy Dhawu: A History of Writing in Aboriginal Languages.* Adelaide: University of South Australia.

Gara, T. (2003) Explorers and prospectors. In J. Turner (ed.) *Trust* (pp. 15–22). Warburton: Warburton Arts Project.

Gee, J.P. (1996) *Social Linguistics and Literacies: Ideology in Discourses.* London: Routledge/Taylor and Francis.

Gee, J.P. (2000) The new literacy studies: From 'socially situated' to the work of the social. In D. Barton, M. Hamilton and R. Ivanic (eds) *Situated Literacies: Reading and Writing in Context* (pp. 180–196). London: Routledge.

Gee, J.P. (2003) *What Video Games Have to Teach Us About Learning and Literacy.* New York, NY: Palgrave Macmillan.

Gee, J.P. (2004) *Situated Language and Learning: A Critique of Traditional Schooling*. London and New York, NY: Routledge.

Gee, J.P. (2005) Semiotic social spaces and affinity spaces. In D. Barton and K. Tusting (eds) *Beyond Communities of Practice: Language, Power and Social Context* (pp. 214–232). Cambridge: Cambridge University Press.

Geertz, C. (1973) *The Interpretation of Cultures*. New York, NY: Basic Books Inc.

Giddens, A. (1991) *Modernity and Self-Identity: Self and Society in the Late Modern Age*. Cambridge: Polity Press.

Giddens, A. (1994) Living in a post-traditional society. In U. Beck, A. Giddens and S. Lash (eds) *Reflexive Modernization: Politics, Tradition and Aesthetics in the Modern Social Order* (pp. 56–109). Cambridge: Polity Press.

Giddens, A. (1999) *Runaway World: How Globalisation is Reshaping Our Lives*. London: Profile Books.

Giles, E. ([1899] 1995) *Australia Twice Traversed: The Romance of Exploration Being a Narrative Compiled from the Journals of Five Exploring Expeditions into and through South Australia and Western Australia from 1872–1876*. Western Australia: Hesperian Press.

Gilmore, P. (1986) Sub-rosa literacy: Peers, play and ownership in literacy acquisition. In B.B. Schieffelin and P. Gilmore (eds) *The Acquisition of Literacy: Ethnographic Perspectives* (pp. 155–168). Norwood, NJ: Ablex.

Glass, A. (1973) Bilingual education for Aborigines: Discussion and proposal supplement. *Aboriginal Affairs Planning Authority Newsletter* 1 (3), 1–16.

Glass, A. (1974) A new era: Learning in two languages. *Department of Aboriginal Affairs, Western Australia, Newsletter* 1 (8), 43–45.

Glass, A. (1980) *Cohesion in Ngaanyatjarra Discourse*. Unpublished Masters thesis. Canberra: The Australian National University.

Glass, A. (1997) *Into Another World: A Glimpse of the Culture of the Ngaanyatjarra People of Central Australia*. Berrimah, NT: Summer Institute of Linguistics.

Glass, A. (2000) *History of Ngaanyatjarra Literacy*. Unpublished manuscript, Alice Springs.

Glass, A. (2006) *Ngaanyatjarra Learner's Guide*. Alice Springs: IAD Press.

Glass, A. and Hackett, D. (1970) *Pitjantjatjara Grammar: A Tagmemic View of Ngaanyatjarra (Warburton Ranges) Dialect*. Canberra: AIAS.

Glass, A. and Hackett, D. (eds) ([1969] 1979) *Ngaanyatjarra Texts: New Revised Edition of Pitjantjatjara Texts*. Canberra: AIAS.

Glass, A. and Hackett, D. (2003) *Ngaanyatjarra and Ngaatjatjarra to English Dictionary*. Alice Springs: IAD Press.

Glass, A. and Newberry, D. (eds) (1990 [1979]) *Tjuma: Stories from the Western Desert*. Warburton: Warburton Community Council Inc.

Goddard, C. (1983) *A Semantically-Oriented Grammar of the Yankunytjatjara Dialect of the Western Desert Language*. Unpublished PhD thesis. Canberra: The Australian National University.

Goddard, C. (1987) *A Basic Pitjantjatjara/Yankunytjatjara to English Dictionary*. Alice Springs: IAD Press.

Goddard, C. (1990) Emergent genres of reportage and advocacy in the Pitjantjatjara print media. *Australian Aboriginal Studies* 2, 27–47.

Goddard, D., Anderson, B., Hill, A. and Hodgins, B. (2000) *Review and Report on the Provision of Secondary Education for Students in the Kimberley and the Ngaanyatjarra Lands for the Education Department of Western Australia*. Perth: Simpson Norris International.

Goddard, D., Ashton, N. and Anderson, B. (2005) *Final Report for the Review of the Ngaany-atjarra Education Area Memorandum of Agreement and the Development of a Shared Responsibility Agreement*. Perth: Simpson Norris International Consultants.

Goffman, E. (1956) *The Presentation of Self in Everyday Life*. Edinburgh: Social Sciences Research Centre, University of Edinburgh.

Goffman, E. (1981) *Forms of Talk*. Philadelphia, PA: University of Pennsylvania Press.

Goodwin, C. (2000) Action and embodiment within situated human interaction. *Journal of Pragmatics* 32, 1489–1522.

Goody, J. (ed.) (1968) *Literacy in Traditional Societies*. Cambridge: Cambridge University Press.

Goody, J. (1977) *The Domestication of the Savage Mind*. Cambridge: Cambridge University Press.

Gordon, J. (2006) *High School Audit (12–16 yrs): Ngaanyatjarra Lands*. Unpublished manuscript. Alice Springs: Ngaanyatjarra Council.

Gould, R.A. (1969) *Yiwara: Foragers of the Australian Desert*. New York, NY: Charles Scribner's Sons.

Gould, R.A. (1980) *Living Archaeology*. Cambridge: Cambridge University Press.

Graff, H.J. (1979) *The Literacy Myth: Literacy and Social Structure in the Nineteenth-century City*. New York: Academic Press.

Graff, H.J. ([1982] 1994) The legacies of literacy. In J. Maybin (ed.) *Language and Literacy in Social Practice* (pp. 151–167). Clevedon: Multilingual Matters Ltd.

Graff, H.J. (1987) *The Legacies of Literacy: Continuities and Contradictions in Western Culture and Society*. Bloomington and Indianapolis, IN: Indiana University Press.

Grayden, W. (1957) *Adam and Atoms: The Story of the Warburton Aborigines*. Perth: Frank Daniels Pty Ltd.

Grayden, W.L. (2002) *A Nomad was our Guide: The Story through the Land of the Wongi – the Central Desert of Australia – 1953*. Perth: N.H. Holdings Publications.

Green, J. (2009) *Between the Earth and the Air: Multimodality in Arandic Sand Stories*. Unpublished PhD thesis, University of Melbourne.

Green, N. (1983) *Desert School*. South Fremantle: Fremantle Arts Press.

Green, P. (1976) *Situation Report – Warburton, December 1976*. Unpublished manuscript. Canberra AIATSIS Library.

Greenfield, P.M. (1999) Cultural change and human development. *New Directions for Child and Adolescent Development* 83, 37–59.

Greenfield, P.M. (2004) *Weaving Generations Together: Evolving Creativity in the Maya of Chiapas*. Santa Fe, NM: School of American Research Press.

Grillo, R. (1989) Anthropology, language, politics. In R. Grillo (ed.) *Social Anthropology and the Politics of Language* (pp. 1–24). London and New York, NY: Routledge.

Gudschinsky, S. (1973) *A Manual of Literacy for Preliterate Peoples*. Ukarumpa: Summer Institute of Linguistics.

Gumperz, J.J. and Hymes, D. (1964) The ethnography of communication. *American Anthropologist* 66 (6), 103–114.

Gumperz, J.J. and Hymes, D. (1972) *Directions in Sociolinguistics: The Ethnography of Communication*. New York, NY: Holt, Rinehart and Winston.

Hackett, D. (ed.) (2004) *Tjilkuku-Tjanampa Tjukurrpa Walykumunu: The Children's Book of Wonderful Stories*. Alice Springs: Ngaanyatjarra Bible Project.

Haebich, A. ([1988] 1992) *For Their Own Good: Aborigines and Government in the South West of Western Australia 1900–1940*. Perth: University of Western Australia Press.

Haebich, A. (2005) Nuclear, suburban and black: Middleton's vision of assimilation for Nyungar assimilation. In T. Rowse (ed.) *Contesting Assimilation* (pp. 201–220). Perth: API Network.

Hall, N. (2000) The materiality of letter writing: A nineteenth century perspective. In D. Barton and N. Hall (eds) *Letter Writing as a Social Practice* (pp. 83–108). Amsterdam and Philadelphia, PA: John Benjamins Publishing.

Hamilton, A. (1979) *Timeless Transformation: Women, Men and History in the Australian Western Desert*. Unpublished PhD thesis. Sydney: University of Sydney.

Hamilton, A. (1981) *Nature and Nurture: Aboriginal Child-Rearing in North-Central Arnhem Land*. Canberra: Australian Institute of Aboriginal Studies.

Hanks, W.F. (1990) *Referential Practice: Language and Lived Space Among the Maya*. Chicago, IL: University of Chicago Press.

Hansen, K. and Hansen, L. (1978) *The Core of Pintupi Grammar*. Alice Springs: Summer Institute of Linguistics and Institute of Aboriginal Development.

Harries, P. (1994) *Work, Culture and Identity: Migrant Labourers in Mozambique and South Africa, c. 1860–1910*. Portsmouth: Johannesburg; and London: Heinemann; Witwatersrand University Press; and James Currey.

Hartman, D. and Henderson, J. (eds) (1994) *Aboriginal Languages in Education*. Alice Springs: IAD Press.

Heath, S.B. (1982a) Protean shapes in literacy events: Ever-shifting oral and literate traditions. In D. Tannen (ed.) *Spoken and Written Language: Exploring Orality and Literacy* (pp. 91–117). Norwood, NJ: Ablex.

Heath, S.B. (1982b) What no bedtime story means: Narrative skills at home and school. *Language in Society* 11 (2), 49–76.

Heath, S.B. (1983) *Ways with Words: Language, Life and Work in Communities and Classrooms*. Cambridge: Cambridge University Press.

Heath, S.B. (1984) Oral and literate traditions. *International Social Science Journal* 99, 41–57.

Heath, S.B. (1990) The children of Trackton's children: Spoken and written language in social change. In J.W. Stigler, R.A. Shweder and G. Herdt (eds) *Cultural Psychology: Essays on Comparative Human Development* (pp. 496–519). Cambridge: Cambridge University Press.

Heath, S.B. (1991) The sense of being literate: historical and cross-cultural features. In R. Barr, M.L. Kamil, P. Mosenthal and P.D. Pearson (eds) *Handbook of Reading Research* (Vol. 2) (pp. 3–25). London and New York, NY: Longman.

Heath, S.B. (2008a) Foreward. In J. Simpson and G. Wigglesworth (eds) *Children's Language and Multilingualism* (pp. ix-xiii). London and New York: Continuum.

Heath, S.B. (2008b) Language socialization in the learning communities of adolescents. In P. Duff and N. Hornberger (eds) *Language Socialization (Vol. 8), Encyclopedia of Language and Education* (2nd edn) (pp. 217–230). New York, NY: Springer.

Heath, S.B. (2012) *Words at Work and Play: Three Decades in Family and Community Life*. Cambridge: Cambridge University Press.

Heath, S.B. and McLaughlin, M.W. (eds) (1993) *Identity and Inner-City Youth: Beyond Ethnicity and Gender*. Columbia, NY: Teachers College Press.

Heath, S.B. and Smyth, L. (1999) *ArtShow: Youth and Community Development. A Resource Guide*. Washington, DC: Partners for Livable Communities.

Heffernan, J. and Heffernan, K. (2000) *A Learner's Guide to Pintupi-Luritja*. Alice Springs: IAD Press.

Heslop, J. (1998) Making the schools relevant: School and community partnerships. In G. Partington (ed.) *Perspectives on Aboriginal and Torres Strait Islander Education* (pp. 274–293). Katoomba: Social Science Press.

Hill, J.H. (1999) Styling locally, styling globally: What does it mean? *Journal of Sociolinguistics* 3 (4), 542–556.

Hilliard, W. (1968) *The People in Between: The Pitjantjatjara People of Ernabella*. London: Hodder and Stoughton.

Hinkson, M. (2005) New media projects at Yuendumu: Towards a history and analysis of intercultural engagement. In L. Taylor, G.K. Ward, G. Henderson, R. Davis and L.A. Wallis (eds) *The Power of Knowledge: The Resonance of Tradition* (pp. 157–168). Canberra: Aboriginal Studies Press.

Hoggart, R. (1957) *The Uses of Literacy: Aspects of Working-Class Life with Special Reference to Publications and Entertainments*. Middlesex: Penguin.

Holland, A. (2005) Saving the race: Critics of absorption look for an alternative. In T. Rowse (ed.) *Contesting Assimilation* (pp. 85–99). Perth: API Network.

Holland, D., Lachicotte Jr., W., Skinner, D. and Cain, C. (1998) *Identity and Agency in Cultural Worlds*. Cambridge and London: Harvard University Press.

Holland, D. and Lave, J. (2001) History in person: An introduction. In D. Holland and J. Lave (eds) *History in Person: Enduring Struggles, Contentious Practice, Intimate Identities* (pp. 3–33). Oxford and Santa Fe, CA: James Currey; School of American Research Press.

Holland, D. and Lave, J. (2009) Social practice theory and the historical production of persons. *Actio: An International Journal of Human Activity Theory* 2, 1–15.

Hoogenraad, R. (2001) Critical reflections on the history of bilingual education in Central Australia. In J. Simpson, D. Nash, M. Laughren, P. Austin and B. Alpher (eds) *Forty Years On: Ken Hale and Australian Languages* (pp. 123–150). Canberra: Pacific Linguistics, ANU.

Howell, H. (1996) *Ngaanyatjarra Wangka Walykumunu: Ngaanyatjarra is a Good Language*. Unpublished manuscript, Warburton Ranges.

Howitt, R. (1990) *'All They Get is the Dust': Aborigines, Mining and Regional Restructuring in Western Australia's Eastern Goldfields. ERRRU Working Paper No. 1*. Sydney: University of Sydney.

Hoyle, S.M. and Adger, S.T. (eds) (1998) *Kids Talk: Strategic Language Use in Later Childhood*. Oxford and New York, NY: Oxford University Press.

Huebner, T. (1987) A socio-historical approach to literacy development: A comparative case study from the Pacific. In J.A. Langer (ed.) *Language, Literacy and Culture: Issues of Society and Schooling* (pp. 178–196). Norwood, NJ: Ablex.

Hughes, H. and Hughes, M. (2009) *Revisiting Indigenous Education*. Sydney: The Centre for Independent Studies.

Hughes, H. and Warin, J. (2005) A new deal for Aborigines and Torres Strait Islanders in remote communities. *The Centre for Independent Studies: Issue Analysis* 54, 1–20.

Hughes, M. and Dallwitz, J. (2007) Ara Irititja: Towards culturally appropriate IT best practice in remote Indigenous Australia. In L.E. Dyson, M. Hendriks and S. Grant (eds) *Information Technologies and Indigenous People* (pp. 146–158). London and Melbourne: Information Science Publishing.

Hull, G. and Schultz, K. (eds) (2002) *School's Out! Bridging Out-of-School Literacies with Classroom Practice*. Columbia, NY: Teachers College Press.

Hull, G.A. (2003) At last. Youth culture and digital media: New literacies for new times. *Research in the Teaching of English* 38 (2), 229–233.

Hull, G.A. and Nelson, M.E. (2005) Locating the semiotic power of multimodality. *Written Communication* 22 (2), 224–261.

Hull, G.A. and Stornaiuolo, A. (2010) Literate arts in a global world: Reframing social networking as cosmopolitan practice. *Journal of Adolescent and Adult Literacy* 54 (2), 85–97.

Hulsemeyer, A. (ed.) (2003) *Globalization in the Twenty-First Century: Convergence or Divergence?* Hampshire and New York, NY: Palgrave Macmillan.

Human Rights and Equal Opportunity Commission (1997) *Bringing Them Home: National Inquiry into the Separation of Aboriginal and Torres Strait Islander Children from their Families.* Sydney: Commonwealth of Australia.

Hutchins, E. (1996) *Cognition in the Wild.* Cambridge, MA: Massachusetts Institute of Technology.

Hymes, D. (1964) Introduction: Towards Ethnographies of Communication. *American Anthropologist* 66 (6), 1–34.

Hymes, D. (1972) On communicative competence. In J.B. Pride and J. Holmes (eds) *Sociolinguistics* (pp. 269–293). Harmondsworth: Penguin.

Ito, M., Baumer, S., Bittanti, M., Boyd, D., Cody, R., Herr-Stephenson, B., Horst, H.A., Lange, P.G., Mahendran, D., Martínez, K.Z., Pascoe, C.J., Perkel, D., Robinson, L., Sims, C. and Tripp, L. (2010) *Hanging Out, Messing Around and Geeking Out: Kids Living and Learning with New Media.* Cambridge, MA: The MIT Press.

Ivanic, R. and Hamilton, M. (1990) Literacy beyond school. In D. Wray (ed.) *Emerging Partnerships* (pp. 4–19). Clevedon: Multilingual Matters.

Jacobs, A.M. (1988) A descriptive study of the bilingual language development of Aboriginal children in the Eastern Goldfields of Western Australia. *Australian Journal of Human Communication Disorders* 16 (2), 3–16.

James, T. (1993) The winnowing of organizations. In S.B. Heath and M.W. McLaughlin (eds) *Identity and Inner-City Youth: Beyond Ethnicity and Gender* (pp. 176–195). New York, NY: Teachers College Press.

Jebb, M.A. (2002) *Blood, Sweat and Welfare: A History of White Bosses and Aboriginal Pastoral Workers.* Perth: University of Western Australia Press.

Jessor, R., Colby, A. and Shweder, R.A. (eds) (1996) *Ethnography and Human Development: Context and Meaning in Social Inquiry.* Chicago, IL: The University of Chicago Press.

Johns, G. (2006) *Aboriginal Education: Remote Schools and the Real Economy.* Canberra: Menzies Research Centre.

Jones, G.M. and Schieffelin, B.B. (2009) Talking text and talking back: 'My BFF Jill' from Boob Tube to YouTube. *Journal of Computer-Mediated Communication* 14, 1050–1079.

Jones, P. (2007) *Ochre and Rust: Artefacts and Encounters on Australian Frontiers.* Adelaide: Wakefield Press.

Kalman, J. (1999) *Writing on the Plaza: Mediated Literacy Practices Among Scribes and Clients in Mexico City.* Cresskill, NJ: Hampton Press.

Kapitzke, C. (1995) *Literacy and Religion: The Textual Politics and Practice of Seventh-day Adventism.* Amsterdam and Philadelphia, PA: John Benjamins Publishing.

Katz, C. (2004) *Growing Up Global: Economic Restructuring and Children's Everyday Lives.* London and Minneapolis, MI: University of Minnesota Press.

Kendon, A. (1988) *Sign Languages of Aboriginal Australia: Cultural, Semiotic and Communicative Perspectives.* Cambridge: Cambridge University Press.

Kerr, B. (1989) *Tjuma Purlkanya – A Big Story. A Research Paper that looks at Education in Remote Communities in the Kalgoorlie Education District.* Kalgoorlie: Education Department of Western Australia.

Kerr, B., Booth, L. and Johnson, B. (2001) *The Big Picture Ten Years On: A Research Paper that Examines the Issues from a Teacher's Perspective of Living and Working in a Remote Community in the Goldfields.* Kalgoorlie: Education Department of Western Australia.

Klapproth, D. (2004) *Narrative as Social Practice: Anglo-Western and Australian Aboriginal Oral Traditions.* Berlin and New York, NY: Mouton de Gruyter.

Kral, I. (2000) *The Socio-Historical Development of Literacy in Arrernte: A Case Study of Writing in an Aboriginal Language and the Implications for Current Vernacular Literacy Practices.* Unpublished Masters thesis, University of Melbourne.

Kral, I. (2007) *Writing Words – Right Way! Literacy and Social Practice in the Ngaanyatjarra World.* Unpublished Ph.D thesis, The Australian National University.

Kral, I. (2010a) *Generational Change, Learning and Remote Australian Indigenous Youth. CAEPR Working Paper No. 68.* Canberra: Centre for Aboriginal Economic Policy Research, The Australian National University.

Kral, I. (2010b) *Plugged In: Remote Australian Indigenous Youth and Digital Culture, CAEPR Working Paper No. 69.* Canberra: Centre for Aboriginal Economic Policy Research, The Australian National University.

Kral, I. (2011) Youth media as cultural practice: Remote Indigenous youth speaking out loud. *Journal of the Australian Institute of Aboriginal and Torres Strait Islander Studies* 1, 4–16.

Kral, I. and Ellis, E.M. (2008) Children, language and literacy in the Ngaanyatjarra Lands. In G. Wigglesworth and J. Simpson (eds) *Children's Language and Multilingualism: Indigenous Language Use at Home and School* (pp. 154–172). London: Continuum Publishers.

Kral, I. and Falk, I. (2004) *What is All That Learning For? Indigenous Adult English Literacy Practices, Training, Community Capacity and Health.* Adelaide: NCVER.

Kral, I. and Ward, D. (2000) *Report on the Review of Education and Training in the Ngaanyatjarra Lands.* Alice Springs: Ngaanyatjarra Council.

Kress, G. (2003) *Literacy in the New Media Age.* London and New York, NY: Routledge.

Kress, G. (2010) *Multimodality: A Social Semiotic Approach to Contemporary Communication.* London and New York, NY: Routledge, Taylor and Francis Group.

Kress, G. and Van Leeuwen, T. (2001) *Reading Images: The Grammar of Visual Design.* London: Routledge.

Kulick, D. (1992) *Language Shift and Cultural Reproduction: Socialization, Self and Syncretism in a Papua New Guinean Village.* Cambridge: Cambridge University Press.

Kulick, D. and Stroud, C. (1993) Conceptions and uses of literacy in a Papua New Guinean village. In B. Street (ed.) *Cross-Cultural Approaches to Literacy* (pp. 30–61). Cambridge: Cambridge University Press.

Labov, W. (1972) *Language in the Inner City.* Philadelphia, PA: University of Pennsylvania Press.

Lam, W.S.E. (2008) Language socialization in online communities. In P. Duff and N. Hornberger (eds) *Language Socialization* (pp. 301–311). *Encyclopedia of Language and Education* (Vol. 8) (2nd edn). New York, NY: Springer.

Langlois, A. (2004) *Alive and Kicking: Areyonga Teenage Pitjantjatjara.* Canberra: Pacific Linguistics, Research School of Pacific and Asian Studies.

Laughren, M. (1978) *Directional Terminology in Warlpiri* (Vol. 8). Launceston: Tasmanian College of Advanced Education.

Lave, J. (1988) *Cognition in Practice.* Cambridge: Cambridge University Press.

Lave, J. (1990) The culture of acquisition and the practice of understanding. In J.W. Stigler, R.A. Shweder and G. Herdt (eds) *Cultural Psychology: Essays on Comparative Human Development* (pp. 309–327). Cambridge: Cambridge University Press.

Lave, J. (1996) Teaching, as Learning, in Practice. *Mind, Culture and Activity* 3, 149–164.

Lave, J. and Wenger, E. (1991) *Situated Learning: Legitimate Peripheral Participation*. Cambridge: Cambridge University Press.

Lawrence, D. and Low, S. (1990) The built environment and spatial form. *Annual Review of Anthropology* 19, 453–505.

Lefebvre, H. ([1974] 1991) *The Production of Space*. Oxford and Cambridge, MA: Basil Blackwell.

Lester, J.Y. (1981) Pages from an Aboriginal book: History and the land. In B. Menary (ed.) *Aborigines and Schooling: Essays in Honour of Max Hart* (pp. 21–30). Adelaide: Texts in Humanities, Adelaide College of the Arts and Education.

Levine, K. (1986) *The Social Construction of Literacy*. London: Routledge and Kegan Paul.

Levine, K. (1998) Definitional and methodological problems in the cross-national measurement of adult literacy: The case of the IALS. *Written Language and Literacy* 1 (1), 41–61.

Levinson, B.A., Foley, D.E. and Holland, D.C. (eds) (1996) *The Cultural Production of the Educated Person: Critical Ethnographies of Schooling and Local Practice*. New York, NY: State University of New York Press.

Levinson, B.A.U., with Borman, K.M., Eisenhart, M., Foster, M., Fox, A. E. and Sutton, M. (eds) (2000) *Schooling and the Symbolic Animal: Social and Cultural Dimensions of Education*. Lanham, ML: Rowman and Littlefield Publishers.

Levinson, S.C. (1996) Language and space. *Annual Review of Anthropology* 25, 353–382.

Levinson, S.C. and Wilkins, D.P. (eds) (2006) *Grammars of Space: Explorations in Cognitive Diversity*. New York, NY: Cambridge University Press.

Levy-Bruhl, L. (1923) *Primitive Mentality*. London: George Allen and Unwin.

Lewis, D. (1976) Observations on route finding and spatial orientation among the Aboriginal peoples of the Western Desert region of Central Australia. *Oceania* 46, 249–282.

Liberman, K. (1985) *Understanding Interaction in Central Australia: An Ethnomethodological Study of Australian Aboriginal People*. Boston, MA: Routledge and Kegan Paul.

Liddelow, W. (1979) *R.W. Schenk, the Establishment of Wongutha Mission Training Farm and the Fight for Native Land Settlement on the Esperance Plains*. Unpublished manuscript, Perth.

Livingstone, S. (2002) *Young People and New Media*. London: Sage.

Long, J. (1964) Papunya: Westernization in an Aboriginal Community. In M. Reay (ed.) *Aborigines Now: New Perspectives in the Study of Aboriginal Communities* (pp. 72–82). Sydney: Angus and Robertson.

Long, M., Frigo, T. and Batten, M. (1999) *The School to Work Transition of Indigenous Australians: A Review of the Literature and Statistical Analysis*. Canberra: Department of Education Science and Training.

Long, T. (1969) The role of the Department of Native Welfare for Western Australia. In *Thinking about Australian Aboriginal Welfare with Particular Reference to Western Australia* (pp. 24–28). Perth: University of Western Australia.

Luke, A. (1988) *Literacy, Textbooks and Ideology: Postwar Literacy Instruction and the Mythology of Dick and Jane*. London: Falmer Press.

Luria, A.R. (1976) *Cognitive Development: Its Cultural and Social Functions*. Cambridge, MA: Harvard University Press.

Makihara, M. and Schieffelin, B.B. (eds) (2007) *Consequences of Contact: Language Ideologies and Sociocultural Transformations in Pacific Societies*. Oxford and New York, NY: Oxford University Press.

Makin, C.F. (1977) The teaching of Aboriginal children. In R. Berndt (ed.) *Aborigines and Change: Australia in the 70s* (pp. 210–236). Canberra: Australian Institute for Aboriginal Studies.

Marks, S.R. (1960) Mission Policy in Western Australian History 1846–1959. *University Studies in Western Australian History* 3 (4), 60–106.

Maushart, S. ([1993] 2003) *Sort of a Place Like Home: Remembering Moore River Native Settlement*. Perth: Fremantle Arts Centre Press.

Maybin, J. (ed.) (1994) *Language and Literacy in Social Practice*. Clevedon: Multilingual Matters.

McCarty, T.L. and Wyman, L.T. (2009) Indigenous youth and bilingualism: Theory, research, praxis. *Journal of Language, Identity, and Education* 8, 279–290.

McClure, P. (2000) *Participation Support for a More Equitable Society: Final Report of the Reference Group on Welfare Reform, July 2000*. Canberra: Department of Family and Children's Services.

McConvell, P. (1991) Understanding language shift: A step towards language maintenance. In S. Romaine (ed.) *Language in Australia* (pp. 143–155). Cambridge: Cambridge University Press.

McDermott, R. and Varenne, H. (1995) Culture *as* disability. *Anthropology and Education Quarterly* 26 (3), 324–348.

McDonald, H. (2001) *Blood, Bones and Spirit: Aboriginal Christianity in an East Kimberley Town*. Melbourne: Melbourne University Press.

MCEETYA (2004) *National Report on Schooling in Australia 2004. Preliminary Paper: National Benchmark Results Reading, Writing and Numeracy Years 3, 5 and 7*. Canberra: Commonwealth of Australia.

McGrath, P. (2004) *Assimilation, Atom Bombs, Aboriginal Activists and W.L. Grayden's 1957 film 'Manslaughter'*. Unpublished MA Prelim. thesis, LaTrobe University.

McGrath, P. (2010) *Hard Looking: A Historical Ethnography of Photographic Encounters with Aboriginal Families in the Ngaanyatjarra Lands, Western Australia*. Unpublished PhD thesis, The Australian National University.

McGrath, P.F. and Brooks, D. (2010) Their Darkest Hour: The films and photographs of William Grayden and the history of the "Warburton Ranges controversy" of 1957. *Aboriginal History* 34, 115–140.

McLaughlin, M.W., Irby, M.A. and Langman, J. (1994) *Urban Sanctuaries: Neighborhood Organizations in the Lives and Futures of Inner-City Youth*. San Francisco, CA: Jossey-Bass Publishers.

Mead, M. ([1970] 1978) *Culture and Commitment: The New Relationships Between the Generations in the 1970s*. New York, NY: Columbia University Press.

Mendoza-Denton, N. (2007) *Homegirls: Symbolic Practices in the Making of Latina Youth Styles*. Oxford: Blackwell.

Merlan, F. (1998) *Caging the Rainbow: Places, Politics and Aborigines in a North Australian Town*. Honolulu: University of Hawai'i Press.

Merlan, F. (2005) Explorations towards intercultural accounts of socio-cultural reproduction and change. *Oceania* 75 (3), 167–182.

Michaels, E. (1986) *The Aboriginal Invention of Television: Central Australia 1982–1986*. Canberra: AIAS.

Miller, E.P. (1966) Factors affecting vocational training of Aborigines in the Northern Territory and Western Australia. In I.G. Sharp and C.M. Tatz (eds) *Aborigines in the Economy: Employment, Wages and Training* (pp. 17–42). Brisbane: Jacaranda Press.

Miller, P.J. (1996) Instantiating culture through discourse practices: Some personal reflections on socialization and how to study it. In R. Jessor, A. Colby and R.A. Shweder (eds) *Ethnography and Human Development: Context and Meaning in Human Development* (pp. 183–204). London and Chicago, IL: The University of Chicago Press.

Milnes, P. (1987) *A History of the Education of the Aborigines in Western Australia with Particular Reference to the Goldfields District Since 1927*. Unpublished PhD thesis, University of New England.

Mollenhauer, S. (2002) Warburton Mission: A brief history. In V. Plant and A. Viegas (eds) *Mission Time in Warburton: An Exhibition Exploring Aspects of the Warburton Mission History 1933–1973* (pp. 65–75). Warburton: Warburton Arts Project.

Morgan, M. (1986) *Mt Margaret: A Drop in a Bucket*. Lawson: Mission Publications of Australia.

Munn, N. ([1973] 1986) *Walbri Iconography: Graphic Representation and Cultural Symbolism in a Central Australian Society*. Chicago, IL: The University of Chicago Press.

Munn, N.D. (1992) The cultural anthropology of time: A critical essay. *Annual Review of Anthropology* 21, 93–123.

Murray, T. ([1969] 1979) A traditional story of the turkey. In A. Glass and D. Hackett (eds) *Ngaanyatjarra Texts: New Revised Edition of Pitjantjatjara Texts* (pp. 1–14). Canberra: AIAS.

Musharbash, Y. (2003) *Warlpiri Sociality: An Ethnography of the Spatial and Temporal Dimensions of Everyday Life in a Central Australian Aboriginal Settlement*. Unpublished PhD thesis, The Australian National University.

Musharbash, Y. (2004) Red bucket for the red cordial, green bucket for the green cordial: On the logic and logistics of Warlpiri birthday parties. *The Australian Journal of Anthropology* 15 (1), 12–22.

Musharbash, Y. (2009) *Yuendumu Everyday: Contemporary Life in Remote Aboriginal Australia*. Canberra: Aboriginal Studies Press.

Myers, F.R. (1986) *Pintupi Country, Pintupi Self: Sentiment, Place and Politics among Western Desert Aborigines*. Berkeley, CA: University of California Press.

Myers, F.R. (1988) Burning the truck and holding the country: Pintupi forms of property and identity. In E.N. Wilmsen (ed.) *We Are Here: The Politics of Aboriginal Land Tenure* (pp. 15–42). London: University of California Press.

Myers, F.R. (2002) Ways of place-making. *La Ricerca Folklorica* 45, 101–119.

Myers, F.R. (2010) All around Australia and overseas: Christianity and indigenous identities in Central Australia 1988. *The Australian Journal of Anthropology* 21 (1), 110–128.

Myers, F.R. (2011) Fathers and sons, Trajectories of self: Reflections on Pintupi lives and futures. In U. Eickelkamp (ed.) *Growing Up in Central Australia: New Anthropological Studies of Aboriginal Childhood and Adolescence* (pp. 82–100). Oxford and New York, NY: Berghahn Books.

Nelson, E., Smith, S. and Grimshaw, P. (2002) *Letters from Aboriginal Women of Victoria, 1867–1926*. Department of History Monograph Series: University of Melbourne.

Neville, A.O. (1947) *Australia's Coloured Minority: Its Place in the Community*. Sydney: Currawang Publishing Co.

New London Group (1996) A pedagogy of multiliteracies: Designing social futures. *Harvard Educational Review* 66 (1), 60–92.

Ngaanyatjarra Bible Project (1999) *Mama Kuurrku Wangka Marlangkatjanya: The New Testament in Ngaanyatjarra and English*. Canberra: The Bible Society in Australia.

Ngaanyatjarra Bible Project (2003) *Turlku Pirninya: Tjiitjaku Wanalpayi Pirniku*. Alice Springs: Ngaanyatjarra Bible Project.

Ngaanyatjarra Bible Project (2007) *Mama Kuurrku Wangka: Ngarnmanytjatjanya Puru Marlangkatjanya. Portions of the Old Testament in Ngaanyatjarra Together with the New Testament in Ngaanyatjarra and English*. Minto: The Bible Society in Australia.

NLLIA (1996) *Desert Schools: An Investigation of English Language and Literacy among Young Aboriginal People in Seven Communities* (Vol. 1, 2 and 3). Canberra: DEETYA and NLLIA South Australian Teaching and Curriculum Centre.

Ochs, E. (1988) *Culture and Language Development: Language Acquisition and Language Socialization in a Samoan Village*. Cambridge and New York, NY: Cambridge University Press.

Ochs, E. (1990) Indexicality and socialization. In J.W. Stigler, R.A. Shweder and G. Herdt (eds) *Cultural Psychology: Essays on Comparative Human Development* (pp. 287–308). Cambridge and New York, NY: Cambridge University Press.

Ochs, E. (1993) Constructing social identity: A language socialization perspective. *Research on Language and Social Interaction* 26 (3), 287–306.

Ochs, E. (1996) Linguistic resources for socializing humanity. In J.J. Gumperz and S.C. Levinson (eds) *Rethinking Linguistic Relativity* (pp. 407–438). Cambridge: Cambridge University Press.

Ochs, E. and Shohet, M. (2006) The cultural structuring of mealtime socialization. *New Directions for Child and Adolescent Development* 111, 35–49.

Ogbu, J.U. (1990) Cultural model, identity and literacy. In J.W. Stigler, R.A. Shweder and G. Herdt (eds) *Cultural Psychology: Essays on Comparative Human Development* (pp. 520–541). Cambridge and New York, NY: Cambridge University Press.

Ogilvie, E. and Van Zyl, A. (2001) Young Indigenous males, custody and the rites of passage. *Trends and Issues in Crime and Justice, Australian Institute of Criminology* 204, 1–6.

Olson, D.R. (1977) From utterance to text: The bias of language in speech and writing. *Harvard Educational Review* 47 (3), 257–281.

O'Malley, P. (1994) Gentle genocide: The government of Aboriginal peoples in Central Australia. *Social Justice* 21 (4), 46–66.

Ong, W.J. (1982) *Orality and Literacy: The Technologizing of the Word*. London and New York, NY: Methuen.

Ortner, S.B. (1984) Theory in anthropology since the Sixties. *Comparative Studies in Society and History* 26, 126–166.

Ortner, S.B. (1989) *High Religion: A Cultural and Political History of Sherpa Buddhism*. Princeton, NJ: Princeton University Press.

Ortner, S.B. (2006) *Anthropology and Social Theory: Culture, Power, and the Acting Subject*. Durham, NC: Duke University Press.

O'Shannessy, C. (2011) Young children's social meaning making in a new mixed language. In U. Eickelkamp (ed.) *Growing Up in Central Australia: New Anthropological Studies of Aboriginal Childhood and Adolescence* (pp. 131–155). Oxford and New York, NY: Berghahn Books.

Paisley, F. (2005) Mary Bennett and Chief Protector Neville: Protection, absorption and the future of the Aborigines. In T. Rowse (ed.) *Contesting Assimilation* (pp. 71–84). Perth: API Network.

Palmer, K. (2005) Dependency, technology and governance. In L. Taylor, G.K. Ward, G. Henderson, R. Davis and L.A. Wallis (eds) *The Power of Knowledge: The Resonance of Tradition* (pp. 101–115). Canberra: Aboriginal Studies Press.

Paradise, R. and Rogoff, B. (2009) Side by side: Learning by observing and pitching in. *Ethos* 37 (1), 102–138.

Parliament of Australia (2011) *Doing Time – Time for Doing: Indigenous Youth in the Criminal Justice System. House of Representatives Standing Committee on Aboriginal and Torres Strait Islander Affairs Report.* Canberra: Commonwealth of Australia.

Pearson, N. (2000) *Our Right to Take Responsibility.* Cairns: Noel Pearson and Associates.

Pelto, P. (1973) *The Snowmobile Revolution: Technology and Social Change in the Arctic.* Menlo Park, CA: Benjamin Cummings.

Pennycook, A. (2003) Global Englishes, Rip Slyme, and performativity. *Journal of Sociolinguistics* 7 (4), 513–533.

Peterson, N. (1977) Aboriginal involvement with the Australian economy in the Central Reserve during the winter of 1970. In R.M. Berndt (ed.) *Aborigines and Change: Australia in the 70s* (pp. 136–146). Canberra: Australian Institute of Aboriginal Studies.

Peterson, N. (1993) Demand sharing: Reciprocity and the pressure for generosity among foragers. *American Anthropologist* 95 (4), 860–874.

Peterson, N. (2000) An expanding Aboriginal domain: Mobility and the initiation journey. *Oceania* 70 (3), 205–218.

Pfaffenberger, B. (1992) Social anthropology of technology. *Annual Review of Anthropology* 21, 491–516.

Philips, S.U. (1983) *The Invisible Culture: Communication in Classroom and Community on the Warm Springs Indian Reservation.* New York, NY: Longman.

Plant, V. (1995) *Warburton Mission History.* Unpublished manuscript. Alice Springs: Ngaanyatjarra Council.

Plant, V. and Viegas, A. (eds) (2002) *Mission Time in Warburton: An Exhibition Exploring Aspects of the Warburton Mission History 1933–1973.* Warburton: Warburton Arts Project, Tjulyuru Regional Arts Gallery.

Poirier, S. (2005) *A World of Relationships: Itineraries, Dreams and Events in the Australian Western Desert.* Toronto: University of Toronto Press.

Powell, R. and Kennedy, B. (2005) *Rene Baker: File #28/E.D.P.* Perth: Fremantle Arts Centre Press.

Prinsloo, M. (1995) Provision, acquisition and culture: Literacy research in South Africa. *International Journal for Educational Development* 15 (4), 449–460.

Prinsloo, M. and Breier, M. (eds) (1996) *The Social Uses of Literacy: Theory and Practice in Contemporary South Africa.* Amsterdam and Philadelphia, PA: John Benjamins Publishing.

Proctor, G. and Viegas, A. (1990) *Minymalu Kanyirrantja: Women's Form and Aesthetics from the Western Desert (Exhibition Catalogue).* Alice Springs: Ngaanyatjarra Council.

Purves, A.C. and Jennings, E.M. (eds) (1991) *Literate Systems and Individual Lives.* Albany, NY: State University of New York Press.

Putt, J., Payne, J. and Milner, L. (2005) Indigenous male offending and substance abuse. *Trends and Issues in Crime and Criminal Justice* 293, 1–6.

Rajkowski, P. (1995) *Linden Girl: A Story of Outlawed Lives.* Perth: University of Western Australia Press.

Rampton, B. (1995) *Crossing: Language and Ethnicity among Adolescents.* London: Longman.

Rampton, B. (1999) Styling the Other: Introduction. *Journal of Sociolinguistics* 3 (4), 421–427.

Read, P. (1981) *The Stolen Generations.* Sydney: NSW Government Printer.

Reder, S. and Green, K.R. (1983) Contrasting patterns of literacy in an Alaska fishing village. *International Journal of the Sociology of Language* 42, 9–39.

Reder, S. and Wikelund, K.R. (1993) Literacy development and ethnicity: An Alaskan example. In B.V. Street (ed.) *Cross-Cultural Approaches to Literacy* (pp. 176–197). Cambridge: Cambridge University Press.

Reid, J. (1983) *Sorcerers and Healing Spirits: Continuity and Change in an Aboriginal Medical System*. Canberra: Australian National University Press.

Rennie, E. and Featherstone, D. (2008) The potential diversity of things we call TV: Indigenous community television, self-determination and the advent of NITV. *Media International Australia Incorporating Culture and Policy* 129, 52–66.

Richards, J.W. (1997) *Warlawurru Manngutjarra: The Eagle's Nest*. Broome: Magabala Books.

Riemer, F.J. (2008) Becoming literate, being human: Adult literacy and moral reconstruction in Botswana. *Anthropology and Education Quarterly* 39 (4), 444–464.

Robben, A.C.G.M. (1989) Habits of the home: Spatial hegemony and the structuration of house and society in Brazil. *American Anthropologist* 91 (3), 570–588.

Rogoff, B. (1990) *Apprenticeship in Thinking: Cognitive Development in Social Context*. Oxford: Oxford University Press.

Rogoff, B. (2003) *The Cultural Nature of Human Development*. Oxford and New York, NY: Oxford University Press.

Rogoff, B. and Lave, J. (1984) *Everyday Cognition: Its Development in Social Context*. Cambridge, MA: Harvard University Press.

Rogoff, B., Mistry, J., Goncu, A. and Mosier, C. (1993) Guided participation in cultural activity by toddlers and caregivers. *Monographs of the Society for Research in Child Development* 58 (8), 1–183.

Rogoff, B., Paradise, R., Arauz, R.M., Correa-Chavez, M. and Angelillo, C. (2003) Firsthand learning through intent participation. *Annual Review of Psychology* 54, 175–203.

Rose, D. (2001) *The Western Desert Code: An Australian Cryptogrammar*. Canberra: Pacific Linguistics, The Australian National University.

Rowley, C.D. ([1970] 1972) *The Remote Aborigines*. Ringwood: Penguin.

Rowse, T. (1998) *White Flour, White Power: From Rations to Citizenship in Central Australia*. Cambridge: Cambridge University Press.

Rowse, T. (2005a) The certainties of assimilation. In T. Rowse (ed.) *Contesting Assimilation* (pp. 237–249). Perth: API Network.

Rowse, T. (2005b) Introduction. In T. Rowse (ed.) *Contesting Assimilation* (pp. 1–24). Perth: API Network.

Sackett, L. (1977) Liquor and the Law: Wiluna, Western Australia. In R. Berndt (ed.) *Aborigines and Change* (pp. 90–99). Canberra: AIAS.

Sackett, L. (1978a) Clinging to the Law: Leadership at Wiluna. In M.C. Howard (ed.) *'Whitefella Business': Aborigines in Australian Politics* (pp. 37–48). Philadelphia, PA: Institute for the Study of Human Issues.

Sackett, L. (1978b) Punishment in ritual: Man-making among Western Desert Aborigines. *Oceania* 49 (2), 110–127.

Sackett, L. (1990) Welfare colonialism: developing divisions at Wiluna. In R. Tonkinson and M.C. Howard (eds) *Going it Alone: Prospects for Aboriginal Autonomy. Essays in Honour of Ronald and Catherine Berndt* (pp. 201–217). Canberra: Aboriginal Studies Press.

Sahlins, M. (1981) *Historical Metaphors and Mythical Realities: Structure in the Early History of the Sandwich Islands Kingdom*. Ann Arbor, MI: University of Michigan Press.

Sanders, W.G. (1986) *Access, Administration and Politics: The Australian Social Security System and Aborigines*. Unpublished PhD thesis, The Australian National University.

Sansom, B. (1980) *The Camp at Wallaby Cross: Aboriginal Fringe Dwellers in Darwin*. Canberra: Australian Institute of Aboriginal Studies.

Sansom, B. ([1988] 1994) A grammar of exchange. In I. Keen (ed.) *Being Black: Aboriginal Cultures in 'Settled' Australia* (pp. 159–177). Canberra: Aboriginal Studies Press.

Schapper, H.P. (1970) *Aboriginal Advancement to Integration: Conditions and Plans for Western Australia*. Canberra: Australian National University Press.

Schenk, R. (1936) *The Educability of the Native*. Perth: Service Printing Company.

Schieffelin, B.B. (1990) *The Give and Take of Everyday Life: Language Socialization of Kaluli Children*. Cambridge: Cambridge University Press.

Schieffelin, B.B. (2002) Marking Time: The dichotomizing discourse of multiple temporalities. *Current Anthropology* 43, S5–S17.

Schieffelin, B.B. (2007) Found in translating: Reflexive language across time and texts in Bosavi, Papua New Guinea. In M. Makihara and B.B. Schieffelin (eds) *Consequences of Contact: Language Ideologies and Sociocultural Transformations* (pp. 140–165). Oxford and New York, NY: Oxford University Press.

Schieffelin, B.B. and Gilmore, P. (eds) (1986) *The Acquisition of Literacy: Ethnographic Perspectives*. Norwood, NJ: Ablex Publishing Corporation.

Schieffelin, B.B. and Ochs, E. (eds) (1986) *Language Socialization Across Cultures*. Cambridge: Cambridge University Press.

Schmidt, A. (1985) *Young People's Dyirbal: An Example of Language Death from Australia*. Cambridge: Cambridge University Press.

Schmidt, A. (1990) *The Loss of Australia's Aboriginal Language Heritage*. Canberra: Aboriginal Studies Press.

Schofield, R.S. (1968) The measurement of literacy in pre-industrial England. In J. Goody (ed.) *Literacy in Traditional Societies* (pp. 311–325). Cambridge: Cambridge University Press.

Schwab, R.G. (2001) 'That school gotta recognise *our* policy!': The appropriation of educational policy in an Australian Aboriginal community. In M. Sutton and B.A.U. Levinson (eds) *Policy as Practice: Toward a Comparative Sociocultural Analysis of Educational Policy* (pp. 243–264). Westport, CT: Ablex.

Scollon, R. and Scollon, S. (1981) *Narrative, Literacy, and Face in Interethnic Communication*. Norwood, NJ: Ablex.

Seely Brown, J. (2002) The social life of learning: How can continuing education be reconfigured in the future? *Continuing Higher Education Review* 66, 50–69.

Serpell, R. (1993) *The Significance of Schooling: Life Journeys in an African Society*. Cambridge: Cambridge University Press.

Shamgar-Handelman, L. and Handelman, D. (1991) Celebrations of bureaucracy: Birthday parties in Israeli Kindergartens. *Ethnology* 30 (4), 293–312.

Shaw, G. (2002) *An Ethnographic Exploration of the Development in Child Rearing Style Among the Ngaanyatjarra People from the Pre-Contact Era to the Present*. Unpublished Masters thesis, University of New South Wales.

Shuman, A. (1986) *Storytelling Rights: The Uses of Oral and Written Texts by Urban Adolescents*. Cambridge: Cambridge University Press.

Simpson, J., Caffery, J. and McConvell, P. (2009) *Gaps in Australia's Indigenous Language Policy: Dismantling Bilingual Education in the Northern Territory. AIATSIS Research*

Discussion Paper No. 24. Canberra: Australian Institute of Aboriginal and Torres Strait Islander Studies.

Simpson, J. and Wigglesworth, G. (eds) (2008) *Children's Language and Multilingualism: Indigenous Language Use at Home and School*. London and New York, NY: Continuum.

Smith, D. (1986) The anthropology of literacy acquisition. In B.B. Schieffelin and P. Gilmore (eds) *The Acquisition of Literacy: Ethnographic Perspectives* (pp. 261–275). Norwood, NJ: Ablex.

Smyth, J. and Hattam, R. (2004) *'Dropping Out', Drifting Off, Being Excluded: Becoming Somebody Without School*. New York, NY: Peter Lang.

Sneath, D., Holbraad, M. and Pederson, M.A. (2009) Technologies of the imagination: An introduction. *Ethnos* 74 (1), 5–30.

Snow, C.E. and Ferguson, C.A. (eds) (1977) *Talking to Children: Language Input and Acquisition*. Cambridge: Cambridge University Press.

Soep, E. (2006) Beyond literacy and voice in youth media production. *McGill Journal of Education* 41 (3), 197–213.

Spicer, I. (1997) *Independent Review of the CDEP Scheme*. Canberra: Aboriginal and Torres Strait Islander Commission.

Spindler, G.D. (ed.) (1974) *Education and Cultural Process: Toward an Anthropology of Education*. New York, NY: Holt, Rinehart and Winston.

Spolsky, B., Engelbrecht, G. and Ortiz, L. (1983) Religious, political and educational factors in the development of biliteracy in the Kingdom of Tonga. *Journal of Multilingual and Multicultural Development* 4 (8), 459–469.

Stanton, J. (1983) Old business, new owners: Succession and 'the Law' on the fringe of the Western Desert. In N. Peterson and M. Langton (eds) *Aborigines, Land and Land Rights* (pp. 160–171). Canberra: Australian Institute of Aboriginal Studies.

Stanton, J. (1988) Mt Margaret: Missionaries and the aftermath. In T. Swain and D.B. Rose (eds) *Aboriginal Australians and Christian Missions: Ethnographic and Historical Studies* (pp. 292–307). Adelaide: Australian Association for the Study of Religions, SACAE.

Stanton, J. (1990) Autonomy and dependency: The experience at Mt Margaret. In R. Tonkinson and M.C. Howard (eds) *Going it Alone: Prospects for Aboriginal Autonomy. Essays in Honour of Ronald and Catherine Berndt* (pp. 219–233). Canberra: Aboriginal Studies Press.

Staples, C. and Cane, E. (2002) *Ngaanyatjarra Community Law and Justice Submission to the Attorney General of Western Australia the Hon. J.A. McGinty MLA*. Warburton: Shire of Ngaanyatjarraku and Warburton Community Inc.

Stornaiuolo, A., Hull, G. and Nelson, M.E. (2009) Mobile texts and migrant audiences: Rethinking literacy and assessment in a new media age. *Research Directions: Language Arts* 86 (5), 382–392.

Storry, K. (2006) Tackling literacy in remote Aboriginal communities. *Issue Analysis. Centre for Independent Studies* 73, 1–11.

Strauss, G. (1978) *Luther's House of Learning: Indoctrination of the Young in the German Reformation*. Baltimore, MD: Johns Hopkins University Press.

Street, B.V. (1984) *Literacy in Theory and Practice*. Cambridge: Cambridge University Press.

Street, B.V. (ed.) (1993a) *Cross-Cultural Approaches to Literacy*. Cambridge: Cambridge University Press.

Street, B.V. (1993b) Introduction: The new literacy studies. In B.V. Street (ed.) *Cross-Cultural Approaches to Literacy* (pp. 1–21). Cambridge: Cambridge University Press.

Street, B.V. (1994) Cross-cultural perspectives on literacy. In J. Maybin (ed.) *Language and Literacy in Social Practice* (pp. 139–150). Clevedon: Multilingual Matters Ltd.

Street, B.V. (1995) *Social Literacies: Critical Approaches to Literacy in Development, Ethnography and Education*. London and New York, NY: Longman.

Street, B.V. (ed.) (2001) *Literacy and Development: Ethnographic Perspectives*. London and New York, NY: Routledge.

Sullivan, P. (2010) The Aboriginal community sector and the effective delivery of services: Acknowledging the role of Indigenous sector organisations. *Working Paper 73*, 1–13.

Sutton, P. (2009) *The Politics of Suffering: Indigenous Australia and the End of Liberal Consensus*. Melbourne: Melbourne University Press.

Taussig, M. (1993) *Mimesis and Alterity: A Particular History of the Senses*. London and New York, NY: Routledge.

Taylor, C. (2004) *Modern Social Imaginaries*. Durham, NC: Duke University Press.

Taylor, D. and Dorsey-Gaines, C. (1988) *Growing Up Literate: Learning from Inner-City Families*. Portsmouth, NH: Heinemann.

Thurlow, C. and Mroczek, K. (eds) (2011) *Digital Discourse: Language in the New Media*. Oxford and New York, NY: Oxford University Press.

Thurtell, J. (2003) *Ngaanyatjarra Council – Doing Business with Government*. Alice Springs: Ngaanyatjarra Council (Aboriginal Corporation).

Tomlinson, J. (2007) *The Culture of Speed: The Coming of Immediacy*. Thousand Oaks, CA: Sage.

Tonkinson, R. (1974) *The Jigalong Mob: Aboriginal Victors of the Desert Crusade*. Menlo Park, CA: Cummings.

Tonkinson, R. (1978) *The Mardudjara Aborigines: Living the Dream in Australia's Desert*. New York, NY: Holt, Rinehart and Winston Inc.

Tonkinson, R. (1988) Reflections on a failed crusade. In T. Swain and D.B. Rose (eds) *Aboriginal Australians and Christian Missions: Ethnographic and Historical Studies* (pp. 60–73). Adelaide: Australian Association for the Study of Religions, SACAE.

Toyne, P. and Vachon, D. (1984) *Growing Up the Country: The Pitjantjatjara Struggle for their Land*. Ringwood: Penguin Books.

Trigger, D. (1992) *Whitefella Comin': Aboriginal Responses to Colonialism in Northern Australia*. Cambridge: Cambridge University Press.

Tri-State Project (1990) *Tri-state Project Draft Report: Improving Aboriginal Student Learning Outcomes through Co-Operative Education Services*. Unpublished manuscript, Perth.

Trudinger, R.M. (1943) Grammar of the Pitjantjatjara dialect, Central Australia. *Oceania* 13 (3), 205–223.

Turner, J. (2003) *Trust: Mining Exhibition Catalogue*. Warburton: Warburton Arts Project.

United Nations (2005) *World Youth Report 2005: Young People Today, and in 2015*. New York, NY: United Nations.

van Dijck, J. (2007) *Mediated Memories in the Digital Age*. Stanford, CA: Stanford University Press.

van Toorn, P. (2006) *Writing Never Arrives Naked: Early Aboriginal Cultures of Writing in Australia*. Canberra: Aboriginal Studies Press.

Varenne, H. and McDermott, R. (eds) (1999) *Successful Failure: The School America Builds*. Boulder, CO: Westview Press.

von Sturmer, J. (2002) *Warburton One and Only: 'Click Go the Designs': Presencing the Now in 1000 Easy Pieces*. Unpublished manuscript.

Warburton Arts Project (1993) *Yarnangu Ngaanya: Our Land – Our Body*. Perth: Perth Institute of Contemporary Arts Press.

Warburton Arts Project (1999) *Ngayulu-Latju Palyantja: We Made These Things*. Exhibition catalogue. Warburton: Warburton Arts Press.

Watson, C. (1997) Re-embodying sand drawing and re-evaluating the status of the camp: The practice and iconography of women's public sand drawing in Balgo, WA. *The Australian Journal of Anthropology* 8 (1), 104–124.

Weil, S. (1986) The language and ritual of socialisation: Birthday parties in a Kindergarten context. *Man* 21 (2), 329–341.

Wells, G. (1985) Pre-school literacy related activities and success in school. In D.R. Olson, N. Torrance and A. Hildyard (eds) *Literacy, Language and Learning: The Nature and Consequences of Reading and Writing* (pp. 229–255). Cambridge: Cambridge University Press.

Wells, M. (2002) I remember. In V. Plant and A. Viegas (eds) *Mission Time in Warburton: An Exhibition Exploring Aspects of the Warburton Mission History 1933–1973* (pp. 51–54). Warburton: Warburton Arts Project.

Wenger, E. (1998) *Communities of Practice: Learning, Meaning and Identity*. Cambridge: Cambridge University Press.

Western Australia Parliament (1956) *Report of the Select Committee of the Legislative Assembly appointed to inquire into Native Welfare Conditions in the Laverton-Warburton Range Area*. *V&P* (Vol. 3). Perth: Government of Western Australia.

Western Australia Parliament (1976) *Report of the Royal Commission to Inquire into and Report upon Certain Incidents in which Aborigines were Involved in the Laverton Area*. *V&P* (Vol. 8). Perth: Government of Western Australia.

White, I. (1981) Generational moieties in Australia: Structural, social and ritual implications. *Oceania* 52 (1), 6–27.

Wilkins, D.P. (1997) Alternative representations of space: Arrernte narratives in sand. In M. Biemans and J. van de Weijer (eds) *Proceedings of the CLS Opening Academic Year '97, '98* (pp. 133–164). Tilburg University: Centre for Language Studies.

Wilkins, D.P. (2004) The verbalization of motion events in Arrernte. In S. Strömqvist and L. Verhoeven (eds) *Relating Events in Narrative: Typological and Contextual Perspectives* (pp. 143–157). Mahwah, NJ: Lawrence Erlbaum Associates.

Wilkins, D.P. (2006) Towards an Arrernte grammar of space. In S.C. Levinson and D.P. Wilkins (eds) *Grammars of Space: Explorations in Cognitive Diversity* (pp. 24–62). New York, NY: Cambridge University Press.

Williams, R.M. (1998) *A Song in the Desert*. Sydney: Angus and Robertson.

Willis, P. (1977) *Learning to Labour: How Working Class Kids get Working Class Jobs*. Westmead: Saxon House.

Wilson, A. (2000) Absolutely truly brill to see from you: Visuality and prisoners' letters. In D. Barton and N. Hall (eds) *Letter Writing as a Social Practice* (pp. 179–198). Amsterdam and Philadelphia, PA: John Benjamins Publishing.

Wilurarra Creative (2010) *Lurrtjulu-La Palyanma: Let's Keep Doing it Together*. Warburton: Wilurarra Creative.

Woenne, S.T. (1980) 'The true state of affairs': Commissions of Inquiry concerning Western Australian Aborigines. In R. Berndt and C. Berndt (eds) *Aborigines of the West: Their Past and Present* (pp. 324–356). Perth: University of Western Australia Press.

Wogan, P. (1994) Perceptions of European literacy in early contact situations. *Ethnohistory* 41 (3), 407–429.

Wolcott, H. (1967) *A Kwakiutl Village and School*. New York, NY: Holt, Rinehart and Winston.

Wyman, L.T. (2012) *Youth Culture and Linguistic Survivance*. Bristol: Multilingual Matters.

Young, M. (1988) *The Metronomic Society: Natural Rhythms and Human Timetables*. Cambridge, MA: Harvard University Press.

Index